To Whom Was

The Promised Land

Promised?

*Some Fundamental Truths About The
Arab-Israeli Conflict*

Abraham A. Sion, Ph.D. (Cantab.)

D1251578

Mazo Publishers

To Whom Was The Promised Land Promised?
Copyright © 2020 – Abraham A. Sion
U.S. Copyright Registration TXu002204728

ISBN 978-1-946124-75-3 – Soft Cover
ISBN 978-1-946124-83-8 – Hard Cover

Contact The Author
absion@gmail.com

Mazo Publishers
Chaim Mazo, Publisher
Website: www.mazopublishers.com
Email: mazopublishers@gmail.com

In memory of my late wife Sima

Remembering the kindness of thy youth
when thou went after me in the wilderness
in a land that was not sown

Jeremia II 2

And
to Sabina

Table of Contents

Part I: The Balfour Declaration

    A. The Declaration – A Binding Document

    B. The Declaration – A Document of International standing
       and Recognition

    A. Background of the Declaration

    B. Chain of Events Leading to the Final Draft of the Declaration

    C. Meaning of National Home for the Jewish People

      (aa) What are Jewish Zionist Aspirations

      (bb) Literal Interpretation of National Home for the Jewish
         People

       • National Home

       • The Jewish People

      (cc) Purposive Interpretation of the Declaration

      (dd) Perception of National Home by the Public

       • Perception of National Home by the Press

       • Perception of National Home by World Statesmen

       • Perception of National Home by the Jewish People

       • Perception of National Home by the Arabs

      (ee) The Provisos as a means of Interpretation of the term
         National Home

       • Background

       • Civil and Religious Rights as Opposed to National
         Rights or Status

       • Meaning of Civil and Religious Rights

List of Maps

List of Abbreviations

BDFA – British Documents on Foreign Affairs
Cmd – Command Papers
CAB – Cabinet Papers
DBFP – Documents on British Foreign Policy
ZMFI – The Zionist Movement and the Foundation of Israel

---

[1] The term Trans-Jordan is normally used with a hyphen, although in some places, Transjordan is used without a hyphen. Transjordania is usually used in British documents to signify Trans-Jordan before the first partition (1917-1922). The term 'Jordan' came into use after 1948 as a result of the annexation of the West Bank to the Kingdom of Jordan.

Foreword

The object of this treatise is to ascertain who owned the legal right to the territory of Mandatory Palestine under international law. The two competitors were the Arab nation on the one hand and the Jewish people on the other. This research is concerned with the legal aspects of the century-long Arab-Israeli conflict. Its aim is not to do justice to either side. It does not seek to establish who is morally right or wrong in this conflict, or who has been the aggressor or the victim among the parties. This would require further research, even though these attributes could be sporadically deduced from the historical facts described in this work. In the same vein, the book is not a political dissertation. It does not consider the issue from a political point of view, e.g., whether territories captured during the Six-Day-War should be exchanged for peace or whether a Palestinian State should be established in the West Bank and the Gaza Strip. The aim of this research is to juxtapose the legal rights under international law of both parties in relation to the territory of Mandatory Palestine for the purpose of determining who acquired the legal title to this land.

I believe the foregoing question would have been more easily answered if Palestine would have been referred to as Judea or the land of Israel and the West Bank as Judea and Samaria. In fact, the name Palestine was hardly ever used before the conquest of the Middle East by the Allied Powers, mainly by Britain, in WWI. During Ottoman rule, the nucleus of the territory later known as Palestine was referred to by the Turks as the Sanjaq of Jerusalem. The term Palestine was revived by the British for the sole purpose of detaching it from Syria and establishing within it a National Home for the Jewish people on the footing of the Balfour Declaration. In fact, the term Palestine is a misnomer, so is the West Bank. In both cases the reason for adopting these names seems to stem from an endeavor to obliterate any connection of these territories to the Jewish people.[1] Nevertheless, in my treatise I preferred to use Palestine and the West Bank rather than the land of Israel or Judea and Samaria, for the sake of convenience, since the former terms are used as a matter of course in major contemporary international decisions and documents.

My interest in the legal aspects of the conflict began after the Six-Day-War in 1967, when I was a Ph.D. student at the University of Cambridge (U.K.). The war hardly ended and United Nations resolutions put Israel on the international dock. In fact, Israel has been incessantly criticized since 1967 for its occupation of the West Bank and Gaza, and almost every activity Israel assumed there was condemned as illegal and a war crime, the implication being that it had no right to these territories. In fact, the West Bank and Gaza, which were captured by Israel in a purely defensive war, were from the outset considered *Palestinian Arab territory*, and Israel was required by the majority of the international community, to withdraw from them. The question immediately arose: how did these areas become Palestinian Arab territories?

This book is the result of serious study and analysis of the legal aspects of the conflict at the Center for Law and Mass Media at Ariel University which I chaired for over 10 years and as a lecturer on International Law in courses relating to the conflict. I have also engaged myself in writing articles in periodicals and pamphlets on the subject, and submitted papers in academic and non-academic conferences on the issue. I appeared on television and radio programs and had for over a decade a weekly program on the Voice of Israel Channel B Radio regarding, inter alia, this issue. Prior to setting myself to compose this book, I refused to

---

[1] The term Palestine originates from Philistine, a coastal strip around Gaza which was for a time occupied and settled by the Philistine invaders from across the sea. It was only after the destruction of the Jewish second Temple and the crushing of the Jewish uprising that followed, that Hadrian, the Roman Emperor, officially renamed the former Jewish Kingdom as Palestina or Syria-Palestina, and Jerusalem as Aelia Capitolina, in an effort to wipe out Jewish nationhood and statehood. Similarly, the name Judea was abolished to obliterate its historic Jewish identity. See Bernard Lewis – "Palestine: On the History and Geography of a Name", *The International History Review,* Vol. 2, No. 1 (Jan. 1980), pp. 1-12.

accept the contention of a few that the majority of the international community and international organizations were wrong about Israel's legal standing in the area. After conducting a five-year intensive research, I was surprised to see how wrong I was.

The five-year research began in 2015-2016 at Stanford Law School where I spent a year as a visiting professor. The research was aimed at first to suggest a legal solution to the Arab-Israeli conflict other than the *Two State Solution*, which has failed. This inevitably led me to investigate more thoroughly the origin of the conflict. My research involved close study of authentic letters, memorandums and protocols of the British Cabinet, the British Foreign and Colonial Offices and of treaties and resolutions of international bodies and organizations, as well as memoirs and treatises of those who were directly involved in the making of history, such as David Lloyd George, Col. Richard Meinertzhagen, Chaim Weizmann, Sir Herbert Samuel and others. Ultimately, my conclusion was that, under international law, the Jewish people have a solid claim to the whole of Palestine – the Arab nation, and the Arabs of Palestine in particular, on the other hand, have no such claim. This research refutes the findings of mainstream writers and contradicts political and judicial decisions on the subject.

Finally, I have set forth to carry out my research in a spirit of fairness and objectivity, and while approaching the subject from a Jewish-Israeli angle, I strove to fulfill this task without prejudice or partiality. It is my hope that I have succeeded in this endeavor.

A.A.S.
June 2020

Acknowledgements

It is with great pleasure that I thank Dr. Michael Maoz of Ariel University for reading the manuscript and offering valuable editing remarks and comments. I have also had the advantage of gaining the goodwill of Professor Michael Zinigrad, Rector, and of Professor Albert Pinchasov, Vice President, both of Ariel University, through my long journey. I had many useful and inspiring conversations with my daughter Snunit Sion Zafrani, LL.B., LL.M. lecturer at Ariel University, from which I benefited and for which I am grateful. I am also indebted to Professor Oded Mudrik of Ariel University and former deputy President of the Tel-Aviv District Court for reading the first part of my manuscript and making valuable comments.

I would also like to acknowledge my gratitude to the staff of the libraries at Stanford University, UCLA and Ariel University for their invaluable assistance.

I am grateful to the Geospatial Information section of the United Nations for allowing me to use a map displaying the second partition plan, being Annex A to Resolution 181 (II) of the General Assembly, dated November 29th 1947.

Last but not least, I owe an immense debt to my children and their spouses, Snunit and Lior, Ophir and Sharon, Nadav and Osnat, to my grandchildren, and to Sabina Heller, my friend and companion, for their encouragement and interest in my work and for the patience and sympathetic understanding they demonstrated during the long hours I had been locked up in my study.

Introduction

It has often been stated that Judea and Samaria (widely known as the West Bank),[1] East Jerusalem, and the Gaza Strip constitute Palestinian Arab territory. This view became almost axiomatic in the parlance of international organizations such as the Security Council and the General Assembly of the United Nations, the International Court of Justice (ICJ), the International Committee of the Red Cross (ICRC), and the majority of legal scholars. As a result, the international community has considered the establishment of Israeli settlements in these areas illegal under international law, violating Article 49 of the Fourth Geneva Convention of 1949. These international bodies have all affirmed that the Fourth Geneva Convention applies to the West Bank. So did the representatives of the High Contracting Parties to the reconvened Geneva Convention, who declared in 2014 that the settlements were illegal,[2] as did the ICJ and the ICRC.

Soon after the Six-Day-War of June 1967, the Security Council and General Assembly adopted resolutions aimed at deterring the Israeli Government from taking steps towards the unification of Jerusalem and later the annexation of its eastern parts. They were

---

[1]   During the British Mandate this area generally was referred to in its original biblical name as Judea and Samaria. The name 'West Bank' was given to the area by Trans-Jordan after having occupied it in the war of 1948, and subsequently annexed it in 1950. The annexation was universally considered illegal and void also by the Arab League and Arab States. It was only recognized by Britain and Pakistan. Apparently, the name was given to disconnect the area from its biblical origin. For more details see Eyal Benvenisti – *The International Law of Occupation*, Oxford University Press, 2nd ed. 2012, p. 204.

[2]   Conference of High Contracting Parties to the Fourth Geneva Convention Declaration, December 17th 2014, para. 8, which was convened pursuant to General Assembly Resolution 64/10 of December 1st 2009. This Resolution recommended that the Swiss Government take all necessary steps to reconvene a Conference of High Contracting Parties to the Fourth Geneva Convention for the purpose of enforcing the Convention in "the Occupied Palestinian Territory, including East Jerusalem.", para. 5. http://www.news.admin.ch/NSBSubscriber/message/attachments/37764.pdf

also against the establishment of Jewish settlements in Judea and Samaria, partly in areas that were inhabited by Jews prior to 1948 and then abandoned during the Arab invasion of Palestine. For this purpose, they repeatedly stated in their resolutions that the acquisition of territory by military conquest is inadmissible.[3] The Security Council and General Assembly claimed that any legislative or administrative measures or actions aimed at changing the legal status of Jerusalem were invalid and could not change its status.[4] In their view, the Fourth Geneva Convention relative to the Protection of Civilian Persons in Time of War was applicable 'to the Arab territories occupied since 1967, including Jerusalem' and that the establishment of settlements in the Palestinian territories occupied since 1967 had no legal validity.[5] Therefore, the Security Council called upon Israel 'to desist from taking any action which would result in changing the legal status and geographical nature and materially affecting the demographic composition of the Arab territories occupied since 1967, including Jerusalem, and, in particular not to transfer part of its own civilian population into the occupied Arab territories.'[6] The General Assembly made similar demands.[7]

In subsequent resolutions, the General Assembly went even further in recognizing the right of the Palestinian people

---

[3] Security Council Resolutions 252, May 21st 1968; 267, July 3rd 1969; 298, September 25th 1971; 476, June 30th 1980; 478, August 20th 1980; see also General Assembly Resolutions ES-10/13, October 27th 2003; ES-10/14, December 12th 2003.

[4] Security Council Resolutions 252, May 21st 1968; 267, July 3rd 1969; 298, September 25th 1971; 476, June 30th 1980 and 478, August 20th 1980. General Assembly Resolutions 2253, July 4th 1967; 2254, July 14th 1967. The United Nations never explained what was the status of Jerusalem before the 1967 war that could not be changed.

[5] Security Council Resolutions 446, March 22nd 1979; 452, July 20th 1979 and 465, March 1st 1980; 2334, December 23rd 2016. General Assembly Resolutions 3092, December 7th 1973; A/41/63, December 3rd 1986; A/RES/ ES-10/13, October 27th 2003; A/RES/ ES-10/14, December 12th 2003.

[6] Security Council Resolutions 446, 452, 465 and 2334, Ibid.; see also General Assembly Resolutions 3092, December 7th 1973; A/RES/ES-10/14, December 12th 2003.

[7] For example: General Assembly Resolution 3092, December 7th 1978.

'to self-determination in accordance with the Charter of the United Nations' and in reaffirming 'the inalienable rights of the Palestinian people in Palestine.'[8] Thereafter, General Assembly resolutions provided the Arabs of Palestine with full national rights to the whole of Palestine, namely, 'the right of return, the right of self-determination, and the right to national independence and sovereignty in Palestine [not restricted to the West Bank and Gaza Strip alone], in accordance with the Charter of the United Nations'.[9] The General Assembly then saw fit to declare that the Camp David Accords had no validity in so far as they purport to determine the future status of the Palestinian people and the occupied Palestinian territories.[10] This led to the adoption on November 29th 2012 by the General Assembly of a resolution 'to accord to Palestine non-member observer State status in the United Nations' after 'reaffirming the right of the Palestinian people to self-determination, including the right to *their* independent State of Palestine'.[11] [Italics added]. Consequently, the Legal Counsel to the United Nations instructed that 'for United Nations purposes, Palestine may now generally be referred to as a State or country; and its authorities may generally be identified as the Government of Palestine'. Also, they insisted that Palestine should be referred to as the 'State of Palestine', and that the geographical area of the Palestinian territory occupied by Israel since 1967 should be addressed as 'occupied Palestinian territory, including East Jerusalem'.[12]

The International Committee of the Red Cross followed suit. It defined the 'occupied Palestinian territories' as constituting 'the West Bank, East Jerusalem and the Gaza Strip' and, therefore,

---

8 General Assembly Resolution 3236 (XXIX), November 22nd 1974.

9 General Assembly Resolution 34/65 B, December 12th 1979, para. 2.

10 Ibid., para. 4.

11 General Assembly Resolution 67/19, December 4th 2012, see 8th recital and para. 2.

12 Patricia O'Brien – *Issues related to General Assembly Resolution 67/19 on the status of Palestine in the United Nations*, United Nations Inter-Office Memorandum, December 21st 2012, paras. 3, 7 and 8. O'Brien served as Under-Secretary-General for Legal Affairs and the Legal Counsel at the United Nations.

in its view, the Fourth Geneva Convention applied to these territories as a matter of course. As a result, the establishment of Jewish settlements in these areas was considered illegal.[13] This conception gained credit in international circles despite the fact that these areas were captured in 1948 by invading Arab forces into Palestine, including the armies of Trans-Jordan and Egypt, in a clear act of aggression; despite the fact that neither Trans-Jordan nor Egypt acquired sovereignty over any of these territories; and despite the fact that these areas had no recognized frontiers but were delineated by armistice agreements concluded in 1949 between Israel and Trans-Jordan for the West Bank, and between Israel and Egypt for the Gaza Strip. These agreements emphasized that they should not be interpreted in any sense as establishing political or territorial boundaries.[14]

Similarly, the European Union has repeatedly emphasized that it did not recognize Israel's sovereignty over the Gaza Strip and the West Bank including East Jerusalem, and would not recognize any changes to pre-1967 *borders* [italics provided], other than those agreed upon by the parties in the Middle East Process. Therefore, in the EU's view, the establishment of settlements by Israel in the "Palestinian Occupied Territories, including East Jerusalem', has no legal validity and constitutes a flagrant violation of international law. On the basis of this policy, the European Union issued guidelines intended to preclude the application of agreements with Israel to the West Bank and East Jerusalem. These agreements constitute mainly grants, prizes and financial instruments funded by the European Union. The guidelines specifically absolved the Arabs living in the same areas of the West Bank and East Jerusalem from the application of these restrictions.[15]

---

[13] Peter Maurer – *Challenges to International Humanitarian Law: Israel's Occupation Policy*, International Review of the Red Cross, Vol. 94, No. 888, Winter 2012.

[14] Jordanian-Israeli General Armistice Agreement, April 3rd 1949, Art. II (2) and Art. VI (8). Egyptian-Israeli General Armistice Agreement, February 24th 1949, Articles IV (3) and V (2) and (3).

[15] Guidelines on *The Eligibility of Israeli Entities and their Activities in the Territories Occupied by Israel since June 1967 for Grants, Prizes and*

Most striking is the fact that none of these international organizations made any reference to the original treaties and resolutions that shaped the legal structure of the Middle East at the beginning of the Twentieth Century, viz., the McMahon pledge, the Balfour Declaration, the San Remo Resolution, the Treaty of Sèvres, and most of all the Mandate for Palestine which conferred on Britain the task of establishing in Palestine a National Home for the Jewish people. The rights derived from these binding international commitments made to the Jewish people were still valid when Israel occupied the West Bank, pursuant to Article 80 of the United Nations' Charter which provides:

> Nothing in this Chapter[16] shall be construed in or of itself to alter in any manner the rights whatsoever of any states or any peoples or the terms of existing international instruments to which members of the United Nations may respectively be parties.

Only by ignoring or overlooking these original treaties and resolutions could the international community arrive at the decisions adopted incessantly by the United Nations and other international organizations. These fundamental truths are ignored by the international community, and they are treated as if they never existed.

Most interesting is the advisory opinion of the ICJ regarding the construction of parts of the Security Barrier in the West Bank in which it axiomatically referred to the latter as 'Occupied Palestinian Territory'.[17] Yet, the ICJ provided no explanation as to how this area, which was to form an integral part of the Jewish National Home, became Palestinian Arab territory, particularly

---

Financial Instruments Funded by the EU from 2014 Onwards, Official Journal of the European Union, July 19th 2013, C 205/9-11; see also report by the European Union, September 30th 2019, on 'Israeli settlements in the occupied West Bank, including East Jerusalem' (reporting period January-June 2019).

16 Chapter XII – International Trusteeship System, Articles 75-85.

17 International Court of Justice – *Legal Consequences of the Construction of a Wall in the Occupied Palestinian Territory,* July 9th 2004, para. 70.

when there has never been any Palestinian Arab state before then. In fact, the Jewish population of Palestine by the end of British rule in Palestine numbered around 600,000, forming more than one third of the total population, and they were also regarded as Palestinians. In ascertaining the status of the West Bank, the ICJ made no reference to any of the above-mentioned original international documents. In fact, the ICJ hardly touched upon the historical background which led to the establishment of the Palestine Mandate. On the legal history of Palestine and the West Bank, the ICJ made a brief comment stating:

> Palestine was part of the Ottoman Empire. At the end of the First World War, a class 'A' Mandate for Palestine was entrusted to Great Britain by the League of Nations, pursuant to paragraph 4 of Article 22 of the Covenant.

The next relevant step in the sequence of events, in the ICJ's view, was:

> In 1947 the United Kingdom announced its intention to complete evacuation of the mandated territory by 1 August 1948, subsequently advancing that date to 15 May 1948...[18]

Evidently, the ICJ totally disregarded the period beginning with the Balfour Declaration, a period of three decades, in which binding international treaties and resolutions shaped the Middle East after the First World War. The ICJ, which was to pronounce its opinion on the legality of the construction of the Security Barrier in the western part of the West Bank, and as a result, on the legality of Israel's right to control these territories, attached no significance to the San Remo Resolution and the Mandate which gave birth to rights that were still valid under Article 80 of the United Nations Charter.

The Israeli Government, for its part, refused to apply the

---

[18] Ibid., para. 71.

Geneva Convention in the territories, and since 1977 Israel has voted in the General Assembly against the applicability of the Geneva Convention while the vast majority of its members voted in the diametrically opposite direction. However, Israel stated that it would apply voluntarily its humanitarian provisions. On this basis, the Israeli Supreme Court applied the humanitarian provisions of the Convention as a matter of course, even if it proved a detriment to Israeli interests. Surprisingly, the Supreme Court never found it necessary to base its refusal to apply the Geneva Convention de jure on the right of the Jewish people to a National Home in Palestine under the Mandate, a right that was still valid pursuant to Article 80 of the United Nations Charter. Perhaps, for this reason, the Supreme Court consistently avoided any decision on the legality of the settlements.[19]

As will be revealed in this book, based on historical facts: shortly after the First World War, the Principal Allied Powers, who 'inherited' the sovereignty over the Middle East from the defunct Ottoman Empire, decided to divide the Middle East under a mandatory system between the two contenders at the time. These were the Arab nation as a whole, represented by the Sherif of Mecca (later King Hussein of Hedjaz), and the Jewish people as a whole, represented by the Zionist Organization. Their decision was to grant the Arab nation independence in the entire Middle East except Palestine, and simultaneously, to confer upon Britain the Mandate for Palestine to be held in trust for the purpose of establishing there a National Home for the Jewish people, which could evolve, if the experiment proved successful, into a Jewish State. Documentary evidence demonstrates that Britain was responsible for the establishment of a Jewish, not Arab, National Home in Palestine, while the civil and religious rights of the non-Jewish population of Palestine, as a future minority, were to be well protected.

The reason behind British promises to both the Arab nation and Jewish people was the desire to induce them to join forces

---

[19] Daphne Barak-Erez – *Israel: The security barrier – between international law, constitutional law, and domestic judicial law,* 4 Int'l J. Const. L. 540, 548.

with the Allied Powers, particularly Britain, in their war efforts against the Axis Powers, mainly Germany and the Ottoman Empire. The Arabs of Hedjaz under Hussein and Feisal joined forces with the Allied Powers, mainly with Britain. The Jews also played their part in the bargain. After the war, the two competing parties came forward and made their claims at the Paris Peace Conference. Accordingly, the Allied Powers divided the Middle East to suit the pledges that were made to the Arab nation and Jewish people.

The legal authority of the Allied Powers to dispose of the territories in the Middle East after the war was based on the renunciation by the Ottoman Empire of its sovereignty over the Middle East in favor of the Allied Powers, who decided against annexation and in favor of establishing Mandates under the Covenant of the League of Nations, leading eventually, in all cases except for Palestine, to the independence of the native population. In consequence, Syria, Lebanon and Mesopotamia, in addition to the Hedjaz and other Arab entities in the Arabian Peninsula, were established as Arab independent States subject to certain requirements, while Palestine was conferred in trust to Britain as a Mandatory – for the sole purpose of giving effect to the Balfour Declaration for the establishment of a Jewish National Home in that country. These two decisions were taken simultaneously and constituted a package deal that could not be separated. In this way, both pledges, to the Arabs and Jews alike, were fulfilled in the eyes of the Allies.

The pledge to the Jewish people was made by the British Government on November 2nd 1917, in a document known as the Balfour Declaration, in which Britain undertook to facilitate the establishment of a National Home for the Jewish people in Palestine coupled with an understanding that nothing shall be done that might jeopardize the civil and religious rights of the existing non-Jewish inhabitants of that country. The pledge referred to a National Home, but not to a State, for the reason that the whole project was an experiment at its beginning depending on Jewish enterprise to immigrate en mass to Palestine to form a majority and take over the country. But a National Home was envisaged from the very beginning by Prime Minister Lloyd George, Foreign Secretary Arthur James Balfour, and other members of the British Cabinet, to lead, if successful, to a Jewish State. The Balfour Declaration was affirmed and endorsed by all the Allied and Associated Powers. It was then confirmed by the Allied Powers at San Remo, in the Treaty of Sèvres, and was made part of the Mandate for Palestine. The Mandate received the formal confirmation of the League of Nations and its 51 members.

Two years earlier, on October 24th 1915, McMahon, the British High Commissioner in Cairo, promised Hussein that the British would recognize Arab independence in an area bordered in the north by a line connecting Alexandretta with Diarbekir, in the east bordered by Persia and the Persian Gulf, in the south by the Indian Ocean, and in the west by the Red Sea and the Mediterranean, except the littoral area lying west of the towns of Aleppo, Homs, Hama and Damascus, and territories in which France had interests. The British contended all along that these exceptions clearly included Palestine as it was west of the four enumerated towns in Syria, and, in any case, Palestine clearly falls within the area in which France had abiding interests. At first, Hussein and Feisal showed no objection to the British interpretation of the McMahon pledge, demonstrated in Feisal's speeches at the Paris Peace Conference and in his agreement with Weizmann. But five years later, when Feisal lost the throne in Syria, and the Arab inhabitants of Palestine began to show resistance to Feisal's acquiescence, the Sherifian family changed its attitude and opposed the exclusion of Palestine from the area assigned for Arab independence.

This disagreement between the British and the Sherifian family was never resolved, but either way it should be clearly emphasized that the McMahon pledge had no significance in international law. At the most, it could be contended that it was a British commitment which included Palestine. This, as pointed out, had been emphatically denied by all British Governments since the making of the pledge. The McMahon pledge was never granted international recognition. Unlike the Balfour

Declaration, it was not confirmed, ratified or endorsed by any state other than Britain, having not been part of any treaty and never been confirmed by the League of Nations. While the Balfour Declaration was immediately published and received worldwide recognition, the McMahon pledge was not made public until 1938, twenty-three years after its issuance.

The Arab nation relied on three more documents in an effort to include Palestine in the British pledge to the Arabs. These were the Hogarth Message, the Declaration to the Seven, and the Anglo-French Declaration all concluded in 1918. The first two were created while the war was still being fought and the third just at its end. None of them amounted to a pledge regarding the inclusion of Palestine within the Arab hemisphere and, in any case, none had any significance in international law.

Notably, the McMahon pledge was made to Hussein as representative of the Arab nation as a whole. The Arabs of Palestine, forming part of that nation, accepted his leadership and, in fact, Hussein was acting on their behalf too. The pledge was not given specifically to the Arabs of Palestine, who fought alongside the Turkish Army in the war, and Britain owed them no consideration. At any rate, the Arabs of Palestine did not then form a separate entity that made them eligible to a separate independence.

Nevertheless, the commitment to the establishment of the Jewish National Home was watered down due to violent Arab resistance, which cast a heavy burden on the British taxpayer in order to keep the peace and restore law and order. Deadly riots initiated by Arabs against Jewish inhabitants in Palestine occurred in 1920, 1921, 1929, 1933, and 1936. British policy in Palestine gradually changed and restrictions were imposed on immigration and land settlement. By 1939, the McDonald White Paper decreed a complete halt to Jewish immigration within five years, in total violation of the Mandate and the other binding international instruments. Originally, the Jewish National Home was to be established on both sides of the Jordan River. However, Palestine was partitioned for the first time in 1921 to provide a State for Emir Abdullah, second son of the Sherif of Mecca, on its eastern part, located east of the Jordan River, namely, Trans-Jordan. It was then planned to be partitioned for the second time in 1947, pursuant to General Assembly Resolution 181 (II), in an endeavor to create yet another Arab State, leaving the Jewish people with only a small portion of the original promised territory. Nevertheless, even this move was rejected by the Arabs, who claimed the whole of Palestine and, consequently, began the war of 1948 with an avowed object to destroy by military force the newly born Jewish State.

Now, for the purpose of determining the legality of Jewish settlements in the West Bank, including East Jerusalem and the Gaza Strip, the international community, and notably the ICJ, consider that only events that took place as a result of the 1967 Six-Day-War should count, thus disregarding altogether the Balfour Declaration, the San Remo Resolution and the Mandate for Palestine. This view is deeply in error. This is because the legal position of the West Bank goes back 50 years when the Middle East was shaped by the Principal Allied Powers, the only authority to decide on how to dispose of the Middle East at the time, with the legal and political structure of the Middle East decided between 1915 and 1923. During this time, the McMahon pledge was made in favor of the Arab Nation as a whole and the Balfour Declaration together with the San Remo Resolution and the Mandate for Palestine were made in favor of the Jewish people as a whole. The rights and privileges acquired in these documents cannot be discarded, and they continue to prevail under Article 80 of the UN Charter even after the League of Nations' era and the constitution of the United Nations. The Arabs were promised independence throughout the whole of the Middle East except Palestine, while the Jews were promised to have their National Home established in Palestine.

Has any post-1923 event affected the right of Jews to settle anywhere in Palestine including the West Bank, East Jerusalem, and the Gaza Strip? In view of the following survey, it seems not.

Arguably, the first pertinent event was General Assembly Resolution 181 (II). However, its implementation was aborted due to Arab rejection. It was drafted subsequent to British appeal to the United Nations on April 2nd 1947, pursuant to Article 10 of the Charter to propose a settlement in Palestine. Article 10 provides that 'the General Assembly... may make *recommendations* to the members of the United Nations or to the Security Council or to both on any such questions or matters'.[20] [Italics added]. The General Assembly decided to adopt the partition plan, which was suggested by a Special Committee on Palestine (UNSCOP) that it appointed for this purpose. Accordingly, the General Assembly recommended that Palestine west of the Jordan be divided into three entities, one forming a Jewish State, the other forming an Arab State, and the third, concerning the City of Jerusalem, was to be held under an international trustee system, administered by the United Nations as *Corpus Separatum*.

However, the General Assembly's partition plan lacked any binding force. It was a recommendation made to the parties, free to adopt or reject it. The Jewish representatives accepted the recommendation. However, the Arabs vehemently rejected it. Julius Stone, quoting Elihu Lauterpacht, maintained that 'the 1947 partition resolution had no... legislative character as to vest territorial rights in either Jews or Arabs'.[21] Evidently, the Jewish side was not bound by the Resolution. In the first place, this was because the Arabs had rejected it and subsequently aborted it by a war of aggression launched against Israel. Secondly, as noted, the Resolution was a recommendation to the parties which was rejected. For the Resolution to have had a binding effect, it should have been accepted by both parties and made part of an agreement which would confer sovereignty over the Jewish State and the Arab State, while subjecting Jerusalem to UN administration as *Corpus Separatum*. However, such an agreement was never achieved. Consequently, Resolution 181 (II) carries no international significance.[22]

---

[20] Referring to questions or matters "within the scope of the present Charter or relating to the powers and functions of any organs provided for in the present Charter". (Article 10).

[21] Julius Stone – *Israel and Palestine: Assault on the Law of Nations*, Johns Hopkins University Press, Baltimore, 1981, pp. 60-61.

[22] Ibid., pp. 62-63.

Another notable event was the armistice agreements signed in 1949. In consequence of the 1948 war, the Arab armies who invaded Palestine managed to occupy parts of it. Trans-Jordan occupied Judea and Samaria and named it the West Bank, ostensibly to disconnect the area from its original biblical name. Egypt occupied the Gaza Strip. By the end of the war, separate armistice agreements were signed between Egypt, Trans-Jordan, Syria, and Lebanon on the one hand and Israel on the other. These agreements did not alter in any way the right of the Jewish people to settle anywhere in Palestine. The armistice line between the State of Israel and the West Bank followed the cease fire line that was established at the end of the Arab-Israeli war of 1948-1949. This line was susceptible to change either as a result of a political settlement or another war between the Parties. The Jordanian-Israeli Armistice Agreement specifically stated 'that no provision of this Agreement shall in any way prejudice the rights, claims and positions of either Party hereto in the ultimate peaceful settlement of the Palestine question, *the provisions of this agreement being dictated exclusively by military considerations*'.[23] [Italics added]. The same applied to the Egyptian-Israeli Armistice Agreement.[24]

Of further importance was the annexation of the West Bank, including East Jerusalem, by Trans-Jordan. Egypt never attempted to apply sovereignty over the Gaza Strip, which remained in Egyptian occupation for 19 years until the Six-Day-War of 1967, while Trans-Jordan decided to annex the West Bank unlawfully after occupying it in an unprovoked act of aggression aimed at destroying the newly born Jewish State. This purported annexation was not recognized by any country save for Britain and Pakistan. Recognition was even denied by other Arab countries and also by the Arab League. Trans-Jordan's invasion into Palestine in 1948 constituted a use of force in violation of Article 2 (4) of the United Nations Charter, and, therefore, did not acquire any legal title under international law over the West

---

[23] Jordanian-Israeli General Armistice Agreement, April 3rd 1949, Article II (2).

[24] Egyptian-Israeli General Armistice Agreement of February 24th 1949, Article IV (3).

Bank. Neither did it acquire the rights of a legitimate sovereign over this territory. In any case, in 1988 Jordan[25] abandoned all claims to the West Bank.[26] Consequently, the annexation did not alter the original legal position of the West Bank.

In Blum's view 'in a case like the present where the ousted state never was the legitimate sovereign, those rules of belligerent occupation aimed at safeguarding the sovereign's reversionary rights, have no application'.[27] In addition, in view of the San Remo Resolution, the Treaty of Sèvres and the Mandate, the Arabs of Palestine never acquired national rights in any part of Palestine west of the Jordan River. Thus, when Israeli forces took over the West Bank in a purely defensive war, they occupied that same land that was pledged to the Jewish people as their National Home through binding international treaties and resolutions. According to the Mandate for Palestine, Jews had the right to settle in any part of Palestine, including the West Bank. The same rule that allowed Jewish settlements in Tel Aviv, Haifa, and Beersheba applied to East Jerusalem, Hebron, and Bethlehem.[28] In fact, before the 1948-1949 Arab-Israeli war, Jewish settlements existed in the West Bank such as in Hebron and in East Jerusalem, but they were destroyed as a result of the Arab invasion and their Jewish inhabitants violently evicted.

A fundamental contradiction exists in the attitude of the United Nations and other international organizations towards the establishment of Jewish settlements in the West Bank. On the one hand, it is accepted that the occupation of the West Bank in

---

[25] As a result of the annexation of the West Bank, Trans-Jordan was renamed Jordan.

[26] This move was taken in favor of the Palestinians. However, Jordan could not transfer rights that it never had.

[27] Yehuda Blum – *The Missing Reversioner: Reflections on the Status of Judea and Samaria,* Is.L.R. 3(2)279, 293; This view was supported by other jurists, see Adam Roberts – *Prolonged Military Occupation: The Israeli Occupied Territories Since 1967,* AJIL, Vol. 84, No. 1, Jan. 1990, p. 79 expressing the view that the idea that the West Bank would revert to Jordan "was effectively dead".

[28] Eugene V. Rostow – *Are the Settlements Legal? Article 1: Bricks and Stones – Settling for Leverage; Palestinian Autonomy,* The New Republic, April 23rd 1990.

1967 by Israel was the outcome of a purely defensive act, and, therefore, there was hardly any claim that Israel's occupation of the West Bank was illegal.[29] Furthermore, there could be no doubt that during the Mandate, Jews had the right to settle anywhere in Palestine, including the West Bank. Those rights did not fade away. They were preserved and safeguarded by virtue of Article 80 of the United Nations Charter. Yet, the international community and the United Nations incessantly claim that Jewish settlements in the West bank are illegal under Article 49 of the Geneva Convention, which, as claimed internationally, applies to the territories. These two positions cannot be reconciled. Indeed, the Mandate should take preference over Article 49 of the Geneva Convention according to the well-known maxim: *lex specialis derogat legi generali*, since the former applies specifically to Palestine including the West Bank, while Article 49 applies to occupied territories in general.

Notably, the Mandate for Palestine differs from the other mandates established in the Middle East in the sense that the latter were trusts for the benefit of the native population whilst the former was held in trust for the purpose of establishing a National Home for the Jewish people, founded on international recognition of the Jewish historical connection to Palestine.

Another significant event is Security Council Resolution 242, which was adopted in consequence of the Six-Day-War. The circumstances in which it was passed give rise to the question of whether its adoption affected the right of Jews to settle in any part of the West Bank. Here too, the answer is in the negative. In the Six-Day-War of June 1967, Israel occupied territories far larger than its own. It occupied the entire Sinai Peninsula, the Golan

---

[29] Adam Roberts, op. cit., p.67, n.79: Roberts pointed out that the term 'illegal occupation' with regard to Israel was hardly used in UN resolutions. It was only used in General Assembly Resolutions 32/20 of November 25th 1977 and 33/29 of December 7th 1978, but these were the exceptions to the rule. The General Assembly and the Security Council have not stated that the fact of the occupation is in itself illegal; see e.g. General Assembly Resolutions 41/63 December 3rd 1986 and 43/58A-G December 6th 1988. The omission of the term 'illegal occupation' in the Arab-Israeli conflict is in sharp contrast to its repeated use in the resolutions on Namibia.

Heights, the West Bank, East Jerusalem and the Gaza Strip. It is generally acknowledged that of all United Nations resolutions on the occupied territories, Security Council Resolution 242 was the most important. It was accepted as binding by all the belligerent Parties: Israel, Egypt, Jordan and Syria. The main theme of Resolution 242 was the unanimous demand by the Security Council of all belligerent States in the area to arrive at a just and lasting peace on the following principles: (a) Withdrawal of Israeli troops 'from *territories* occupied in the recent conflict' to secure and recognized boundaries [Italics added], and (b) 'Termination of all claims or states of belligerency and respect for and acknowledgement of the sovereignty, territorial integrity and political independence of every State in the area and their right to live in peace'.[30] Security Council Resolution 338, adopted after the October 1973 War, also known as the Yom Kippur War, called upon the parties to undertake the implementation of Resolution 242, thus adding more weight to its binding force.[31] In none of these two major Resolutions were the Palestinian Arabs mentioned as a separate entity eligible for the right of self-determination or to having acquired any legal title over the West Bank, East Jerusalem, or the Gaza Strip.

It has been consistently contended by Arab States, as well as by European, Soviet, and some American officials, that Resolution 242 was deliberately ambiguous and, therefore, open to various interpretations. Eugene Rostow, who served as Under-Secretary of State for Political Affairs between 1966 and 1969, and took an active part in its production, firmly rejected these allegations stating:

> Nothing could be further from the truth. Resolution 242...calls on the parties to make peace and allows Israel to administer the territories it occupied in 1967 until 'a just and lasting peace in the Middle East' is achieved. When such a peace is made, Israel is required to withdraw its forces 'from territories' it

---

30 Security Council Resolution 242, November 22nd 1967, Article 1.
31 Security Council Resolution 338, October 22nd 1973.

occupied during the Six Day War – *not from 'the' territories nor from 'all' the territories, but from some of the territories,* which included the Sinai Desert, the West Bank, the Golan Heights, East Jerusalem, and the Gaza Strip. [Italics added].

The missing definite article in Resolution 242 was, therefore, deliberate and intentional. Rostow emphasized that the final text was the result of over five months of intensive deliberations which made clear what Resolution 242 meant. Many drafts were proposed demanding total withdrawal of Israeli forces from *all* the territories occupied in the 1967 conflict. However, these demands were defeated both in the Security Council and the General Assembly. Rostow reiterated: 'Speaker after speaker made it explicit that Israel was not to be forced back to the 'fragile' and 'vulnerable' Armistice Demarcation Lines, but should retire once peace was made to what Resolution 242 called 'secure and recognized' boundaries, agreed by the parties.'

Following the Peace Treaty with Egypt and Jordan, Israel withdrew from all the Sinai Peninsula and rectified the frontier with Jordan. Thus, it withdrew from most of the territories occupied during the Six-Day-War. It should be emphasized that Resolution 242 never required Israel to withdraw from each of the occupied territories. Israel was not required specifically to withdraw from the West Bank, East Jerusalem or the Gaza Strip. On the contrary, it was clear from Rostow's statement that Israel was not required or expected to return to the fragile and vulnerable 1948 demarcation lines.

The agreement signed between the Israeli Government and the Palestine Liberation Organization (PLO) on September 13th 1993 entitled Declaration of Principles on Interim Self-Government Arrangements is another event of importance. It was followed by a series of agreements generally known as the Oslo Accords.[32]

---

[32] Key agreements were: Agreement on the Gaza Strip and the Jericho Area, signed on May 4th 1994 in Cairo, also known as the Cairo Agreement, and Israeli-Palestinian Interim Agreement on the West Bank and the Gaza Strip of September 28th 1995, also known as the Oslo II Accord.

The purpose of the Agreement was to achieve peace between the parties 'after decades of confrontation and conflict'[33] on the one hand and, on the other, "to establish a Palestinian interim self-Government Authority...for a transitional period not exceeding five years leading to a permanent settlement based on Security Council Resolutions 242 and 338'.[34] As a prerequisite to signing the Declaration of Principles, Yasser Arafat, PLO Chairman, solemnly made the following commitments to Yitzhak Rabin, Prime Minister of Israel:[35]

> The PLO commits itself to the Middle East peace process, and to a peaceful resolution of the conflict between the two sides and declares that all outstanding issues relating to permanent status will be resolved through negotiations.
>
> The PLO considers that the signing of the Declaration of Principles constitutes a historic event, inaugurating a new epoch of peaceful coexistence, free from violence and all other acts which endanger peace and stability. Accordingly, *the PLO renounces the use of terrorism and other acts of violence* and will assume responsibility over all PLO elements and personnel in order to assure their compliance, prevent violations and discipline violators. [Italics added].

On the basis of these commitments, Israel began peace negotiations with the PLO.[36] As a result of these negotiations, each party recognized the 'legitimate and political rights' of the other party, and, consequently, the Palestinians were granted self-rule after holding democratic elections in the territories. These elections would 'constitute a significant interim preparatory step

---

[33] Declaration of Principles on Interim Self-Government Arrangements, Preamble.

[34] Ibid., Article I.

[35] Letter by Chairman Arafat to Yitzhak Rabin Prime Minister of Israel on September 9th 1993, four days before signing the Declaration of Principles in Washington.

[36] See Yitzhak Rabin's reply the next day to Arafat's letter.

toward the realization of the legitimate rights of the Palestinian people and their just requirements.'[37] The jurisdiction of self-rule would cover the West Bank and the Gaza Strip as one unit, except for specified excluded areas such as Jewish settlements and army barracks and installations, until the conclusion of final negotiations on the permanent status of the West Bank and the Gaza Strip. Final negotiations would include the following issues: Jerusalem, refugees, settlements, security arrangements, borders, relations with other neighbors, and other issues of common interest. Significantly, the Declaration of Principles made no mention of a Palestinian sovereign State necessarily emerging as a result of the final negotiations. Neither did it specify the borders and limits of the Palestinian entity. These were subject to negotiations between the parties and conditional to Israel's acceptance. In any case, it was highly unlikely that the Palestinians would have been able to keep the entire area of the West Bank and the Gaza Strip. At best, they would have been allowed to keep part of these territories in consequence of negotiations that would have led to a compromise by Israel.

Be that as it may, the Oslo Accords were violated, frustrated and finally abolished as a result of deadly acts of Palestinian terror that began soon after the signing of the Declaration, culminated by the second intifada of July 2002 that brought about the murder of hundreds of civilians in major Israeli cities towns and villages. Under these circumstances, the Israeli Government ceased troop withdrawals, and, in consequence, the Agreement became defunct, devoid of any international significance.[38]

The resolutions of the United Nations referring to East Jerusalem as Palestinian Arab territory are even more perplexing. Soon after the Israeli occupation, Security Council resolutions

---

[37] Declaration of principles on Interim Self-Government Arrangements, Article III (3).

[38] The main objective and rationale of the Oslo accords was the achievement of peace between Israel and the Palestinians and a commitment that all conflicts would be solved through negotiations. The initiation of terrorist activities against Israeli civilians soon after the Oslo Accords were signed was a complete violation of these Agreements, severely jeopardizing its purpose and raison d'être.

warned Israel against changing the legal status of East Jerusalem but deliberately refrained from stating what that status was.[39] General Assembly resolutions followed suit,[40] at some stage referring to East Jerusalem, and sometimes to the whole of Jerusalem, as Palestinian Arab territory. However, international pledges to establish a Jewish National Home in Palestine made no exception to Jerusalem or to any part of it. Furthermore, in General Assembly Resolution 181 (II) regarding the partition plan, neither Jerusalem, nor any part of it, was assigned to the Arabs of Palestine. Jerusalem, as recalled, was to be administered by the United Nations as a *Corpus Separatum*. Chronologically, Palestine was under Ottoman sovereignty for 400 years preceding the British Mandate, and later was illegally occupied by Jordan. It is, therefore, not clear on what grounds the United Nations termed Jerusalem or East Jerusalem as Arab or Palestinian territory. At no time in modern history was Jerusalem under legitimate Arab sovereignty or control. It is, therefore, inexplicable how Jerusalem, which was under Ottoman sovereignty, then passed to British Mandatory rule, and then occupied illegally by Trans-Jordan came to be designated Palestinian Arab territory. The ICJ also refers to Jerusalem as occupied Palestinian Territory without mentioning the legal basis for its assertion.[41]

This book is not about the grievances or injustices that might have been suffered by either party. It is entirely concerned with exploring the legal rights to Mandatory Palestine of each of the two contending parties, the Arab Nation on the one hand and the Jewish people on the other. For this purpose, it was necessary to thoroughly examine the original international treaties and resolutions which shaped the legal and political structure of the Middle East at the beginning of the Twentieth Century: namely,

---

[39] Security Council Resolutions 252, May 21st 1968; 267, July 3rd 1969; 298, September 25th 1971.

[40] General Assembly Resolutions 2253, July 4th 1967; 2254, July 14th 1967.

[41] It is illuminating that during the 19 years of unlawful occupation of the West Bank and East Jerusalem by Jordan the United Nations never condemned it for changing the legal status of the eastern parts of Jerusalem by its formal annexation. Julius Stone, op. cit., pp. 110-11.

the McMahon pledge of 1915, the Balfour Declaration of 1917, the San Remo Resolution of 1920, the Treaty of Sèvres of 1920, and the Mandate for Palestine of 1922, which became part of international law. Significantly, these original treaties and regulations were unjustifiably ignored or cast aside by the United Nations and other international organizations in consistently and incessantly condemning the establishment of Jewish settlements in the occupied territories as having no legal validity and constituting a flagrant violation of international law.

Part I

The Balfour Declaration

Chapter I

The Foundations of Zionism

The Jewish people lived in the Diaspora for almost 2000 years after the destruction of their second Temple. They were scattered as religious minorities all over the world. Jewish national revival began in 1897 with Theodor Herzl, the first Jewish leader to bring the Jewish question out into the open as a national problem. Herzl came to the conclusion, after the political scandal of the Dreyfus affair in 1894,[1] that the only solution to anti-Semitism and Jewish persecution was the reconstruction of a Jewish state as a homeland for the Jewish people. In his seminal treatise *The Jewish State* (*Der Judenstaat*), published in Vienna in 1896,[2] he argued that the end of anti-Semitism could be accomplished either through total assimilation (i.e. effectively the end of the Jewish people) or by re-establishing a state of their own for Jews to live in, free from persecution and oppression. Herzl was referring to a state with full sovereignty and not to any entity short of that sovereign designation.

For Herzl, the Jewish question emanated from irrefutable conditions of historical reality: Wherever they (the Jews) live in perceptible numbers, they are more or less persecuted. Their equality before the law, granted by statute, has become practically a dead letter. They are debarred from filling even moderately high positions, either in the army, or in any public

---

[1] Alfred Dreyfus served as a captain in the French Artillery Corps when he was falsely accused of treason for allegedly communicating French military secrets to the Germans. Apparently, Dreyfus was convicted for no other reason, but for the fact that he was a Jew. He was sentenced to life imprisonment and was sent to serve his sentence in Devil's Island in French Guiana. His conviction proved to be a striking example of miscarriage of justice. Dreyfus was finally exonerated in 1906 and reinstated as a major in the French Army. He served during The First World War ending his service with the rank of Lieutenant-Colonel. He died in 1935.

[2] Edition published by the American Zionist Emergency Council, 1946, translated from the German by Sylvie D'Avigdor; www.jewishvirtuallibrary. org/jsource/Zionism/herzl2.html

or private capacity, and attempts are made to thrust them out of business too: Don't buy from Jews.[3] All of which leads to the same conclusion: Juden Raus! (Out with the Jews!). Now, the question arises: where to?

At first, Herzl, in *The Jewish State*, was not yet sure where the Jewish State would be established. He preferred Palestine, but other options were entertained.[4] In the case of Palestine, the Ottoman Sultan would need to grant the establishment of a Jewish State. Herzl saw the Jewish question as a 'national question, which can only be solved by making it a political world question to be discussed and settled by the civilized nations of the world in council.'[5] He argued that its essence was political and national (not individual), that had to be dealt with in the sphere of international law. Therefore, it would have to be settled legally and openly.

How then can the Jewish people be transferred to their newly established state from all corners of the earth? Herzl answered: 'No human being is wealthy or powerful enough to transplant a nation from one habitation to another. An idea alone can achieve that, and this idea of a state may have the requisite power to do so.'[6]

Herzl was preceded by others, particularly Dr. Leon Pinsker, an assimilated Jewish physician from Odessa. In his pamphlet *Auto-Emancipation*, he came to the same conclusion following anti-Jewish riots in Tsarist Russia in 1881. Only by establishing a state of their own could Jews avoid anti-Semitism. This state could only be established in Palestine.[7] Even before the publication of *The Jewish State*, local Zionist activities had already sprouted up in eastern Europe, particularly in Russia. These revolved around

---

[3] Theodor Herzl – *The Jewish State*, Vienna 1896, Jewish virtual Library, p.7. https://www.jewishvirtuallibrary.org/quot-the-jewish-state-quot-theodor-herzl

[4] In Herzl's words: 'Palestine is our ever memorable historic home' and 'Next year in Jerusalem is our old phrase.'

[5] Ibid., p. 2.

[6] Ibid., p. 3.

[7] Israel Cohen – *The Zionist Movement*, ZOA New York, 1946, p. 64.

promoting Jewish immigration to Palestine, although for various reasons Herzl seems to have been unaware of them. Nevertheless, Herzl was undoubtedly the founder of political Zionism, the first Jewish leader to project the Jewish question into the international arena.

The movement that began under Herzl's leadership first convened in Basel, Switzerland, in 1897. This congress represented the first secular gathering of Jews from different nations to formulate a Zionist plenum. It declared that 'Zionism seeks to establish a home for the Jewish people in Palestine secured under Public Law.'[8] Following the first Zionist Congress, the World Zionist Organization was established as a representative of the Jewish people, with Herzl elected its president. Herzl famously wrote in his personal diary on September 3rd 1897: 'If I were to sum up the Basel Congress in one word…it would be this: at Basel I founded the Jewish State.'[9]

Herzl chaired six congresses from 1897 till 1902, during which national settlement options other than Palestine were considered: Uganda, Wadi El Arish in the Sinai Peninsula, and Cyprus. These deliberations were, in fact, the outcome of despair caused by unsuccessful negotiations with the Ottoman Sultan to secure a Charter for large scale Jewish settlement in Palestine. Regardless, the majority of the delegates were almost unanimously in favor of Palestine as a National Home for the Jewish people. Herzl died in 1904 at the age of 44, leaving much to be accomplished.

---

[8]   http://www.jewishvirtuallibrary.org/first-to-twelfth-zionist-congress-1897-1921

[9]   Israel Cohen, op. cit., p.78.

Chapter II

The Status of the Balfour Declaration

The Zionist movement created by Herzl was at first no more than an internal movement within the Jewish people unrecognized by any international body or state. Public recognition to Jewish aspirations was first granted by the British Government on November 2nd, 1917 in a declaration later known as the Balfour Declaration. The Declaration was given in the form of a letter signed by the British Foreign Secretary, Lord Arthur James Balfour. Its addressee was Lord Lionel Walter Rothschild, the honorary president of the English Zionist Federation. The letter, which was soon made public, stated the following:

> I have much pleasure in conveying to you, on behalf of his Majesty's Government, the following declaration of sympathy with Jewish Zionist aspirations which has been submitted to, and approved by, the Cabinet:
>
>> His Majesty's Government view with favour the establishment in Palestine of a national home for the Jewish people, and will use their best endeavours to facilitate the achievement of this object, it being clearly understood that nothing shall be done which may prejudice the civil and religious rights of existing non-Jewish communities in Palestine, or the rights and political status enjoyed by Jews in any other country.
>
> I should be grateful if you would bring this declaration to the knowledge of the Zionist Federation.[1]

---

[1] David Lloyd George – *The Truth About the Peace Treaties,* Victor Gollancz Ltd., London, 1938, Vol. II, p. 1136.

A. The Declaration – A Binding Document

The primary objective of the Balfour Declaration is apparent in the phrase 'the establishment in Palestine of a National Home for the Jewish people.' The Declaration was a commitment taken by the British Government on behalf of the Jewish people to 'use their best endeavours to facilitate the achievement of this object.' Importantly, the pledge was given to the Jewish people as a whole and not only to Jews then living in Palestine.[2] True, the Declaration was not a contract in the strict legal sense of the word. However, it was regarded by its initiators as a binding commitment made in the framework of a contract.[3] It was, in essence, a quid pro quo deal, one morally and politically binding, a fact never denied by the British Government. The British had their own objectives in formulating the Declaration, the most crucial of which were determined mainly by considerations of war policy and propaganda. The *raison d'être* behind the Declaration was its potential usefulness in winning the War. In fact, it was believed that world Jewry could contribute substantially to the achievement of this military goal.

As noted, the Balfour Declaration was made at a critical juncture due to war time political conditions. Lloyd George testified before the Peel Commission 'that while the Zionist cause had been widely supported in Britain and America before November 1917, the launching of the Balfour Declaration at that time was due to propagandist reasons.'[4] In his treatise *The Truth About the Peace Treaties* published a year later in 1938, Lloyd George recalled:

---

[2] Lloyd George, ibid., Vol. II, p. 1182 ; it was again reaffirmed in a letter from Prime Minister Ramsay MacDonald to Weizmann on February 13th 1931; and again by Sir Winston Churchill speaking in the House of Commons on May 23rd 1939, see Parliamentary Debates, Vol. 347, c. 2171; see also Isaiah Friedman – *The Question of Palestine 1914-1918*, Transaction Publishers, New Brunswick & London, 2nd edition, 1992, p. 311, n.18.

[3] See pp. 54 et seq., infra.

[4] Cmd. 5479, Palestine Royal Commission Report, July 1937, headed by William Robert Wellesley, Earl Peel, [hereinafter the Peel Report], p.23.

In 1917 the issue of the war was still very much in doubt… (The Germans) had smashed the Roumanians. The Russian Army was completely demoralised by its numerous defeats. The French Army was exhausted and temporarily unequal to striking a great blow. The Italians had sustained a shattering defeat at Caporetto. The unlimited submarine campaign had sunk millions of tons of our shipping. There were no American divisions at the front, and when I say at the front, I mean available at the trenches.[5]

Therefore, every strategic avenue which could make a difference in winning the war was exploited.

The Allies were then in desperate need of US military intervention,[6] even as the latter continued its hesitation to join the war effort.[7] However, in April 1917, Lord Balfour noticed on an official visit to the United States that 'American opinion might be favourably influenced if His Majesty's Government gave an assurance that the return of the Jews to Palestine had become a purpose of British policy'.[8] While there, Lord Balfour met with Louis Brandeis, Justice of the United States Supreme Court and a close friend to President Wilson. Prior to his nomination, Brandeis acted as President of the Zionist Organization of America. The meeting convinced Lord Balfour that a declaration, as suggested by the Zionists, would well serve the purposes of Great Britain.

The British also needed the goodwill of Russia. The situation there was deteriorating rapidly. It was feared that due to her descent into bloody revolution, Russia would be tempted to betray the

---

[5] Lloyd George, op. cit., Vol. II, p.1119; See also Michael J. Cohen – *The Origins and Evolution of the Arab-Zionist Conflict*, University of California Press, Berkeley 1987, pp. 46-47.

[6] J.C. Hurewitz, ed. – *The Middle East and North Africa in World Politics, A Documentary Record*, Vol. II (British – French Supremacy 1914 – 1915, p. 102, Yale University Press , New Haven & London, 1979.

[7] Ernst Frankenstein – *The Meaning of the Term "National Home for the Jewish People"*, 1 Jewish Y.B. Int'l L. 27, 30, 1948.

[8] British Cabinet Papers, C.P. 60 (23), January 1923, p. 2.

Allied cause and abandon the eastern theater of war. By making a separate peace treaty with Germany, the Central Powers could secure supplies of grain, oil and copper from Russia's vast natural resources. As Lloyd George noted, 'A friendly Russia would mean not only more food and raw material for Germany, but fewer German and Austrian troops on the Eastern front and, therefore more available for the West.'[9] It was, therefore, important to keep Socialist Russia (then in the first stages of the Revolution) from leaving the war.[10] Both the Allies and the Central Powers knew that the Jews had considerable influence in new Bolshevik Russia. Lloyd George emphasized that 'the Zionist Movement was exceptionally strong in Russia and America... The support of the Zionists for the cause of the Entente, would mean a great deal as a war measure.'[11]

However, the Jews of Russia were not only hostile towards the Allied Powers, due to long time Russian pogroms and persecutions. They also tended to be active disseminators of German pacifist propaganda encouraging Russian withdrawal from hostilities. By 1917, they had done much to bring about Russia's disintegration through the Bolshevik Revolution. The British Government, nevertheless, assumed that 'if Great Britain declared for the fulfillment of the Zionist aspirations in Palestine under her own pledge, one effect would be to bring Russian Jewry to the cause of the Entente.'[12] Therefore, as early as March 1916, and again in April 1917, the British Government consulted the British Ambassador in Petrograd on the effect in Russia of a declaration by the Entente of sympathy for Jewish national aspirations. It was thought that such a declaration 'might counteract Jewish pacifist propaganda in Russia'.[13]

As a result, on March 13th 1916, the British Embassy in Petrograd presented an *aide-memoirs* to the Russian Foreign

---

9   Lloyd George, op. cit., Vol. II, p. 1121.

10 Hurewitz, op. cit., p. 102; C.P. 60 (23), p.2.

11 Lloyd George, op. cit., Vol. II, p. 1121

12 Harold W.V. Temperley, ed – *A History of the Peace Conference of Paris*, Vol. VI, p. 173, The British Institute of International Affairs, London 1924.

13 British Cabinet Papers, C.P. 60 (23)

Minister, Sazanoff, pushing forward in its conviction that 'by means of utilizing the Zionist idea, important political results might be achieved. One of these would be the conversion to the side of the Allies of Jewish elements in the East, in the U.S.A., and other places, whose present attitude towards the cause of the Allies is, to a considerable extent, hostile.' It goes on to refer to an agreement or transaction to be made with the Jews to seek their support, stating that 'the only object of His Majesty's Government is to devise some agreement which will be sufficiently attractive to the majority of Jews to facilitate the conclusion of a transaction securing Jewish support.'[14]

The Allies were, therefore, anxious to rally public opinion in the United States and Russia in their favor, and Lloyd George stressed in his memoirs that 'we had every reason at that time to believe that in both countries the friendliness or hostility of the Jewish race might make a considerable difference.'[15] The wooing of the Jewish people was then part of British general strategy. The British used propaganda, *inter alia*, to weaken the ties and loyalties of oppressed nations serving under Turkish, German, and Austro-Hungarian rule, mobilizing public opinion in those countries in favor of the Allied cause. To implement this strategy, Britain announced publicly her intentions to liberate minorities oppressed by enemy regimes, and it thus notably succeeded to disintegrate the solidarity of such minorities towards their Governments.[16]

By the end of 1917, the British Cabinet was eager to make a declaration in favor of establishing a Jewish National Home in Palestine, giving it maximum publicity out of real concern that the Germans would beat them to making a similar declaration for the purpose of gaining Jewish support. They had no doubt that if Jewish support decisively shifted to the Central Powers, the

---

[14] Leonard Stein – *Zionism*, Kegan Paul, Trench, Trubner &Co. Ltd., London 1932 pp. 82, 112-3; Temperley, op. cit., 171.

[15] Lloyd George, op. cit., Vol. II, 1118; Leonard Stein – *The Balfour Declaration*, The Magnus Press, Jerusalem and The Jewish Chronicle Publications, London 1983 (first published in 1961), p. 550.

[16] Lloyd George, op. cit., Vol. II, p. 1118.

Germans would have a great advantage over the Allied Powers.[17]

In fact, the Germans were the first to realize the war value of the Jews and in 1916 had consequently urged the Turks to reconcile with Jewish demands in Palestine to be guaranteed by the German Government. As Lloyd George put it, 'By September 1917 the German Government were making very serious efforts to capture the Zionist Movement... but the Turks were too stupid to understand or too sluggish to move.'[18] On October 4th 1917, the War Cabinet discussed German machinations to entice the Jews to their side, in consequence of which the Secretary of State for Foreign Affairs, Balfour, urged the Cabinet to forthwith make a decision on the issuance of the Declaration as 'the German Government were making great efforts to capture the sympathy of the Zionist Movement.'[19]

Balfour was not acting in a vacuum. The British Foreign Office came to a final conclusion that if the Declaration was not made by the end of 1917 'the result might be to throw the Zionists into the arms of the Germans and to put an end to the prospect of attracting valuable support for the Allied cause from the Zionist forces in Russia and the United States. The German press was taking up the Zionist question, and the British Government might at any moment find itself confronted with a German move'.[20] It was for this reason that the Foreign Office urged the Cabinet to make the Declaration without any further delay. It was acknowledged in British circles that the moment the Zionists received the Declaration, they 'would be prepared to start active propaganda in the interests of the Allies in all parts of the world.'[21] On October 31st 1917, the day the decision to make the Declaration was taken, Balfour stated in the War Cabinet that a declaration favorable to the aspirations of the

---

[17] Howard Grief – *The Legal Foundation and Borders of Israel Under International Law*, Mazo Publishers, Jerusalem, 2008, p. 79.

[18] Lloyd George, op. cit., Vol. II, pp. 1117, 1121.

[19] Minutes of War Cabinet Papers, No. 245, October 4th 1917, p. 5; Cabinet Papers C.P. 60 (23); Lloyd George, ibid., 1140-41; Walter Laqueur – *History of Zionism*, Weidenfeld and Nicolson, London 1972, p. 202.

[20] Cabinet Papers, C.P. 60 (23); Walter Laqueur, op. cit., 202.

[21] Leonard Stein, *The Balfour Declaration*, op. cit., p. 544.

Jewish nationalists should be made 'from a purely diplomatic and political point of view'.[22] The Declaration was not solely a British interest, but applied to all the Allied Powers seeking to prevent 'the incalculable and universal influence of Jewry being exerted on the side of the Central Powers – as indeed it was, to a serious extent, then being exerted – and to transfer this highly important influence to the cause of the Entente.'[23]

Parenthetically, the Turks did indeed announce their intention to make limited concessions to the Jewish people, but it was too little, too late. At the time of the Balfour Declaration, the German Government was doing all it could to win the Zionist Movement to its side. However, no serious or substantial move was taken by the Turks until after the Balfour Declaration was announced. The Germans then urged their Turkish allies to make a rival proposition. By the end of 1917, the Turks were inclined to accept a scheme whereby some kind of chartered company would be created for German Zionists to take care of the Jewish settlements in Palestine with a degree of autonomy. More specifically, the Jews would be granted a limited form of local self government and a right of immigration into Palestine.[24] In an interview with Julius Becker, a correspondent for the *Vossische Zeitung*, published on December 31st 1917, Talaat Pasha, one of the triumvirate who then ruled the Ottoman Empire, promised to cancel the restrictions on Jewish immigration to Palestine. He also declared that Turkey would be open to discussion on Jewish immigration, land purchase in Palestine, and autonomy. He invited a delegation of Jewish organizations in Germany to visit Constantinople to begin negotiations.[25] By this time, however, Jerusalem was already in British hands, and these efforts by the Central Powers proved to be in vain.

One further reason for the Balfour Declaration was strategic: Palestine is situated geographically as a buffer zone between

---

[22] Minutes of the War Cabinet, No. 261, October 31st 1917, p.5., para.12; Cabinet Papers C.P. 60 (23), January 1923, p.3.

[23] Temperley, op. cit., Vol. VI, p. 171.

[24] Peel Report, op. cit., pp. 23-24.

[25] Isaiah Friedman, op. cit., pp. 296-7, 298; Israel Cohen, op. cit., p. 120.

Turkey and the Suez Canal. The Suez Canal was the nerve center of the British Empire in the Middle East, and the British Government regarded its protection with the utmost importance. At the outset of the War, the British High Command considered the Sinai desert to be an impenetrable wasteland and a buffer zone between the Suez Canal and the Turks. However, this view was shattered in February 1915 when a Turkish contingent force, guided by German experts, crossed the desert and disrupted Canal traffic for a few days. This had a strong psychological effect on the British High Command. In consequence they came to view Palestine as strategically imperative.[26] The establishment of a National Home for the Jewish people in Palestine, which would naturally be pro-British, could serve as a powerful wall against enemy attack from the north or east of the Suez Canal.[27]

Furthermore, the British Government was aware of Palestine's geographical importance for safeguarding British lines of communication to India and the Far East. Post-war, it was assumed that Palestine could serve as an important imperial node in the promotion of British economic, political, and military interests.[28] A Jewish National Home in Palestine loyal to Britain would therefore be of great strategic value to Britain – without having to annex Palestine or occupy it as a colony, a move which would antagonize France, Italy, and the United States.

Another incentive to make the Declaration was the British desire to find a persuasive excuse to bypass the Sykes-Picot Agreement of May 16th 1916. This secret pact divided the Middle East between Great Britain and France, creating an international regime in Palestine to be jointly administered by Britain and France in consultation with their allies, Russia and Italy as an international condominium.[29] However, by 1917 the British

---

[26] Michael J. Cohen, op. cit., p. 42; see also Herbert Samuel, *Memoirs*, The Cresset Press, London, 1945, p. 147.

[27] CAB 24/4/33, G. 182, December 12th 1917, p.3; Temperley, op. cit., p. 171.

[28] Samuel, op. cit., p. 148; Grief, op. cit. p. 79.

[29] The Sykes-Picot Agreement, also known as Asia Minor Agreement, was an understanding reached secretly between the British and French Governments, in May 1916, through Sir Mark Sykes, the British Representative and Francois Georges-Picot the French Representative, while World War I was still in

Government was inspired by a policy of change towards the Middle East, i.e., of keeping Palestine under unilateral British influence.[30] This could be achieved, it was believed, only through creating a Jewish National Home in Palestine loyal to Britain. The British Government, therefore, saw support of Zionist aspirations as a means of extricating itself from the Sykes-Picot Agreement.[31] For this purpose Sykes, who soon realized his mistake devising the Agreement, urged British Zionist leaders to secure French approval for the Declaration. The task was given to Nahum Sokolow who went on a mission to Paris to convince the French Government that the Zionists desired a British protectorate, as the sole power in Palestine.[32] He returned from Paris with an encouraging letter dated June 4th 1917, signed by the French Foreign Minister, Jules Cambon, which read as follows:[33]

> You were good enough to present the project to which you are devoting your efforts, which has for its object the development of Jewish colonization in Palestine. You consider that, circumstances

---

progress. According to the Agreement the Middle East, except for a major part of Palestine, was to be divided between the two Powers. The Blue area and the 'A' Zone were to be allocated to France, and the Red area and 'B' zone were to be allocated to Britain. In the Blue and Red areas France and Britain (respectively) were allowed to assume full control and administration, while in the 'A' and 'B' Zones France and Britain were prepared to "recognize and protect" an Arab state or a confederation of Arab states under the suzerainty of an Arab chief, but would have, each in the Zone allotted to him, priority of right of enterprise and loans and the right to supply advisors. A major part of Palestine, marked with a brown color, was to be excluded from the rest of the Middle East territories, and there, an international administration was to be established, the form of which was to be decided in consultation with Russia, with the other Allies, and with the Sherif of Mecca. See map No. 1 on p. 158 infra. https://www.britannica.com/event/Sykes-Picot-Agreement. More details on pp. 157-62 infra.

[30] Grief, ibid., p. 79.

[31] Leonard Stein, *The Balfour Declaration*, op. cit., p. 549.

[32] Hurewitz, op. cit., p. 102; Michael Cohen, op. cit., p. 46.

[33] Nahum Sokolow, *History of Zionism 1600-1918*, Vol. II, p. 53, Ktav Publishing House, New York, 1969 (first published by Longmans, Green & Co., London, 1919).

permitting, and the independence of the Holy Places being safeguarded on the other hand, it would be a deed of justice and of reparation to assist, by the protection of the Allied Powers, *in the renaissance of the Jewish nationality in that land from which the people of **Israel** were exiled so many centuries ago.*

The French Government, which entered this present war to defend a people wrongfully attacked, and which continues the struggle to assure the victory of right over might, *can but feel sympathy for your cause,* the triumph of which is bound up with that of the Allies.

I am happy to give you herewith such assurance.

Please accept, Sir, the assurance of my most distinguished consideration.

[Italics added, emphasis in the original].

This letter of assurance, regarded by members of the British Cabinet as 'a very sympathetic declaration', accelerated the British issuance of the Declaration. It was discussed in the War Cabinet on October 4th 1917, at which time Balfour read aloud the French declaration. He added that President Wilson was extremely favorable to the Zionist Movement. Less than a month later, on October 31st 1917, the Cabinet decided to issue the Balfour Declaration.[34]

What then was expected from Zionist organizations in return? As David Lloyd George plainly stated:

Zionist leaders gave us a definite promise that, if the Allies committed themselves to giving facilities for the establishment of a National Home for the Jews in Palestine, they would do their best to rally to the Allied cause Jewish sentiment and support throughout the world. They kept their word in the letter and the spirit, and the only question that remains now is whether we mean to honour ours.[35]

---

[34] Minutes of the War Cabinet No. 245, October 4th 1917; C.P. 60 (23), January 1923, p. 3.

[35] Lloyd George, op. cit., Vol. II, p. 1139.

Lloyd George then went on to outline the implementation of the Jewish commitment:

> Immediately the Declaration was agreed to, millions of leaflets were circulated in every town and area throughout the world where there were known to be Jewish communities. They were dropped from the air in German and Austrian towns, and they were scattered throughout Russia and Poland.
>
> I could point out substantial, and in one case decisive advantages derived from this propaganda amongst the Jews. In Russia the Bolsheviks baffled all the efforts of the Germans to benefit by the harvests of the Ukraine and the Don, and hundreds of thousands of German and Austrian troops had to be maintained to the end of the war on Russian soil, whilst the Germans were short of men to replace casualties on the Western front.
>
> I do not suggest that this was due entirely, or even mainly, to Jewish activities. But we have good reason to believe that Jewish propaganda in Russia had a great deal to do with the difficulties created for the Germans in Southern Russia after the peace of Brest-Litovsk. The Germans themselves know that to be the case, and the Jews in Germany are suffering to-day [1938] for the fidelity with which their brethren in Russia and in America discharged their obligations under the Zionist pledge to the Allies.[36]

The Declaration was, therefore, a quid pro quo given in exchange for Jewish commitments to use their best efforts in support of the Entente's war efforts. Lloyd George pointed out that for these Jewish considerations, the British Government was impelled in 1917 to make 'a contract with Jewry'.[37]

---

[36] Ibid. Vol. II, 1139-40.

[37] Lloyd George, ibid., Vol. II, p. 1122; Blanche Dugdale, Balfour's niece and biographer, stated, however, in her biography on Balfour, that 'The Balfour Declaration was not part of a bargain, nor a reward for services rendered' see

As much was confirmed by the eminent historian Temperley, who noted –

> that it is in purpose a definite contract between the British Government and Jewry represented by the Zionists is beyond question. In spirit it is a pledge that in return for services to be rendered by Jewry, the British Government would 'use their best endeavours' to secure the execution of a certain definite policy in Palestine. No time limit is set for performance; completion alone appears to have been intended as the conclusion of the contract. It would thus seem to be an agreement incapable of being greatly varied except by consent.[38]

Subsequently, the Declaration was accepted and endorsed by France, Italy, and Japan.

Ample evidence found in British and League of Nations official documentation supports this transactional view. Lord Curzon, later Foreign Secretary, stated in 1918: 'We have pledged ourselves, if successful, to secure Palestine as a National Home for the Jewish people… [If the Turkish flag were to continue to fly over Jerusalem]… It would destroy the remotest chance of fulfillment of Jewish aspirations'.[39]

Blanche Dugdale, Balfour's biographer and niece, referred to the Balfour Declaration as no less than a pledge or promise made by the British Cabinet, after the most thorough consideration, in support of the establishment of a Jewish National Home in Palestine.[40] In fact, Balfour himself told Lord Beaverbrook, the

---

Arthur James Balfour 1906-1930, Vol. II, G.P. Putnam's Sons, New York, 1937, p. 165, n. 1; yet Lloyd George in his treatise *The Truth About the Peace Treaties*, published in 1938, ibid., Vol. II, p. 1122, specifically stated that the negotiations with the Zionist Organization led to 'a contract with Jewry'. Dugdale did not specify the basis of her statement.

[38] Temperley, op. cit. pp. 173-74.

[39] F.O.371/3388/1396, p. No. 30340, minutes by Graham and Balfour, February 17th 1918, cited in Friedman, op. cit., p. 296.

[40] Blanche Dugdale – *Arthur James Balfour 1906-1930*, op. cit., p.155.

Minister of information, that Britain was 'definitely committed' to this policy which had won the public support of her Allies and which should be promoted by propaganda.[41] As Colonial Secretary, Winston Churchill made it abundantly clear:

> The British Government have passed their word, by the mouth of Mr. Balfour, that they will view with favour the establishment of a National Home for Jews in Palestine, and that inevitably involves the immigration of Jews into the country. This declaration of Mr. Balfour and of the British Government has been ratified by the Allied Powers who have been victorious in the Great War; and it was a declaration made while the war was still in progress, while victory and defeat hung in the balance. It must therefore be regarded as one of the facts definitely established by the triumphant conclusion of the Great War. It is upon this basis that the mandate has been undertaken by Great Britain, it is upon this basis that the mandate will be discharged; I have no doubt that it is on this basis that the mandate will be accepted by the Council of the League of Nations.[42]

And in a subsequent meeting on the same day, Churchill told the Jewish delegation (Deputation of Representatives of the Jewish Community in Palestine): 'I have told the [Arab Delegation] quite plainly that there can be no question of our departing from the principles enunciated by Mr. Balfour in his declaration.'[43]

In a statement on principles of policy from October 1923, arrived at by a special committee of the British Cabinet, later dispatched by the Duke of Devonshire, then Colonial Secretary,

---

[41] F.O.371/3383/747, August 16th 1918, cited in Friedman, op. cit. p. 297.

[42] During a meeting held in Palestine with the Arab Delegation (Deputation of the Executive Committee of the Haifa Congress), on March 28th 1921, CAB 24/126, C.P. 3123, p. 150.

[43] CAB 24/126, C.P. 3123, p. 155.

to Sir Herbert Samuel, High Commissioner of Palestine, it was stated:

> The key-note of British policy in Palestine, as conducted since the establishment of a civil administration at Jerusalem, is to be found in the Balfour Declaration of November 1917... The policy of the declaration was accepted by the principal Allied Powers at the San Remo Conference in April 1920; its text was embodied verbatim in the treaty signed at Sèvres in August 1920, and again in the mandate approved by the Council of the League of Nations in July 1922. It formed an essential part of the conditions on which Great Britain accepted the Mandate for Palestine, and thus constitutes an international obligation from which there can be no question of receding.[44]

In the House of Commons, William Ormsby-Gore, acting as Under-Secretary of State for the Colonies, noted on July 4th 1922, that it would be 'absolutely dishonourable' to go back on the Balfour Declaration.[45] And later on, as Colonial Secretary, while testifying as the representative of the British Government before the Permanent Mandates Commission at the League of Nations on August 18th 1937, on the question of partition, he stated emphatically that 'the Balfour Declaration was still a binding obligation, and would remain so until replaced by an independent Jewish State. It was only if the suggested plan of partition were accepted, and eventuated in the creation of a Jewish State, that the Balfour Declaration would reach its fruition and cease to be binding.'[46]

---

[44] Cmd. 1989, *Palestine: Proposed Formation of an Arab Agency – Correspondence with the High Commissioner for Palestine*, HMSO London, November 1923: in the dispatch Devonshire stressed that 'the whole matter was most carefully examined by the Committee of the Cabinet' and was presented to the Cabinet as a whole.

[45] Friedman, op. cit., p. 310.

[46] League of Nations, 32nd session, Minutes of the Permanent Mandates Commission, August 18th 1937.

On June 17th 1918, Ormsby-Gore, while speaking at a Jewish conference in Jaffa, made it clear that Britain and her Allies had no intention of annexing territories acquired during the war. 'They are fighting for an ideal,' he said. Soon after, Dr. Ami, representing the British Ambassador to Washington, told a Zionist Convention in Pittsburgh held on June 23rd-27th 1918, that Britain was taking Palestine not for herself, but for the Jewish people. 'It is the policy of England to do everything reasonably within her power to put the Jews back in the home of their ancestors.'[47]

Sir Ronald Graham, assistant under secretary of state for foreign affairs, underscored the language of British commitment: 'We are committed and must support it wholeheartedly if we wish to reap the full political results.'[48]

In November 1918, Sir Mark Sykes considered it essential to make it clear to the Arabs of Palestine that while their interests would be safeguarded, the Balfour Declaration was a 'settled part of [British] policy... concurred in by the Entente as a whole.'[49]

General Jan Smuts, a member of the Imperial War Cabinet, referred to the Declaration as 'the foundation of a great policy of international justice. The greatest, most ancient historic wrong has at last been undone.'[50] Later, in October 1930, Smuts commented to then Prime Minister Ramsay MacDonald that the Declaration was 'a definite promise to the Jewish world'.[51]

Neville Chamberlain was explicit that Britain was 'definitely pledged' and that he would oppose any attempt to renounce it. David George Hogarth,[52] in his introduction to Philip Graves'

---

[47] F.O. 371/3388/1495, British Embassy Washington to Balfour, July 30th 1918; the *Jewish Chronicle* July 26th, August 16th 1918, cited in Friedman op. cit., p. 300.

[48] F.O. 371/3055/87895, p. 240635, December 21st 1917, cited in Friedman, ibid., p. 310.

[49] F.O. 371/3386/856, Report by Sir Mark Sykes (Jerusalem), November 15th 1918, cited in Friedman, ibid., p. 310.

[50] The *Jewish Chronicle*, November 1st 1918, cited in Friedman, ibid., 309.

[51] Parliamentary Debates, February 13th 1931, cc. 751-57, cited in Friedman, ibid. p. 309.

[52] A British Archaeologist and scholar who worked closely with T.E. Lawrence to plan the Arab Revolt.

book, *Palestine, the Land of the Three Faiths,* wrote that the Balfour Declaration was as binding an agreement as Britain had ever entered into which should be carried out even within the narrower interpretative limits of the 1922 White Paper.[53]

In a debate carried out in the House of Lords on June 27th 1923 on the subject of Palestine,[54] Lord Islington opposed the Declaration policy, but he referred to it as an 'undertaking' by the British Government. Lord Milner held that 'it would be totally impossible for the Government either of the United States, or of France, or of Italy to dissociate itself entirely from the policy of that Declaration', all the more Great Britain. The Duke of Devonshire, then Secretary of State for the Colonies, stated that the Balfour Declaration was not 'something which we could take up or lay aside just to suit our own convenience… The Mandate is not merely a national obligation, it is an *international obligation,* and the Balfour Declaration was the basis on which we accepted from the principal Allied Powers the position of Mandatory Power in Palestine.' [Italics added]. Viscount Grey of Falladon, the fourth and last speaker in the debate, also referred to the Balfour Declaration as a pledge noting that 'Now we are in great difficulties with regard to that pledge.'[55]

At the Peace Conference, in a session held by the Supreme Council early in 1920, Lord Curzon referred to the Declaration as a formal declaration, a pledge made to the Jewish people and that 'the Jews regarded the declaration of Mr. Balfour in its entirety as the charter of their rights.'[56]

Churchill, in his speech in the House of Commons on the White Paper of 1939, famously framed the Balfour Declaration as 'a solemn engagement into which Britain has entered before

---

[53] Friedman, op. cit., p.311.

[54] Parliamentary Debates, H.L., Vol. 54, cc. 654-82, June 27th 1923

[55] Difficulties arising from Arab opposition. See Parliamentary Debates, H.L., Ibid.

[56] Lloyd George, op. cit., Vol. II, pp. 1182 and 1188; Documents on British Foreign Policy 1919-1939, First Series, Rohan Butler & J.P.T. Bury, ed. HMSO London, 1958, [hereinafter DBFP], Vol. VIII (1920), p. 159.

the world'.[57] The Declaration was also referred to by members of the Cabinet as 'a pledge to be redeemed by the acceptance of the Mandate under the League of Nations'.[58] Churchill added that the establishment of a Jewish National Home in Palestine was a 'paramount pledge and obligation' made by the British Government, and the establishment of self-governing institutions, alluded to in the 1922 White Paper, was to be subordinated to that pledge and obligation.[59]

Churchill pointed out that these views were not his alone, but represented the entire government. In a dispatch he made as Colonial Secretary, he stressed: 'The position is that his Majesty's Government are bound by a pledge which is antecedent to the Covenant of the League of Nations, and they cannot allow a constitutional position to develop in a country for which they have accepted responsibility to the Principal Allied Powers which may make it impracticable to carry into effect a solemn undertaking given by themselves and the Allies.'[60]

Churchill vehemently attacked the White Paper of 1939 which severely constrained Jewish immigration to Palestine as 'alien to the spirit of the Balfour Declaration'.[61] He added that by restricting or stopping immigration 'there is the violation of the pledge; there is the abandonment of the Balfour Declaration; there is the end of a vision, of the hope, of the dream… [tantamount to a] … unilateral denunciation of an engagement'.[62] Churchill saw the Declaration in the stark terms of a warning: 'Either there will be a Britain which knows how to keep its word on the Balfour Declaration, and is not afraid to do so, or we shall find ourselves relieved of many oversea responsibilities.'[63]

The Declaration, therefore, represented a valid and binding British commitment, publically and formally approved by the

---

[57] Parliamentary Debates, H.C., May 23rd 1939, Vol. 347, c. 2168.
[58] Parliamentary Debates, H.C., ibid., c. 2169.
[59] Ibid., c. 2170.
[60] Ibid., c. 2171.
[61] Ibid.
[62] Ibid., c. 2173.
[63] Ibid., c. 2177.

Cabinet, to use 'its best endeavors to facilitate the establishment in Palestine of a National Home for the Jewish people'. As noted, it was transactional in nature based on services rendered by the Jewish people in the form of rallying global Jewry to the Allied cause in a difficult War in which Jewish influence and support could prove a significant factor in victory. The British acknowledged that the Jews 'kept their word in the letter and the spirit'.[64] No better witness to this agreement can be found than Lloyd George, the Prime Minister of Great Britain, under whose auspices and consent the Declaration was issued and promulgated. Thus, a binding contract was established between the Zionists, representing the majority of the Jewish people, and the British Government, backed and later endorsed by the Allied Powers.

Other lesser reasons informed the issuance of the Balfour Declaration; for instance, the Biblical redemption of the Holy Land, from Dan to Beersheba, from Muslim control. Lloyd George mentioned this factor as clearly stated by Lord Curzon at a War Cabinet meeting on December 12th 1917, while the war still waged over Palestine. The belief that the Turks should never again be allowed to resume possession and control of Palestine was rooted in a Crusader zeal quite apart from considerations of Realpolitik. The expulsion of the Turks from the Holy Land and the return of Christian banners hoisted over the walls of Jerusalem proved to be a strong motive.[65] It was believed that Palestine was to be recaptured and rescued from Turkish rule, and once redeemed it should become one and indivisible. In this context, as Lloyd George noted: 'The Sykes-Picot agreement perished in its fire.'[66]

Another factor was sympathy for Zionist aspirations, representing the British decision to come to terms with Jewry. The Jews were scattered all over the world with no home of their own. Both Balfour and Lloyd George were 'influenced by a desire

---

[64] Lloyd George, op. cit., Vol. II, p. 1139.

[65] CAB 24/4/33, G. 182, December 12th 1917, p.3.

[66] Lloyd George, op. cit., Vol. II, p. 1116.

to give the Jews their rightful place in the world; a great nation without a home is not right.'[67] They were devout Christians, believers in the Old Testament. As Weizmann insightfully noted: 'Those British statesmen of the old school were genuinely religious. They understood as a reality the concept of the Return. It appealed to their tradition and their faith.'[68] Of course, the Bible contains abundant prophesies envisaging the return of the Jewish people to their homeland, the land of ancient Israel. In fact, the expression 'from Dan to Beersheba' was often invoked by British statesmen.

Dugdale recalled that 'Balfour's interest in the Jews and their history was lifelong. It originated in the Old Testament training of his mother, and in his Scottish upbringing. As he grew up […] the problem of the Jews in the modern world seemed to him of immense importance. He always talked eagerly on this, and I remember in childhood imbibing from him the idea that Christian religion and civilization owes to Judaism an immeasurable debt, shamefully ill repaid.'[69] Balfour regarded Zionism as providing him with one of his greatest life opportunities. As she put it, 'Near the end of his life he said to me that on the whole he felt that what he had been able to do for the Jews had been the thing he looked back upon as the most worth his doing.'[70]

Indeed, Walter Laqueur noted:

> Balfour believed, as Lloyd George did, that the Jews had been wronged by Christendom for almost two thousand years and that they had a claim to reparation. The whole culture of Europe, he said in a speech in 1922, had been guilty of great crimes against the Jews, and the British had at last taken the initiative in giving them the opportunity of

---

[67] Richard Meinertzhagen – *Middle East Diary 1917-1956,* The Cresset Press, London 1959, p. 9, February 7th 1918.

[68] Chaim Weizmann – *Trial and Error*, Schocken Books, New York, 1949, p. 178.

[69] Blanche E.C. Dugdale – *Arthur James Balfour, 1848-1906,* Vol. I, G.P. Putnam's Sons, New York, 1937, p. 324.

[70] Dugdale – *Arthur James Balfour 1906-1930*, Vol. II, op. cit., p. 171.

developing in peace the great gifts which in the past they had been able to apply only in the countries of the Diaspora. Balfour thus had the feeling that he was instrumental in writing a wrong of world historical dimensions, quite irrespective of the changing world situation. There was a similar element in Lloyd George's thinking.[71]

It was apparent to members of the British Government that the Jews were yearning for an opportunity to make Palestine their home again, and it was only right and just that this should be so. In the words of Lloyd George, 'Men like Mr. Balfour, Lord Milner, Lord Robert Cecil, and myself were in whole-hearted sympathy with Zionist ideal. The same thing applied to all the leaders of public opinion in our country and in the Dominions, Conservative, Liberal and Labour.'[72]

A third suggested reason propelling the Declaration may have been recent Allied championing of freedom for oppressed peoples and small nations. This emerged as somewhat of an Allied slogan, informed to some extent by genuine altruistic motives. Naturally, in the ranks of oppressed peoples who deserved freedom and justice there was room for the Jewish people.[73]

Herbert Samuel, who served as a member of the British Government and later as the first High Commissioner to Palestine, echoed this relatively new attitude in his memoirs:

A genuine sympathy with the aspirations of Jews for a restoration in Palestine, as a factor of spiritual and moral value to them, and indirectly to some degree to the world; a belief that to bring to Palestine that new economic and cultural element would be the best means of promoting the regeneration of a land, of deep historic interest to mankind, that was now

[71] Walter Laqueur, op. cit., p. 203, citing Stein, *The Balfour Declaration*, op. cit., pp. 160, 552.

[72] Lloyd George, op. cit., Vol. II, p.1122; see also Herbert Samuel, op. cit., p. 147.

[73] Temperley, Vol. 6, op. cit., p. 171.

almost derelict.[74]

Indeed, some British politicians felt that the establishment of a Jewish National Home in Palestine would bring about the regeneration of the entire Middle East. For centuries, since Jewish exile from their homeland, Palestine turned into barren land beyond any hope of recovery. It was thought that Jewish energy, skills, and knowledge would enhance the economic cultural and political situation of the region far more effectively than importing foreign capitalists, technicians, and administrators.[75]

Yet another motive for the Declaration was financial, the belief that it would secure Jewish capital, particularly in the United States, at a time when the Entente had exhausted their resources.[76]

Last but not least was the exceptional personal acquaintance of Dr. Chaim Weizmann, a Zionist leader and Don in Chemistry at Manchester University, with Lloyd George. The latter regarded him as 'one of the greatest Hebrews of all time'.[77] He noted that 'Dr. Weizmann enlisted my adhesion to his ideals at a time when, at my request, he was successfully applying his scientific skill and imagination to save Britain from a real disaster over the failure of wood alcohol for the manufacture of cordite.' [78] Lloyd George's deep gratitude for Weizmann's crucial contributions during the war was no doubt conducive to the final formulation of the Declaration.

B. The Declaration: A Document of International Standing and Recognition

The Balfour Declaration was not a mere statement of policy undertaken by the British Government in favor of the Jewish people

---

[74] Herbert Samuel, op. cit., p. 147.

[75] Leopold S. Amery – *My Political Life*, Vol. II, Hutchinson & Co. (Publishers) Ltd., London 1953, p. 116.

[76] Lloyd George, op. cit., Vol. II, p. 1122.

[77] Lloyd George, ibid., Vol. II, p. 1117.

[78] Ibid.

with no international significance, as argued by some scholars.[79] On the contrary. It was made public soon after it was delivered to Lord Rothschild and received maximum publicity. Importantly, it was not kept secret like the Sykes-Picot Agreement or private like the McMahon-Hussein correspondence. Made openly before the whole world, the Declaration was internationally recognized, representing the consensus of other governments before and after the Declaration was announced.[80] Prior to the issuance of the Declaration the Allied Powers, France, Italy and Russia, had given it their approval.[81] The United States, even though not involved in the war with Turkey, also expressed its prior approval of the Declaration.[82] So did Greece, China, Serbia and Siam.[83] In fact, the Balfour Declaration was not issued until the prior approval of France, Italy, and the United States was assured.[84]

Lloyd George elaborated on the importance of United States pre-approval: 'The views of President Wilson should be obtained before any declaration was made.'[85] As Lloyd George wrote:

> When the matter was brought to the attention of the Cabinet on the 3rd of September 1917, it was decided to communicate with President Wilson

---

[79] See, for example Howard Grief, op. cit., p. 18.

[80] This fact was expressed in a speech made by Viscount Milner in the House of Lords a few years later (in 1923). Lord Milner was a member of the War Cabinet at the time the Declaration was made, and was instrumental in making it. He said: 'It is quite certain that it (the Declaration) has received on a number of occasions the express approval of other Powers, our Allies in the great war…I think it would be totally impossible for the Government either of the United States, or of France or of Italy to dissociate itself entirely from the policy of that Declaration.' Parliamentary Debates, H.L., June 27th 1923, Vol. 54, cc. 654-82.

[81] Samuel, op. cit., p. 148; Friedman, op. cit., p. 309.

[82] War Cabinet Papers, No. 245, of October 4th 1917, p. 6.

[83] Lloyd George, op. cit., Vol. II, p. 1184.

[84] Stein, *Zionism*, op. cit., pp.89, 90; Lloyd George, op. cit., Vol. II, p. 1138.

[85] Based on minutes taken by the War Cabinet, see War Cabinet Papers No. 227 of September 3rd 1917, p. 3, to be found in Destani, Beitullah, ed. – *The Zionist Movement and the Foundation of Israel 1839-1972*, Vol. II, 1917-1918, Archive Editions, 2004, p.367, [hereinafter ZMFI].

informing him that the Government were being pressed to make a Declaration in sympathy with the Zionist Movement, and seeking his views as to the advisability of such a Declaration being made. It took some weeks to obtain his personal opinion on the subject, but, when it arrived, Mr. Balfour reported that 'President Wilson was extremely favourable to the Movement'.[86]

President Wilson's comment was made after the wording of the Declaration was brought to his attention. The Palestine Royal Commission (also known as the Peel Commission) confirmed in 1937 that 'the text of the Declaration had been approved by him [President Wilson] before its publication.'[87]

Later on, after the Declaration was made public, both the French and Italian Governments openly endorsed it, and so did both Houses of Congress with the approval of the President of the United States. First to endorse the Declaration was the French Government on the February 14th 1918. A formal and public communiqué from the French Minister for Foreign Affairs, Mr Pichon, was addressed to Nahum Sokolow, as representative of the Zionist Organization: 'There was complete agreement between the French and British Governments in all matters which concern the establishment of a Jewish national home in Palestine' ('un etablissement Juif en Palestine').[88] The French Government stated further that this communiqué was sent to the press and made public to show its definite views 'on the subject of Zionist aspirations with regard to the creation of a Jewish national home in Palestine'.[89]

---

[86] Lloyd George, op. cit., Vol. II, p. 1135.

[87] The Peel Report, July 1937, Cmd. 5479, op. cit., p. 22.

[88] Sokolow – op. cit., p.128; translation of the text from French by Mr Sokolow.

[89] Sokolow – ibid.; Friedman, op. cit., p. 309: In a dispatch to Lord Curzon dated May 19th 1919, Lord Balfour, while referring to the letters sent by M. Pichon and Marquis Imperiali to Dr. Nahum Sokolow of February 14th 1918 and May 9th 1918, respectively, stated clearly that "both the French, United States and Italian Governments have approved the policy set forth in my letter to Lord Rothschild of November 2nd 1917. See DBFP, op. cit., Vol. IV, p. 281, n. 4.

Next to endorse the Declaration was the Italian Government through the Italian Ambassador in London on May 9th 1918, assuring the Zionist Organization of its desire to facilitate the establishment in Palestine of a Jewish National Centre ('un centro nazionale ebraico').[90]

The American endorsement came almost four years later with a Joint Resolution of the Sixty-Seventh Congress unanimously adopted by the Senate on May 3rd 1922 and the House of Representatives on June 30th 1922. It was approved by President Harding on September 21st 1922, in favor of 'the establishment in Palestine of a national home for the Jewish people, it being clearly understood... etc.'[91]

In November 1918 the Imperial Japanese Government joined the other Principal Allied Powers in approving the Balfour Declaration, and authorized its Ambassador in London to issue the following declaration of sympathy with Jewish national aspirations: 'The Japanese Government gladly take note of the Zionist aspirations to establish in Palestine a National Home for the Jewish people, and they look forward with a sympathetic interest to the realization of such desire upon the basis proposed.'[92]

Lord Balfour summed up the Declaration as a 'settled policy among the Allied and Associated Powers before ever the Armistice came into existence. It was accepted in America, it was accepted in this country, it was published all over the world, and, if ever there was a Declaration which had behind it a general consensus of opinion, I believe it was the Declaration of November 1917.' [93]

---

[90] Sokolow – ibid., 129; translation of the text from Italian by Nahum Sokolow.

[91] Statutes of the United States of America, Vol. XLII, Sixty Seventh Congress, Session II, Chap. 372, p. 1012, Joint Resolution by the Senate and House of Representatives, September 21st 1922; *Cf.* Stein, *Zionism,* op. cit., p. 91, n.2.

[92] C.L. Torley Duwel ed., – *Bulletin de L'Institut Intermediaire International,* Publication trimestrielle, the Hague, 1919, p. 245; Stein*, Zionism,* ibid., p. 90.

[93] Parliamentary Debates, H.L. June 21st 1922, Vol. 50, cc. 994-1033; See also DBFP, Vol. VIII, op. cit. p. 159.

Chapter III

Interpretation and Object of the Declaration

As mentioned, the Declaration was a deliberate product of British foreign policy. It was not the act of a single idiosyncratic politician, nor delivered in haste or lightheartedly. It should be understood in the context of the intentions of its initiators and its literal wording and purpose should be parsed closely. To what end was the Declaration made, and what did the decision makers and the drafters wish it to achieve? It is also important to examine its background and the stages that culminated in the delivery of the Declaration. The primary formulators and decision-makers were Lloyd George and Balfour. Other members of the British Cabinet included Lord Milner and General Smuts. The actual drafters of the final version were Leopold Stennett Amery and Viscount Alfred Milner. As for the government officials involved in negotiations and daily progress towards making the Declaration a reality, Mark Sykes and William Ormsby-Gore (later, Lord Harlech) were prominent. Thus, the Declaration should be examined through its creation and reception by British statesmen, press, Zionists, and anti-Zionists. Other notable viewpoints include the Jewish people as a whole, Arab dignitaries, as well as President Wilson.

The main source of information on the genesis of the Declaration is Lloyd George. Without his pro-Zionist policy, consent, and permission no declaration would have been possible. Lloyd George based his memoirs on personal notes, recollections, and secret Cabinet documents. Another crucial source of information is Lord Balfour himself, associated with the Declaration by name. The intention and purpose of Lloyd George and Balfour, together with other members of the British Cabinet, is most valuable in the interpretation of the Declaration. No less important are now public British Cabinet papers and decisions. Other valuable sources are memoirs and treatises authored by those with first hand information on the drafting of the Declaration. These include Dr. Chaim Weizmann, Sir Herbert

Samuel, Leopold Amery, Nahum Sokolow, Leonard Stein, and others.

It may be conclusively shown that the ultimate purpose of the Declaration was to give the Jewish people the opportunity to reconstitute a National Home in Palestine as an independent sovereign state: that is, Palestine in its historical and Biblical borders, from Dan to Beersheba, situated on both sides of the Jordan River. It was obvious, since most of the Jewish people then lived outside Palestine, that such a reconstruction of an independent State could not be achieved instantly. Gradual stages would have to allow for immigration, establishment of Jewish settlements, and revival of Jewish culture, language and economic stability. Finally, by forming a substantial majority, and consequently by erecting a central Government, the Jews would assume control over the country. In other words, the ultimate purpose was 'the recreation of Palestine as it was before the days of the dispersion'.[1]

However, before going into any details to substantiate the above, it calls for a preliminary survey of the background and history of the Declaration.

A. Background of the Declaration

When the Balfour Declaration was announced on November 2nd 1917, Palestine was still in the hands of the Turks. British Forces under the command of General Sir Edmund Allenby did not enter Jerusalem until a month later, on December 9th 1917 and Palestine was not fully occupied until October 31st 1918. At the time of the Declaration, there was no such place or country as Palestine. Under the Turks the area was divided between the *Sanjaq* of Jerusalem and the *vilayets* of Syria and Beirut. Therefore, when speaking of Palestine in this context, the British Government meant 'the old Scriptural Palestine, extending from Dan to Beer-Sheba, i.e. from Banias to Bir Saba. This is a country of less than 10,000 square miles, including 4,000 to the east of

---

[1] Lord Curzon's statement of opinion to the British Cabinet, October 26th 1917, cited in Lloyd George, op. cit., Vol. II, p. 1124.

the Jordan.'[2] The population of Palestine, given the highest estimate, ranged between 600,000 and 700,000, with less than one quarter Jewish and the remainder (except for small Christian communities or settlements) Muslim.

Under Turkish rule, the country was, as described by Lord Curzon, 'in a condition of abject debasement. Its soil was barren, it was devastated by centuries of neglect and misrule. It was a poor land, containing no mineral, no coal, no iron ore, no copper, gold or silver. It depended entirely on live stock (i.e. mainly goats which crop the bare hills) and agriculture.'[3]

The country, therefore, had primitive industry and agriculture. It was in no position to receive the entirety of the Jewish people, nor even a substantial number of them. The global Jewish population at the time numbered approximately 12 million, and was scattered in all parts of the world. To assemble them in one place was no easy task. The hot weather in Palestine was not fit for Europeans from northerly climates, and malaria was prevalent along with ophthalmia and other ailments. The Jews were not known to be farmers and it was uncertain if they could cultivate the land. Therefore, even if implemented, the Declaration was by itself no guarantee of national prosperity. It was an experiment and only the future would reveal if it could succeed. These were the bare conditions under which the Balfour Declaration was issued.

The following phrasal components of the Balfour Declaration require careful consideration:

- Sympathy with Jewish Zionist aspirations
- View with favour
- National Home
- Jewish people
- Best endeavours
- To facilitate the achievement of this object
- Civil and religious rights
- Existing non-Jewish communities in Palestine

---

[2] War Cabinet Papers, G.T. 2406, October 26th 1917, p.2; see also Lloyd George, ibid., Vol. II, p. 1126.

[3] War Cabinet Papers, ibid.; Lloyd George, ibid., Vol. II, p. 1128.

- The rights and political status enjoyed by Jews in any other country

B. Chain of Events Leading to the Final Draft of the Declaration

After three years of intensive negotiations with prominent British officials, and after a number of formulae were considered, Lord Rothschild, on behalf of the British Zionist Federation, was able to submit to Lord Balfour, on July 18th 1917, a draft of the proposed declaration. Weizmann pointed out that in phrasing the proposal, every effort was made to stay 'within the limits of the general attitude on the subject which prevailed among the leading members of the Government'.[4] Weizmann saw fit to emphasize that 'this is something to be borne in mind for the reconstruction of the complete picture'.[5]

The proposed draft read as follows:[6]

1. His Majesty's Government accepts the principle that Palestine should be reconstituted as the National Home of the Jewish people.

2. His Majesty's Government will use its best endeavours to secure the achievement of this object, and will discuss the necessary methods and means with the Zionist Organization.

This draft was approved by the Foreign Office and by both Lloyd George and Lord Balfour.[7] In August 1917, Lord Balfour sent a reply to Lord Rothschild:[8]

In reply to your letter of July 18th, I am glad to be in a position to inform you that his Majesty's

---

[4] Weizmann, op. cit. p. 203.

[5] Ibid.

[6] War Cabinet Papers, G.T. 1803, July 18th 1917.

[7] Weizmann, op. cit. p. 204.

[8] War Cabinet Papers, G.T. 1803. op. cit.

> Government accept the principle that Palestine should be reconstituted as the national home of the Jewish people.
>
> His Majesty's Government will use their best endeavours to secure the achievement of this object and will be ready to consider any suggestions on the subject which the Zionist Organization may desire to lay before them.

Lord Balfour thus endorsed the draft submitted to him by Lord Rothschild almost verbatim, with minor variation in wording of the two drafts of no real consequence. It was now ready to receive the approval of the War Cabinet.

However, at this stage final approval was sabotaged. Incredibly, the saboteurs were affluent, assimilated anti-Zionist Jews, mainly of British birth – and no one else. In the words of Weizmann, 'There cannot be the slightest doubt that without outside interference, *entirely from Jews*, [italics in the original] the draft would have been accepted early in August, substantially as we submitted it.'[9] Weizmann described these Jews as a 'well-to-do, contented and self-satisfied minority, a tiny minority who rebelled against making the Declaration.'[10] They were organized in two major groups: The Anglo Jewish Association and the Board of Deputies of British Jews. As Weizmann described them, in their view 'the Jews were a religious community and nothing more. The Jews could not claim a National Home. The utmost that could be demanded for the Jews of Palestine was enjoyment of religious and civil liberty, 'reasonable' facilities for immigration and colonization, and such municipal privileges in towns and colonies as may be shown to be necessary.'[11]

The most outspoken and prominent representative of Jewish anti-Zionism in Britain was Lord Edwin Montagu, who some weeks before the debates in the Cabinet was appointed the Secretary of State for India. In this capacity he was a member

---

[9] Weizmann, op. cit.

[10] Weizmann, ibid. p. 200.

[11] Weizmann, ibid. p. 202.

of the Government and had access to meetings of the War Cabinet. No Zionist activist enjoyed a privilege similar to his. The Declaration was discussed in four War Cabinet meetings. Although Montagu had to leave for India, he made sure to participate in the first two Cabinet meetings, and to state his case. He was thus responsible for important changes in the phrasing of the final draft, detrimental to the Zionist cause. He dispatched before or after each meeting a detailed memorandum critical of the Declaration in the form Zionists wanted it.

Soon after Montagu received the Rothschild-Balfour correspondence, he submitted a counter-memorandum. This was presented to the War Cabinet on August 23rd 1917, with the provocative title, *Anti-Semitism of the present (British) Government*. Its purpose was to suppress any declaration of the establishment of a National Home for the Jewish people in Palestine. When the War Cabinet convened on September 3rd 1917 for the first time to discuss the Declaration,[12] on the basis of the correspondence between Lord Rothschild and Lord Balfour, they had before them Montagu's memorandum. However, the Declaration's major supporters, Lloyd George and Lord Balfour, were absent. To this meeting Lord Alfred Milner, a member of the War Cabinet, presented an alternative draft to that which was agreed upon by Balfour and Lloyd George. The Milner draft provided as follows:

> His Majesty's Government accepts the principle that every opportunity should be afforded for the establishment of a home for the Jewish people in Palestine, and will use its best endeavours to facilitate the achievement of this object, and will be ready to consider any suggestions on this subject which the Zionist Organizations may desire to lay before them.[13]

---

[12] War Cabinet meeting of September 3rd 1917, No. 227, Minutes of which would be found in the ZMFI, op. cit., p. 365.

[13] War Cabinet Papers, G.T. 1803A, entitled The Zionist Movement, Alternative to Draft Declaration, by Lord Milner, referring to the draft submitted by Lord Rothschild and accepted by Balfour and the Foreign Office, *Cf.* War Cabinet Papers G.T. 1803, July 18th 1917.

Milner's draft, which apparently came as a response to Montagu's strong opposition, in fact, suggested substantial changes in the original Rothschild-Balfour proposal. Instead of the term 'reconstituted' in the phrase 'accepts the principle that Palestine should be reconstituted as the national home' which indicated the Jewish historical connection to Palestine, Milner suggested the neutral term 'establishment'. Instead of 'the National Home' Milner's version omitted the significant 'National' and substituted the indefinite for the definite article. Instead of 'to secure' (in the phrase, 'His Majesty's Government will use their best endeavours to <u>secure</u> the achievement of this object'), Milner offered the weaker 'to facilitate'. In other words, the original version approved by the Foreign Office and the Prime Minister had been watered down substantially.

Even so, Montagu was not satisfied. He opposed the use of the phrase 'a home for the Jewish people' in Milner's proposal. In his opinion, this 'would vitally prejudice the position of every Jew elsewhere.'[14] Ultimately, Montagu's intervention caused the withdrawal of the item from the agenda.[15] It was decided in the Cabinet to postpone a decision on the merits, meanwhile obtaining the views of President Wilson 'as to the advisability of such a declaration being made'.[16]

Accordingly, President Wilson was approached by the British Government: On September 12th 1917, Lord Robert Cecil, Acting Foreign Secretary, received a telegram from Colonel Edward M. House, presidential chief advisor. In President Wilson's opinion, 'the time is not opportune for any definite statement further perhaps than one of sympathy, provided it can be made without conveying any real commitment. Things are in such a state of flux at [the] moment that he does not consider it advisable to go further.'[17] Following this response, on September 19th 1917 Weizmann cabled Judge Brandeis, a close friend of the President.

---

[14] War Cabinet Papers, Meeting No. 227, September 3rd 1917, p. 366.

[15] Weizmann, op. cit., p. 204.

[16] War Cabinet Papers, Meeting No. 227, op. cit. p. 367.

[17] War Cabinet Papers, G.T. 2015, September 12th, 1917.

He asked him to enquire 'what President Wilson's views were regarding declaration'. A week later, on September 27th 1917, Brandeis replied that the President 'is in entire sympathy with declaration quoted in yours of the 19th, as approved by Foreign Office and Prime Minister. I, of course heartily agree.'[18]

The second War Cabinet meeting on the Declaration was scheduled for October 4th 1917. On September 14th 1917, prior to the meeting, Lord Montagu dispatched a detailed letter to Lord Robert Cecil in an incessant effort to suppress the issuance of a declaration. If a declaration was to be issued, he wanted it to refrain from using words which may imply 'that there is a Jewish people in the political sense'.[19] In the meeting of October 4th, both Lloyd George (in the chair) and Balfour were present. This meeting proved to be crucial and set the tone for the final draft. Lord Milner was not entirely happy with the alternative draft that he had presented to the Cabinet in the meeting of September 3rd and therefore asked Amery for assistance.[20] In *My Political Life*, Amery described the amazing story as to how the phrasing of the proposed Declaration went through new changes:

> Half an hour before the meeting Milner looked in from his room in the Cabinet offices, next door to mine, told me of the difficulties, and showed me one or two alternative drafts which had been suggested, with none of which he was quite satisfied. Could I draft something which would go a reasonable distance to meeting the objectors, both Jewish and pro-Arab, without impairing the substance of the proposed

---

[18] War Cabinet Papers, G.T. 2158, September 26th 1917.

[19] War Cabinet Papers, G.T. 2191, September 14th 1917.

[20] Leopold Amery served as Parliamentary Under-Secretary in Lloyd George's Government, later as Colonial Secretary. He was described by Weizmann, who knew him personally, as being of large stature and superior abilities. He was the most open-minded of all British Officials who were involved in the issue of the Declaration. 'He realized the importance of a Jewish Palestine in the British imperial scheme of things more than anyone else. He also had much insight into the intrinsic fineness of the Zionist Movement... He, in particular, was incensed when the leading Jews attacked the scheme openly in 1917'. Weizmann, op. cit., p. 182.

declaration? I sat down and quickly produced the following:

> His Majesty's Government view with favour the establishment in Palestine of a National Home for the Jewish race, and will use their best endeavours to facilitate the achievement of this object, it being clearly understood that nothing shall be done which may prejudice the civil and religious rights of the existing non-Jewish communities in Palestine or the rights and political status enjoyed by Jews in any other country who are contented with their existing nationality.[21]

Amery's draft was thus prepared in haste, thirty minutes before commencement of the meeting. There was no time to consider with any depth the repercussions of the two provisos that were now included for the first time in the declaration. Amery's main aim was to please Lord Montagu and the Jewish anti-Zionists who opposed the Declaration, for the Declaration to go through. He did not mean to change the substance or the purpose of the Declaration nor the intentions of its makers. Amery later explained: 'The various provisos gave away nothing that was not self-evident. Anyhow it served its immediate purpose and was agreed with the Jewish leaders subject to two minor alterations.'[22]

The pro-Arabs Amery was referring to were presumably Lord Montagu and Lord Curzon. The first asserted that the establishment of a National Home for the Jewish people might mean 'Mohammadans and Christians are to make way for the Jews'.[23] The latter wondered 'How was it proposed to get rid of the existing majority of Mossulman inhabitants and to introduce

---

[21] Amery, op. cit., p. 117.

[22] Ibid., With regard to the two alterations see p.76, infra.

[23] See a memorandum by Edwin Montagu on the Anti-Semitism of the Present (British) Government, August 23rd 1917, jewishvirtuallibrary.org/jsource/History/Montagumemo.html.

the Jews in their place?'[24] Milner submitted the draft to the Cabinet over strong objections raised by Lord Montagu against making any declaration stating that Palestine was the National Home of the Jewish people.

Weizmann gave a vivid description of the proceedings regarding the October 4th Cabinet meeting. He recalled in his memoirs that on the day of the meeting he came to the office of Lloyd George's secretary and asked if he could wait there in case he was asked for, but the secretary advised him to leave, since no private citizen has ever been admitted to Cabinet meetings. Weizmann, however, did not leave. Instead he went to the office of Ormsby-Gore, which was close by and waited there.

As Weizmann recalled:

> When the Palestine item was laid before the War Cabinet, Edwin Montagu made a passionate speech against the proposed move… There was nothing new in what he had to say, but the vehemence with which he urged his views, the implacability of his position, astounded the Cabinet. I understand the man almost wept. When he had ended, Balfour and Lloyd George suggested that I be called in, and messengers were sent for me. They looked for me high and low – and I happened to be a few doors away in the office of Ormsby-Gore. I missed a great opportunity.[25]

Nevertheless, Lord Balfour supported the issuance of the Declaration. With the two contradictory telegrams, the one received from Colonel House and the one received from Judge Brandeis, laid before the Cabinet, Balfour stated that 'he knew that President Wilson was extremely favourable to the [Zionist] movement.'[26] He also alluded to 'a very sympathetic declaration by the French Government which had been conveyed

---

[24] Ibid.

[25] Weizmann, op. cit. p. 206.

[26] War Cabinet Papers, No. 245, October 4th 1917. Minute 18, p. 5.

to the Zionists'.[27] He saw nothing inconsistent between the establishment of a Jewish focus in Palestine and the complete assimilation and absorption of Jews into the nationality of other countries. However, Montagu's obstruction drove the Cabinet into reaching a decision not to make a decision. They decided to postpone the meeting and meanwhile to ask for additional opinions from three quarters: Leaders of the Zionist movement, representatives of Anglo-Jewry opposed to Zionism, and President Wilson, on the latest version of the proposed declaration, the one drafted by Amery.

In accordance with the Cabinet decision, the Milner-Amery draft was submitted to ten prominent Jewish leaders, six in favor of the Declaration (or of the Declaration with slight amendments) and four against it (including Lord Montagu). Out of the amendments suggested by these leaders only two were finally adopted, namely those suggested by the Chief Rabbi Dr. Joseph Herman Hertz, Dr. Weizmann, Sokolow, and Lord Rothschild:

> (1) The term 'Jewish race' to be substituted for the expression 'Jewish people'.
> (2) The words following the phrase '… of Jews in any other country' to be deleted.[28]

However, a proposal made to the Cabinet by Weizmann and Sokolow, each separately, to substitute the word 're-establishment' for 'establishment' in the original draft was not adopted at this stage, even though it was not officially rejected. This small amendment was designed to secure an official recognition of the historical connection of the Jewish people with their homeland. Five years later, this was given officially and internationally in the instrument of the British Mandate for Palestine.[29]

---

27 Ibid.

28 War Cabinet Papers, G.-164, CAB. 24/4/14, October 17th 1917, p. 9.

29 The second recital in the preamble of the British Mandate stipulates as follows: 'Whereas recognition has already been given to the historical connection of the Jewish people with Palestine and to the grounds for *reconstituting* their national home in that country.' [Italics added].

The third War Cabinet meeting concerning the Declaration was scheduled for October 25th 1917. However, the meeting was adjourned before it began due to a statement made by Lord Curzon announcing that 'he had a Memorandum on the subject in course of preparation' which will be ready for submission later on.[30] The Memorandum, entitled *The Future of Palestine,*[31] was submitted to the War Cabinet the next day. In it, Curzon did not object to 'a systematic settlement of Jewish emigrants in Palestine'. Rather, he was concerned with the hardships arising from the realization of the Declaration, and the risk that it would be raising false expectations among the Jewish people regarding the feasibility of a resettlement in Palestine, a country of barren soil, the size of Wales. The country was not considered apt to absorb the whole of the Jewish people, numbering at the time around twelve million.

Speaking of hardships, Curzon was aware of the half million 'Syrian Arabs' already living in Palestine composing a mixed community of Arab, Hebrew, Canaanite, Greek, Egyptian, and possibly crusaders blood, who 'will not be content either to be expropriated for Jewish immigrants, or to act merely as hewers of wood and drawers of water to the latter'.[32] Curzon believed that 'Palestine would appear to be incapacitated by physical and other conditions from ever becoming in any real sense the national home for the Jewish people'. He was clearly of the opinion that 'the population of Palestine had already reached its possible limits of expansion, certainly on anything like a big scale.'[33]

However, war tension and pressure brought to the fore the need to make a declaration favorable to the aspirations of the Zionists for the purpose of wooing world Jewry to the side of the Allies. The War Cabinet felt the time was ripe for such a declaration. It reconvened on October 31st 1917 for the fourth time for a

---

[30] War Cabinet Papers No. 257, October 25th 1917, Minute 12, p. 6.

[31] War Cabinet Papers, G.T. 2406, October 26th 1917.

[32] Ibid.

[33] Ibid.; see also Lloyd George, op. cit., Vol. II, pp. 1122-23, 1132-33.

final decision. The Cabinet had before them the views of the ten prominent Jewish leaders and also Lord Curzon's memorandum. Lord Balfour, as Foreign Secretary, urged the Cabinet forward: 'If we could make a declaration favourable to such an ideal [the Zionist ideal...] we should be able to carry on extremely useful propaganda both in Russia and America.'[34] In consequence, the War Cabinet adopted the Milner-Amery version with the two minor amendments: 1) substituting Jewish race for Jewish people and 2) deleting 'by such Jews who are fully contented with their existing nationality' from the final clause of the second proviso.

On October 31st 1917, the War Cabinet authorized the Secretary of State for Foreign Affairs to take a suitable opportunity of making the following declaration of sympathy with the Zionist aspirations:

> His Majesty's Government views with favour the establishment in Palestine of a National Home for the Jewish people, and will use its best endeavours to facilitate the achievement of this object, it being clearly understood that nothing shall be done which may prejudice the civil and religious rights of existing non-Jewish communities in Palestine, or the rights and political status enjoyed by Jews in any other country.[35]

There is no evidence in British official documents that the Arabs took any part in opposing the Declaration or its wording. Dugdale explained that Balfour was never called upon to express an opinion on the Arab attitude to the Declaration, 'for the simple reason that no hostility had been evinced by Sherif Hussein, Emir of Mecca, and his sons – then the acknowledged representatives of Arab nationalism – when they became aware of the promise of a National Home in Palestine for the Jews. They had no objection in fact to the policy in itself, as was proved by the attitude of the Emir Feisal at the Peace Conference, nor did they claim that it

---

[34] War Cabinet Papers, No. 261, October 31st 1917, p. 5.

[35] Ibid. p. 6.

was a breach of any promise to themselves.'[36]

The changes the Declaration went through were mostly, if not entirely, the outcome of Jewish anti-Zionist activities, particularly those of Lord Montagu, who happened to be a member of the British Government at the time. Weizmann wrote later: 'certain it was that Montagu's opposition, coupled with the sustained attacks which the tiny anti-Zionist group had been conducting for months, their letters to the press, the pamphlets, some of them written pseudonymously by Lucien Wolf, their feverish interviews with Government officials – was responsible for the compromise formula.'[37]

C. Meaning of *National Home for the Jewish People*

(aa) What are Jewish Zionist Aspirations

The cornerstone of the Balfour Declaration lies mainly in the interpretation of the term: 'National Home for the Jewish people'. To fully appreciate the meaning of this term, its interpretation should be linked to the phrase 'Jewish Zionist aspirations' mentioned in the preamble. This phrase may assist in the interpretation of the term 'National Home for the Jewish people'. At the time, Jewish aspirations or aims were not kept a secret: They were well known both to members of the British Government and Cabinet and to Zionist leaders, with whom negotiations for a declaration took place.

In *The Jewish State* (1896), Herzl found no solution to Jewish persecution and anti-Semitism except through the establishment of an independent Jewish State. He invoked a model state, with sovereignty granted to the Jewish people 'over a portion of the globe large enough to satisfy the rightful requirements of a nation.'[38] Mass immigration from the Jewish Diaspora to the

---

[36] Blanche Dugdale, op. cit., Vol. II, pp. 159-60.

[37] Weizmann, op. cit., p. 206.

[38] www.jewishvirtuallibrary.org/jsource/Zionism/herzl2.html, p.6; In his treatise Herzl was not yet decisive whether that portion of the globe would be Palestine or Argentina. This was decided in the first Zionist Congress, a year later in 1897 in Basle, where it was concluded that there was no other place on the globe for Jewish independence except in Palestine.

Jewish State was, therefore, required. Only the idea of a Jewish State had the requisite power to draw the masses of Jews. Herzl believed that the departure of Jewish masses to the Jewish State was the implementation of their dream, through the long nights of their history, to return to their ancient homeland, praying for 19 centuries 'next year in Jerusalem'. In fact, Herzl did envision such Jewish mass immigration: 'Their exodus will have no resemblance to a flight, for it will be a well-regulated movement under control of public opinion. It will be inaugurated with absolute conformity to law.'[39] Through gradual and continuous movement covering many decades, Jewish immigrants would cultivate the soil, build settlements and dwellings, construct roads, bridges, railways and telegraph installations. It would create trade, trade would create markets, and markets would attract new settlers to build the country.[40]

The First Zionist Congress which took place in Basle Switzerland, on August 30th 1897, declared the goals and aspirations of the Zionist movement: 'Zionism seeks to establish a home for the Jewish people in Palestine secured under public law.'[41] The primary means of its achievement was promotion of settlements in Palestine by Jewish farmers, artisans, and manufacturers. For political considerations and convenience, the term 'Home' (Heimstaette) was used instead of 'State' (Stadt) in the original, along with 'Public Law' (Oeffentlich-rechtlich) instead of 'International Law' (Voelkerrechtlich).

One reason for this change apparently was, as Grief noted, to avoid antagonizing the Turks from whom Herzl hoped to obtain a Charter for the establishment of a Jewish State. His aim was to convince the Turkish Sultan to promote Jewish settlements in Palestine and overcome the ban on Jewish immigration into

---

[39] Ibid., p. 3.

[40] Ibid., p. 6.

[41] Another translation from German would be: "Zionism seeks to secure for the Jewish people a publicly recognized, legally secured homeland in Palestine". See *The Jubilee of the First Zionist Congress 1897-1947*, ed. S.U. Nahon, the Publishing Department of the Jewish Agency for Palestine, the Jerusalem Press Ltd. Jerusalem 1947, p. 76.

the country. Guided by the instructions they had received, the drafters of the Resolution, headed by Dr. Max Nordau, 'deliberately omitted any reference to either a Jewish State or to international law, to keep the door open for further negotiations with the Sultan.'[42] However, the use of 'Home' instead of 'State' in the 1897 Resolution did not alter the aim and aspirations of the founders of Zionism to establish in the long run a Jewish State in Palestine. A good proof of that would be Herzl's entry in his diary on September 3rd 1897, regarding the creation in Basle of the Jewish State.[43]

Jewish aspirations came up often in conversations held between Zionist leaders and British statesmen prior to the announcement of the Declaration, some of which paved the way to its making. Thus, in 1906, Weizmann convened with Lord Balfour in Manchester, at Balfour's request, and briefed him on the motive forces behind Jewish national revival, Zionist ideology, and the need to return to Palestine and no other part of the globe. Dugdale recalled years later that it was this conversation 'which in years to come was to bear fruit undreamed of by them both, and to set its impress on history, in the Balfour Declaration of 1917.'[44] Dugdale noted that 'Balfour for his part told me often about the impression the conversation made on him. (He said): 'It was from that talk with Weizmann that I saw that the Jewish form of patriotism was unique. Their love for their country refused to be satisfied by the Uganda scheme. It was Weizmann's absolute refusal even to look at it that impressed me.'[45]

Later, while addressing the War Cabinet on October 4th 1917, Balfour referred to Zionist aspirations informed by intense national consciousness, self-regard as one of the great historic races of the world, and having an original home in Palestine: 'These Jews had a passionate longing to regain once more this ancient National Home.' It is self-evident that the term 'ancient

---

[42] Grief, op. cit. pp. 74-75.

[43] See p. 38, n. 9, supra.

[44] Dugdale, Vol. I, op. cit., p. 323.

[45] Dugdale, ibid., p. 325.

National Home' in Balfour's address was used as a substitute for state.[46]

Herbert Samuel mentioned in his memoirs that he had discussed with Sir Edward Grey, then Foreign Secretary, On November 9th, 1914, British opportunities, following victory over the Turks, to bring about the fulfillment of 'the ancient aspiration of the Jewish people and the restoration there of a Jewish State'.[47] To this Dugdale pointed out that 'through Mr. Samuel, Sir Edward Grey's personal attitude was discovered. He was in full sympathy with the Zionist ideal.'[48] Early in 1915, Samuel submitted to the Cabinet a memorandum entitled *The Future of Palestine*, urging that 'We should take Palestine, into which the scattered Jews would in time swarm back from all quarters of the Globe, and in due course obtain Home Rule.'[49]

In a Foreign Office memorandum by Eric G. Forbes Adam,[50] of December 30th 1919, the natural implications which Zionists had given to the term National Home were explained: 'i.e. an attempt to make Palestine a state in its natural geographical and historic frontiers and by gradual immigration and special economic facilities to turn this state into a Jewish state'.[51]

In the years preceding the announcement of the Declaration, Zionist aspirations and aims were discussed intensively with many British politicians and statesmen. One of these was Lord Bertie, the British Ambassador to France. In his diary of January 1915, he mentioned a meeting in Paris with Weizmann in which an 'absurd scheme', as he put it, was discussed. 'It contemplates the formation of Palestine into an Israelite State under the

---

[46] War Cabinet Papers, No. 245, October 4th 1917, p. 5; see also Lloyd George, op. cit., Vol. II, p. 1136.

[47] Samuel, op. cit., pp. 140-41.

[48] Dugdale, Vol. I, op. cit., p. 164.

[49] Israel Cohen – *The Zionist Movement*, op. cit., p. 113. See also Weizmann, op. cit., pp. 150-51.

[50] Eric Graham Forbes Adam was 3rd Secretary in the British Peace Delegation to the Paris Peace Conference of 1919, and later first Secretary to the Foreign Office.

[51] DBFP, Vol. IV, No. 409, Memorandum by Mr. Eric G. Forbes Adam on *France and Northern Frontier of Palestine*, December 30th 1919, p. 608.

protectorate of England, France or Russia, preferably England.'[52]

To sum up Jewish Zionist aspirations, these consisted of the return of the Jewish people from all corners of the earth to their ancient homeland, to Palestine, to rebuild the land, become a substantial majority, enough to finally re-establish a state. The idea was not to create a focus of Jewish culture but to erect a Jewish sovereign State, not immediately but in due course. As demonstrated, these aspirations were very well known to the British Government and Cabinet.

Saying all that, one cannot ignore Sokolow's remark in his introduction to his treatise, *History of Zionism 1600-1918,* in which he denied that there was any truth in the anti-Zionist claim that Zionism aims at the creation of an independent Jewish State. He wrote: 'The Jewish State was never a part of the Zionist programme. The Jewish State was the title of Herzl's first pamphlet, which had the supreme merit of forcing people to think. This pamphlet was followed by the first Zionist Congress, which accepted the Basle programme – the only programme in existence.'[53]

This quotation totally contradicted the beliefs and ideology Sokolow had been fighting for. In the same introduction, Sokolow referred to Jewish aspirations in a collective way, as a nation, as a people, and not as individuals. He stressed that 'for two thousand years after the loss of political independence the Jews believed with passionate intensity in their future as a nation in Palestine.'[54] That the Jews never forgot the old holy home which they had left, they never forgot Jerusalem, they never forgot their old nationality. They always considered it their duty to be bound together not only by a common past but by ideas, aspirations and hopes, for a national future. Sokolow highlighted the unshaken belief the Jews had in Bible prophecies for the return of the Jewish people to their homeland in the form

---

[52] *The Diary of Lord Bertie of Thame, 1914-1918,* Vol. I, ed. Lady Algernon Gordon Lennox, George H. Doran Company, New York, 1924, p. 105.

[53] Sokolow, op. cit., Vol. I, p. XLV

[54] Sokolow, ibid., p. XXXIV.

of national restoration. He added in Appendix I of his book a detailed survey of these prophecies.[55]

Sokolow also published a Manifesto, in conjunction with E.W. Tschlenow and Chaim Weizmann, soon after the Balfour Declaration was made public, stating that the aim of the Jewish people since the first Zionist Congress was to 'achieve a national resurrection'.[56] Sokolow commented openly and clearly that 'Zionists want a commonwealth of Jewish colonization and labour, a settlement of Jewish pioneers and workers who will be able to create and develop a civilization of their own, undisturbed by restrictions. This is possible only in Palestine, and is the paramount necessity of the whole Jewish people all over the world.'[57] There can be little doubt that the only way to achieve these objects would have been through the establishment of a Jewish State. However, it seems very likely that Sokolow's denial of the final goal to create a Jewish State was motivated by the desire to conceal true Zionist aspirations to avoid conflicts with anti-Zionists – whether Jews, Arabs, or gentiles.[58]

(bb) Literal Interpretation of *National Home for the Jewish People*

National Home

The term 'home' originated from a similar expression adopted in the first Zionist Congress Resolution, namely that 'Zionism seeks to establish a *home* for the Jewish people in Palestine secured under public law.'[59] [Italics added]. The term was extensively used in Zionist literature prior to its appearance in the Balfour Declaration. Interestingly, 'national' was added to

---

[55] See for example Deuteronomy XXX, 3-5: 'That then the Lord thy God ... will return and gather thee from all the peoples wither the Lord thy God hath scattered thee...And the Lord thy God will bring thee into the land which thy fathers possessed, and thou shalt possess it'; see also Isaiah XI, 12, and Ezekiel XXXVI, 24.

[56] Sokolow, op. cit, Vol. II, p. 124.

[57] Sokolow, op. cit. Vol. I, p. XLVI.

[58] Grief, op. cit., pp. 85, 86.

[59] See p. 37 supra.

'home' by Sokolow as a substitute for 'state.' In fact, National Home can be seen as an innovation in international law as it was introduced for the first time in the Balfour Declaration.[60] It is highly probable that no precedent can be found for its use. Herzl advocated for the establishment of a Jewish State in *Der Judenstadt*, and this continued to be the ultimate aim of the Zionist movement. However, for political reasons the Congress determined to formulate Zionist goals in less forthright words.

What does the term 'national' indicate? In most definitions, this term, when used as an adjective, relates to a nation as a whole acting as an independent political unit and is controlled by a national, as opposed to local, Government.[61]

'National' derives from the word 'nation'. A 'nation' is defined as a distinct race or people, characterized by common descent, language or history, usually organized as a separate political state and occupying a definite territory.[62] 'A nation means people, and land on which to toil and live.'[63]

What is meant by 'home'? A home for a people is the centre of their life. The place where it lives, to which it belongs, the one

---

[60] Frankenstein, op. cit., pp. 27, 28.

[61] Thus in the Cambridge English Dictionary the term 'national' is defined as 'relating to all parts of a nation or to a nation as a whole rather than to any part of it'; and in the Miriam Webster English Dictionary, the term 'national' is defined as 'relating to the entire nation or country, owned and controlled or operated by a national Government'. In Dictionary.com, the term is defined as 'relating to or maintained by a nation as an organized whole or independent political unit'. The MacMillan Dictionary, stipulates that if the term 'national' comes before a noun, its connotation would be 'owned or controlled by the Government' as in 'national park', on the same footing as 'National Home'; also 'relating to one particular nation and not including other nations'. In the Shorter Oxford Dictionary 'national' implies 'of a nation or belonging to a nation'. The Oxford Advanced Learner's Dictionary defines 'national' as 'common to or characteristic of a whole nation'. Chambers Dictionary defines 'national' as pertaining to a nation; belonging to a nation, peculiar to a nation, characteristic of a nation, or controlled by a nation. Chambers Twentieth Century Dictionary, revised edition, London, 1901, 1966.

[62] The Shorter Oxford Dictionary; see also Chambers Dictionary, which defines Nation as a body of people marked off by common descent, language, culture, or historical tradition or, in other words, the people of a state.

[63] Felix Frankfurter, (later Justice of the United States Supreme Court), *The Palestine Situation Restated*, 9 Foreign Aff. 409, 417 (1930-1).

place in the world which is always open to it, and to which no one else has access except with the consent of the people. One's own country.[64]

'An Englishman's home is his castle' – We should understand 'home' used in the British Declaration in this respect. Accordingly, it is a place where one lives, or has the right to live, permanently, and he may exercise power legally to prevent access to anyone who does not belong to that home. A home provides safety and protection from outside danger and a sanctuary in case of foreign attack. It gives the sense of community, of living together. What makes a home different from any other place is the fact that access is open at any time to members of that home and to no one else.

As Frankfurter noted, 'A national home for the Jewish people in Palestine implies something wholly different from individual and isolated Jews living as they had lived or might live in Poland or Rumania. Land, the Jews may own in other countries; industries, they may acquire in other lands; but an integrated national life – a well rounded civilized society – is the very essence of the Palestinian home.'[65] A National Home is where a nation can develop its language, and culture without outside interference. The word 'National Home' in the Declaration, therefore, was expressly aimed at distinguishing the Jewish home in Palestine from that in any other country. In the words of Gribetz: "The word 'Jewish' identifies the people; the word 'national', the sovereignty inherent in a nation." [66]

---

[64] Frankenstein, op. cit., p. 28; see also the Shorter Oxford Dictionary which defines 'home' as a dwelling place, the fixed residence of a household, the dwelling in which one habitually lives or which one regards as one's proper abode; a place, region, or state to which one properly belongs, in which one's affections center or where one finds rest, refuge, or satisfaction; one's own country, one's native land, the place where one's ancestors dwelt; the seat, center or native habitat. So does Chambers Dictionary, op. cit., define 'home' as one's own country, the mother country, habitual abode or the place felt to be such; residence of one's family; the scene of domestic life with its emotional associations.

[65] Felix Frankfurter, op. cit., p. 417.

[66] Louis J. Gribetz – *The Case for the Jews: An Interpretation of their Rights under the Balfour Declaration and the Mandate for Palestine*, Bloch Publishing Company, New York, 1930, pp. 21-22.

By the same token, Jews lived in Palestine for many centuries in addition to being its indigenous inhabitants from Biblical times. At the time of the Declaration, they formed a clear majority in Jerusalem. However, they had not developed national aspirations. They lived among their Muslim and Christian neighbors as individual citizens or as a religious community of the Jewish faith. Palestine was where they lived, but it was not their National Home. The Zionist movement strove to turn Palestine into the National Home of the Jewish people.

In view of the above, National Home has all the necessary characteristics attributed to an independent State. Its connotation is thus collective, referring not to the home of individuals, but to a nation as a whole. The term is defined as a nation's own country, native land, and mother country – a native habitat which provides refuge and freedom to its people. Refuge in this context means free access to members of the home and denial of access to those who do not belong to that home. A nation cannot exercise these powers without possessing full control of that home; that is, having a state with a central government.

The National Home was to be for the Jewish people as a whole, not merely the Jews in Palestine. As Feinberg noted, 'It is granted not to Zionists or to Jews who have settled in Palestine or who will settle there, but to all Jews wherever they may be.'[67] This was substantiated not only by the wording of the Declaration, but also by high ranking British statesmen. In 1931, Prime Minister J. Ramsay MacDonald submitted to the House of Commons a letter he had sent to Weizmann on British policy in Palestine. He wrote that the undertaking of the Mandate incorporated into the Balfour Declaration 'is an undertaking to the Jewish people and not only to the Jewish population of Palestine.'[68] In 1939, Winston Churchill addressing the House of Commons posed the question: 'To whom was the pledge of the Balfour Declaration made? It was not made to the Jews of Palestine, it was not made to those who were actually living in Palestine. It was made to world

---

[67] Nathan Feinberg – *The Recognition of the Jewish People in International Law*, 1 Jewish Y.B. Int'l L. 1, 1948, p. 17.

[68] Parliamentary Debates, H.C., February 13th 1931, Vol. 248, c. 751.

Jewry.'[69] Churchill also added that 'the pledge was made to an entity which never before had been recognized in international law.'[70] At a meeting of the Supreme Council held in San Remo on April 24th 1920, Lord Curzon stated that the Declaration was a pledge 'that Palestine was in future to be the National Home of the Jews throughout the world.'[71]

The beneficiary of the National Home was, therefore, not the Jewish population of Palestine, but the newly recognized entity, the Jewish people. Hence, in spite of not being in actual possession of the country and inhabiting it, every Jew in the world had the right (though not the obligation) to return to his National Home: 'Every Jew [was] a potential inhabitant of Palestine.'[72] As Van Rees, Vice Chairman of the Permanent Mandates Commission pointed out, 'the Jewish people is virtually part of the population of Palestine.'[73]

The Jewish People

It was only with the Balfour Declaration that Jews were recognized as a nation in the modern era. Until then, Jews were simply co-religionists, believers in Judaism and members of one of the oldest monotheistic religions. Strong disagreement over the very nature of what constituted the Jewish people prevailed even among Jews. Some Jews thought that Judaism was no more than a faith tradition. Due to historical dispersion, Jews effectively no longer existed as a people or nation. Others, particularly members of the Zionist movement, believed that the Jewish people were not only followers of a particular religion (Judaism), but also constituted a nation and political entity. Lord Balfour was well versed in the Bible, and affirmed the uniqueness of the Jewish people as one nation and one religion, with a special affiliation to one country – and that was Palestine.

---

[69] Parliamentary Debates, H.C., May 23rd 1939, Vol. 347, cc 2171; see also Feinberg, op. cit., p. 17; Gribetz, op. cit. p. 22.

[70] Frankenstein, op. cit., p. 39.

[71] DBFP, Vol. VIII. op. cit. p.159.

[72] Ernst Frankenstein, *Palestine in the Light of International Law,* Narod Press, London, 1946, p. 35, cited in Friedman, op. cit., p. 325, n. 83.

[73] Cited in Feinberg, op. cit., p. 17.

The most prominent Jew who strongly opposed the claim that Jews formed a nation was Lord Edwin Montagu. Montagu was the only Jew to serve in the British Government at the time. He sent memorandums to the War Cabinet and participated in two of the deliberations on the Declaration. In his memorandum of August 23rd 1917, he referred to the Jews as 'a new nation with a new home in Palestine'.[74] For Montagu, there was no Jewish nation. He regarded Jews exclusively as a religious community and self-identified as a Jewish Englishman.[75] He urged the British Government that no words should be used to imply that 'there is a Jewish people in the political sense'.[76] The common Jewish denominator for Montagu was only religion: 'To bring the Jews back to form a nation in the country from which they were dispersed would require divine leadership'.[77]

Other prominent anti-Zionist Jewish leaders shared the same view. Sir Philip Magnus, in his reply to the British War Cabinet, stated that 'I cannot agree that the Jews regard themselves as a nation.'[78] This was echoed by Claude G. Montefiore, President of the Anglo-Jewish Association: 'I deprecate the expression "a national home" for it assumes that the Jewish race constitutes a "nation", or might profitably become a nation, both which propositions I deny.'[79] The same denial of Jewish national aspirations was made by L.L. Cohen, chairman of the British Board of Guardians.[80] Notwithstanding this Jewish opposition, the British Cabinet gave recognition to the Jews as a people deserving of a National Home in Palestine.

Although the term 'Jewish people' was applied in various international documents (e.g., the Balfour Declaration and the Mandate instrument), no formal definition of the term was ever

---

[74] http://www.jewishvirtuallibrary.org/montagu-memo-on-british-government-s-anti-semitism.

[75] War Cabinet Papers No. 245, of October 4th 1917, p. 6.

[76] Letter addressed to Lord Robert Cecil, a member of the War Cabinet, on September 14th 1917.

[77] Ibid.

[78] War Cabinet Papers, G-164, CAB 24/4/14, October 17th 1917, pp. 5-6.

[79] Ibid., p. 7.

[80] Ibid., p. 8.

specified. In addition, no exact criteria for inclusion in the Jewish people was ever codified. It was accepted then that a Jew was any person who according to his general conviction felt a Jew. As the representative of the Jewish Agency before the United Nations Special Committee on Palestine noted: 'Generally, we accept as Jews all who say they are conscious of being Jews.'[81] Notwithstanding, according to Jewish religious law, the definition of who is a Jew is quite clear – namely, any person born to a Jewish mother or who has gone through the formal process of conversion.

As noted, a 'National Home' constitutes the home of a nation. Members have free access to their nation and control its borders. This cannot be achieved under the domination of a foreign power. For the Jewish people, this longing for a National Home was intensified as the vast majority of the Jewish population lived in diaspora communities outside Palestine. An essential component of this national rebirth was free Jewish immigration to Palestine. For a foreign power to impose restrictions on immigration, much less bring it to a halt, was the antithesis of the concept of a National Home. The National Home was to provide housing, land, and jobs for arriving immigrants. But without Jewish authority to control immigration, this task would have been almost impossible. Implementing the Balfour Declaration would have stood no chance if there was outside intervention.

No better proof of the need for Jewish autonomy in determining its national destiny exists than the White Paper of 1939. The White Paper was aimed at bringing to a halt Jewish immigration to Palestine and was decried as a severe violation of the Balfour Declaration even in British circles. For Lloyd George, no restriction or cessation of Jewish immigration to Palestine was ever considered by anyone engaged in the issuance of the Declaration: 'That would have been regarded as unjust and as a fraud' on the Jewish people.[82] Churchill expressed similar criticism in the House of Commons in 1939:

---

[81] Feinberg, op. cit., p.18, n. 33-34.

[82] Lloyd George, op. cit., Vol. II, p.1139.

This pledge of a home of refuge, of an asylum, was not made to the Jews in Palestine but to the Jews outside Palestine … But what sort of National Home is offered to the Jews of the world when we are asked to declare that in five years' time the door of that home is to be shut and barred in their faces? The idea of home to wanderers is, surely, a place to which they can resort.[83]

It should be observed that later British restrictions on Jewish immigration were considered by British statesmen themselves as a total violation of the Balfour Declaration.

In the context of the Declaration, 'National Home' was, therefore, equivalent to a political entity free from foreign intervention with all the qualities of an independent state. Its literal interpretation is thus very close to that of a contemporary nation state. However, the literal interpretation does not stand alone; it is complemented by a purposive interpretation: i.e. one that looks into the purpose of the Declaration and the intention of its initiators. The purposive interpretation adds to the literal one and is a supplement to it. It was stated by Williams J. in 1863, in the case of Behn v. Burness, following the need to evaluate a statement in a charter party that:

The court must be influenced in the construction of the contract not only by the language of the instrument, but also by the circumstances under which, and the purposes for which, the charter-party was entered into.[84]

Similarly, it was stated by Parke, B. in Graves v. Legg that:

The court must ascertain the intention of the parties, to be collected from the instrument and the circumstances legally admissible in evidence with

---

[83] Parliamentary Debates, H.C., May 23rd 1939, c. 2173.

[84] *Behn v. Burness* (1863) 3 B. & S. 751, 757.

reference to which it is to be construed.[85]

(cc) Purposive Interpretation of the Declaration

It has been stated by various scholars that the Balfour Declaration was vague and ambiguous, open to various interpretations.[86] This claim turns out to be mostly empty. As noted, on many occasions 'Jewish National Home' was used interchangeably with 'Jewish State' – the two were treated as one and the same. Be that as it may, there can be little doubt as to the true intentions of the Declaration's initiators.

The two most prominent figures responsible for the Declaration, without whom the Declaration would never have come to pass, were obviously Lloyd George and Balfour. Their intentions and aims in issuing the Declaration should be sought first and foremost. On a second level of importance, the intentions and aims of other Cabinet members and statesmen who had direct influence on the issue of the Declaration, should also be examined. Then it would be necessary to examine how the Declaration was received and understood by the public at large and by the press.

The idea propounded by Lloyd George and Balfour, and approved by the Cabinet, was that the Declaration would eventually pave the way to a Jewish State, with Palestine as a British, French or American protectorate in the interim period. When Jews would form a majority of the population due to mass migration, they would take over control of the land. That is, Jewish statehood in Palestine would not be accomplished immediately but by stages. In his statement to the War Cabinet just before approving the final wording of the Declaration, Balfour was quoted as saying:

As to the meaning of the words 'National Home'

---

[85] *Graves v. Legg* (1854), 9 Exch. 709, cited in Cheshire and Fifoot on *The Law of Contract*, Butterworths, 8th edition, London 1972, p. 121.

[86] See Stein, *The Balfour Declaration*, op. cit., p.552; Friedman, op. cit., p. 311; Laqueur, op. cit., p.201; Meinertzhagen, op. cit., pp. 8-9, February 7th 1918.

to which the Zionists attach so much importance, he (Balfour) understood it to mean some form of British, American, or other protectorate, under which full facilities would be given to the Jews to work out their own salvation and to build up, by means of education, agriculture and industry, a real centre of national culture and focus of national life... It did not necessarily involve the early establishment of an independent Jewish State, which was a matter for gradual development in accordance with the ordinary laws of political evolution.[87]

Hence, mass immigration of the Jewish people was a prerequisite for the attainment of a majority in Palestine. There was no reason to insist on a majority unless the ultimate plan was to establish a Jewish State in Palestine. The White Paper of 1939 was attacked by Lloyd George for this reason as a scheme to derail statehood: 'The notion that Jewish immigration would have to be artificially restricted in order to ensure that the Jews should be a permanent minority never entered into the heads of anyone engaged in framing the policy. That would have been regarded as unjust and as a fraud on the people to whom we were appealing.'[88]

Lloyd George also clarified the meaning of 'National Home' in the context of the Declaration: 'There has been a good deal of discussion as to the meaning of the words "Jewish National Home" and whether it involved the setting up of a Jewish National State in Palestine. I have already quoted the words actually used by Mr. Balfour when he submitted the Declaration to the Cabinet for its approval. They were not challenged at the time by any member present, and there could be no doubt as to what the Cabinet then had in their minds.'[89] He noted that the success of the enterprise depended not on British goodwill and

[87] War Cabinet Papers No. 261, Oct. 31st 1917 p. 5; also quoted in Lloyd George, op. cit., Vol. II, p. 1137.

[88] Lloyd George, ibid., pp. 1138-39.

[89] Lloyd George, ibid., p. 1138; Friedman, op. cit. p. 279.

protection alone, but also on Jewish immigration, settlement, and development. In Lloyd George's words: 'All the representatives of the Dominions, and the leaders of public opinion in our country of every party, welcomed the Declaration and pronounced themselves wholeheartedly in favour of the policy.'[90] If the policy succeeded, there could be no doubt that its final aim was the establishment of an independent Jewish State in Palestine.

Lloyd George expressed on several occasions that he was very keen to see a Jewish State established in Palestine.[91] He was quoted by Lord Beaverbrook, Minister of Information, as writing to Balfour that 'I have always been a strong supporter of your policy on the question of Zionism, and nothing that was said by Henry, Swaythling or Philip Magnus in the least affected my opinion.'[92]

Balfour's views on Zionism and its ultimate aim to establish a Jewish State in Palestine, on the same footing as had existed before the dispersion were quite clear. In the Cabinet, he referred to the Zionist Movement as one of intense national consciousness, whose original home was Palestine: 'These Jews had a passionate longing to regain once more this ancient national home.'[93] Balfour explained his support of Zionism to Paul Cambon, the French Ambassador to London. Inter alia, he mused that 'it would be an interesting experiment to reconstitute a Jewish Kingdom.'[94] In an interview with Weizmann on February 15th 1919, he referred to

---

[90] Lloyd George, ibid., p. 1138.

[91] Lloyd George confided with Herbert Samuel in November 1914, soon after the beginning of World War I, see Stein – *The Balfour Declaration*, op. cit., p. 143; Samuel, op. cit., p. 142.

[92] Stein, *The Balfour Declaration*, ibid., p. 566. The names mentioned by Lloyd George were Anti-Zionists of the Jewish faith, who opposed vehemently the issuance of the declaration. Sir Charles Henry served as treasurer of the league of British Jews, Lord Swaythling was Louis Montagu 2nd Baron Swaythling, and Sir Philip Magnus was a Member of Parliament and a co-founder of the Anti-Zionist League of British Jews.

[93] War Cabinet Papers, No. 245, October 4th 1917, p. 5; see also Lloyd George, op. cit., Vol. II, p. 1136.

[94] Lennox – *The Diary of Lord Bertie 1914-1918*, Vol. II, op. cit., entry of December 30th 1917, p. 233.

the National Home as a 'Jewish Commonwealth'.[95] Balfour said as much to a Jewish audience of the English Zionist Federation at the Royal Albert Hall on July 12th 1920, referring to Palestine as given to the Jewish people, as the land of their forefathers, and as the object of hundreds of years of Jewish yearning.[96]

As Dugdale noted, the Jews and their history held an enduring fascination for Balfour: 'It originated in the Old Testament training of his mother, and in his Scottish upbringing. As he grew up...the problem of the Jews in the modern world seemed to him of immense importance.' Balfour's philosemitism was also informed by a strong sense of historical injustice. Dugdale remarked that Balfour saw 'Christian religion and civilization [owing] to Judaism an immeasurable debt, shamefully ill repaid'.[97] It was Balfour who initiated the first meeting with Weizmann. It was clear to Dugdale that Balfour's ardor for Zionism only intensified: 'The more he (Balfour) thought about Zionism, the more his respect for it, and his belief in its importance, grew.'[98] Amery, in his memoir, *My Political Life*, gave a vivid description of Balfour's curiosity about Zionism. Sometime in 1916, Balfour invited Weizmann to dinner, and Amery goes on:

> At a reasonable hour Weizmann excused himself. It was a lovely full moon and Balfour offered to accompany his guest for the 200 yards from 1 Carlton Gardens to the Duke of York's column. At the column he persuaded Weizmann to turn back again to complete the point they were then discussing – and so, pacing backwards and forwards for another two

---

[95] Reported in an article by Stephen Wise entitled: "The Balfour Declaration – Its significance in the U.S.A.", published in Paul Goodman ed. – *The Jewish National Home*, Dent & Sons, London 1943, p. 45, cited in Friedman, op. cit., p. 319.

[96] Balfour in that speech referred to Palestine as a territory 'being given to the people who for all these years have been separated from it – but surely have a title to develop on their own lines in the land of their forefathers...'. See *Speeches on Zionism*, delivered by the Right Honorable the Earl of Balfour, ed. By Israel Cohen, Arrowsmith, London 1928, pp. 24-25.

[97] First hand evidence of Blanche Dugdale, Balfour's biographer and niece, in *Arthur James Balfour*, op. cit., Vol. I, p. 324.

[98] Ibid. p. 326.

hours, Balfour drew out all that was in Weizmann's mind and heart about Zionism and much else.'[99]

From this anecdote, it can be seen that Balfour's interest in Jewish Zionism was literally indefatigable.

Dugdale noted the centrality of Zionist activism in Balfour's own self-conception of his life achievements. She recalled that Balfour 'looked upon Zionism as having provided one of his two greatest opportunities in life, his work as Chief Secretary for Ireland being the other'. Most revealing were his words to his niece near his death. He confessed to her that 'what he had been able to do for the Jews had been the thing he looked back upon as the most worth his doing'.[100]

Balfour expressed his views in many forums: speeches, writing, private conversations, and interviews. One exchange occurred in a private meeting on February 7th 1918 with high dignitaries, in which Colonel Richard Meinertzhagen, Middle East Chief political officer, was present. Meinertzhagen bluntly asked Balfour if the Declaration was a 'reward or bribe to the Jews for past services and given in the hope of full support during the war?' Balfour immediately responded: 'Certainly not; both the Prime Minister and myself have been influenced by the desire to give the Jews their rightful place in the world; a great nation without a home is not right.' Meinertzhagen then probed with a more strategic question: 'At the back of your mind do you regard this declaration as a charter for ultimate Jewish sovereignty in Palestine, or are you trying to graft a Jewish population on to an Arab Palestine?' Apparently, Balfour paused before answering with measured words: '*My personal hope is that the Jews will make good in Palestine and eventually found a Jewish State. It is up to them now; we have given them their great opportunity.*'[101] [Italics added].

---

[99] Amery, op. cit., p. 114.

[100] Dugdale, op. cit., Vol. II (1906-1930), p. 171; This was echoed in Weizmann autobiography: Balfour in retrospect confessed that he 'looked upon it (the Declaration that bears his name) as the great achievement of his life'. Weizmann, op. cit., p. 211.

[101] Meinertzhagen, op. cit., p. 9.

Balfour was asked to write an introduction to Nahum Sokolow's *History of Zionism 1600-1918*. According to Carroll Quigley, Balfour sent the draft for corrections to Alfred Zimmern, a well-known classicist then working in the Political Intelligence Section of the Foreign Office. Zimmern 'drew his (Balfour's) attention to the hazards in the policy opened by the Declaration leading to a Jewish State in Palestine.' Balfour wrote back to Zimmern on September 19th 1918: 'I am sure you are right in your warning about "the eventual Jewish State". *Personally, this is what I should like to see.* But it may prove impossible, and in any case it is not likely to become more possible if it is permanently discussed.'[102] [Italics added].

Therefore, motivated by caution, Balfour was reticent in the wording he used in his Introduction. He hardly mentioned a Jewish State, even though he hinted at it several times:

> [If] Zionism can be developed into a working scheme, the benefit it would bring to the Jewish people... would be great and lasting. It is not merely that large numbers of them would find a refuge from religious and social persecution; but that they would bear corporate responsibilities and enjoy corporate opportunities of a kind which, from the nature of the case, they can never possess as citizens of any non-Jewish State.[103]

Lord Curzon also envisaged a Jewish State as the ultimate goal of the Declaration. In his memorandum of October 26th 1917, entitled *The Future of Palestine*, which he submitted to the Cabinet a few days before the Declaration was decided upon,[104] he posed the following practical question: 'What is the meaning of the phrase "a National Home for the Jewish Race

---

[102] Article by Carroll Quigley, *Lord Balfour's Personal Position on the Balfour Declaration,* Middle East Journal, Vol. 22, No. 3 (Summer 1968) pp. 340-45.

[103] Forward to Sokolow's treatise *History of Zionism 1600-1918,* Vol. I, op. cit., p. LX.

[104] Supra, p. 30.

in Palestine?"' Curzon detected a fundamental disagreement and contradiction among Jewish leaders as to the scope and nature of Zionism,[105] and commented that:

> A National Home for the Jewish race or people would seem, if the words are to bear their ordinary meaning, to imply a place where the Jews can be reassembled as a nation, and where they will enjoy the privileges of an independent national existence. Such is clearly the conception of those who... speak of the creation in Palestine of 'an autonomous Jewish State', words which appear to contemplate a State, i.e. a political entity, composed of Jews, governed by Jews, and administered mainly in the interests of Jews. Such a State might naturally be expected to have a capital, a form of Government, and institutions of its own. It would possess the soil or the greater part of the soil of the country. It would take its place among the smaller nations of the earth. [106]

However, Curzon had some reservations about the tension this project of Jewish national renewal might cause with the Arab population. Therefore, Curzon expressed a hope that 'the wisest of the Zionists will forgo any claim to the recovery of Jerusalem, as the centre and capital of the revived Jewish State, since the city was sacred to Moslems too.'[107]

As indicated, Curzon detected other concepts within the Jewish community, which seem to suggest a much less definite form of political existence for the Jews in Palestine or which regarded the National Home to be no more than a spiritual center or a reservoir of Jewish culture, but these were the ideas of a minority.[108]

---

[105] Supra, p. 29.

[106] War Cabinet Papers, G.T. 2406, October 26th 1917; cited in Lloyd George, op. cit., Vol. II, p. 1124.

[107] Ibid.

[108] Ibid.

General Smuts, a member of the Imperial War Cabinet, speaking at Johannesburg on November 3rd 1919, also predicted mass Jewish immigration into Palestine and 'in generations to come a great Jewish State rising there once more'.[109] The contemplation of the eventual establishment of a Jewish State was also articulated or implied by Mr. Winston Churchill in 1920, Lord Robert Cecil in 1917, and Sir Herbert Samuel in 1919. Churchill envisaged 'in our own lifetime, by the banks of the Jordan, a Jewish state, under the protection of the British Crown, which might comprise three or four millions of Jews.'[110] Lord Cecil, speaking at a great demonstration in London on December 2nd 1917, put it succinctly in the context of a general British support for ethnic nationalism in the region: 'Our wish is that Arabian countries shall be for the Arabs, Armenia for the Armenians, and Judea for the Jews.'[111] The implied meaning of these words is that Cecil was clearly referring to a Jewish State in Palestine in which Arabs could not claim national rights, just as Jews could not claim national rights in Arabian countries or in Armenia.[112] Herbert Samuel, in a speech delivered at the London Opera house, on the second anniversary of the Balfour Declaration (November 2nd 1919), declared that the policy propounded before the Peace Conference, was 'the promotion to the fullest degree that the conditions in the country allow of Jewish immigration and of Jewish land settlement... in order that with the minimum of delay the country may become a fully self-governing Commonwealth under the auspices of an established Jewish majority'[113]. In the same speech, he stated that the ideal

---

[109] Text in a brochure published by the South African Zionist Federation jointly with the south African Jewish Board of Deputies, cited in Stein, *The Balfour Declaration*, op. cit., p. 662.

[110] Illustrated Sunday Herald, February 8th 1920, Cited in Israel Cohen, *The Zionist Movement*, ZOA New York, 1946, p. 121. See Friedman, op. cit. p. 314.

[111] Israel Cohen, ibid.

[112] Grief, op. cit., p. 99.

[113] Soon later to become the first High Commissioner of Palestine. His speech was published in a pamphlet issued by the Zionist Organization entitled *Zionism – Its Ideals and Practical Hopes*, London 1919, quoted in Grief, p. 87, n. 24.

of Zionism would not be fully attained unless Palestine became a State. As Grief noted, his reference to the creation of 'Zionist Palestine [was] a code word for a Jewish State'.[114]

Lord Milner, an assertive Member of the War Cabinet, who was directly responsible for the final wording of the Declaration, said publicly: 'If the Arabs think that Palestine would become an Arab country, they are very much mistaken.'[115] Milner was convinced that only the Jews were capable of rebuilding Palestine as a functional modern state. Ronald MacNeill, M.P., who later in 1922-4 served as Under Secretary of State for Foreign Affairs, submitted to the Cabinet that the future of Palestine was one of the problems that had to be solved 'and [that] the proposal to make that country the domain of a reconstituted Jewish state, the "National Home of the Jewish people", had attractions both from a political and historical point of view.'[116]

In a word, these were the intentions and objectives of the decision-makers in the British Cabinet in making the Declaration. They manifestly did not have in mind the establishment of a cultural-religious center. Rather, they envisaged the gradual re-establishment of a Jewish State. Powerful and well-informed members of the Secretariat of the War Cabinet proved instrumental in the consolidation of the Declaration. This group included accomplished secretaries such as Mark Sykes, Leopold Amery, William Ormsby-Gore and Ronald Storrs. Amery reported that Mark Sykes, as secretary to the War Cabinet, 'practically took charge of all the negotiations which led up to the Balfour Declaration, and that in his doing, the Zionist Movement owed [him] a lot, at a critical moment in its history'.[117] Sykes was a strong supporter of Palestine becoming a Jewish State and was also praised by Weizmann: 'I cannot say enough regarding the

---

[114] Grief, ibid., p. 87.

[115] Weizmann, op. cit., p. 178-79.

[116] F.O. 371/3083/143082, Memorandum by Ronald MacNeill M.P. entitled 'Note on the Secretary of State for India's Paper on Anti-Semitism of the Government', [undated but presumably end of August 1917], cited in Friedman, op. cit. p. 260.

[117] Amery, op. cit., p. 115.

services rendered us by Sykes.'[118] Amery also supported Jewish Palestine, with Weizmann ranking him as a man 'of larger stature and superior abilities... the most open-minded of all that group... [who] realized the importance of a Jewish Palestine in the British imperial scheme of things more than anyone else'.[119]

Eric G. Forbes Adam, a British diplomat and first Secretary to the Foreign Office, in his memorandum of December 30th 1919, succinctly summed up British policy at the time: '[The Declaration was] an attempt to make Palestine a state in its natural geographical and historic frontiers, and by gradual immigration and special economic facilities to turn this state into a Jewish state. Only time and experience can show how far the Zionist aspiration is realisable...Behind British policy, therefore, is the recognition of the principle of Jewish nationality, which is the essence of Zionism and the intention to lay in the Turkish Peace Settlement the foundation for the reconstruction of a Jewish Palestine, as of an Armenia for the Armenians.'[120]

Beyond the Cabinet, the tremendous influence of President Woodrow Wilson on the Declaration should not be underestimated. In President Wilson's words: 'I am persuaded that the Allied nations, with the fullest concurrence of our Government and our people, are agreed that in Palestine shall be laid the foundations of a Jewish Commonwealth.'[121] Lloyd George commented that these words were President Wilson's true interpretation of the Declaration. At the Paris Peace Conference, President Wilson remained consistent. At a meeting held on May 3rd 1919, he pointed out that what was promised to the Jews by the British and American Governments was a State, albeit with problems in Palestine stemming from Arab intransigence. In 1919, he assured Rabbi Stephen Wise, an American Zionist leader: 'Have no fear,

---

[118] Weizmann, op. cit., p. 189.

[119] Weizmann, ibid. p. 182.

[120] DBFP, Vol. IV, op. cit., No. 409, p. 608. Memorandum by Mr. Eric G. Forbes Adam on France and Northern frontier of Palestine, December 30th 1919.

[121] Lloyd George, op. cit. Vol. II, p. 1139; Peel Report op. cit., p. 24, para. 21; Weizmann, op. cit. p. 211; Friedman, op. cit. p. 302.

Palestine will be yours.'[122]

The general American policy was consistent with President Wilson as demonstrated in a document prepared for the President and his Plenipotentiaries on January 21st 1919, entitled, *Report and Recommendations of the intelligence Section of the American Delegation to the Peace Conference.* In Article 3, it recommended the following:

> It is recommended that the Jews be invited to return to Palestine and settle there, being assured by the Conference... that it will be the policy of the League of Nations to recognize Palestine as a Jewish state as soon as it is a Jewish state in fact.

The Report goes on to explain the rationality behind this Article:

> It is right that Palestine should become a Jewish state, if the Jews, being given the full opportunity, make it such. It was the cradle and home of their vital race, which has made large spiritual contributions to mankind, and is the only land in which they can hope to find a home of their own; they being in this last respect unique among significant peoples.[123]

(dd) Perception of *National Home* by the Public

Perception of *National Home* by the Press

As noted, the Declaration was the outcome of a British commitment in return for Jewish wartime support of the Allies.[124] We shall now examine how this commitment was perceived and understood in the British and Foreign press. It seemed obvious

---

[122] Stephen Wise – *Challenging Years*, London 1961, p. 123, cited in Friedman, op. cit., p. 302.

[123] David Hunter Miller – *My Diary at the Conference of Paris*, Vol. IV, self-published by Appeal Printer Co., New York, 1924, Document 246, pp. 263-64.

[124] See pp. 40 et seq., supra.

to the British Cabinet that the proposed declaration had to meet Jewish Zionist aspirations. Judging from the press, it was taken for granted that the final goal of the Declaration would be the establishment of an independent Jewish State in Palestine. Stein noted the headlines in the British newspapers: 'A State for the Jews' in the *Daily Express*, 'Palestine for the Jews' in *the Times*, *Morning Post* and *Daily News... The Spectator* wrote of 'the proposal for the establishment of a Jewish State in Palestine'. The *Manchester Guardian* saw the Declaration as leading to "the ultimate establishment of a Jewish State'. *The Observer* wrote: 'It is no idle dream that by the close of another generation the new Zion may become a State.'[125]

The *New Statesman* of July 8th 1916 printed an editorial on 'The Meaning of Zionism' and referred to 'The creation of an autonomous Jewish State in Palestine'. Lord Cromer, writing in *The Spectator* on August 12th 1916 concluded his article with the words: 'Zionism stands for a national revival'. *The Review of Reviews* of September 1916 defined Zionism as a complete spiritual and national Jewish rebirth – 'a re-settling of Jews in their own ancient home'.[126]

On March 10th 1917, *Common Sense* advocated that 'the British Government will regard it as a duty to obtain a Hebraic Palestine as one of the terms of peace.' In *The Daily Chronicle* of March 30th 1917, its military correspondent wrote that:

> There can be no doubt that we should revive the Jewish Palestine of old, and allow the Jews to realize their dream of Zion in their homeland...The New Jewish State, under British or French aegis, would become the spiritual and cultural centre of Jewry throughout the world. The Jews would at least have a homeland and nationality of their own. The national dream that has sustained them for a score of centuries and more will have been fulfilled.[127]

---

[125] Stein, *The Balfour Declaration*, op. cit., pp. 562-63.

[126] Sokolow, op. cit., pp. 73-74.

[127] Sokolow, ibid., pp. 78-79.

A leading article in the same issue (March 30th 1917), entitled 'The Victory in Palestine' announced: 'The project for constituting a Zionist State there under British protection has a great deal to commend it.'[(128)]

An article published in the *New Europe* on April 19th 1917, under the title *Great Britain, Palestine and the Jews,* stated that 'a British Palestine must be a Jewish Palestine, the home of a restored Jewish people, the spiritual centre of the whole Jewish race.' The *Liverpool Courier* of April 24th 1917 ran an article entitled 'Rebuilding Zion,' with the exhortation: 'A British Palestine must be a Jewish Palestine.' In another issue, the same paper, in an article captioned 'The Future of Palestine' stated: 'It must be the business of the Allies, in pursuance of their policy of liberation, to restore to Palestine its liberties, and to provide a centre of nationhood for the Jewish race.' *The Glasgow Herald* of May 29th 1917, in an article on 'Zion Re-edified', underscored that the Zionists are not merely looking forward to a re-edified (i.e. rebuilt) Zion, 'but to the establishment of a Jewish State, under the suzerainty of some strong Christian power'.[(129)]

The Times Literary Supplement of August 16th 1917, in an article entitled '*After Many Years'*, noted the success of Jewish colonization in Palestine as such that 'Palestine may slowly grow from a State with the status say of the Anglo-Egyptian Sudan – and develop into an autonomous protected State, with its own native sovereign and administration and forming part of the Empire in just the same way as do many States which are in full control of their internal liberties.' As for Jews who elected to remain citizens of their host countries, the *New Europe* of September 27th 1917 thought it likely that 'the existence of a Jewish State would certainly react, and react healthily, upon the position of Jews who might elect to remain in the Dispersion.'[(130)] In the larger geopolitical picture, the *Manchester Guardian* of October 19th 1917 proposed that 'Syria should be given to France, and

---

[128] Sokolow, ibid., p. 79
[129] Sokolow, ibid., pp. 75, 76.
[130] Sokolow, ibid.

Palestine to a Jewish state dependent on this country.'[131]

The Methodist Times, The Globe, The Weekly Dispatch, The Irish Times, The Liverpool Courier and the Liverpool Post, of October 20th 1917, expressed themselves in similar manner. In the United States, the press also used the term Jewish National Home interchangeably with Jewish State, Jewish Republic, and Jewish Commonwealth.

In the Swiss French daily, *Le Matin* of February 27th 1919, Zionist aspirations were understood as meaning at the minimum, bestowal of special rights on the Jewish community in Palestine. Maximally, they meant 'the constitution of a true Jewish state in Palestine... [although] the aim in either case is the same.' In Germany, the press saw the Balfour Declaration as British sponsorship of Jewish statehood.[132]

Perception of *National Home* by World Statesmen

Theodore Roosevelt in the peace program of the Republican Party included, inter alia, the making of Palestine into a Jewish State. At a party meeting in New York, he suggested that an Allied condition for peace should be that Palestine be made into a Jewish State.[133] The former American Consul in Jerusalem, Otis Glazebrook, was also in favor of the prospect of a Zionist State. Another voice of American pro-Zionist sentiment was that of Senator Charles McNary, who supported the settlement of the 'Jewish people in the old-new home to make Palestine a veritable state'.[134]

The French were conflicted over the future of Palestine. However, in February 1919, M. Tardieu, a French representative on the Council of Ten, issued an official statement that France would not oppose the formation of a Jewish State.[135] Berthelot

---

[131] Friedman, op. cit., p. 277.

[132] Friedman, ibid., pp. 277, 312-13.

[133] Friedman, ibid., pp. 301, 313.

[134] Glazebrook spoke at a Thanksgiving celebration at Carnegie Hall, New York, on December 26th 1917. See *The Jewish Chronicle*, September 13th and November 18th 1918, cited in Friedman, ibid., pp. 312-13.

[135] Friedman, ibid., p. 313.

followed up this sentiment at the Supreme Council held at San Remo on April 24th 1920, with the endorsement that the whole world was sympathetic to the aspirations of the Jews to establish a National Home in Palestine, referring to the National Home as a 'new projected State'.[136]

In Germany, the Balfour Declaration was generally interpreted as a 'British sponsored State for the Jewish people'. Support was also apparent in Greece, when the Greek Foreign Minister noted to the editor of the Salonica Jewish organ, *Pro-Israel*, that 'the establishment of a Jewish State meets in Greece with full and sincere sympathy' adding that 'a Jewish Palestine would become an ally of Greece', a position repeated on other occasions by Greek officials.[137]

Perception of *National Home* by the Jewish People

Generally speaking, the understanding of the Jewish people was to interpret the Balfour Declaration as a commitment by the British Government to facilitate the gradual establishment of a Jewish State in Palestine. This view seems to have been shared by Jews in Britain and abroad – by Jewish Zionist and anti-Zionist alike. For this reason, Zionists were jubilant and anti-Zionists reserved or dismayed. Before the Declaration was formally issued, the War Cabinet decided (on October 4th 1917) to seek the opinions of British Zionists and anti-Zionist Jewish representatives.[138] Consequently, the Milner-Amery version was submitted to ten Jewish leaders, partly Zionists or pro-Zionists and partly anti-Zionists. Regardless of the substance of their replies, all were under the impression that the Declaration envisioned a Jewish State in Palestine in its final stage.

Thus, Sir Philip Magnus M.P., who opposed the Declaration in its Milner-Amery form, pointed out that any British pronouncement 'to take steps to establish for Jews, and Jews only, a "national home in Palestine" might be interpreted as implying

---

[136] DBFP, Vol. VIII, op. cit., p. 160.

[137] *The Near East*, December 21st 1917, cited in Friedman, ibid. p. 313.

[138] War Cabinet Papers, No. 245, p. 6; War Cabinet Papers, G-164, October 17th 1917, p. 1.

that the Government of that country would, under certain conditions, be transferred to the Jews'.[139] Magnus was referring to Zionist rumors that the British desired an independent Jewish Palestine as a buffer state between Turkey and Egypt – that is, a country governed by Jews as a British protectorate. These rumors reflect the widespread consensus that the establishment of a Jewish State in Palestine was eminently feasible.

Another anti-Zionist, L.L. Cohen, Chairman of the Jewish Board of Guardians, who denied that the Jews were a nation, also referred to the creation of a Jewish State in Palestine as well within the bounds of possibility: 'What is now proposed is optional emigration to the new State (Section 6)... The creation of a Jewish State in Palestine will scarcely solve it [i.e. the Jewish question].' Cohen was echoing an anti-Zionist argument of the time – that Palestine would not be large enough to contain the entirety of Europe's Jewish population.[140]

It can thus be inferred that the creation of a Jewish State was the Declaration's *terminus ad quem* – even if not dressed in the language of statehood. As can be seen from words of the Chief Rabbi of Great Britain, Dr. Joseph Hertz, the Declaration was broadly understood by the hopeful masses of Jews in Jewish restorative terms (i.e., the re-establishment of a historical Jewish State): 'To millions of my brethren throughout the world it [the proposed Declaration] will mean the realisation of Israel's undying hope of a restoration.'[141]

Lord Walter Rothschild alluded in his reply to the same historical and inviolable right of the Jews to the land of their forefathers. He stated that the greater part of Zionists and pro-Zionists 'hold that they, as Jews, have a historical and inviolable right to a national home, and moreover, a home in Palestine, the land of their forefathers'. He referred to a chief aim of the Zionist Federation as 'obtaining as large a measure of autonomy

---

[139] War Cabinet Papers, G-164, ibid., p. 6.

[140] Ibid., p. 8, sec. 6-8.

[141] Ibid., p. 2.

as possible' in Palestine.[142] As Stein noted, Rothschild was very clear on the goal of the establishment of a Jewish State: 'At Sykes' conference with leading Zionists on 7 February 1917, Rothschild had said that 'he sympathised fully with the development of a Jewish State under the British Crown.' In fact, Rothschild endorsed the 'establishment of an autonomous Jewish State under the aegis and protection of one of the Allied Powers'.[143]

In the same way, oppositional voices construed the Declaration as culminating in Jewish statehood of some kind. For instance, Claude Montefiore, President of the Anglo-Jewish Association, stated in his reply to the British Cabinet that he opposed the expression 'a National Home' which implied that Jews constitute a nationality. He echoed the common anti-Zionist fear that Jews forming themselves into a nationality in Palestine might prejudice the character and position of Jews as nationals in other countries. His fear would have required no articulation if the Declaration lacked a foundational intention to eventually establish a Jewish State. Indeed, nationality can be defined as 'the relationship between a State and its nationals.[144] Montefiore, therefore, was in favor of a scenario in which the British would confer local or municipal autonomy on the Jewish people in contrast to national autonomy.[145]

Lord Montagu, the staunchest of all anti-Zionists, who vehemently opposed the wording of the Declaration, was aware of Zionist aims to eventually establish a political national entity in Palestine. When raising his objections in the War Cabinet, he was aiming at nullifying Zionist claims, 'that the Jewish settlers in Palestine should be (1) recognized as possessing a national character in a political sense; and (2) invested with certain special

---

[142] Ibid., p. 3.

[143] Stein, *The Balfour Declaration*, op. cit., p. 523, quoting Rothschild's letter to *the Times*, May 28th 1917.

[144] Paul Weiss – *Nationality and Statelessness in International Law*, 2nd edition, Sijthoff and Noordhoff 1979, p. 29.

[145] War Cabinet Papers, CAB 24/4/14, G-164, ibid., p. 7.

rights in excess of those enjoyed by the rest of the population'.[146] On October 9th 1917, he submitted a memorandum in which he based his arguments on a review received from Gertrude Bell, Assistant Political Officer in Baghdad, who explicitly referred to the eventual establishment of an independent Jewish State in Palestine, albeit She ruled out the conception of such a State from practical politics, because of Arab objection.[147]

The same impression was given by senior officers in the Cabinet with no ideological stake in the Declaration. For instance, Maurice P.A. Hankey, the able secretary of the War Cabinet, who assembled the aforesaid Zionist and Anti-Zionist opinions into a bundle to be presented to the Cabinet, was not content with a mere ten opinions, and included in the same bundle newspaper articles and miscellaneous information mostly from Eastern Europe and Russia concerning Zionist activities there. In these articles, references to a Jewish State can be found amid information on various Zionist demonstrations, conferences, and meetings for the implementation of Zionist aspirations. One such article was by Sir Alfred Mond, M.P. and published in the *Weekly Dispatch* on April 8th 1917. Mond made reference to the practicability of an 'autonomous Jewish State' in Palestine, and wondered whether 'the foundation of an independent Jewish State comes within the domain of practical politics'.[148] Reports from Eastern Europe stated that in Samarkand (now in modern-day Uzbekistan) a meeting of five thousand Jews adopted a resolution in favor of a Jewish Palestine. A similar resolution was also promulgated in a Zionist Conference held in Petrograd (present day Saint Petersburg) in May 24th 1917, invoking the 'restoration of a national autonomous centre in its historic home, Palestine ... and that its moral and historic right to Palestine is

---

[146] This was mentioned in a letter addressed to Lord Robert Cecil of September 14th 1917, War Cabinet Papers, G.T. 2191. So did the Presidents of the Board of Deputies of British Jews and the Anglo-Jewish Association who likewise dissociated themselves from Zionist aims, see Stein, *Zionism*, op. cit., p. 85.

[147] War Cabinet Papers, G.T. 2263.

[148] War Cabinet Papers, G-164, ibid., Appendix III, p. 13.

incontestable and irremovable'.[149]

Later, anti-Zionist organizations, more specifically, the Board of Deputies of British Jews and the Anglo-Jewish association, adjusted themselves gradually to Zionist ascendency. As Stein noted, they began to identify with the Declaration, subject only to one condition – that it must not 'be held to imply that Jews constitute a separate political nationality all over the world, or that the Jewish citizens of countries outside Palestine owe political allegiance to the government of that country'[150] It can be inferred that anti-Zionists would not have made these stipulations had the Jewish National Home not been construed as a separate political nationality in Palestine – one in which Jews would be expected to show allegiance to its government.

The unconcealed use of the language of Jewish statehood was also on display in the United States. For instance, the Provisional Executive Committee for General Zionist Affairs interpreted the Declaration to mean 'a promise to establish a Jewish State'. Likewise, Felix Frankfurter discussed 'the political and legal foundations of the Jewish State' at the 1918 convention of American Zionists held at Pittsburgh on June 23rd-27th 1918, in the presence of a representative of the British Embassy.[151] In the same year, the American Jewish Congress passed a resolution in Philadelphia supporting the establishment of a Jewish Commonwealth under the trusteeship of Great Britain.[152] The Jewish Ministers' Association of New York also adopted a resolution resolving that all Jewish Rabbis of America should petition the President and both Houses of Congress to 'favourably consider the restoration of Palestine to the Jewish people'.[153]

As noted, in Eastern Europe, and particularly in Poland, the Jews received the Declaration with great enthusiasm. They took it to mean that the British would aid the Jews in establishing an independent self-governing entity. In the Yiddish daily,

---

[149] Ibid., Appendix III, pp. 15, 16.

[150] Stein, *The Balfour Declaration*, op. cit., p. 566.

[151] Friedman, op. cit., p. 312.

[152] Meeting on December 17th 1918, Friedman, ibid., p. 301.

[153] War Cabinet Papers (CAB 24/4/14), G-164, ibid., p. 18.

Lemberger Tageblatt, of November 18th 1917, Britain was praised for assisting the Jewish people 'in order to lift it up once more into the ranks of the independent self-governing races'.[154]

In Russia too, the Declaration was understood to mean a promise that Palestine would be given to the Jews. On November 30th 1917, a delegation of local Rabbis went to meet with the British Consul in Odessa to offer their appreciation. While doing so, Jewish youth organizations vowed to build a Jewish State in Palestine, and thus implement the Declaration. On May 5th-8th, 1918, a Zionist conference was convened in Moscow, attended by sixty delegates, and acclaimed the Balfour Declaration as 'the first step to international recognition of a Jewish Palestine'. In Petrograd, the Jewish community congratulated 'the British Government on its intention to establish a Jewish Government in Palestine'. The same jubilation held true in southeastern European Jewish communities, such as in Rumania. There, the Declaration had an 'electrifying effect' on the Jewish population. Even hitherto anti-Zionists and Jews indifferent to Zionism became very enthusiastic about the idea of a Jewish State. They declared their wish to settle in Palestine and invest capital in the country 'to promote the political, economic and cultural development of the Jewish State'.[155]

There was also considerable support for the Declaration across the Jewish religious spectrum. For instance, Orthodox Jewish delegates of Agudath Israel from various countries met in Zurich on 18th-25th February 1919 to urge the Peace Conference 'to recognize Palestine as the country of the people of Israel'.[156] Isaac Halevi Herzog, the Chief Rabbi of Belfast at the time, saw the Declaration in redemptive terms as a 'preparatory stage leading towards redemption and restoration of Israel.'[157] It was evident that Jews saw in the Balfour Declaration the great

---

[154] Stein, *The Balfour Declaration*, op. cit., p. 569.

[155] Friedman, op. cit., pp. 292, 294, 312, 296, respectively.

[156] Friedman, ibid., p. 307.

[157] *The Jewish Chronicle*, April 12th 1918, cited in Friedman, ibid., p. 311-12. Rabbi Herzog was later the Chief Rabbi of Ireland, and subsequently the Ashkenazi Chief Rabbi of the British Mandate for Palestine and of Israel after its independence in 1948.

promise of the return to them of their own country. Meinertzhagen recorded in his Middle East Diary what he had heard from Weizmann on January 29th 1919, as being Zionist aims: viz, to secure 'the recognition of the League of Nations to the historic title of the Jewish people to Palestine, and the right of the Jews to reconstitute in Palestine their national home'. Here, in this context, the term National Home was used interchangeably with State. The expression 'historic title to Palestine' was widely known to be equivalent to historic ownership, which alluded to pre-exilic national sovereignty.[158]

Perception of *National Home* by the Arabs

The Arab inhabitants of Palestine fought with the Turks against the Allied Powers during the First World War. During that period there was no line of communication between the British Government and the Arabs of Palestine.[159] Nevertheless, Emir Feisal[160] was recognized by both the Arabs and the British Government as representing the entire Arab population of the Middle East, including Palestine. Feisal made assertions that Palestine would be given to the Jewish people. Therefore, as Stein put it, through Feisal, the Arabs conceded that 'in return for an undertaking by the Zionists to do their best for the welfare of the future Arab State, Palestine unencumbered by any Arab claim, had, in effect been set apart for the Jews'.[161] As such, when Feisal addressed the Peace Conference on February 6th 1919, he asked 'for the independence of all the Arab-speaking peoples of Asia' and did so explicitly with the exception of Palestine. 'Palestine... he left on one side for the consideration of all parties interested'.[162] However, a few weeks after signing the agreement with Weizmann early in January 1919, Feisal, in

---

[158] In the meantime Weizmann asked that 'the sovereign possession of Palestine to be vested in the League of Nations and the Government to be entrusted to Great Britain as Mandatory Power'. Meinertzhagen, op. cit., p. 13. On the establishment of the Jewish State in stages, see pp. 128 et seq., infra.

[159] Lloyd George, op. cit., Vol. II, p. 1140.

[160] Acting on behalf of his father Hussein bin Ali, the Sherif of Mecca.

[161] Stein, *The Balfour Declaration*, op. cit., p. 642.

[162] British Documents on Foreign Affairs, [hereinafter BDFA], Part II, Series I, Vol. 2, *The Paris Peace Conference of 1919*, pp. 109, 110.

an interview reported in a Paris newspaper, gave the impression that he went through a change of heart regarding Arab relations with the Zionist Movement. But even then, his position was one of opposition to a 'Jewish Commonwealth in Palestine'.[163]

In a letter addressed to Felix Frankfurter dated March 1st 1919, Feisal expressed deep sympathy for the Zionist cause:

> We Arabs, especially the educated among us, look with the deepest sympathy on the Zionist Movement. Our Deputation here in Paris is fully acquainted with the proposals submitted yesterday by the Zionist Organization to the Peace Conference, and we regard them as moderate and proper. We will do our best, in so far as we are concerned, to help them through: we will wish the Jews a most hearty *welcome home.'* [Italics added].[164]

Feisal ended his letter to Frankfurter in the following paragraph:

> I look forward and my people with me look forward to a future in which we will help you and you will help us, so that *the countries* in which we are mutually interested may once again take their place in the community of the civilized peoples of the world'.[165] [Italics added].

The Zionist proposals to which Feisal referred pointed towards the objective of the eventual re-establishment of a Jewish State in Palestine. As a representative of the Zionist Organization at the Peace Conference, Sokolow invoked the '[Jewish] historic claim to Palestine', referring to it as 'the land of Israel'. He emphasized that 'the Allies promised to help the Jews found a Jewish national center in the place where the real home of the Jewish people

---

[163] Stein, *The Balfour Declaration*, op. cit., p. 643.

[164] Meinertzhagen, op. cit., p. 16; Stein, *The Balfour Declaration*, ibid., p. 643-44.

[165] Ibid.

had always been.' For Sokolow, the transformative potential of Zionism was evident such that old Jewish traditions 'could again be introduced in the land of their ancestors... thus leading to a reconstitution of a people and the transformation of a country'. He then urged that, in the interim, the League of Nations should take sovereign possession of Palestine and its government should be entrusted to Great Britain as a Mandatory of the League. Ultimately, however, this arrangement should 'render possible the creation of an autonomous Commonwealth'. Weizmann said much the same – at first Palestine should be governed by a British Mandatory Power until such time as the Jews will build up a nationality and 'so make Palestine as Jewish as America is American or England English.'[166] Feisal, speaking at the conference in the name of the Arab people, must, therefore, have known that the final Zionist goal was to lay the foundation to a Jewish State in Palestine. Moreover, he found Zionist proposals 'moderate and proper', and promised that the Arabs will do their best to help them through. He again wished the Jewish people a hearty welcome home, the home of their ancestors.

That the Declaration would eventually lead to a Jewish State was not only understood by Emir Feisal as the representative of the Arab people. Other less prominent Arab leaders shared the same understanding. One proof of this understanding could be found in a resolution adopted by the Syrian Congress which opposed the Declaration. The Congress declared: 'We reject the claims of the Zionists for the establishment of a Jewish Commonwealth in that part of Southern Syria which is known as Palestine, and we are opposed to Jewish immigration into any part of the country.'[167]

(ee) The Provisos as a means for the interpretation of the term *National Home*

As mentioned earlier, the final draft of the Declaration bore

---

[166] BDFA, Part II, Series I, Vol. 2, *The Paris Peace Conference of 1919*, op. cit., pp. 259-65.

[167] General Syrian Congress resolutions, Para. 7, Damascus, July 2nd 1919, reported in Stein, *The Balfour Declaration*, op. cit., p. 643.

two provisos as follows:

> It being clearly understood that nothing shall be done which may prejudice the civil and religious rights of existing non-Jewish communities in Palestine, or the rights and political status enjoyed by Jews in any other country.

Background

Both provisos were the outcome of fierce Jewish anti-Zionist opposition to the wording of the Declaration. Arab opposition was not yet born in as coherent a form. The first proviso was intended to balance the second – the main reason for the insertion of the provisos in the first place. Lord Montagu and the conjoint Committee, comprising the Anglo-Jewish Association and the Board of Deputies of British Jews, were their primary cause. Montagu submitted three memorandums to the Cabinet on the eve of the Declaration. This was to prevent the Cabinet from using the term 'National Home for the Jewish People' in the Declaration. The Conjoint Committee carried out intensive work to convince members of the Cabinet to forestall the making of the Declaration as phrased.

The *raison d'être* of this opposition was the assumption that 'the use of the phrase "National Home for the Jewish People" would vitally prejudice the position of every Jew elsewhere.'[168] The anti-Zionists were afraid of having their patriotism challenged. They feared that Zionism would create a vicious public backlash threatening their age-old struggle for assimilation – perhaps even leading to expulsion from England to Palestine. To this, *The Times* replied dismissively: 'Only an imaginative nervousness suggests that the realization of territorial Zionism, in some form, would cause Christendom to turn round on the Jews and say: "Now you have a land of your own, go to it."'[169]

In his Cabinet memorandum of August 23rd 1917, Montagu

---

[168] War Cabinet Papers, No. 227, September 3rd 1917; Lloyd George, op. cit., Vol. II, p. 1133.

[169] Weizmann, op. cit., p. 202; Ben Halpern – *The Idea of the Jewish State*, Harvard University Press, Cambridge, Massachusetts, 1961, p. 174.

expressed his concern that 'when the Jews are told that Palestine is their national home, every country will immediately desire to get rid of its Jewish citizens.'[170] He then emphasized the equal claim to Palestine of Muslims and Christians. Finally, he reiterated: 'When the Jew has a national home, surely it follows that the impetus to deprive us of the rights of British citizenship must be enormously increased. Palestine will become the world's Ghetto. Why should the Russian give the Jew equal rights? His national home is Palestine.... All Jews will be foreign Jews, inhabitants of the great country of Palestine.' With the reality of dual citizenship perhaps unknown to Montagu, he concluded that the Jew will have to choose between the country he loved and thought he belonged to, where now he is no longer welcome, and a country whose people are foreigners to him but his Christian fellow-countrymen tell him he shall belong to.[171] As Frankfurter noted, from the 'published diaries of Edwin S. Montagu... the only opposition within the British Government to the support of the Jewish cause came from its Jewish member.'[172]

Dugdale also commented on Montagu's vigorous anti-Declaration stance grounded in radical Jewish assimilation:

> But there was one formidable enemy inside the Cabinet, and that enemy was the only Jew in the Cabinet, Edwin Montagu, Secretary of State for India. He was the spearhead of that opposition to the Balfour Declaration, which never came from gentile quarters, but from assimilated and semi-assimilated Jews of Western Europe and the United States. It came from within the Jewish people themselves, it came from that type of Jewish person who still survives in those countries of Europe where anti-Semitism is either non-existent or ... latent.[173]

---

[170] https://www.jewishvirtuallibrary.org/montagu-memo-on-british-government-s-anti-semitism

[171] http://www.jewishvirtuallibrary.org/jsource/History/Montagumemo.html. Mentioned in War Cabinet Papers No. 227 0f September 3rd 1917.

[172] Felix Frankfurter, *The Palestine Situation Restated*, op. cit., p. 413.

[173] Blanche Dugdale, "The Balfour Declaration: Its Origins", in *The Jewish National Home*, ed., Paul Goodman, J.M. Dent & Sons, London, 1943, p.4.

Jewish opposition, spearheaded by Montagu in actual fact argued: 'Jews who earned their emancipation and equal stratum in the countries they lived in might imperil their position if they considered themselves as a separate nation from the people among whom they lived. Therefore they were justified in opposing the Declaration'. This attitude seemed intransigent. However, as Dugdale put it, at the moment of truth, it was Balfour who stood up to Montagu, 'and had to fight from the Jewish Zionist Nationalist standpoint against the British assimilated Jew. He had to fight and he won the fight'.[174]

Montagu even used himself as a cautionary example if the Declaration were to be adopted. His position service in the government would effectively become contradictory. Referring to himself in the third person, he exclaimed in the Cabinet somewhat rhetorically: 'How would he (Montagu) negotiate with the peoples of India on behalf of His Majesty's Government... if the world had just been told that His Majesty's Government regarded his national home as being in Turkish territory?'[175] These 'well-to-do' anti-Zionist British Jews feared that the draft Declaration would jeopardize their status as British subjects and their rights to participate in a British Government. They were anxious to demonstrate their undivided loyalty to Great Britain, as proud citizens of the Jewish faith. Rothschild formula was therefore rejected by the Cabinet on September 3rd 1917, not because of the wording of the formula 'that Palestine should be reconstructed as the national home for the Jewish people', nor because of any opposition from the then inhabitants of Palestine, but rather to 'allay the apprehension of upper-crust English Jews who feared that the rights and political status they enjoyed in Britain would be adversely affected by issuing the draft Declaration as it was then formulated'. [176]

Lucien Wolf was another prominent opponent of the Declaration. On behalf of the Conjoint Committee, he met

[174] Blanche Dugdale, in Goodman's *Jewish National Home*, ibid., p. 5.
[175] War Cabinet Papers No. 245, October 4th 1917; Lloyd George, op. cit., Vol. II, p. 1134.
[176] Grief, op. cit., p. 93.

with Balfour at the end of January 1917. He similarly based his opposition to a Jewish State in Palestine on the possibility that it might be understood to 'claim the allegiance of the Jews of Western Europe, who are satisfied with their local nationalities', and might demand a privileged status for the Jews in Palestine which may 'compromise the position and aims of Jews in other countries'.[177]

Similar reservations were submitted by other Jewish anti-Zionists.[178] Sir Philip Magnus was an MP who opined that 'national' should be withdrawn from the proposed formula since Jews do not constitute a nation, instead suggesting 'centre of Jewish culture.'[179] Claude G. Montefiore, President of the Anglo-Jewish Association, went even further, declaring:

> I deprecate the expression "a national home," for it assumes that the Jewish race constitutes a "nation" or might profitably become a nation, both which propositions I deny. The phrase "a national home for the Jewish race" appears to assume and imply that the Jews generally constitute a nationality. Such an implication is extremely prejudicial to Jewish interests, as it is intensely obnoxious to an enormous number of Jews.[180]

It was for these reasons that Amery introduced the second proviso into the Declaration draft. But why was the first proviso introduced? And who were the 'pro-Arabs' Amery was asked by Milner to go 'a reasonable distance' in appeasing? It would seem that the main advocates of the Arab cause were, in fact, Lord Montagu and other influential anti-Zionist Jews.

Montagu expressed his concern regarding the Arabs living in Palestine in his memorandum on August 23rd 1917: 'I do not

---

[177] Stein, *The Balfour Declaration*, op. cit., p. 444.

[178] War Cabinet Papers, G.-164, CAB 24/4/14, October 17th 1917, Appendix I, pp. 5-7.

[179] Ibid. p. 6.

[180] Ibid, p. 7.

know what this involves (the reconstitution of a national home for the Jewish people in Palestine), but I assume that it means that Mohammedans and Christians are to make way for the Jews and that the Jews should be put in all positions of preference.'[181] After the Milner-Amery draft was introduced, Montagu continued in a similar vein. This time he framed his concern as a rhetorical question: As the population of Palestine could not be greatly increased due to geographic constraints, 'what part of the existing population is it (the Jewish national home) proposed to dispossess?'[182]

Magnus was similarly preoccupied with Arab rights in Palestine. In his response to the Cabinet, pending the issuance of the Declaration, he warned that it was essential 'that any privileges granted to the Jews should be shared by their fellow-citizens of other creeds.'[183] Before restoring the country to the Jews under a British protectorate, as was rumored in Zionist circles, Magnus urged the British Government to 'consult the existing inhabitants of Palestine as to the ruling power under which they would desire to live'.[184] He suggested a ruling power in Palestine other than Jewish – Great Britain or one of its Allies. In fact, the future of the local non-Jewish population of Palestine was discussed in the Cabinet, with Curzon noting the region's ethnic diversity.[185]

Thus, concern expressed in the Cabinet for the local population, even if expressed indirectly, and not by the local population, may have motivated the inclusion of the first proviso. Once Montagu's protests led to a stipulation that the Declaration should not impact

---

[181] http://www.jewishvirtuallibrary.org/jsource/History/Montagumemo.html.

[182] Montagu's memorandum of October 9th 1917, War Cabinet Papers, G.T. 2263.

[183] War Cabinet Papers G.-164, CAB 24/4/14, October 17th 1917.

[184] Ibid. p. 6.

[185] War Cabinet Papers, G.T. 2406, October 26th 1917. In a memorandum submitted to the Cabinet on October 26th 1917 entitled *The Future of Palestine,* Curzon raised the question of the local communities in Palestine that should be reckoned with. Those were a mixture of Arab, Hebrew, Canaanite, Greek, Egyptian, Christian, possibly of Crusader's blood, Circassian, Mohammedans, Druses and Muslims from Algeria, Bulgaria and Egypt.

the status of Jews in other countries, it was somewhat natural to add a similar clause in favor of non-Jewish communities in Palestine. If not for Jewish anti-Zionists, the original Zionist draft submitted by Lord Rothschild to Balfour, and approved by the latter, would probably have constituted the official version of the British Government, with no additional provisos.[186]

The anti-Zionist efforts to bring about the deletion of 'National Home' from the text of the Declaration ultimately proved fruitless. However, they did manage to cause a change in wording via the two provisos. Notably, Amery commented in his memoirs that they 'gave away nothing that was not self-evident',[187] and that they served their immediate purpose of avoiding endless delays. Nevertheless, the first proviso was later instrumental in interpretations meant to dilute the British commitment to the Jewish people. Weizmann was fully aware of the extent of the campaign waged by Montagu and his allies: 'certain it was that Montagu's opposition, coupled with the sustained attacks which the tiny anti-Zionist group had been conducting for months – their letters to the press, the pamphlets, some of them written pseudonymously by Lucien Wolf, their feverish interviews with Government officials – was responsible for the compromise formula which the War Cabinet submitted to us a few days later'.[188]

Weizmann had clearly weighed the situation carefully:

> It is one of the ifs of history whether we should have been intransigeant, and stood by our guns. Should we then have obtained a better statement? Or would the Government have become wearied of these internal Jewish divisions, and dropped the whole matter? Again, the result might have been such a long delay that the war would have ended before an agreement was reached, and then all the advantage of a timely decision would have been lost. Our judgment was to

---

[186] Halpern, op. cit., p. 175; Michael Cohen, op. cit., pp. 54, 55.

[187] Amery, op. cit. p. 117.

[188] Weizmann, op. cit., p. 206.

accept, to press for ratification.[189]

Civil and Religious Rights as Opposed to National Rights or Status

'Nothing shall be done' as a condition or stipulation was inserted into the wording of the Declaration for the purpose of asserting that the establishment of a National Home for the Jewish people would not jeopardize the civil and religious rights of the existing non-Jewish communities in Palestine. If the British Government saw the Declaration as merely a pledge to facilitate the establishment of a Jewish cultural/religious center in Palestine, then there would be no need for this clause. Only if the pledge were intended to go further would there be any requirement for a protective condition. It should also be noted that it was mainly intended for a Jewish audience. It could not be addressed to the Arabs of Palestine as they were in no way party to the negotiations – in fact the Arabs of Palestine then fought alongside the Turks and were considered for all intents and purposes the enemy. Lloyd George stated as much concerning the Arabs wartime allegiances: 'Most of the Arab races fought throughout the War for their Turkish oppressors. Arabia was the only exception in that respect. The Palestinian Arabs fought for Turkish rule.'[190]

Meaning of Civil and Religious Rights

It is not entirely clear what the British meant in the Declaration by safeguarding the civil and religious rights of non-Jewish communities in Palestine – were their rights to match those applied then in Great Britain or should they correspond with those applied and practiced in Palestine, then under Ottoman rule? Be that as it may, it should be noted that non-Jewish communities in Palestine were only granted civil and religious, but not national, rights. The concept of civil rights then looked very different from what they are conceived of today. 'In fact, the term "civil rights" then, did not refer to a unified, coherent category; the

---

[189] Weizmann, ibid., p. 207-8.

[190] Lloyd George, op. cit., Vol. II, p. 1119.

content of the term was open, changing, and contradictory.'[191] However, civil and national/political rights were and remained distinguishable at least until the mid-Twentieth Century. The Stanford Encyclopedia of Philosophy suggests that 'one should think of civil rights as the general category of *basic rights* needed for free and equal citizenship'[192] [italics added]. The jurist Gribetz noted the distinction between civil/religious and national/political rights in the context of the Declaration:

> Political rights are directly concerned with the institution and administration of government. Different opinions may be entertained as to the meaning and construction of the term "National Home" as contemplated in the Declaration, but the basis of National Home is essentially political. The two sets of rights in the Declaration are, for these reasons, easily distinguishable. They differ completely in quality and in their consequences.[193]

The distinction between Civil and Political Rights was again stated in a treatise on *Defining Civil and Political Rights: The Jurisprudence of the United Nations Human Rights Committee*:

> The term civil and political rights implies a distinction between two different, but related sets of rights. While civil rights are those rights which are calculated to protect an individual's physical and mental integrity, to ensure that they are not the victims of discrimination, and to preserve their right to a fair trial, political rights are those which ensure that individuals are able to participate fully in civil society. Such rights include rights of democratic

---

[191] Riso L. Goluboff – *The thirteenth Amendment and the Lost Origins of Civil Rights*, Duke Law Journal, Vol. 50, No. 6 (April 2001), p. 1609.

[192] https://plato.stanford.edu/entries/civil-rights/. Stanford Encyclopedia of Philosophy, *Civil Rights*, ed. Andrew Altman, Stanford University, 2003 (substantive revision 2012).

[193] Gribetz, op. cit., p. 50.

participation, such as the right to vote and to participate in the public life of the State, freedom of expression and assembly, and freedom of thought, conscience and religion.'[194]

This distinction was also maintained by Henriques, who defined civil rights as including protection from wrong both to person and property, while political rights guarantee the freedom of taking part in the legislation and government of the country.[195] Similarly, *Black's Law Dictionary*[196] distinguishes between civil and political rights: civil rights are defined as rights that 'belong to every citizen of the state or country, or, in a wider sense, to all its inhabitants, and are not connected with the organization or administration of government. They include the rights of property, marriage, protection by the laws, freedom of contract, trial by jury, etc. [197] And political rights are 'those which may be exercised in the formation or administration of the government'.[198] Again, political rights were defined in court cases as 'rights of citizens established or recognized by constitutions which give them the power to participate directly or indirectly in the establishment or administration of government'.[199]

Interpretation of *National Home* in Light of the Provisos

As we have seen, the variations found in civil rights definitions did not blur the clear distinction between civil and political rights. It appears that the drafters of the Declaration were aware of this distinction: the first proviso did not affirm political rights

[194] By Alex Conte and Richard Burchill, Ashgate Publishing Company, 2nd edition, Surrey, U.K. 2009.

[195] Henry S.Q. Henriques – *The Civil Rights of English Jews*, The Jewish Quarterly Review, Vol. 18, No. 1, (October 1905), p. 40.

[196] Henry Campbell Black – Black's Law Dictionary, Revised 4th Edition, West Publishing Co. Minn. U.S.A., 1968. http://i-uv.com/wp-content/uploads/2014/05/BlacksLaw4th.pdf

[197] Winnett v. Adams, 71 Neb. 817, 99 N.W. 681. Cited in Black's Law Dictionary, ibid.

[198] People v. Morgan, 90 Ill. 563. Cited in Black's Law Dictionary, ibid.

[199] People v. Barrett, 203 Ill. 99, 67 N.E.742, 96 Am. St. Rep. 296; Winnett v. Adams, 71 Neb. 817, 99 N.W. 684. Cited in Black's Law Dictionary, ibid.

for non-Jewish communities in Palestine, while the second proviso affirmed 'political status' for Jews in other countries. The omission in the first proviso, therefore, can be assumed not to be accidental. The British Government made this deliberate feature part of the Declaration because they never contemplated non-Jewish political rule in Palestine.

Moreover, if a Jewish National Home were not envisioned as a possible interim stage towards the formation of a Jewish State, both provisos would have been totally pointless and would not have made any sense at all. There was no likelihood of non-Jewish civil and religious rights being impacted if the British intention was to do no more than establish a cultural or religious center for the Jewish people in Palestine. Apprehension could only arise if Jews majority rule and establishment of a government in Palestine was a probable scenario. Only then could such a Jewish political apparatus conceivably apply restrictions on the civil and religious rights of minorities. The same inevitable logic applies to Jews outside of Palestine. Only a Jewish sovereign government could confer nationality on world Jewry. The fear of Jews in England, such as Montagu, Montefiore, and Wolf, that their political status would be jeopardized rested on the probability of a Jewish National Home eventually leading to a Jewish State – with the power to confer its nationality on Jews in other countries. The non-Zionists worried that this conferment of nationality on Jews living outside Palestine would promote anti-Semitism, resulting in mass expulsions. However, Amery wisely anticipated this issue: 'This judicious blend [i.e. the compromise formula]... conveyed no suggestion that Jews, as such, belonged to Palestine.'[200] In sum, the second proviso was inserted into the Declaration to allay anti-Zionist fears, and this led to the insertion of the first proviso.[201]

---

[200] Amery, op. cit., p. 117.

[201] Frankenstein, op. cit., pp. 29-30. See also Grief, op. cit., p.77: "The two provisos would never have been inserted in the Balfour Declaration or made any sense at all if no Jewish State was intended or assumed"; Gribetz, op. cit., pp. 58-59.

Existing Non-Jewish Communities

While the Declaration specifically made reference to the 'Jewish people', it did not use the same language of peoplehood to describe the existing non-Jewish population of Palestine. This was a deliberate omission. Arabs in Palestine were then living under Turkish rule. They regarded themselves, and were viewed by others, as part of a larger Syrian Arab bloc. In fact, the Arabs of Palestine were no different from Arabs living in Syria, Mesopotamia or any other part of the Levant. They were also not the only community inhabiting Palestine, even though they formed a clear majority. Palestine did not constitute a separate administrative unit and its Arabic-speaking population was not a recognized entity. According both to Ormsby-Gore and Yale, in Palestine as in Syria, there was a 'kaleidoscope of races and creeds'; national history, tradition and sentiment were practically absent.'[202]

As the Peel Report stated:

> In the twelve centuries and more that had passed since the Arab conquest, Palestine had virtually dropped out of history… In economics as in politics Palestine lay outside the main stream of the world's life. In the realm of thought, in science or in letters, it made no contribution to modern civilization. Its last state was worse than its first. In 1914, the condition of the country was an outstanding example of the lethargy and maladministration of the pre-war Ottoman regime. [203]

It is no wonder, therefore, that the Balfour Declaration did not regard non-Jews dwelling in Palestine as a single entity, but as a plurality of communities. As noted, Curzon, who had considerable knowledge of the many ethnic groups under Britain's vast imperial rule, mentioned some of the existing non-Jewish communities in Palestine: Turkmans, Circassian, Kurds,

---

[202] Friedman, op. cit., p. 330.

[203] Peel Report, op. cit., p. 6.

Syrian Arabs, Canaanites, Druses, Greek Orthodox, Roman Catholics, Protestants, and Muslims.[204] He referred to the Arabs of Palestine as 'Syrian Arabs'. They were but one of at least ten or more distinct non-Jewish communities dwelling in Palestine.

The term 'existing non-Jewish communities' meant, in actual fact, non-Jewish communities of different religions and creeds living in Palestine, and they were to be taken into consideration as separate entities. Grief found external evidence to support the contention that non-Jewish communities were, in fact, interchangeable with religious affiliation. For example, Marquis Imperiali of Italy, when writing to Sokolow on May 9th 1918 that his Government endorsed the Balfour Declaration, he used the words 'nothing shall be done to prejudice the existing juridical and political status of the existing *religious* communities', thus replacing the word 'non-Jewish' with 'religious'. Similarly, in the Lodge-Fish joint resolution of both Houses of Congress, signed by President Warren Harding on September 21st 1922, the proviso read: 'It being clearly understood that nothing shall be done which may prejudice the civil and religious rights of *Christian* and other non-Jewish communities, and that the holy places and religious buildings and sites in Palestine shall be adequately protected'.[205] [Both italics added].

In conclusion, the Arabs of Palestine were not mentioned in the proviso by name. They constituted one out of ten or more non-Jewish communities inhabiting Palestine, with no particular significance. They were regarded as Syrian Arabs with no contributions made to modern civilization or the prosperity of the country.

The Declaration also alluded specifically to *existing* non-Jewish communities in Palestine. While the Declaration attributed the National Home to the entire Jewish people, the first proviso was concerned only with the existing non-Jewish population of Palestine. '*Existing*' hinted at not allowing any influx of non-Jewish immigration. It was understood that non-Jewish

---

[204] War Cabinet Papers, G.T. 2406, October 26th 1917.

[205] Grief, op. cit., p. 96-97.

population growth in Palestine could only increase by natural means. In contrast, massive Jewish immigration was part of the design to facilitate reaching a majority population on the way to acquiring Jewish rule. As such, no Arab living outside Palestine had any rights in Palestine. That is, Palestine, in its original (i.e. biblical) borders was not intended as a home for the Arab people. According to Lloyd George and Balfour, the Arabs had received an abundant share of territory as well as independence.[206]

The existence of the first proviso, therefore, argues against any original intention to establish another state in Palestine – apart from the Jewish one.[207] However, this was falsely claimed later on when a change of heart occurred in some high British circles. The primary goal of the Declaration was the establishment of a National Home for the Jewish people. It was intended to solve the Jewish national problem, not the national problem of any non-Jewish community living in Palestine.[208] The National Home was the main theme of the Declaration, with the provisos subsidiaries stemming from its main theme.

---

[206] Lloyd George, op. cit., Vol. II, pp.1118-19: 'No race has done better out of the fidelity with which the Allies redeemed their promises to the oppressed races than the Arabs. Owing to the tremendous sacrifices of the Allied nations, and more particularly of Britain and her Empire, the Arabs have already won independence in Iraq, Arabia, Syria, and Trans-Jordania, although most of the Arab races fought throughout the war for their Turkish oppressors. Arabia was the only exception in that respect. The Palestinian Arabs fought for Turkish rule'. In a speech delivered on July 12th 1920 Balfour said; '[So] far as the Arabs are concerned...I hope they will remember... (that) the Great Powers, and among all the great powers especially Great Britain has freed them, the Arab race, from the tyranny of their brutal conqueror... I hope they will remember it is we who have established the independent Arab sovereignty of the Hejaz. I hope they will remember that it is we who desire in Mesopotamia to prepare the way for the future of a self-governing autonomous Arab State, and I hope that remembering all that, they will not grudge that small notch' [meaning Palestine], would be given to the Jewish people. Israel Cohen ed. – *Speeches on Zionism*, Arrowsmith, London 1928, pp. 24-25.

[207] If there was any intention to establish another state in Palestine, apart from a Jewish State, the first proviso would not have been necessary; or, alternatively, it would have been necessary to add a similar proviso to safeguard civil and religious rights of Jews living in the other state.

[208] Gribetz, op. cit., p. 59.

D. The Pledge and Its Object

The pledge of the British government to the Jewish people was embodied in the wording of the Declaration. Its visible expression took the form of phrases such as 'view with favour', 'will use their best endeavours', and 'to facilitate the achievement of this object'. The term 'view with favour' means to regard with support, approval or goodwill[209], or to be for someone or something[210], or to advocate[211], or to be in agreement with something: such as a plan or idea, or support something and want to help it succeed[212]. By viewing with favor the establishment of a Jewish National Home in Palestine, the British Government expressed its desire to carry out this venture with support, approval and advocacy and wished it to succeed. As Gribetz noted: favor 'not only means countenancing, approving, sanctioning, or acquiescing in the idea of a Jewish National Home in the sense of not hindering, resenting or obstructing it; but in the positive sense of promoting, befriending and protecting it'.[213]

As for 'best endeavours', this is a common and well-known phrase, often used in contracts and commercial commitments in England. The phrase has a legal meaning, reigning supreme on the scale of commitments ranging from 'reasonable endeavours' (i.e. minimal commitment) to 'best endeavours' (i.e. maximal commitment).[214] The leading legal precedent on 'best endeavours' dates back to 1911, rather close in time to the Declaration. In this case, the Great Central Railway made a commitment to the Sheffield District Railway to use its best

---

[209] Cambridge English Dictionary http://dictionary.cambridge.org/dictionary/english/favour; The Shorter Oxford English Dictionary, Oxford 1933; Chambers' Twentieth Century Dictionary (Revised Edition) London 1939.

[210] See Ralph Barton Perry, in *General Theory of Value*, Harvard University Press 1967, p. 115, cited in David Havens Newhall – *Requiredness, Fact, and Value*, Journal of Philosophy, Vol. 47, No. 4 (Feb 16th 1950), p. 87.

[211] Collins English Dictionary, https://www.collinsdictionary.com/dictionary/english/favor.

[212] Longman Dictionary of Contemporary English, http://www.ldoceonline.com/dictionary/favour.

[213] Gribetz, op. cit., p. 24.

[214] In American parlance 'best endeavours' is used as 'best efforts' and 'reasonable endeavours' is used as 'reasonable efforts.'

endeavors to develop the latter's business. The court stated that 'best endeavours' implies 'what the words say; they do not mean second best endeavours... The words mean that the Great Central Company *must, broadly speaking, leave no stone unturned* to develop traffic on the Sheffield District Line' [Italics added].[215] By stating that no stone should remain unturned the court emphasized that the obligation is onerous and demanding.

In another case from many years later, it was found that the interpretation of the term has been slightly modified but not materially changed. The court reviewed a contract containing a stipulation requiring a purchaser to use his 'best endeavours' to obtain planning permission. Buckly L.J. pronounced judgement as follows: 'I can feel no doubt that, in the absence of any context indicating to the contrary, this should be understood to mean that the purchaser is to do all he reasonably can to ensure that the planning permission is granted.'[216]

In yet another case decided in the Chancery Division, the court decided that 'best endeavours' are something less than efforts which go beyond the bounds of reason – but are considerably more than casual and intermittent activities: 'There must at least be the doing of all that reasonable persons reasonably could do in the circumstances.'[217] In *Terrell v. Mabie Todd & Co Ltd* (1952), 'standard of reasonableness' was defined as 'that of a reasonable and prudent board of directors acting properly in the interests of their company and applying their minds to their contractual obligations.'[218] [219]

---

[215] *Sheffield District Railway Co. v. Great Central Railway Co.*(1911) 27 TLR, 451. Discussed in Marcel Fontaine & Filip De Ly – *Drafting International Contracts*, Martinus Nijhoff Publishers, Leiden – Boston, 2009.

[216] *IBM United Kingdom Ltd. v. Rockware Glass Ltd.* (1980) FSR 335. See also Fontaine & De Ly, ibid.

[217] *Pips (Leisure Productions) Ltd. v. Walton* (1980)43 P & CR 415. See also Fontaine & De Ly, ibid.

[218] *Terrell v. Mabie Todd & Co. Ltd.* [1952] 2 TLR 574 (Q.B.D.). See also *the Digest*, Annotated British, Commonwealth and European Cases, Volume 36 (3) 2125, published by LexisNexis (2009, 3rd issue).

[219] American cases did not fall far behind the English ones. Thus in *National Data Payment Systems, Inc. v. Meridian Bank*, 212 F. 3d, 849, it was decided

'To facilitate' means to make it possible or easier for something (an action or process) to happen[220], to help bring it about, to free it from obstruction or difficulty,[221] and also to help forward or further an action or a process, or to pave the way for the achievement of a goal.[222] It had 'more than a passive connotation; it meant to give active aid'.[223] Thus, the promise of the British Government was not merely to tolerate, but pave the way for the establishment of the Jewish National Home in Palestine.[224]

In sum, the British Government made a serious commitment

---

that 'the contractual duty of "best efforts" has diligence as its essence and is more exacting than the usual contracting duty of good faith. See also Black's Law Dictionary, 8th Edition, under 'best efforts' (p. 169). It was further decided in *Bloor v. Falstaff Brewing Corp.*, 454 F. Supp. 258, affirmed 601 F.2d, 609, that by the term 'best efforts' as used in contract, the party undertaking it 'was bound to use its best efforts to merchandise products in good faith and to the extent of its own total capabilities.' In another case it was decided that 'the phrase 'best endeavours' requires that the party put its muscles to work to perform with full energy and fairness the relevant express promises and reasonable implications there-from'. *Stabile v. stabile*, 774 N.E.2d, 673, 55 Mass. App. Ct. 724. All three cases mentioned in Words and Phrases (Permanent Edition), Vol. 5, Thomson – West.

[220] Cambridge English Dictionary, op. cit.; Longman Dictionary of Contemporary English, op. cit.; English Oxford Living Dictionaries https://en.oxforddictionaries.com/definition/facilitate; MacMillan Dictionary http://www.macmillandictionary.com/dictionary/british/facilitate; Chambers Twentieth Century Dictionary, op. cit., Webster's Encyclopedic Unabridged Dictionary of the English Language, Cramerey Books, N.Y. 1989; Standard Dictionary of the English Language, International Edition, Funk & Wagnale, N.Y. 1958;

[221] Merriam Webster Dictionary, https://www.merriam-webster.com/dictionary/facilitate, see also Webster's Third New International Dictionary, published by G. & C. Merriam Company, Mass., U.S.A. 1969; The Heritage Illustrated Dictionary of the English Language, ed. William Morris, Published by The American Heritage Publishing Company, Boston, U.S.A. 1969.

[222] The Shorter Oxford English Dictionary, op. cit.; see also Dictionary. Com http://www.dictionary.com/browse/facilitate?s=t; The Free Dictionary http://www.thefreedictionary.com/facilitate; The New Century Dictionary, ed. H.G. Emery & K.G. Brewster, Collier and Son Corporation, N.Y. 1942 ; The Macquarie Encyclopedic Dictionary, Published by the Macquarie Library Pty. Ltd., Australia 1990.

[223] Friedman, op. cit. p. 322.

[224] Stein, *Zionism*, op. cit. p. 191.

to the Jewish people. This commitment was endorsed by the victorious powers, mainly France, Italy and Japan. They first stated their support, and then approved and advocated the establishment of a National Home for the Jewish people in Palestine. Subsequently, they made a solemn pledge to do everything in their power to facilitate the achievement of this end. That is, they would leave no stone unturned in order to pave the way for a Jewish National Home. Their commitment was to make possible the accomplishment of this national project, free from any hindrance, obstruction or difficulty.

It should be noted that a statement of such magnitude made by a major world power carries tremendous weight. It places an onerous obligation on its maker to see through its total implementation. Arguably, Great Britain was a major World Power then. The British were the ones who fought the war against the Turks in the Middle East almost alone. Their Declaration was accordingly authoritative, solemn, and made public, carrying with it a clear and understood obligation. They were certainly in a position to fulfill it if the war was won. As such, the Declaration was a binding commitment on behalf of the British Government.

E. Statehood in Stages

It might be asked why the Zionist Organization never asked for an explicit declaration to establish a Jewish State by the British Government, as this was always their ultimate goal. Zionist leaders seemed content with the more ambiguous formula of 'National Home for the Jewish people'. This is especially so, since this was the formula that they submitted to the British Government as a basis for the Declaration. The main reason was that when the Declaration was issued, Jews formed a significant minority in Palestine. The vast majority of the global Jewish population, estimated at 12 million, lived outside of Palestine. The Jews living in Palestine at the time of the Declaration numbered 125,000 as opposed to 600,000-700,000 non-Jews.[225]

---

[225] War Cabinet Papers, G.T. 2406, the figures taken from Lord Curzon's memorandum – *The Future of Palestine*, which was submitted to the British Cabinet on October 26th, 1917, pp. 1-2.

Therefore, unlike Iraq or Syria, it was impracticable to form an ethno-state at this stage. To impose a Jewish minority government on Palestine's non-Jewish population was against the wishes of the Zionist Movement and would have been unacceptable to the British.

As a result, the contemplated Jewish State had to wait. There was a preliminary need to gradually build up a nationality through education, agriculture, industry, colonizing activities, and cultural development. There was also a need for the revival of the ancient Hebrew language, development of Jewish institutions, and first and foremost immigration. The Jewish presence in Palestine would gradually become transformed from a minority into a majority. Then, along with other prevailing conditions, it would assume control over the government. To achieve this, a major power would have to act as a protectorate to safeguard and enable the evolution of the Jewish State free of destabilizing intervention.

This scheme of demographic engineering through immigration was of the essence of the Balfour Declaration, even though it was not mentioned explicitly in the Declaration.[226] It was implied in policy-making. For instance, in the proceedings held in San Remo on April 24th 1920, Curzon explained to Berthelot that the Balfour Declaration 'contemplated, first, the creation of a National Home for the Jews, whose privileges and rights were to be safeguarded under a military Power. Secondly, it was of the highest importance to safeguard the rights of minorities; first the rights of the Arabs, and then of the Christian communities.'[227] Curzon's allusion to Arabs as 'minorities' (even though they then constituted a clear majority) is proof that the British Government ultimately intended for the Jews to attain majority status, thus paving the way for the establishment of a Jewish State.

This gradualist approach to state formation was also expressed

---

[226] See p. 87 supra, where Lloyd George and Churchill were quoted as saying that restricting Jewish immigration to Palestine contradicted the Balfour Declaration.

[227] DBFP, op. cit. , Vol. VIII, p. 161; Friedman, op. cit., pp. 326-27; Feinberg, op. cit., p. 15.

by Weizmann: 'states must be built up slowly, gradually, systematically and patiently'.[228] In his address of May 20th 1917 to a special conference of delegates from the constituent Zionist societies of Great Britain, held in London, he noted:

> One reads constantly in the press, and one hears from friends, both Jewish and none-Jewish, that it is the endeavour of the Zionist movement immediately to create a Jewish State in Palestine. Our American friends have gone further, and they have even determined the form of this State, by advocating a Jewish Republic. While heartily welcoming all these demonstrations as a genuine manifestation of the Jewish national will, we cannot consider them as safe statesmanship.[229]
>
> We, therefore, say that while the creation of a Jewish Commonwealth is our final ideal... the way to achieve it lies through a series of intermediary stages. And one of those intermediary stages which I hope will come about as a result of this war, is that... Palestine will be protected by such a mighty and just power as Great Britain. Under the wing of this Power, Jews will be able to develop and set up the administrative machinery which, while not interfering with the legitimate interests of the non-Jewish population, would enable us to carry out the Zionist scheme.

He added that the British Government was ready to support these plans.[230]

Weizmann repeated this plan of action at the Paris Peace Conference. At a meeting held on February 27th 1919, Weizmann was asked about the correct meaning of the words 'Jewish National Home'. Did that mean an autonomous Jewish Government? Weizmann replied that the Zionist Organization did not want

---

[228] Weizmann, op. cit., p. 200-01.

[229] Ibid.

[230] Stein, *The Balfour Declaration*, op. cit., pp. 450-51, 523.

an autonomous Jewish Government forthwith, but at first it would accept a non-Jewish administration in Palestine, under a mandatory Power, which would allow Jewish immigration to Palestine at the rate of 70,000 to 80,000 annually. In the mean time the Zionist Organization would be authorized to develop Jewish institutions and build Hebrew schools and thus gradually form a large majority enough to build up a nationality which 'would make Palestine as Jewish as America is American, or England English'.[231] At such a rate of immigration, the Jews in Palestine would form a substantial majority within 10-15 years, and take over the Government.

As mentioned, the expectation that a Jewish State would emanate eventually from the Declaration was very much shared by members of the British Cabinet and by the President of the United States. Balfour regarded 'National Home' as –

> some form of British, American, or other protectorate, under which full facilities would be given to the Jews to work out their own salvation and to build up, by means of education, agriculture, and industry, a real center of national culture and focus of national life. It did not necessarily involve the early establishment of an independent Jewish State, which was a matter for gradual development in accordance with the ordinary laws of political evolution.[232]

However, the Zionists were not in favor of any other protectorate save Britain, in which they put their trust. Weizmann explained that the Jewish people as a whole, trusted Britain and knew that with Britain in control, law and order would be preserved, and under its jurisdiction Jewish settlement activities and cultural development would progress unfettered. As a result, the Zionists could hope for a time when they would be strong

---

[231] BDFA, Part II, Series I, Volume 2, op. cit., p. 264; See also Frankenstein, op. cit., p. 36.

[232] Speaking at a War Cabinet meeting, War Cabinet Papers No. 261, October 31st 1917, p. 5; Lloyd George, op. cit., Vol. II, p. 1137; Weizmann, op. cit., pp. 211-12; Friedman op. cit., pp. 278-79.

enough to claim self-government.[233] According to Weizmann, Lord Cecil encouraged him to work for 'a Jewish Palestine under a British protectorate'.[234]

Lloyd George discussed precisely this issue in a section of *The Truth about the Peace Treaties* entitled 'Jewish State Ultimately Envisaged'. In Lloyd George's words:

> There has been a good deal of discussion as to the meaning of the words "Jewish National Home" and whether it involved the setting up of a Jewish National state in Palestine... It was not their [i.e. the Cabinet's] idea that a Jewish State should be set up immediately by the Peace Treaty without reference to the majority of the inhabitants. On the other hand, it was contemplated that when the time arrived for according representative institutions to Palestine, if the Jews had meanwhile responded to the opportunity afforded them by the idea of a National Home and had become a definite majority of the inhabitants, then Palestine would thus become a Jewish Commonwealth.[235]

The views of Lloyd George and Balfour on this matter were also recorded by Meinertzhagen. In 1919, he reported that in answer to a question he put to them both as to what was their own interpretation of the Declaration and the ultimate goal of political Zionism, they replied that 'they envisaged a Jewish sovereign State emerging from the Jewish National Home promised under the terms of the Balfour Declaration.'[236]

In 1921, as Colonial Secretary, Winston Churchill commented on British responsibilities in Palestine following the Balfour Declaration. He declared that the British Government had a responsibility 'to do our best to make an honest effort to give the Jews a chance to make a National Home there for themselves.'

---

[233] Weizmann, ibid., p. 191.

[234] Ibid., p. 192.

[235] Lloyd George, op. cit., Vol. II, p. 1139; Peel Report, op. cit., p. 24, (Lloyd George's testimony); See also Laqueur, op. cit. p. 201.

[236] Meinertzhagen, op. cit., p. 205.

As for the question of ultimate control of the government in Palestine, Churchill was unambiguous: 'If, in the course of many years, they [i.e. the Jews] become a majority in the country, they naturally would take it over.'[237]

Other members of the British government held the same view. The Palestine Royal commission pointed out in its Report that "General Smuts, who had been a member of the Imperial War Cabinet when the Declaration was published, speaking at Johannesburg on November 3rd 1919, foretold an increasing stream of Jewish immigration into Palestine and 'in generations to come a great Jewish State rising there once more'''. The Report also noted: 'Lord Robert Cecil in 1917, Sir Herbert Samuel in 1919, and Mr. Winston Churchill in 1920 spoke or wrote in terms that could only mean that they contemplated the eventual establishment of a Jewish State. Leading British newspapers were equally explicit in their comments on the Declaration.'[238]

The same view was entertained by high ranking British officials. For instance, the diplomat, Eric G. Forbes Adam, in a memorandum submitted to the Foreign Office in 1919 stated:

> The British Government, by their support of Zionism, have to a much greater degree accepted the natural implications which Zionists give to the declaration of a National Home, i.e. an attempt to make Palestine a state in its natural geographical and historic frontiers and by gradual immigration and special economic facilities to turn this state into a Jewish state. Only time and experience can show how far the Zionist aspiration is realizable. [239]

Indeed, Forbes Adam contended: 'Behind British policy therefore, is the recognition of the principle of Jewish nationality, which is the essence of Zionism and the intention to lay in the Turkish Peace Settlement the foundation for the reconstruction

---

[237] Lloyd George, op. cit., Vol. II, p. 1193. In a statement made to the Imperial Cabinet, June 22nd 1921.

[238] Peel Report, op. cit., p. 25.

[239] DBFP, op. cit., Vol. IV, 1919, No. 409, p. 608, Memorandum by Forbes Adam on France and the Northern Frontier of Palestine.

of a Jewish Palestine, as of an Armenia for the Armenians.'[240] Forbes Adam's position was accepted without any expression of dissent even by such foreign policy stalwarts as Curzon.[241]

On the American side, President Wilson had come to a similar understanding. His address to the American public on March 3rd 1919 was clear on this point: 'I am persuaded that the Allied nations, with the fullest concurrence of our Government and our people, are agreed that in Palestine shall be laid the foundations of a Jewish Commonwealth.'[242] Lloyd George even invoked Wilson in his treatise under the heading, 'Wilson's clear statement'.[243]

Similarly, the Intelligence Section of the American Delegation at Paris foresaw the establishment of a Jewish State only at a later stage. They recommended –

> that the Jews be invited to return to Palestine and settle there, being assured by the Conference of all proper assistance in so doing that may be consistent with the protection of the personal (especially religious) and the property rights of the non-Jewish population, and being further assured that it will be the policy of the League of Nations to recognize Palestine as a Jewish state as soon as it is a Jewish state in fact. It is right that Palestine should become a Jewish state, if the Jews, being given the full opportunity, make it such.'[244]

In sum, the Balfour Declaration was an unprecedented experiment. It promised to facilitate the establishment of a National Home for the Jewish people. It did not, and could not, at that stage promise the establishment of a Jewish State. Much depended on the Jewish people themselves – whether they

---

[240] Ibid., Stein remarks that Forbes Adam was the Foreign Office official then specializing in the Palestine question. See Stein, *The Balfour Declaration*, op. cit. p. 554.

[241] Stein, ibid.

[242] Lloyd George, op. cit., Vol. II, p. 1139, Peel Report, op. cit., p. 24.

[243] Lloyd George, ibid.

[244] David Hunter Miller – *My Diary at the Conference of Paris*, op. cit., Vol. IV, pp. 263-64; See also *The Middle East and North Africa in World Politics 1914-1915*, ed. J.C. Hurewitz, Yale University Press, Doc. 34, p. 136.

would immigrate in masses to an under-developed, desolate, and malaria-stricken country; whether they would establish self-contained industry, agriculture, and commerce; and whether they would be able to develop institutions, culture, and a common language. However, the British Government did promise to do its utmost to facilitate immigration and provide, through the interim solution of the National Home, the opportunity for the Jewish people to become a majority and develop the country into a Jewish State.

This was the essential message of the Report of the Palestine Royal Commission from 1937:

> It is obvious in any case that His Majesty's Government could not commit itself to the establishment of a Jewish State. It could only undertake to facilitate the growth of a Home. It would depend mainly on the zeal and enterprise of the Jews whether the Home would grow big enough to become a State.

The Report went on to confirm the British realization that –

> a Jewish State might in course of time be established, but it was not in a position to say that this would happen, still less to bring it about of its own motion. The Zionist leaders, for their part, recognized that an ultimate Jewish State was not precluded by the terms of the Declaration, and so it was understood elsewhere.[245]

In his evidence before the Royal Commission, Winston Churchill reiterated that there was nothing in the phraseology of the Declaration to preclude or prohibit the ultimate establishment of a Jewish State in Palestine.[246]

---

[245] Peel Report, op. cit., p. 24.

[246] Ibid., p. 33; Feinberg, op. cit., p. 15.

Chapter IV

Significance of the Declaration

The high esteem and profound significance attached to the Balfour Declaration impacts any interpretation of the term 'National Home'. For one thing, it would not have been described so superlatively if it were merely intending the establishment of a cultural, social or religious center in Palestine. Something fundamental and extraordinary, such as paving the way for the reconstruction of a state for the Jewish people in their ancient and historic homeland after almost 2000 years of Diaspora, was clearly what prompted intense worldwide approbation.

Amery described the Balfour Declaration as a 'charter to Zionism – one of the most momentous declarations made in recent history'. General Smuts referred to it in world-historical terms as 'the foundation of a great policy of international justice. The greatest, most ancient historic wrong has at last been undone'.[1] On the first anniversary of the Declaration he wrote that among the most striking outcomes of the war were 'the liberation of Palestine and its recognition as the Home of Israel'.[2] Isaac Halevi Herzog, at the time Rabbi of Belfast, saw in the Declaration 'an epoch-making event... the preparatory stage leading towards redemption and restoration of Israel'.[3]

Weizmann looked on the Declaration as 'the Magna Carta of Jewish liberties'.[4] He described Jewish emotions after the Balfour Declaration as a high 'spirit of elation':

> A spirit shared by non-Jews and Jews alike: on the Jewish side the expectation of imminent redemption, on the non-Jewish side the profound satisfaction awakened by a great act of restitution ... Viscount

---

[1] Friedman, op. cit., p. 309.
[2] Stein, *Zionism*, op. cit., p. 190; Grief, op. cit., p. 101.
[3] Friedman, op. cit., p. 311-12.
[4] Friedman, ibid., p. 283.

> Robert Cecil, one of the founders of the League of
> Nations, considered the Jewish Homeland to be of
> equal importance with the League itself.[5]

Robert Crewe-Milnes, 1st Marquess of Crewe, made an explicit comparison between the Balfour Declaration and the decree of Artaxerxes in 458 BCE on the Jewish return from exile to Jerusalem to rebuild their Temple.[6] This decree followed the proclamation of Cyrus the Great in 538 BCE after conquering Palestine. It allowed the Jews of the Diaspora to go to Jerusalem to rebuild their Temple and effectively marked the beginning of the Second Temple era. The Zionists in England approved of Lord Crewe's comparison and felt that 'nothing comparable in historical significance had occurred since the proclamation of Cyrus the great in 538 B.C.'[7]

The British historian and diplomat, Charles Webster, saw the Declaration as 'the greatest act of diplomatic statesmanship of the First World War. There was no precedent for what the Zionists were asking'.[8] Herbert Samuel also referred to it as 'the charter of the Zionist movement'.[9] He described it as an event 'of such outstanding importance in the modern history of the Jewish people; touching the sentiment of millions and directly affecting the lives of hundreds of thousands; an event noteworthy even in the history of the British Empire'.[10]

The same language invoking the Declaration as a charter was used by Lord Curzon, then Foreign Secretary, at a session held by the Supreme Council of the Peace Conference on April 24th 1920, where he stated that the Jews regarded the Declaration 'in

---

5 Weizmann, op. cit., p. 211.

6 In July 1920, speaking at a meeting in London, Stein – *Zionism*, op. cit., p. 190.

7 Friedman, op. cit., p. 291; See the Old Testament, the book of Ezra, Cap I:2-4.

8 Sir Charles Kingsley Webster, *The Founder of the National Home*, Weizmann Science Press, Rehovoth, Israel, 1955, pp. 14-15, cited in Friedman, op. cit., p. 282.

9 Herbert Samuel, op. cit., p. 146.

10 Ibid., p.147.

its entirety as the charter of their rights'.[11] Baron Israel Sieff echoed Curzon and added that it represented 'the political charter of the Jewish Nation', 'the first post bellum act of reconstruction in the new world'.[12] Rabbi Joseph Herman Hertz, Chief Rabbi of Great Britain spoke of the Declaration in epochal terms, that it 'will mark an epoch in Jewish history. To millions of my brethren throughout the world it will mean the realization of Israel's undying hope of a restoration – a hope that has been the spiritual lodestar of Israel's wanderings for the last 1800 years.'[13]

Sir Mark Sykes, speaking as a Christian, attested that in helping Zionism he felt that he was doing something to make 'a great amend'.[14] In Robert Cecil's view, 'a Jewish Palestine was the first constructive effort in the new settlement of the world after the war.'[15] Curzon also saw the Declaration as a means of redressing historical injustice. For him, a National Home for the Jewish people 'meant so much more' than granting equal rights for the Jewish community in Palestine.[16]

The historian Isaiah Friedman remarked that the Declaration consolidated Jewish support of Britain beyond all expectations. As Friedman noted: 'Messages from Jewish communities in various parts of the world poured into London expressing gratitude and appreciation. Whether in Greece, Italy or South America, in the Entente or neutral countries, the Declaration aroused a wave of mystic elation which enhanced British prestige.'[17] The Jewish correspondence Bureau in the Hague asserted that 'Britain had secured a place of honor in Jewish history: the Jews would never forget that it was the first Great Power to recognize their

---

[11] DBFP, op. cit., Vol. VIII, p. 167; Lloyd George, op. cit., Vol. II, pp. 1182, 1188; Feinberg, op. cit., p. 9.

[12] Friedman, op. cit., pp. 291-92.

[13] War Cabinet Papers, G.-164, CAB 24/4/14, October 17th 1917.

[14] *The Manchester Guardian*, December 10th 1917, quoted in Friedman, op. cit., p. 290.

[15] *The Jewish Chronicle*, November 1st 1918, quoted in Friedman, ibid.

[16] Curzon's memorandum to the War Cabinet, War Cabinet Papers, G.T. 2406, October 26th 1917, p. 3; Lloyd George, op. cit., Vol. II, p. 1131.

[17] On November 10th 1917, Friedman, op. cit., p. 291.

claim to Palestine.' [18] In England Zionists were in a state of 'near euphoria' while in Russia the Declaration had 'an almost volcanic effect'.[19]

Some English newspapers such as *the Manchester Guardian* of November 9th 1917, saw in the Declaration 'at once the fulfilment of an aspiration and the signpost of a destiny'. For *the Daily Chronicle* of November 9th the Declaration was 'epoch making', while the Daily News of November 10th averred that it 'may prove to be an event of the first importance in the history of the world.'[20]

Balfour regarded the destruction of Judea by the Romans as 'one of the great wrongs' and 'a national tragedy' for the Jews, which the Allied Powers were attempting to redress.[21] In a letter to Leonard Stein from ten years after the Declaration, Balfour reflected: 'The experiment was admittedly a bold one, dealing with an unique situation in a manner wholly without precedent in history.' For Balfour, Palestine was the land 'immemorially associated' with the Jews.[22]

Dugdale concisely described the Declaration as 'the Charter of Jewish national rights'. But perhaps the most convincing words came from Balfour himself. As noted, Dugdale reported that Balfour looked 'upon Zionism as having provided one of his two greatest opportunities in life, his work as Chief Secretary for Ireland being the other. Near the end of his days he said to me that on the whole he felt that what he had been able to do for the Jews had been the thing he looked back upon as the most worth of his doing'.[23] Balfour had a very rich political career, serving as Prime Minister, Foreign Secretary, and Chief Secretary for Ireland. It seems very doubtful that he would have regarded paving the way for the establishment of another Jewish cultural/religious center, this time in Palestine – similar to colonization

---

[18] Friedman, ibid., p. 291.

[19] Friedman, ibid., pp.291-92.

[20] Stein, *The Balfour Declaration*, op. cit., p. 561.

[21] Friedman, op. cit., p. 290.

[22] Stein, *Zionism*, op. cit., p. 197.

[23] Dugdale, Vol. II, op. cit., pp. 170, 171; Weizmann, op. cit., p. 211.

projects in Argentina or other parts of the world – as the single greatest achievement of his life.

In fact, the contrast Leonard Stein made between a Jewish National Home in Palestine and Jewish colonies in other parts of the world is quite enlightening. Jewish colonization schemes in Argentina and Brazil in the first three decades of the 20th century resulted in thirty thousand Jews settled in agricultural communities by the Jewish Colonization Association. But as Stein noted:

> The 30,000 colonists have created nothing beyond their farms. They have not made the smallest impression upon the Jewish world at large; nor has anyone ever suggested that from Mauricio shall go forth the Law, and the Word of the Lord from Entre-Rios. Very different, as has been seen, are the results and the prospects of Jewish settlement in Palestine. The contrast is illuminating...[24]

Presumably, if immigration and settlement of Jews in Palestine would have resembled in any way the immigration and settlement of Jews in any other part of the world, this would not have been an event to describe in superlative terms. The extent to which the Declaration was universally held in awe is a powerful indicator that it aimed at something far beyond the establishment of a Jewish cultural home or religious center in Palestine.

---

[24] Stein, *Zionism*, op. cit., p. 196.

Part II

Putting Into Effect the Balfour Declaration

The San Remo Resolution, the Treaties of Sèvres
and Lausanne, and the British Mandate for Palestine

Chapter I

The San Remo Resolution and its Legal Significance

A second major step after the Balfour Declaration, which proved to be an important milestone towards the establishment of legal title of the Jewish people over Palestine, in accordance with international law, was embodied in a resolution carried during an international conference held at Villa Devachan in San Remo, a resort town on the Italian Riviera, on April 24-25, 1920. The Resolution was the outcome of a multilateral agreement by the Principal Allied Powers, comprising Great Britain, France, Italy and Japan with the United States as an observer.(1) It was the culmination of their previous discussions and debates during the years 1918-1920. Among these were the Paris Peace Talks of February 1919 followed by the Conference of London held in February 1920, in which the terms later to be inserted in the San Remo Resolution were drawn.

The San Remo Conference was convoked by the Principal Allied Powers, forming the Supreme Council, with the participation of the United States. Members of the Supreme Council were headed by the following leaders: for Great Britain, David Lloyd George and Lord George Nathaniel Curzon, British Prime Minister and Foreign Secretary, respectively; for France, Alexandre Millerand, Prime Minister and President of the French Council, and Philippe Berthelot of the Ministry of Foreign Affairs; for Italy, Francesco Nitty, Italian Prime Minister and Signor Scialoja; for Japan, Keishiro Matsui; and for the United States, Robert Underwood Johnson, American Ambassador in Rome.[2]

---

[1] Minutes of the San Remo Conference relate the attendance of the American Ambassador in the meetings as one of 'observer only, and not as a representative participant in the (Supreme Council) deliberations'. See *Documents on British Foreign Policy 1919-1939*, ed. Rohan Butler & J.P.T. Bury, First Series, HMSO, London 1958, Vol. VIII, p. 161, [hereinafter DBFP].

[2] DBFP, ibid., Vol. VIII, p. 156.

The San Remo Resolution formed the foundation upon which the British Mandate for Palestine was established. The Resolution incorporated in its entirety the Balfour Declaration, thus giving the latter international recognition. The international validity of the Balfour Declaration was first endorsed in San Remo, then in the Treaty of Sèvres, and later in the British Mandate[3]. The Resolution entrusted Palestine to the British Government for the sole purpose of establishing a National Home for the Jewish people. The Resolution concerning Palestine was not meant to satisfy Arab national aspirations in any part of the country. These were duly catered to in the second paragraph of the Resolution, designating Syria (including Lebanon) and Mesopotamia as future independent Arab states. Great Britain was made responsible, a responsibility she welcomed, to establish the Jewish national home in Palestine, with the caveat that nothing should be done to jeopardize the civil and religious rights of existing non-Jewish communities in Palestine. As noted, a Jewish National Home meant the eventual formation of a Jewish State.[4]

The San Remo Resolution was made openly and publically at the conclusion of an international conference that was convened for the explicit purpose of deciding the future of the captured Ottoman territories. It was the outcome of a full agreement arrived at by the High Contracting Parties comprising the British Empire (namely, Great Britain, Canada, Australia, New Zealand, South Africa, and India), France, Italy, Japan, Armenia, Belgium, Greece, Hedjaz, Poland, Portugal, Romania, the Serb-Croat-Slovene State, and Czechoslovakia.[5] The Resolution incorporated a major modification to the Declaration. It transformed an indecisive British pledge to use 'their best endeavours to facilitate the achievement of this object' (i.e., the object of establishing in Palestine a National Home for the

---

[3] Isaiah Friedman – *The Question of Palestine 1914-1918*, Shocken Books, New York, 1973, p. 309.

[4] See, pp. 89 et seq., supra.

[5] A definition of the High Contracting Parties was given in the Treaty of Sèvres, signed on August 10, 1920. In Art. 95 of the Treaty, the second paragraph of Art. (b) of the San Remo Resolution was inserted verbatim.

Jewish people) to one which made Britain legally 'responsible for putting into effect' this declared objective.

By virtue of the San Remo Resolution, the right of the Jewish people to self-determination within their ancient homeland, from Dan to Beersheba, was internationally recognized, even though the great majority of the Jewish people then lived outside Palestine. The Jewish people were given that right by the Principal Allied Powers, in whose favor the Turks had renounced all their sovereign rights to territories outside Asia Minor, including in the Middle East. The Powers that decided to grant independence to Syria and Mesopotamia were the same who decided simultaneously to grant a National Home to the Jewish people in Palestine. Thus, arguably any challenge to the validity of the establishment of a National Home for the Jewish people in Palestine may be applied to Syria and Mesopotamia as independent sovereign states.

In the Resolution, it was decided that the territories occupied by the Allies would be administered by a mandatory in accordance with Article 22 of the League of Nations Covenant. As to Palestine, the term 'National Home' was regarded by the Allies as a prelude to an eventual independent State, in which the Arabs would form a minority after massive Jewish immigration.

Thus, the San Remo Resolution became part of international law by the very fact that it was the result of a multilateral agreement made by the Principal Allied Powers, at an international conference convoked by the Supreme council. Its terms were embodied verbatim into the Treaty of Sèvres,[6] incorporated again into the Preamble of the British Mandate Charter for Palestine, and approved by the League of Nations, with its 51 members voting all in favor.[7]

At the conclusion of a hectic debate at San Remo, the Principal Allied Powers came to an agreement on April 25th 1920, which

---

[6] The Treaty of Sèvres was signed by the Parties on August 10th 1920, but was not duly ratified because of Turkish refusal. Regarding the legal effect of this fact, see pp.182 et seq., infra.

[7] Howard Grief – *The Legal Foundation and Borders of Israel under International Law*, Mazo Publishers, Jerusalem, 2008, p. 19.

produced the following resolution:[8]

It was agreed:

(a) To accept the terms of the Mandates Article as given below with reference to Palestine, on the understanding that there was inserted in the procès-verbal an undertaking by the Mandatory Power that this would not involve the surrender of the rights hitherto enjoyed by the non-Jewish communities in Palestine...

(b) That the terms of the Mandates Article should be as follows:
    The High Contracting Parties agree to entrust, by application of the provisions of Article 22, the administration of Palestine, within such boundaries as may be determined by the Principal Allied Powers, to a Mandatory, to be selected by the said Powers. The Mandatory will be responsible for putting into effect the Declaration originally made on November 8[9] 1917, by the British Government, and adopted by the other Allied Powers, in favour of the establishment in Palestine of a national home for the Jewish people, It being clearly understood that nothing shall be done which may Prejudice the civil and religious rights of existing non–Jewish communities in Palestine, or the rights and political status enjoyed by Jews in any other country.

Arab national aspirations were taken into consideration in the following paragraph of the San Remo Resolution:

    The High Contracting Parties agree that Syria and Mesopotamia shall, in accordance with the fourth paragraph of Article 22, Part I (Covenant of

---

8   DBFP, ibid., Vol. VIII, pp. 176-77.
9   Should be November 2nd 1917.

the League of Nations), be provisionally recognized as independent States, subject to the rendering of administrative advice and assistance by a mandatory until such time as they are able to stand alone. The boundaries of the said states will be determined, and the selection of the Mandatories made, by the Principal Allied Powers.

The Middle East was, therefore, partitioned between the Arab nation and the Jewish people, both of whom were instrumental in winning the war against the Turks. Syria and Mesopotamia were allotted to the Arabs and Palestine to the Jewish people as their National Home. If there was any intention to allocate any part of Palestine as a National Home for the then existing Arab population of Palestine, the Resolution was the right place to mention it. However, no such mention was made, whether explicitly or implicitly, neither in the San Remo Resolution nor in the Treaty of Sèvres nor in the British Mandate Charter. The administration of Palestine was thus conferred to Britain in trust for the sole purpose of establishing a National Home for the Jewish people.[10] By entrusting the administration of Palestine to Britain, and by the acceptance of this trust, Britain was deemed responsible and under a legal obligation to implement the Balfour Declaration. The responsibility the British Government took upon itself required accountability and liability to fulfill its duty under that trust.[11]

In a legal sense, the term 'entrust' confers upon a trustee a legal burden, heavier than the one conferred upon an ordinary agent. It

---

[10] DBFP, op. cit., Vol. XIII. p. 251; in a briefing to Lord Hardinge of the Foreign office on April 26th 1920, regarding the San Remo Resolution, Curzon stated that the duties entrusted to the mandatory for Palestine, meaning Great Britain, were those defined by the verbatim repetition of the Balfour Declaration.

[11] See the definition of 'entrust' and 'responsible' in the *English Oxford Living Dictionaries*, https://en.oxforddictionaries.com/definition/entrust; *Cambridge English Dictionary*, http://dictionary.cambridge.org/dictionary/english/entrust; *Miriam Webster Dictionary* https://www.merriam-webster.com/dictionary/entrust; and *Dictionary com.* http://www.dictionary.com/browse/entrust.

requires that the trustee fulfill his duty in good faith, coupled with a greater degree of loyalty, reliability, dedication and devotion.[12] Interestingly, the term 'trust' appeared in the Resolution only in relation to the duties of the Mandatory of Palestine. No similar mention is made in the Resolution to the mandates of Syria and Mesopotamia. True, the Resolution had already recognized them provisionally as independent states, but their independence was qualified and made 'subject to the rendering of administrative advice and assistance by a mandatory until such time as they are able to stand alone'.[13] That is, they still had a long way to go until total independence. However, the Mandatories, Britain and France, had not been required to act as trustees for the purpose of leading Syria and Mesopotamia to total independence.

Article 22 of the Covenant of the League of Nations (enacted on June 28th 1919) established the Mandate System. Its avowed object was to prevent the annexation of territories captured during the war; instead, it would establish a system of Mandatory tutelage. This would be on behalf of the League, for the benefit of the native inhabitants of those territories 'not yet able to stand by themselves under the strenuous conditions of the modern world'. The League of Nations applied the principle that the wellbeing and development of peoples inhabiting those territories form a sacred trust of civilization. The method for the realization of this principle was by placing those peoples under the tutelage of advanced nations, the latter acting as Mandatories on behalf of the League of Nations. Article 22 constituted three categories of such peoples, according to their stage of development. The

---

[12] See definitions in above-mentioned dictionaries, ibid.

[13] In his memorandum of August 11th 1919, Balfour made his observation on the significance of granting independence to Syria and Mesopotamia at that stage. He stated that independence, as understood by the Sykes-Picot Agreement, and for that matter, the San Remo Resolution, was qualified by the obligatory presence of foreign advisers: 'Now, by an 'adviser' these documents undoubtedly mean – though they do not say so – an adviser whose advice must be followed; and assuredly no State can be described as really independent which has habitually and normally to follow foreign advice supported, if worst comes to the worst, by troops, aeroplanes, and tanks'. Memorandum by Mr. Balfour (Paris) respecting Syria, Palestine, and Mesopotamia, see DBFP, op. cit., Vol. IV, No. 242, p. 344.

most advanced were those 'communities formerly belonging to the Turkish Empire (who) have reached a state of development where their existence as independent nations can be provisionally recognized, subject to the rendering of administrative advice and assistance by a Mandatory, until such time as they are able to stand alone.'[14]

If the Principal Allied Powers had any intention of establishing an independent Arab state in Palestine, on the footing that the then existing Arab inhabitants formed a large majority of the country, they would have placed Palestine in the same category as Syria and Mesopotamia and invoked the fourth paragraph of Article 22 of the Covenant to recognize Palestine as an independent Arab State. But that was not the intention of the Principal Allied Powers nor the Supreme Council. Their clear objective was to establish in Palestine a National Home for the Jewish people and for no other. However, this could not be immediately carried out since the majority of the Jewish people were not then living in Palestine. The High Contracting Parties, therefore, invoked Article 22 *by application* with the only object of giving legal effect to the Balfour Declaration in favor of the establishment in Palestine of a National Home for the Jewish people, as stipulated in Article (b) of the San Remo Resolution.

As noted, in San Remo, the decision to entrust the administration of Palestine to a Mandatory was made by the High Contracting Parties. But the dominant authority to select the Mandatory,[15] determine the borders of Palestine, and formulate the terms of the mandate was vested with the Principal Allied Powers. The terms of the mandate were to be submitted eventually to the Council of the League of Nations for approval. Simultaneously, the Principal Allied Powers were to select the Mandatory of Syria and Mesopotamia, to determine their borders and to formulate the terms of their mandate, albeit they were

---

[14] Covenant of the League of Nations, Article 22, fourth paragraph. http://avalon.law.yale.edu/20th_century/leagcov.asp

[15] *Cf.*, DBFP, op. cit., Vol. XIII, p. 251. In his briefing to Lord Hardinge on April 26th 1920, Curzon asserted that there was no mention of the Mandatory in the Peace Treaty, but the Supreme Council declared Great Britain as the Mandatory for Palestine by an independent decision.

recognized as independent states.

However, there was a major difference between Syria and Mesopotamia on the one hand and Palestine on the other. In Syria and Mesopotamia, the indigenous inhabitants were granted independence subject to the rendering of administrative advice and assistance by a Mandatory. Palestine, on the other hand, was pledged as a National Home for the Jewish people. The Jewish people then formed a small minority in Palestine. The native inhabitants were mainly Muslim Arabs. The vast majority of the Jewish people were scattered all over the world. A Jewish National Home could only be achieved through immigration, purchase of land, establishment of settlements and the formation of national institutions – safeguarded by a strong military Power, until the Jews turned into a majority in Palestine and could take over the country. Lord Curzon made this exact point in San Remo on April 24th 1920. Curzon noted that the Balfour Declaration 'contemplated, first, the creation of a National Home for the Jews, whose privileges and rights were to be safeguarded under a military Power. Secondly, it was of the highest importance to safeguard *the rights of minorities* [italics added]; first, the rights of the Arabs, and then of the Christian communities'.[16] By referring to the Arabs as a minority in Palestine, even though at the time of the San Remo deliberations they formed a significant majority, he implied that the British Government anticipated the Jewish people eventually forming a majority in Palestine. Other Principal Allied Powers also referred to Arab communities in Palestine as ultimate minorities that would need protection.

Within the Conference Chamber

The San Remo Conference was convened for the purpose of discussing the terms of the Treaty of Peace with Turkey, later known as the Treaty of Sèvres. On April 24th and 25th the Supreme Council discussed the question of mandates for those territories that were severed from the Ottoman Empire after the First World War. The discussion was a prelude to deciding what terms were to be included in the Peace Treaty with Turkey, regarding Syria,

---

[16] DBFP, op. cit., Vol. VIII, p. 161.

Mesopotamia and Palestine.[17]

Lord Curzon made a clear distinction between Syria and Mesopotamia, on the one hand, and Palestine on the other. As for Syria and Mesopotamia, he suggested that since the mandate form was still unsettled, they should be drawn up later by the French and British Governments in mutual consultation and co-operation. However, as regards Palestine, he indicated that the only safe plan was the adoption of the pledge embodied in the Balfour Declaration in the precise form in which it had originally been given. He argued that the Jews themselves attached a 'passionate importance' to the terms of this Declaration and, furthermore, they had been pressing on the British Foreign Office to have the terms of that pledge expanded and improved. However, the British Government decided not to make any changes in the Declaration which was to be inserted in the treaty, and urged the French representatives to accept the proposal to include the Balfour Declaration in the treaty without reservation.[18]

Curzon referred to the Balfour Declaration as a 'formal declaration', which 'had been accepted by the Allied Powers', and whose significance was 'that Palestine was in future to be the National Home of the Jews throughout the world'. Thus, Jews throughout the world had the right to have their National Home in Palestine.[19] He further stated that the Jews 'regarded the declaration in its entirety as the charter of their rights,'[20] and added that in issuing the Balfour Declaration 'the British Government had taken up a position from which it was practically impossible for them to recede'.[21] He reaffirmed that the Declaration contemplated first the creation of a National Home for the Jews and only second the safeguarding of the rights of minorities.[22]

Likewise, Millerand, the French Prime Minister, stated that

---

[17] DBFP, ibid., Vol. VIII, p. 159.

[18] Ibid.

[19] Ibid.

[20] DBFP, ibid., Vol. VIII, p. 167.

[21] Ibid., p. 169.

[22] Ibid., p. 168.

the first question regarding Palestine was 'that there should be a National Home for the Jews, upon that they were all agreed'. Berthelot affirmed that 'the whole world was sympathetic to the aspiration of the Jews to establish a National Home in Palestine, and they would be prepared to do their utmost to satisfy their legitimate desires'. The French Government, he said, would not oppose Britain's wish 'to give the Jews due opportunity to achieve those passionate aspirations.' In making those statements, the French representative referred to the Jewish National Home in Palestine as the 'new projected State'. With this concept in mind, he expressed apprehension that the future establishment of a Jewish State would create great difficulties with the Islamic and Christian worlds.[23]

Signor Nitti of Italy, who presided over the Supreme Council, confirmed that 'they were all agreed on the question of establishing a Jewish home there (in Palestine)'.[24]

As mentioned, the French Government was in favor of the establishment in Palestine of a National Home for the Jewish people. Nevertheless, its main objection was to any mention of the Balfour Declaration, in any way or form, in the peace treaty with Turkey. In their effort to convince the Supreme Council to refrain from doing so, the French representatives raised a large number of reservations, not necessarily consistent with one another. At first Berthelot stated that the Declaration was 'framed in general terms' and that there had never been any official acceptance of the Declaration by the Allied Powers. Lord Curzon then confronted him with the facts: namely, that in February 1918, the Declaration was communicated through Sokolow to Stephen Pichon, then French Minister for Foreign Affairs. Pichon not only endorsed the Declaration on behalf of his Government, but added in his letter to Sokolow that the 'understanding between the French and British governments on this question was complete'. Even so, Berthelot was still adamant. Curzon went further to assert that 'the Italian Government had also expressed its approval of the

---

23 Ibid., p. 160.

24 Ibid., p. 163.

terms of the declaration, which had further been accepted by the President of the United States, and also by Greece, China, Serbia and Siam'. Curzon concluded that the Balfour Declaration had been accepted by France and by a large number of the Allied Powers. However, Berthelot refused to be convinced that Pichon accepted the whole Declaration.[25]

As the deliberations went on, Berthelot raised new arguments. For instance, he claimed that the Balfour Declaration 'had long been a dead letter' and, therefore, there was no necessity to refer to it in the treaty.[26] Later in the discussion, a change in the French attitude was intercepted by the British. Millerand said he was willing to accept the insertion of the Declaration in the treaty provided the following words would be omitted from it, namely, 'putting into effect the Declaration originally made on the November 8th [2nd] 1917, by the British Government and adopted by the other Allied Powers in favour of...'. At some point Lord Curzon lost his patience and fulminated that 'he found it difficult to discover exactly what it was to which the French delegation took exception...He enquired why it was desired to omit this sentence and what injury was done by its inclusion'.[27]

Berthelot continued to stick to his opinion that the Declaration had never been officially accepted by the French Government and went on to give another reason for the French objection. He explained: 'What the French objected to was any reference in an official instrument, such as the Turkish treaty, to an unofficial declaration made by one Power, which had never been accepted by the Allies generally'.[28] A short while earlier it seemed that the French delegation accepted the insertion of the Declaration into the treaty in a modified form. Yet they produced still another argument, apparently a change of ground from the previous one. Moreover, they came up with a French draft, which they proposed to submit to the Supreme Council for adoption.[29]

---

25 Ibid., pp. 160, 162.

26 Ibid., p. 163.

27 Ibid., p. 167.

28 Ibid., p. 168.

29 Ibid., p. 169.

Notwithstanding strong French opposition, the deliberations on this point ended that day, April 24th 1920. Ultimately, the French delegation completely accepted the British proposal to incorporate the Balfour Declaration verbatim into the treaty, with the exception of using a more decisive version; namely, of making the British Government responsible for putting into effect the Balfour Declaration in favor of the establishment in Palestine of a National Home for the Jewish people. This was instead of the original version of using their best endeavors to facilitate the achievement of that object.[30]

From the viewpoint of the British Government, Palestine as a whole, from Dan to Beersheba, was to constitute a National Home for the Jewish people, even if its exact frontiers were not yet determined. This proved obvious from the speeches of both the British Prime Minister and the Foreign Secretary at the Conference. Lord Curzon referred to the Balfour Declaration as a formal declaration that '*Palestine was in future to be the National Home of the Jews throughout the world.*'[31] [Italics added]. Similarly, Lloyd George stated that 'the task of governing Palestine would not be an easy one, and it would not be rendered less difficult by the fact that *it* *was to be* the National Home of the Jews...'. [32] [Italics and emphasis added].

The French delegation made a last-minute effort to expand the rights of the French community in Palestine. They hoped to add political rights to the civil rights as well as religious rights that were already included in the first proviso of the Balfour Declaration. Millerand was aware of the difference between civil and political rights and conveyed to his British counterpart that 'in

---

[30] Ibid., p. 170.

[31] Ibid., p. 159.

[32] Ibid., p. 166; This was later contradicted by the British Government, following a change of heart, which made a distinction between making a Jewish National Home in Palestine and making Palestine a Jewish National Home. In the British White Paper of June 1922, the British Government made use of this distinction to deny any intention to create a 'wholly Jewish Palestine'. The White Paper stated that the terms of the Balfour Declaration 'do not contemplate that Palestine as a whole should be converted into a Jewish National Home, but such a Home should be founded in Palestine'. See British White Paper of June 3rd 1922, Cmd. 1700, Doc. 5, third paragraph.

French Law civil rights were not identical with political rights'. He thus insisted that the Supreme Council should take a stand on the actual wording in the Treaty. However, Curzon refused to make any changes to the original form of the Declaration. He explained that 'in the British language all ordinary rights were included in civil rights'. In any case, at a later stage when the precise form of the mandate would be decided, France would be consulted before submitting it to the Council of the League of Nations. Finally, Millerand agreed not to make any changes in the Resolution as regards political rights, and was satisfied to have the French claim recorded in the procès-verbal.[33]

By 'political rights' Millerand was alluding to 'the right to vote and take part in elections' and nothing more.[34] In fact, it was the French who made the most of showing concern for the non-Jewish communities in Palestine. Yet they were not suggesting that the non-Jewish communities would be granted any type of political rights on a national basis, self-determination or collective aspirations. The French were concerned merely that the non-Jewish inhabitants could vote or be elected to official and public institutions on an individual basis. None of the other Powers had suggested conferring upon the non-Jewish communities, and particularly upon the Arabs then living in Palestine, any type of collective or national rights within the whole of Palestine.

Another major issue which attracted the attention of the Supreme Council was the question of safeguarding the rights of the Christian religious communities in Palestine. The Arabs as such were hardly mentioned or considered in the debate. The main concern was the control and guardianship of the Christian Holy Places. During the Ottoman rule of Palestine, the French acted as their guardians. The French and Italian representatives pressed that this status quo should continue. Britain vehemently opposed this idea, and even thought that it was an insult. The British, said Lloyd George, were not like the Turks. They had the reputation of safeguarding and allowing free access to the

---

[33] Ibid., pp. 169-70.

[34] Ibid., p. 170. See also Howard Grief, op. cit., p. 30.

Holy Places to all religions, and any international rule or joint rule by two powers would cause tremendous difficulties.[35] The debate was mainly concerned with the rights of Christian religious communities: with the Roman Catholics, Protestants, Franciscans and other religious denominations. Finally, it was suggested by Italy that all privileges and prerogatives France enjoyed under the Ottoman Empire should cease to exist, and a Commission would be established in order 'that the whole subject of privileges and rights of various religious communities should be carefully examined by the Council of the League of Nations, with a president appointed by that Council'. The British delegation seconded that suggestion, and the French found themselves obliged to accept it, subject to making a few reservations.[36]

---

[35] Ibid., p. 164.
[36] Ibid., pp. 164, 170.

Chapter II

The Road to the San Remo Resolution

At the commencement of the First World War, Palestine was of no interest to the Allied Powers. It was out of the picture, a forsaken land of no strategic or economic value. During 1917, the whole concept changed and Palestine came to be seen as highly valuable. This conceptual shift by the Allied Powers, and particularly Great Britain, was demonstrated, during and after the war, in a number of decisions and resolutions. These were at times contradictory, but they paved the way to the San Remo Resolution. After the war started, the first major consideration of what British attitudes should be towards Palestine was taken by the De Bunsen Committee. It recommended that Britain should take no part in the retention of Palestine, or in the administration of the Holy Places.

The De Bunsen Committee, June 1915

On April 8th 1915, soon after the beginning of the First World War, in response to a French initiative, British Prime Minister Herbert Asquith appointed an interdepartmental 'Committee on Asiatic Turkey' headed by Sir Maurice de Bunsen, assistant undersecretary of state at the Foreign office 'to consider the nature of British desiderata in Turkey in Asia in the event of a successful conclusion of the war…'. The Report was meant to establish the foundation of British policy in the Middle East, and consequently to provide guidelines for negotiations with France, Italy and Russia on the partitioning of the Ottoman Empire.

The Report was submitted on June 30th 1915, and its main recommendation on Palestine was that 'it will be idle for His Majesty's Government to claim the retention of Palestine in their sphere. Palestine must be recognized as a country whose destiny must be the subject of special negotiations, in which both belligerents and neutrals are alike interested'. However, should Britain prefer to choose a scheme which would include Palestine within its sphere, the Committee saw no reason 'why the sacred places of Palestine should not be dealt with as a separate question.'[1]

The Sykes-Picot Agreement, May 1916

Almost a year later, on May 9th and 16th, the Sykes-Picot Agreement[2] was signed. This was an understanding between Britain and France regarding their share of influence in the Middle East should the war prove successful for the Allies, and hence occupied territories would be freed from Ottoman rule. Lloyd George pointed out that 'the intention of the Allied Powers regarding the future of Palestine up to the end of 1916 are practically embodied in the Sykes-Picot Agreement. The country was to be mutilated and torn into sections. There would be no more Palestine'. The Sykes-Picot Agreement divided the land, later known as Palestine, into three separate parts, placed under three different administrations:

1) The central area, including the Holy Places, colored brown, was to be internationalized;

2) The northern part, including upper and Lower Galilee, colored blue, was to be under French administration;

3) The Negev, from the vicinity of Beersheba southwards, colored red, was to be part of Area B, contemplated to become part of the projected Arab State, placed under British administration.[3]

The main plan in the Sykes-Picot Agreement was to establish an independent Arab State or a confederation of Arab States in

---

[1] J.C. Hurewitz, ed. – *The Middle East and North Africa in World Politics: A Documentary Record,* 2nd Edition, Vol. 2, p. 45, Yale University Press, New Haven & London, 1979.

[2] The Agreement was named after Sir Mark Sykes, the British representative to the negotiations and his French counterpart, Francois Georges-Picot.

[3] See map No. 1 on subsequent page. See also The Palestine Royal Commission Report, HMSO 1937, Cmd. 5479. Headed by Earl Peel [hereinafter referred to as the Peel Report], p. 21.

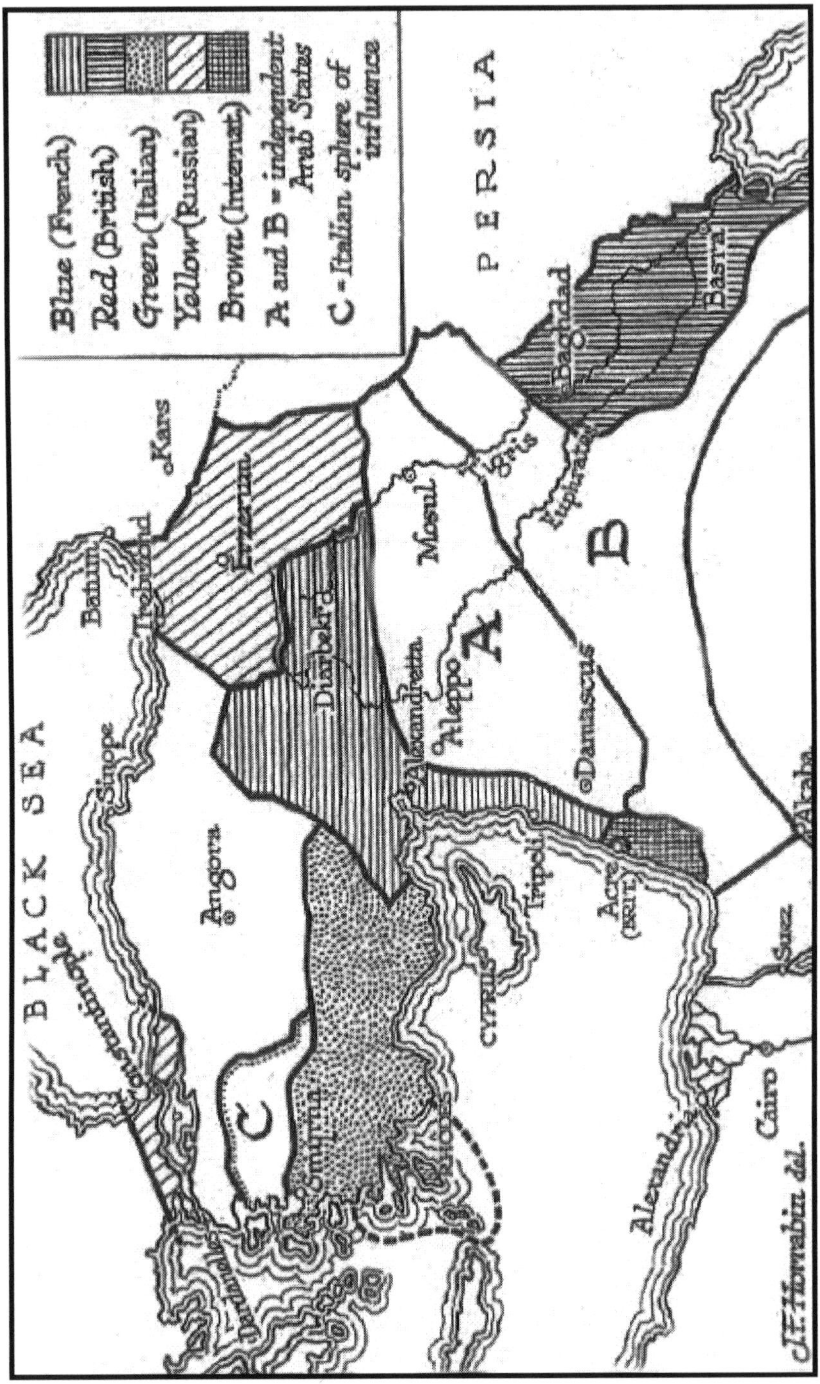

Map No. 1: The Sykes-Picot Agreement 1916. (Arab State A was to be in the French, and B in the British sphere of influence). From David Lloyd George – The Truth About the Peace Treaties, Vol. II, p.1024

areas A and B as marked on the map annexed to the Agreement,[4] roughly including the territories of Syria, Mesopotamia, and part of Arabia. This would leave out the central part of Palestine, i.e., areas identified with the biblical land of Israel to be dealt with separately. This area, colored brown, was marked on the map by a line stretching, in the north, from the Mediterranean, north of Acre, eastwards towards Safed, ending at the northern tip of the sea of Galilee. On the east, bordered by the Jordan River, on the South bordered by a line stretching from the mid-length of the Dead Sea westwards towards the Mediterranean on the southern tip of the Gaza strip. On the west, it was bordered by the Mediterranean. [5]

The relevant wording of the Sykes-Picot Agreement read as follows:

> It is accordingly understood between the French and British Governments:

> That France and Great Britain are prepared to recognize and protect an independent Arab State or a Confederation of Arab States in the areas (A) and (B) marked on the annexed map, under the suzerainty of an Arab chief ...

> That in the Brown area there shall be established an international administration, the form of which is to be decided upon after consultation with Russia, and subsequently in consultation with the other Allies, and the representatives of the Shereef of Mecca.

The Sykes-Picot Agreement was signed almost seven months after the McMahon pledge, and the British Government seemed

---

4   See map No. 1; more on the Sykes-Picot understanding view Part I, pp. 46-47, n. 29 supra.
5   See map No. 1.

to have taken full notice of the latter.[6] The wording of the Agreement, and its illustration on the map annexed to it, indicated that Palestine, from Dan to Beersheba, including the regions of Judea and Samaria and the Holy Places, were excluded from the vast areas which were to form the projected Arab State, or confederation of Arab States.[7] The central part of Palestine, the brown area, was to be placed under international administration, and the northern part, the blue area, was to be placed under French administration. Only the Negev Desert, from the vicinity of Beersheba southwards, was designated to become part of the Arab State under British administration. The form of the international administration in the Brown area would be decided after consultations being held with the Russians, the other Allies and the Sherif of Mecca. It should be noted that the Agreement required Britain and France to hold consultations, and nothing further. It did not require them to seek the approval or consent of any of the other parties to this scheme.

However, as Lloyd George noted:

> 1917 saw a complete change in the attitude of the nations towards this historic land. It was no longer the end of a pipe-line here, the terminus of a railway there, a huddled collection of shrines over which Christian and Moslem sects wrangled under the protection of three great powers in every quarter. It was an historic and sacred land, throbbing from Dan to Beersheba with immortal traditions, the homeland of a spiritual outlook and faith professed by hundreds of millions of the human race and fashioning more and more the destinies of mankind. The carving knife of the Sykes-Picot Agreement was a crude hacking of a Holy Land. At the beginning of the war, Palestine

---

6   On the McMahon pledge, see pp. 354 et seq, infra.

7   According to Pichon, the French Foreign Minister, the Sykes-Picot 'agreement had two objects: first, to detach the Arabs from the Turks; second, to decide the claims of Great Britain and France'. Even so, Biblical Palestine was not included neither in the Arab State or confederation of Arab States nor in the sphere of British or French influence. See Paris Peace Conference, minutes of the Council of Four, May 24th 1919, DBFP, op. cit., Vol. V, p. 1.

was not in the picture. The mind of the Great Powers was on Belgium, Poland and Istria. The destiny of Palestine was left to the haggling of experts in the various Foreign offices of the Allies.[8]

It also became clear to the British Government, as the war progressed, that the Sykes-Picot Agreement could not work – it had been a mistake and needed to be reconsidered. Lloyd George referred to it as a 'foolish document', and Curzon enunciated that the arrangement contained in it was inexplicable and was a display of 'the gross ignorance with which the boundary lines in that agreement were drawn'. Curzon further stated that introducing international administration in Palestine, as contemplated in the Sykes-Picot Agreement, was bound to fail, as it had failed in other oriental countries. Mark Sykes was ashamed of it and later regretted participating in its making.[9] Lloyd George recorded that for many 'practical reasons the Sykes-Picot Pact was discredited, and the British authorities were convinced that in at least two respects amendment was essential. The first was in regard to the severance of Mosul from Mesopotamia... The second was the partition of Palestine into three separate areas under three different administrations'.[10] Lloyd George attested that when meeting with Clemenceau in London after the war, he asked the French Prime Minister to agree that Mosul would be attached to Iraq and that Palestine from Dan to Beersheba would be under British control: 'Without hesitation he agreed... although that agreement was not reduced into writing, he (Clemenceau) adhered to it honourably in subsequent negotiations'.[11]

The Sykes-Picot Agreement was kept secret until it was revealed by the Russian Bolsheviks in the Autumn of 1917. The Arabs were unaware of it, and neither were the Zionists. The

---

[8] David Lloyd George – *The Truth About the Peace Treaties*, Vol. II, Victor Gollancz Ltd. London 1938, pp. 1115-16.

[9] Lloyd George, ibid.,Vol. II, pp. 1025-26, 1145-46; Walter Laqueur – *A History of Zionism*, Weidenfeld and Nicolson, London 1972, pp. 190-91.

[10] Lloyd George, Ibid., Vol. II, pp. 1037-38.

[11] Ibid.

Zionist movement carried out negotiations during 1917 with the British, French, and Italian governments. They were blindfolded, not knowing that the main obstacle to achieving any results was the Sykes-Picot Agreement. Weizmann noted: 'What we did not know in the early stages of our practical negotiations was that a secret tentative agreement, which was later revealed as the 'Sykes-Picot Treaty', already existed between France and England... and months passed... before we understood what it was that blocked our progress.'[12] Weizmann and the leadership of the Zionist movement naturally regarded the Sykes-Picot Agreement as detrimental to the Zionist cause. However, when Britain decided to take control of Palestine, it made every effort to alter its understanding with France. According to Lloyd George, 'the Sykes-Picot Agreement perished' in the flames of the last stages of the war, and he asserted that 'Palestine if recaptured, must be one and indivisible to renew its greatness as a living entity'.[13]

Allied Powers' Policy After the Balfour Declaration

Following the Balfour Declaration, the British Government made meaningful efforts to see it implemented and thus paved the way to secure Palestine as a National Home for the Jewish people, despite Arab opposition and French disapproval. Palestine was treated differently from Syria and Mesopotamia. There was no intention of applying self-determination to the indigenous population of Palestine as was employed in Syria and Mesopotamia. In fact, the right to self-determination was attributed to the Jewish people as a whole, even though its majority then lived outside Palestine.[14] British consistency in

---

[12] Chaim Weizmann – *Trial and Error*, Schocken Books, New York, 1949, p. 188; Lloyd George, ibid., Vol. II, p. 1037. Hurewitz, op. cit., p. 110.

[13] Lloyd George, ibid., Vol. II, p. 1116.

[14] See Friedman, op. cit., p. 325: 'The Declaration was made to the Jewish people as a whole. Hence, as Ernst Frankenstein, the jurist, put it, the beneficiary of the National Home was not the Jewish population of Palestine but the newly recognised entity, the Jewish people, and therefore, in spite of not being in actual possession of the country and not inhabiting it, every Jew in the world had the right though not the obligation to turn towards his National Home. 'Every Jew [was] a potential inhabitant of Palestine'.'

its endeavor to implement the Declaration on this footing was apparent in the course of the proceedings that led to the San Remo Resolution.

On November 7th 1918, soon after the armistice with Turkey, the British and French Governments made an announcement to appease the Arabs who were perturbed that one hated ruling power would be replaced by another. This announcement, better known as the Anglo-French Declaration 1918, declared the disinterest of the Allied Powers in Arab land and pledged to assist in the establishment of national governments in Syria and Mesopotamia. The omission to mention Palestine was not accidental. It was in conformity with the Balfour Declaration, which assigned Palestine as the National Home for the Jewish people.[15]

The announcement in its essential passages declared:[16]

> The goal aimed by France and Great Britain ... is the complete and definite freedom of the peoples so long oppressed by the Turks, and the establishment of national governments and administrations deriving their authority from the initiative and free choice of the native population.
>
> In order to fulfill these intentions, France and Great Britain are agreed in the desire to encourage and assist in the establishment of native governments and administrations in *Syria and Mesopotamia,* at this moment freed by the Allies, and in the territories of which they are attempting the liberation,[17] and on the recognition of these as soon as they are effectively established.[18] [Italics added].

---

15 On the significance of the omission to mention Palestine in the Anglo-French Declaration, see further pp. 400-02 infra.

16 Charles Geddes, ed. – *A Documentary History of the Arab-Israeli Conflict,* Praeger, New York 1991, doc. 10, p.58; Lloyd George, op. cit., pp. 1036, 1089-90.

17 Those territories could not have included Palestine since Palestine was already in British hands at the announcement date.

18 The Peel Commission held a different view as to the omission of Palestine. In their view such a specific mention was not necessary 'since the Arabs had

The same year, 1918, also witnessed President Wilson's statement of principles for peace, delivered to both Houses of Congress, better known as the Fourteen Points speech, to which the Allied Powers promised to adhere in their peace treaties with Germany and Turkey.[19] The main points pertinent to Allied policy in the Middle East were points V and XII:

> (V) [i]n determining all such questions of sovereignty, the interests of the populations concerned must have equal weight with the equitable claims of the government whose title is to be determined.

> (XII) The Turkish portions of the present Ottoman Empire should be assured a secure sovereignty, but the other nationalities which are now under Turkish rule should be assured an undoubted security of life and an absolutely unmolested opportunity of autonomous development...[20]

The Allied Powers pledged that the settlement of Turkey should also take into consideration President Wilson's subsequent pronouncements. One such was his Mount Vernon

---

always regarded Palestine as included in Syria'. See Peel Report, op. cit., p. 25. However, this observation is unreasonable. The Balfour Declaration referred to Palestine as a separate entity. In fact, Palestine was detached from Syria for the sole purpose of establishing a National Home for the Jewish people. Emir Feisal, who represented the Arab people at the Paris Peace Conference, referred to Palestine as a separate entity and so he did in his agreement with Weizmann of January 3rd 1919. Lloyd George recorded that 'when he [Feisal] came to deal with Palestine, he admitted that it was on a different footing to the countries that were traditionally Arab.' Lloyd George, op. cit., Vol. II, p. 1042.

[19] On January 8th 1918 President Wilson delivered to both Houses of Congress his annual speech which included fourteen points as a program of world peace. In a joint note dated November 5th 1918, the Allied Powers promised President Wilson that they would conclude an armistice with Germany on the basis of his Fourteen Points, and similarly felt bound to do the same in their peace treaty with Turkey. See British Documents on Foreign Affairs, Part II, Series I, Vol. 11, p. 136, [hereinafter BDFA]; Geddes, op. cit., doc. 8, p. 45.

[20] Geddes, ibid., doc. 8, pp. 49-50.

address of July 4th 1918, in which he underlined the doctrine of self-determination. In his speech, he asserted that non-Turkish populations formerly subject to Turkey ought to be liberated from Turkish rule to form independent and self-governing states. That would include Arab countries formerly under Ottoman rule. Analogously, it might also be construed to mean the Arabs of Palestine. However, President Wilson held a different view with regard to Palestine. A statement issued to the press by members of the American delegation stated that the President promised his entire support for a 'Jewish Palestine full and unhampered'. He agreed to confer the mandate for Palestine on Britain and gave renewed assurances of his adherence to the Balfour Declaration, emphasizing that no one seriously opposed the purpose which it embodied.[21]

President Wilson's assurances followed recommendations prepared for him by the Intelligence Section of the American delegation to the Peace Conference. It recommended that there be established a separate state in Palestine which would control its own sources of water power and irrigation, and that this state be placed under Great Britain as a mandatory of the League of Nations. It further recommended that:

> The Jews be invited to return to Palestine and settle there, being assured by the Conference of all proper assistance in so doing that may be consistent with the protection of the personal (especially the religious) and the property rights of the non-Jewish population, and being further assured that it will be the policy of the League of Nations to recognize Palestine as a Jewish state as soon as it is a Jewish state in fact. It is right that Palestine should become a Jewish state, if the Jews, being given the full opportunity, make it such. It was the cradle and home of their vital race, which has made large spiritual contributions to

---

[21] DBFP, op. cit., Vol. IV, p. 262 (enclosure 4 in No. 180, letter from President Wilson to Frankfurter, May 16th 1919. See The Times, January 16th, 18th 1919; The Jewish Chronicle, January 17th 1919; both cited in Friedman, op. cit. p. 301. Stein, op. cit., p. 597.

mankind, and is the only land in which they can hope to find a home of their own; they being in this last respect unique among significant peoples.[22]

The aim to safeguard Palestine as a homeland of the Jewish people was further demonstrated in a statement on British foreign policy in the Middle East submitted on February 18th 1919 to the Paris Peace Conference. The British delegation to the Peace Conference made a point in adding a caveat to Wilson's Fourteen points and pronouncements with regard to, inter alia, Palestine:

> 'Self-determination' as provided for above, is subject to certain inevitable limitations ... There are elements, like the Armenians and the Zionist Jews, which for historical reasons or on account of future possibilities, have a claim to special consideration out of proportion to their present numerical strength in the Middle Eastern countries they inhabit. And finally, there are world interests such as ... access to Holy Places in Palestine for all religions ... which are so important that they must, if necessary, take precedence over the wishes of the inhabitants of the localities in which they are situated.[23]

The British expressed the view that even though Jewish agricultural colonists in Palestine formed a clear minority, they were entitled to special consideration out of proportion to their numbers. This was due to their historic past, their superior vigor and ability, the barbarous methods by which their numbers had been reduced, and their reservoirs of potential immigrants, from which their losses could be made good. The British proposed, therefore, to confer a mandate on a single Power for the purpose of transforming Palestine into a State in which all inhabitants would enjoy equal civil, but not political, rights – to secure for the Arabs and Jews representation on the Palestinian administration

---

[22] Hurewitz, op. cit., doc. 34, p. 136.

[23] BDFA, op. cit., Vol. 2, p. 139

in proportion of their respective stakes in the country. It would also train Jews and Arabs to work together so that they should be able to govern themselves in ecclesiastical matters and public education.[24]

British Endeavor to Implement the Balfour Declaration amid Difficulties

The British Government was consistent at this stage in putting the Balfour Declaration into effect in Palestine amid Arab agitation and hostilities, lack of cooperation of the Palestine Administration, French and Italian propaganda, and King-Crane Commission report.

General Clayton, stationed in Cairo, warned Curzon in May 1919 that the Arabs of Palestine desired for themselves what they considered as their country, and would resist Jewish immigration, however gradual, in any way possible including active hostilities. To allay their fears, Clayton suggested that the British make an authoritative announcement that the Zionist scheme will not be imposed on the majority against their wishes. He also warned that the alternative might preclude any local request for a British Mandate for Palestine. Moreover, 'a British mandate for Palestine on the lines of the Zionist programme will mean the indefinite retention of a military force considerably greater than that now in Palestine.' [25]

In the same vein, Major J.N. Camp, Assistant Political Officer at Jerusalem, sent a report to Curzon on August 12th 1919, warning him of widespread Arab antagonism and organization against the Zionist program. He suggested abandoning the substance of the Balfour Declaration, advocating an immigration policy open to all. Britain would obtain the Mandate, but not for a Jewish or Zionist Palestine. He suggested appeasing the Arabs

---

[24] BDFA, ibid., Vol. 2, p. 151-52.

[25] DBFP, op. cit., Vol. IV, p. 272. Telegram from General Clayton to Earl Curzon on May 5th 1919. Other British officers sent similar warnings: On July 17th 1919 Colonel French sent a warning from Cairo to Curzon stating 'that the Zionist programme can only be carried through against the wishes of the people and by force'. See DBFP, ibid., Vol. IV, p. 316.

and refraining from hurting their feelings. He explained:

> Practically all Moslems and Christians of any importance in Palestine are anti-Zionists, and bitterly so… If we mean to carry out any sort of Zionist policy we must do so with military force and adopt a strong policy against all the agitators in the country. We must also be prepared for the possibility of raids by the Gaza, Beersheba, and Trans-Jordan Bedouin. We must also be ready to risk disorders in the Moslem world at large and be prepared for the propaganda that is certain to be made with regard to Jews taking possession of the holy Places and the Holy Land[26].

Meinertzhagen similarly reported to Curzon on September 26th 1919 that there was strong local opposition to Zionism in Syria and Palestine, which had been frequently voiced by nearly all communities and classes. This opposition involved official elements. The question was how to give effect to the Declaration without stirring violent opposition.[27]

The reports arriving from the Near East had little to no effect on British policy towards the Jews and did not deter the British Government from their efforts to carry out the Balfour Declaration. Balfour, commenting on Clayton's request for a British official announcement, stated: 'There can of course be no question of making any such announcement'.[28] He went on to say that the French, United States and Italian Governments have approved the policy set forth in the Declaration of November 2nd 1917, and urged that Clayton emphasize the general unity of opinion among the Allies on this matter in responsible quarters in Palestine.[29]

---

[26] DBFP, ibid., Vol. IV, p. 364.

[27] Ibid., pp. 425-26.

[28] Ibid., p. 281, dispatch from Balfour to Curzon dated May 19th 1919, commenting on Clayton's telegram of May 5th 1919, see note 25 supra.

[29] Ibid. Balfour was basing his argument, inter alia, on Cambon's letter to Sokolow of June 4th 1914 [1918], Pichon's letter to Sokolow of February 14th 1918, the Marquis Imperiali's letter to Sokolow of May 9th 1918; enclosed in

Herbert Samuel, then Chairman of the Advisory Committee on Economic Development of Palestine, investigated Arab agitation in Palestine in June 1919, at the request of Sir William Tyrrell on behalf of the British Government. He revealed that Arab unrest and hostilities were the direct consequence of the fact that until then there had been no definite public announcement on the subject by the British Government. The Arabs, therefore, were still in doubt if the establishment of a Jewish National Home in Palestine was a closed case. They felt that with some agitation, the British would retreat and yield to their demands. To stabilize the situation, Samuel made suggestions that were soon adopted by Balfour, and on his instructions they were dispatched by Curzon to Allenby and to the local administration.[30]

In this dispatch, Curzon sent explicit directives to all heads of the Administration in Palestine and their local representatives, asserting that the terms of Mandate would embody the substance of the Balfour Declaration. He noted that 'American and French Governments are equally pledged to support establishment in Palestine of Jewish National Home. This should be emphasized to Arab leaders at every opportunity and it should be impressed on them that the matter is a *'chose jugée'* and continued agitation would be useless and detrimental'.[31] Similar dispatches were sent to Allenby and Meinertzhagen reaffirming that the establishment of a National Home for the Jewish people in Palestine was a 'settled policy' of the British Government, which could not be influenced by Arab agitation.[32]

Another obstacle the British Government had to overcome came from within their own ranks. It became obvious, not

---

Sokolow's letter of May 15th 1918 to the Foreign office, the correspondence with Sir William Wiseman in October 1917, and President Wilson's letter to Rabbi Wise of August 13th 1918.

[30] DBFP, Vol. IV, ibid., p. 284, June 5th 1919 and p. 301, July 1st 1919. Samuel's recommendations were handed over to Curzon who delivered them to Balfour.

[31] DBFP, ibid., Vol. IV, p. 329. Curzon's instructions via Colonel French in Cairo, August 4th 1919.

[32] DBFP, ibid., Vol. IV, p. 507. Letter from Curzon to Allenby on Meinertzhagen's draft on Zionism, November 7th 1919.

long after the issuance of the Declaration, that the British administrators were not cooperative with their Government's policy in Palestine and did not conduct their relations with the local population on the basis of the Balfour Declaration. On July 2nd 1919, Samuel complained to Sir R. Graham that British Military Authorities who were administering Palestine 'took every opportunity to injure Zionist interests... Local Authorities were not acting in the spirit of the assurances given by Mr. Balfour to the Zionist organization.'[33] Weizmann was even more blunt: British Authorities were showing a marked hostility to the Jews and causing them great injury and humiliation.[34] Immigration to Palestine, for example, even by a few, came to be very difficult. Weizmann, all the more, found it necessary to ask Balfour for the replacement of British officers who showed themselves not only unsympathetic, but even hostile to the Jewish population of Palestine.[35]

The attitude of the British Administration was in total denial of British Government Policy in Palestine. The contrast between the two could be easily detected by comparing this attitude with Balfour's total concurrence with the three conditions Brandeis found essential for the realization of a Jewish homeland in Palestine:

(a) 'that Palestine should be the Jewish homeland and not merely that there be a Jewish homeland in Palestine';

(b) that 'there must be economic elbow room for a Jewish Palestine', adequate borders, and 'not merely a small garden within Palestine', the control of waters in the north, etc.;

(c) that in the future the Jews of Palestine should have control of economic life including the land and natural resources.[36]

Balfour insisted that despite disharmony between the Declaration of November 2nd 1917, and other British commitments, the promise for the establishment of a Jewish homeland in

---

[33] DBFP, ibid., Vol. IV, p. 307.

[34] DBFP, ibid., Vol. IV, p. 308.

[35] DBFP, ibid., Vol. IV, pp. 326-27, letter from Weizmann to Balfour, July 23rd 1919.

[36] DBFP, ibid., Vol. IV, p. 1276-77, memorandum by Frankfurter of a meeting between Balfour and Justice Brandeis in Paris on June 24th 1919.

Palestine should prevail. He reiterated: 'The four Great Powers are committed to Zionism. And Zionism, be it right or wrong, good or bad, is rooted in age-long traditions, in present needs, in future hopes, of far profounder import than the desires and prejudices of the 700,000 Arabs who now inhabit that ancient land'.[37] Notwithstanding the Covenant, the Great Powers had no intention of consulting the inhabitants of Palestine as to who would be their Mandatory.

A further challenge to British Government policy in Palestine was the King-Crane Report.[38] The Report was the result of an American fact-finding Commission appointed by President Wilson. The purpose of this Commission was to get accurate and definite information on the desires of all peoples and classes in the Near East, in order that President Wilson may act on them with full knowledge of the situation. At first, President Wilson suggested at the Paris Peace Conference, at the Council of Four, to appoint an Inter-Allied Commission, comprising representatives of the United States, Great Britain, France, and Italy. The Commission's objective was 'to elucidate the state of opinion and the soil to be worked on by any mandatory'.[39] They should be sent with 'Carte blanche to tell the facts as they found them.'[40] However, France withdrew and then Britain, leaving the United States alone. Thus, a Commission that was meant to be international ended by being American.

Balfour objected to the dispatch of a fact-finding Commission to Palestine because it was in total contradiction to the Declaration. In fact, he wondered how President Wilson could reconcile his adherence to Zionism with the doctrine of self-determination. Balfour was reported to have told Brandeis:

One day in the Council of Four, when the Syrian

---

[37] DBFP, ibid., Vol. IV, p. 345, Memorandum by Balfour (in Paris) respecting Syria, Palestine, and Mesopotamia, August 11th 1919.

[38] Submitted on August 28th 1919 by Dr. Henry Churchill King and Charles R. Crane to the Peace Conference; https://wwi.lib.byu.edu/index.php/The_King-Crane_Report; Hurewitz, op. cit., p. 191.

[39] DBFP, op. cit., Vol. V, p. 12; President Wilson addressing the Council of Four, at the Paris Peace Conference, March 20th 1919.

[40] Ibid.

matter was under dispute, the President suggested the despatch of a Commission to find out what the people really wanted. It began with Syria but the field of enquiry was extended over the whole East. Mr. Balfour wrote a memorandum to the Prime Minister, and he believed it went to the President, pointing out that Palestine should be excluded from the terms of reference because the Powers had committed themselves to the Zionist programme, which inevitably excluded numerical self-determination. Palestine presented a unique situation. We are dealing not with the wishes of an existing community but are consciously seeking to re-constitute a new community and definitely building for a numerical majority in the future.[41]

The American Commission of enquiry began its mission after arriving at Jaffa on June 10th 1919, and submitted their recommendations to the supreme Council on August 28th 1919. They recommended a 'serious modification of the extreme Zionist program for Palestine of unlimited immigration of Jews, looking finally to making Palestine distinctly a Jewish State'.[42] They contended that 'a national home for the Jewish people is not equivalent to making Palestine into a Jewish State' and that the claim to a right to Palestine based on historical connection 'can hardly be seriously considered.' They recommended that Palestine should be included in a united Syrian State and concluded that 'only a greatly reduced Zionist program be attempted by the Peace Conference, and even that, only very gradually initiated. This would have to mean that Jewish immigration should be definitely limited, and that the project for making Palestine distinctly a Jewish Commonwealth should be given up.'[43] The British rejected those recommendations and gave them very little consideration. So did the European powers and the United States.

---

[41] DBFP, ibid., Vol. IV, p. 1277. Memorandum by Frankfurter of a meeting between Balfour and Brandeis, on June 24th 1919, see n. 36, supra.

[42] The King-Crane Report, op. cit., p. 31, para. E, Chapter on Zionism; Hurewitz, op. cit., p. 195.

[43] The King-Crane Report, ibid., p. 32, para. E; Hurewitz, ibid., p. 196.

They remained of academic interest only.[44]

Last but not least were the hurdles laid down by Feisal. At first, he made a clear distinction at the Paris Peace Conference[45] between the Arab State or Confederation of Arab States and Palestine. For all Arabic-speaking peoples in Asia, he asked for total independence from the line of Alexandretta-Diarbekir southward. He spoke of the Arabs as being of one stock, who live in one area with natural frontiers that ensure their unity and all speak one language, Arabic. Socially and economically they form one unit. As Feisal stated: 'There are few nations in the world as homogeneous as this'.[46] His principal aim was Arab unity, and it was for this the Arabs had fought. However, when referring to Palestine, 'in consequence of its universal character, he [Feisal] left on one side for the consideration of all parties interested. With this exception, he asked for the independence of the Arab areas enumerated in his memorandum'.[47] It was clear from his speech that Feisal, who spoke for the Arabs as a whole, did not regard Palestine as part of the Arab sphere. In a Foreign Office memorandum, Forbes Adam asserted that 'the Zionists have several times received satisfactory assurances from Feisal personally as to his attitude towards their general programme'.[48] As Lloyd George put it: 'When he (Feisal) came to deal with Palestine he admitted that it was on a different footing to the countries that were traditionally Arab'.[49]

Later Feisal's appetite grew. Only a month after he had made his speech at the Peace Conference, he convoked the Syrian Congress, a self-constituted body, of which the composition, authority or credentials were unknown. Its intention was to

---

[44] Hurewitz, ibid., p. 192.

[45] At a session held at the Quai d'Orsay in Paris on February 6th 1919.

[46] BDFA, ibid., Vol. IV, p. 109; see also Lloyd George, op. cit., pp. 1039-40.

[47] BDFA, ibid., Vol. IV, p. 110, section (f). In his memorandum to the Supreme Council, January 1st 1919, Feisal enumerated the provinces of Arab Asia as including: Syria, Iraq, Jezireh, Hedjaz, Nejd and Yemen. In his enumeration he did not include Palestine. See Hurewitz, op. cit., p. 131.

[48] DBFP, op. cit., Vol. IV, p. 608. Memorandum by Forbes Adam on *France and the northern frontier of Palestine,* December 30th 1919.

[49] Lloyd George. Op. cit., p. 1042.

declare the complete independence of Syria, including Palestine, and crown him as king, all without consulting the Allied Powers.[50] To avoid Arab hostilities and agitation, Allenby 'strongly advised' the British Government that the Allied Powers 'acknowledge sovereignty of Feisal over an Arab nation or Confederation embracing Syria, Palestine and Mesopotamia, the Administration of Syria being secured to French and that of Palestine and Mesopotamia to British'.[51] But the British and French Governments rejected Allenby's advice and acted in unison to oppose the Arab move in its entirety. They affirmed that the future of territories severed from the Ottoman Empire could only be determined by the Allied Powers, who were the only authority entitled to negotiate a Peace Treaty with Turkey and to decide on the future settlement of the areas that were under the latter's sovereignty. The Allies were adamant that decisions of the Arab Congress could not supersede duties and decisions of the Peace Conference or entitle Feisal to force their hands.[52] Despite British and French opposition, on March 8th 1919 Feisal was crowned King of Syria and Palestine, whilst his brother Abdullah was proclaimed King of Mesopotamia.[53]

Though the British Government had no objection to Feisal being declared King of Syria provided the declaration was made by a 'properly constituted Syrian authority'[54], it opposed any attempt to annex Palestine to Syria, or to crown Feisal as King of Syria and Palestine. In so doing, the British were motivated by the Balfour Declaration and by their desire to put it into effect. In rejecting Allenby's advice, Curzon retorted: 'How would this procedure be applied to Palestine and how would recognition of Feisal as King be reconcilable with Zionist claims?'[55] Allenby, fearing the commencement of Arab hostilities in Syria and Palestine, made further attempts to convince the British

---

50 DBFP, op. cit., Vol. XIII, pp. 221, 226.

51 DBFP, ibid., Vol. XIII, p. 223.

52 DBFP, ibid., Vol. XIII, p. 232.

53 DBFP, ibid., Vol. XIII, p. 231.

54 DBFP, ibid., Vol. XIII, p. 232.

55 DBFP, ibid.

Government to assure the recognition of Feisal at the Peace Conference at least as a representative (not sovereign) of the Arab peoples of Syria and Palestine. The British Government was prepared to assure Feisal of that, 'provided that Feisal comes to Peace Conference with corresponding recognition of special positions of France in Syria and Lebanon and British in Palestine, the latter including obligation to provide a National Home for Zionists in that country.'[56] Allenby doubted whether Feisal would accept such a proposition, since, as Herbert Samuel commented, the only means to combat Zionism was through a united and independent Syria (which would include Palestine).[57]

On another occasion,[58] Curzon, in his effort to give effect to the Balfour Declaration, urged the French Government through its Ambassador in London to agree to a joint line of policy to be pursued with regard to Feisal's position in Syria. The British and French would recognize Feisal as King of Syria if he would be prepared to make special arrangements with France about Syria and Lebanon and with Britain about Palestine. The latter had to include recognition of British commitment 'to secure the fulfilment of the pledges they have entered into with the Jews in Palestine – pledges which have already been recognized by Feisal.'[59] The French, in response, expressed their wish to participate in any arrangement with Feisal.

The British were consistent in separating Palestine from the rest of the territories allocated to the Arabs, and this formed the basis of their policy in the Middle East. Thus, when Feisal expressed his surprise on April 8th 1920 at the concentration of new British forces in Palestine and asked for reasons which led to that decision, Curzon was advised to ignore Feisal's demand 'as any reply to it would be tantamount to recognizing his right

---

[56] DBFP, ibid., Vol. XIII, p. 235.

[57] DBFP, ibid., Vol. XIII, p. 241. Herbert Samuel made this comment in a letter to Curzon on April 2nd 1920, summing up his conclusions on the political situation in Palestine, with reference to the Syrian Congress and the declarations of March 8th 1920 in favor of an independent and united Syria, which would include Palestine under the kingship of Feisal.

[58] DBFP, ibid., Vol. XIII, p. 237. March 30th 1920. See Record by Curzon of a conversation with the French Ambassador on the Syrian question.

[59] DBFP, ibid., Vol. XIII, p. 238, para. 6.

to speak for Palestine.'[60] On the morrow of the San Remo Resolution, Curzon stated flatly: 'We cannot recognize him [Feisal] as King of Palestine'. However, he saw no inconsistency between recognition of Feisal as King of an independent Syrian State and acceptance by Britain of the Mandate for Palestine, 'in as much as he [Feisal] has known throughout that the British Government were pledged by Mr. Balfour's declaration to creating a National Home for the Jews in Palestine and this intention has been acquiesced in by him'.[61] Allenby also reiterated in his communication with Feisal that 'as regards Palestine you have always been aware that his Majesty's Government were pledged to creating a National Home for the Jews in Palestine, an intention in which administration acquiesced.'[62]

The British also had to overcome French, Italian, and Arab propaganda against the Zionist scheme in Palestine. Meinertzhagen reported to Curzon repeatedly on French and Arab anti-Zionist propaganda, adding that 'Italian propaganda is of a more serious and complex nature, and has been conducted in a much more subtle manner'. He also found that the Vatican is violently opposed to Zionism.'[63] On one occasion, he reported to Curzon of information received from an 'absolutely reliable source' that the 'Vatican concurs in deprecating Zionism which they regard as blow to Christian conscience'.[64] Months later, Churchill circulated a memorandum prepared by the General

---

[60] DBFP, ibid., Vol. XIII, p. 250.

[61] DBFP, ibid., Vol. XIII, p. 252. Letter by Curzon to Lord Hardinge on April 26th 1920.

[62] DBFP, ibid., Vol. XIII, p. 253. Letter by Curzon to Feisal dated April 27th 1920. At this stage, after Syria and Mesopotamia were recognized in San Remo as independent states and he was recognized as Head of Syria, Feisal made a complete change of policy over Palestine. His contention now was that Palestine was an inseparable part of Syria and that his acquiescence to the creation of a National Home for the Jewish people in Palestine was misunderstood.

[63] DBFP, ibid., Vol. IV, messages from Meinertzhagen in Cairo to Curzon, on September 12th 1919, p. 383; on September 26th 1919, p. 426; and on November 10th 1919, p. 526.

[64] DBFP, ibid., Vol. IV, p. 443, Report from Meinertzhagen to Curzon on October 7th 1919.

Staff stating: 'French policy is anti-Zionist'.[65] Anti-Zionist propaganda aggravated the situation in Palestine and increased tension between Jews and Arabs, rendering it more difficult for the British Government to implement the Declaration.

On February 17th-21st 1920, the Allies held a conference in London as a prelude to the Conference of San Remo, one of the main themes being Palestine. At this Conference, the French continued to lay obstacles to the establishment of a Jewish home in Palestine. Berthelot used double talk when he said the French would 'do their best to favour the development of a Jewish home in Palestine, so long as this development did not run counter to the wishes of the original inhabitants',[66] knowing full well that the original inhabitants totally opposed Zionism and were against the establishment of a Jewish National Home in Palestine. He also advocated that 'Palestine should be open to all nations'.[67] However, Lloyd George reiterated that 'Great Britain would only accept a mandate for a real Palestine, the Palestine of ancient history, which should not merely include the barren rocks of Judea…The waters of Palestine were essential to its existence. Without those waters, Palestine would be a wilderness.'[68] In making those assertions, Lloyd George had taken into consideration Jewish claims on the importance of the headwaters of the Jordan to the existence of Palestine.

On February 21st 1920, the London Conference adopted, inter alia, the following resolutions to be inserted into the Peace Treaty. Turkey had to renounce 'in favour of the Allied Powers all her rights and titles over Kurdistan, Mesopotamia, Syria, Palestine, Arabia, and the islands still remaining under Turkish sovereignty.'[69] Syria would be under French Mandate and Palestine under British Mandate. The borders of Palestine were to be limited to the historical boundaries from Dan to Beersheba. During the five days of discussion, Lloyd George yielded to

---

[65] CAB 24/107, C.P. 1450, June 8th 1920.

[66] DBFP, Vol. VII, op. cit., p. 103.

[67] Ibid.

[68] DBFP, ibid., Vol. VII, p. 104.

[69] DBFP, ibid., Vol. VII, p. 182. Part IV, para. 2.

Berthelot on this issue, the latter arguing that 'the historic boundaries of Palestine had never extended beyond Dan and Beersheba.'[70] Thus, the watersheds were left out of the borders of Palestine. In a last-minute effort, Brandeis wired Lloyd George via Weizmann, on behalf of the Zionist Organization of America, urging that the northern border of Palestine should include the Litany River and watersheds of the Hermon, but these proposals were rejected.[71] As a result, the British and French Governments decided to accept the boundaries of Dan to Beersheba as the future boundaries of Palestine.

A relatively accurate summing up of British foreign policy in Palestine may be found in a memorandum prepared by Major H.W. Young[72] of the Foreign Office on May 17th 1920 entitled *The Future Control of the Middle East*:[73]

> His Majesty's Government have declared their intention of encouraging in Palestine the formation of a National Home for the Jewish people, while ensuring that the existing rights and privileges of non-Jews should be scrupulously safeguarded. Over 80 percent of the population of Palestine are non-Jews, and hostile to the idea of a Jewish National Home. It appears from this that it is not intended to institute a representative government in Palestine, but to set up a British administration which shall make it possible for a Jewish National Home gradually to be formed there. The Zionists imagine that Palestine is to become eventually a Jewish state. This could only be reconciled with the principle of self-government if the country were developed to an extent that would admit of the immigration of Jews in such large numbers that they would form the Majority of the population.

---

[70] DBFP, ibid., Vol. VII, p. 184.

[71] Ibid. See also Lloyd George, op. cit., Vol. II, pp. 1179-80.

[72] An officer in the Indian Army who was temporarily a member of the Eastern and Egyptian Department of the Foreign Office.

[73] DBFP, op. cit., Vol. XIII, p. 261-62.

Chapter III

The Treaties of Sèvres and Lausanne

The conference of London led to the San Remo Resolution, which in turn led to the conclusion of the Treaty of Peace with Turkey signed at Sèvres on August 10th 1920, better known as the Treaty of Sèvres. The Treaty was signed by the Principal Allied Powers, namely: The British Empire,[1] France, Italy and Japan, together with the other Allied Powers, namely: Armenia, Belgium, Greece, the Hedjaz, Poland, Portugal, Rumania, the Serb-Croat-Slovene State and Czecho-Slovakia, on the one hand, and Turkey on the other hand. The Treaty explicitly dealt with the future of Syria, Mesopotamia, and Palestine. The Principal Allied Powers made sure to insert within its clauses the San Remo Resolutions almost verbatim through Articles 94-97.

Article 94

The High Contracting Parties agree that Syria and Mesopotamia Shall, in accordance with the fourth paragraph of Article 22, Part I (Covenant of the League of Nations), be provisionally recognized as independent States, subject to the rendering of administrative advice and assistance by a mandatory until such time as they are able to stand alone.

A Commission shall be constituted...to trace on the spot the frontier line described in Article 27 II (2) and (3)...[2]

The determination of the other frontiers of the said

---

[1] The British Empire comprising Great Britain, Canada, Australia, New Zealand, South Africa and India. The Treaty was signed by 18 States, on the one hand, and Turkey on the other. On the part of Turkey, the Treaty was signed by three representatives of Sultan Muhammad VI: General Haadi Pasha, Riza Tevfik Bey and Rechad Haliss Bey.

[2] Article 27 II (2) of the Treaty defined the frontier of Turkey with Syria; Article 27 II (3) defined the frontier of Turkey with Mesopotamia.

States, and the selection of the Mandatories, will be made by the Principal Allied Powers.

Article 95

The High Contracting Parties agree to entrust, by application of the provisions of Article 22, the administration of Palestine, within such boundaries as may be determined by the Principal Allied Powers, to a Mandatory, to be selected by the said Powers. The Mandatory will be responsible for putting into effect the Declaration originally made on November 2, 1917, by the British Government, and adopted by the other Allied Powers, in favour of the establishment in Palestine of a national home for the Jewish people, It being clearly understood that nothing shall be done which may Prejudice the civil and religious rights of existing non–Jewish communities in Palestine, or the rights and political status enjoyed by Jews in any other country....

Article 96

The terms of the mandates in respect of the above territories will be formulated by the Principal Allied Powers and submitted to the Council of the League of Nations for approval.

Article 97

Turkey hereby undertakes, in accordance with the provisions of Article 132, to accept any decisions which may be taken in relation to the questions dealt with in this Section.

The authority to act in accordance with Articles 94-97 was vested in the Principal Allied Powers through the following Article:

Article 132

Outside her frontiers as fixed by the present Treaty, Turkey hereby renounces in favour of the

Principal Allied Powers all rights and title which she could claim on any ground over or concerning any territories outside Europe which are not otherwise disposed of by the present Treaty.

Turkey undertakes to recognize and conform to the measures which may be taken now or in the future by the Principal Allied Powers, in agreement where necessary with third Powers, in order to carry the above stipulation into effect.

The Treaty of Sèvres stripped the Ottoman Empire of all her colonies and went further to divide parts of Turkish territory in Asia Minor among the Allied and Associated Powers.[3] The Ottoman Empire, which was severely defeated in the war, was in no position to negotiate a better settlement. This gave rise to strong sentiments among the nationalist Turks headed by Mustapha Kemal Ataturk. As noted by Grief: 'He set up a unified committee called 'the Society for the Defence of Rights in Anatolia and Rumelia', to preserve the unity of the Turkish fatherland in defiance of the victorious Allies'.[4] In May 1919, Ataturk launched a fierce campaign against the Allies with the objective to drive out all foreign armies from Asia Minor, particularly from Smyrna (now Izmir), Antalya, Cilicia, Armenian

---

[3] Lloyd George, op. cit., Vol. II, pp.1337-38: 'The territories severed from Turkey [in the Treaty of Sèvres] were dealt with as follows: Greece was given the islands of Imbros and Tenedos, and the parts of Turkey-in-Europe outside the Constantinople hinterland. Armenia was set up as an independent State, with frontiers settled by the arbitration of President Wilson.

Syria and Mesopotamia were made independent States, subject to supervision by a Mandatory power appointed by the League – the Mandatory of Palestine had the duty of carrying out the promises of the Balfour Declaration in that country.

The Hedjaz was made an independent State. Turkey renounced all rights of suzerainty over Egypt, the Soudan and Libya. She recognized the British protectorate over Egypt and that of France over Tunis and Morocco. The British annexation of Cyprus was accepted, and the Dodecanese Islands were ceded to Italy. Smyrna and a large area of Western Asia Minor were placed under Greek control, with the option of voting within five years for its inclusion in the Greek realm. Kurdistan was accorded local autonomy, with the right to secede in one year from Turkey.

[4] Grief, op. cit., p. 269.

and Kurdish territories in the eastern part of the peninsula, and European Turkey (Eastern Thrace). The nationalists gained power and overthrew the last Ottoman Emperor, Mohammad VI. On the ruins of the Ottoman Empire, they established the new secular state of Turkey. Ataturk managed to achieve most of his goals in Asia Minor, defeating Greek, Armenian, Georgian, Italian, and French forces with their far better equipped armies.[5]

The Treaty of Sèvres stipulated that it had to be ratified in order to acquire binding force.[6] The Treaty was signed by the three plenipotentiaries of the Ottoman Empire, but under the new situation that developed on the battlefield and in consequence of new Turkish gains, Ataturk refused to ratify it. In consequence, the Treaty became defunct.[7] To meet the new situation, new negotiations began, and a new treaty was drafted – the Treaty of Lausanne. This Treaty, which was signed on July 24th 1923 and came into force by its ratification on August 6th 1924, superseded the Treaty of Sèvres. However, in the Treaty of Lausanne, the parties no longer incorporated the clear and precise provisions on Palestine, Syria, and Mesopotamia, namely Articles 94-97 of the Treaty of Sèvres. They also failed to incorporate Article 132 which transferred the sovereignty of these areas from the Ottoman Empire to the Principal Allied Powers. In our view, based on the following, this was not accidental and did not make much difference.

---

5 Ibid. p. 268; Lloyd George, op. cit., Vol. II, pp. 1342-52.

6 At the close of the Treaty of Sèvres it was stipulated that the Treaty should be ratified, and it would come into force only after it had been ratified, by Turkey, on the one hand, and by three of the Principal Allied Powers on the other hand.

7 L. Oppenheim – *International Law, A Treatise*, Vol. I, H. Lauterpacht, ed., 7th edition, Longmans, Green & Co., London, 1948, [hereinafter Oppenheim & Lauterpacht] elucidated the legal concept of ratification: 'Ratification is the term for the final confirmation given by the parties to an international treaty concluded by their representatives, and is commonly used to include the exchange of the documents embodying that confirmation. Although a treaty is concluded as soon as the mutual consent is manifest from acts of the duly authorized representatives, its binding force is, as a rule, suspended till ratification is given. The function of ratification is, therefore, to make the treaty binding; and if it is refused, the treaty falls to the ground in consequence.' p. 813.

By refusing to ratify the Treaty of Sèvres, Turkey did not contest the provisions in the Treaty regarding the detachment of Palestine and the Arab provinces from Turkey. Lloyd George commented that 'Kemal was shrewd enough to know that the Arab countries were irretrievably lost to the Turkish Empire. They might resent the interference of foreign mandatories and the immigration of Jews, but they were not hankering for the return of their Turkish misrulers.'[8] On the other hand, Ataturk had vigorously contested the territorial losses Turkey had suffered in Asia Minor, and their calamitous partition between foreign powers. After restoring those territories to Turkey in battle, the Treaty of Lausanne carved new frontiers for Turkey, taking into consideration the Turkish territorial gains in their national campaign, which lasted from May 19th 1919 till July 24th 1924. By the time the Treaty of Lausanne was signed and ratified, the political map of the Middle East had changed. Consequently, there appeared to be no reason to adopt provisions similar to Articles 94-97 and 132 of the Treaty of Sèvres, which might have been regarded as obsolete by then.

The Treaty of Lausanne was signed almost three years after the Treaty of Sèvres. As mentioned, it did not make any specific reference to Palestine, Syria or Mesopotamia. In place of Articles 94-97 and 132, the Treaty of Lausanne stated in Article 16 as follows:

> Turkey hereby renounces all rights and title whatsoever over or respecting the territories situated outside the frontiers laid down in the present Treaty and the islands other than those over which her sovereignty is recognized by the said Treaty, the future of these territories and islands being settled or to be settled by the parties concerned.[9]

---

[8] Lloyd George, op. cit., Vol. II, p. 1334.

[9] Article 16, in a second paragraph, adds that 'the provisions of the present article do not prejudice any special arrangements arising from neighbourly relations which have been or may be concluded between Turkey and any limitrophe countries'. Grief explains that these special arrangements 'referred to several different border rectifications', none of which involves Palestine. Grief, op. cit. p. 276.

At first sight, it would seem that there was a major discrepancy between Articles 94-97 and 132 on the one hand and Article 16 on the other. For in Article 16 of the Treaty of Lausanne, although Turkey renounced all her rights and title whatsoever over territories outside those over which her sovereignty was recognized, it did not specify in whose favor the renunciation was made. It may be argued that lacking this, there could be no transfer of sovereignty to the Allied Powers, who then could not have the authority to establish mandates and grant independence to territories they occupied during the war. The answer is found in Article 16 itself, stating 'the future of these territories and islands were settled or to be settled by the parties concerned'. The 'parties concerned' could not have been the Turks, since they had accepted the severance of these areas from Turkey in the Treaty. The 'parties concerned' were, therefore, most likely the Principal Allied Powers and their associates.

By the time the Treaty of Lausanne came into force on August 6th 1924,[10] most of the provisions pertinent to the Middle East had already been implemented. The implementation of Articles 94-96 led to the following developments: With regard to Syria and Mesopotamia [Article 94], France had already been selected as the Mandatory for Syria and Lebanon, and Great Britain the Mandatory for Mesopotamia. Both countries accepted the challenge. In the Mandate Charters for Syria and Mesopotamia, the Mandatory was charged with the duty of rendering administrative advice and assistance to the population in accordance with the provisions of Article 22 of the Covenant of the League of Nations. On December 7th 1920 the draft mandate for Mesopotamia was submitted for approval to the League of Nations. Feisal was crowned King of Iraq on August 23rd 1921. The French Mandate for Syria and Lebanon was confirmed by the League of Nations on July 24th 1922.[11] Both Mandates, the French for Syria and Lebanon, and the British for Mesopotamia, came into force on September 29th 1923. The boundaries

---

[10] The Treaty of Lausanne came into force after it had been duly ratified.

[11] League of Nations Official Journal, August 1922, p. 1013.

between the territories under the French and British Mandates were determined and settled between Britain and France by the Franco-British Convention of December 23rd 1920.[12]

The execution of Article 95 of the Treaty of Sèvres was marked by the following events: The draft Mandate for Palestine was submitted to the League of Nations for approval on December 7th 1920. It was then approved on July 24th 1922. The Mandate Charter stipulated in its second recital that the Mandatory shall be responsible for putting into effect the Balfour Declaration in favor of the establishment in Palestine of a National Home for the Jewish people, as required by the Treaty of Sèvres.[13] The Mandate for Palestine came into force on September 29th 1923.[14] In the summer of 1920, a Civil Administration was established in Palestine replacing the Military one, and Sir Herbert Samuel was appointed High Commissioner. In June 1922, the British Colonial Secretary published a statement of British Policy in Palestine.[15] In March 1921, Britain decided to separate West Palestine from East Palestine, creating the Emirate of Trans-Jordan. The boundaries between Palestine and Trans-Jordan were established on September 1st 1922 and were accepted by the League of Nations on September 23rd 1922.[16]

The Principal Allied Powers would not have had the authority to bring about these developments if not for Article 132 of the Treaty of Sèvres. However, the Treaty of Sèvres was

---

[12] *The Franco-British Convention on Certain Points Connected with the Mandates for Syria, Lebanon, Palestine and Mesopotamia*, December 23rd 1920, Cmd. 1195, HMSO, London 1921.

[13] Peel Report, op. cit. p. 32; See the British Mandate Charter, The Avalon Project, Yale Law School. http://avalon.law.yale.edu/20th_century/palmanda.asp;

[14] *Convention between the United States and Great Britain* in Respect to Rights in Palestine, Cmd. 2559, 1925, (signed December 3rd 1924). HeinOnline – 44 stat. 2191, 1925-1927.

[15] Cmd. 1700 – *Palestine: Correspondence with the Palestine Arab Delegation and the Zionist Organization*, HMSO, London, June 1922, pp. 17-21; see also Cmd. 3530, *Report of the Commission on the Palestine Disturbances of August 1929*, (Appendix V), HMSO, London, March 1930.

[16] Gideon Biger – "Britain's Role as a Boundary Maker in the middle East", in Zach Levy and Elie Podeh ed. – *Britain and the middle East, From Imperial Power to Junior Partner*, Sussex Academic Press, Brighton, U.K. 2008, p. 25.

never ratified and the war went on between the Allies and the Turkish nationalist movement until a new Armistice was signed in Mudanya on October 11th 1922,[17] followed by the Treaty of Lausanne of July 24th 1923. During almost three years, the Principal Allied Powers continued to implement Articles 94-97 with respect to Syria, Mesopotamia and Palestine on the premise that Article 132 of the Treaty of Sèvres was still valid, all that with the acquiescence and non-intervention of Turkey under Ataturk.[18]

In fact, the British Government continued to base its arguments, regarding the establishment of a Jewish National Home in Palestine, on the Treaty of Sèvres. Thus, Winston Churchill, as Colonial Secretary, reiterated a statement published in June 1922 on 'British Policy in Palestine'. He noted that the Balfour Declaration 'reaffirmed by the Conference of the Principal Allied Powers at San Remo and *again in the Treaty of Sèvres*, is not susceptible to change'[19] [Italics added]. The Duke of Devonshire, who succeeded Churchill as Colonial Secretary, again based British Cabinet policy in Palestine on the Treaty of Sèvres. In a dispatch sent to the High Commissioner of Palestine on October 4th 1923, he instructed him that:

> [T]he policy of the declaration was accepted by the Principal Allied Powers at San Remo in April 1920; its text was embodied verbatim in *the treaty signed at Sèvres in August 1920* and again in the mandate approved by the Council of the League of Nations in July 1922. It formed an essential part of the conditions on which Great Britain accepted the mandate for Palestine, and thus constitutes an

---

[17] In the Armistice at Mudanya signed between Britain, France and Italy, Greece acceded to the Armistice a few days later to end hostilities between the parties. So did the Grand National Assembly of Turkey.

[18] Grief suggested that 'Even though the Treaty of Sèvres was never ratified, it still had probative legal value as an agreement between the four Principal allied Powers, showing exactly what they had intended to do in disposing of the ex-Turkish territories in the Middle East.' Grief, op. cit., p. 294.

[19] Cmd. 1700, op. cit., p. 19; Peel Report, op. cit., p. 32.

international obligation from which there can be no question of receding.[20] [Italics added].

Similarly, the Peel Commission, as late as 1937, based its argument on the Treaty of Sèvres. In reply to Arab claim, it stated that:

> [T]he acceptance by the Allied Powers and the United States of the policy of the Balfour Declaration made it clear from the beginning that Palestine would have to be treated differently from Syria and Iraq and that this difference in treatment was confirmed by the Supreme Council in *the Treaty of Sèvres* and by the Council of the League sanctioning the Mandate. [Italics added].

Did the Principal Allied Powers acquire the authority to dispose of territories captured from the Turks despite the fact that the Treaty of Sèvres was not expressly ratified? The answer seems to be in the affirmative. According to international law, a treaty may be tacitly ratified by its execution. Oppenheim and Lauterpacht maintained that 'no rule of International Law exists which prescribes a necessary form of ratification. Ratification can, therefore, be given tacitly as well as expressly. Tacit ratification takes place when a state begins the execution of a treaty without expressly ratifying it.'[21] Thus, Turkey, by divesting of former Ottoman territories in the Middle East and by knowingly refraining from contesting the disposition of these territories by the Allied Powers, took a passive part in the implementation of Articles 94-97 of the Treaty of Sèvres. Temperley, the distinguished historian, remarked that 'the view was apparently now advanced [1924] that, despite the non-ratification of the Treaty, these areas, [namely Mesopotamia, Syria and Palestine] had ceased to be under Turkish sovereignty.'[22] Be that as it may,

---

[20] Cabinet Papers, C.P. 433 (23), October 27th 1923.

[21] Oppenheim & Lauterpacht, Vol. I, op. cit., p. 818.

[22] Temperley, Vol. VI, op. cit. p. 37.

Articles 94-97 and 132 became part of international law despite the non-ratification of the Treaty of Sèvres, by their subsequent incorporation into the British Mandate for Palestine, and their confirmation by the League of Nations.

Furthermore, the absence of ratification did not, in actual fact, prejudice the significance of the Treaty of Sèvres. According to Article 25 of the Treaty of Lausanne, Ataturk's Turkey recognized the full force of Article 22 of the Covenant of the League of Nations, which implied the transfer of sovereignty in the Middle East from Turkey to 'certain communities formerly belonging to the Turkish Empire'.

Article 25 provides as follows:

> Turkey undertakes to recognize the full force of the Treaties of Peace and additional Conventions concluded by the other Contracting Powers with the Powers who fought on the side of Turkey...

The Treaties of Peace alluded to in Article 25 were: The Treaty of Versailles signed with Germany on June 28th 1919; the Treaty of St. Germain-en-Laye signed with Austria on September 10th 1919; the Treaty of Neuilly-sur-Seine signed with Bulgaria on November 27th 1919; and the Treaty of Trianon signed with Hungary on June 4th 1920. All of these Peace Treaties, including the Treaty of Sèvres, inserted in their first part, the Covenant of the League of Nations.[23] Article 22 of the Covenant created the Mandate system whereby 'colonies and territories which as a consequence of the late war have ceased to be under the sovereignty of the States which formerly governed them' would eventually reach independence. This would be subject to an interim period in which they would be entrusted to the tutelage of an advanced nation on behalf of the League, who would give them advice and assistance until they could stand alone. This would include former Turkish colonies and territories.

The fourth paragraph of Article 22 of the Covenant refers specifically to colonies and territories which formerly belonged to the Turkish Empire and ceased to be so:

---

[23] https://avalon.law.yale.edu/20th_century/leagcov.asp

Certain Communities *formerly* belonging to the Turkish Empire have reached a stage of development where *their existence as independent nations* can be provisionally recognized subject to the rendering of administrative advice and assistance by a Mandatory until such time as they are able to stand alone... [Italics added].

By signing and ratifying the Treaty of Lausanne, Turkey under Ataturk recognized the full force of Article 22 of the Covenant. In fact, it accepted the reality that territories which were formerly under Turkish sovereignty ceased to be so. Turkey thus also consented to certain communities in those areas eventually achieving independence after having been subjected to a mandatory for a provisional period until they were self-sufficient. This could only mean the acceptance by Turkey, under the Treaty of Lausanne, of the eventual transfer of sovereignty from Turkey to the beneficiaries of those territories. The Turks had full knowledge from Articles 94 and 95 of the Treaty of Sèvres that the beneficiaries in the Middle East were the indigenous populations of Syria and Mesopotamia and the Jewish people with regard to Palestine.

Chapter IV

The British Mandate for Palestine

Legal Significance of the Mandate for Palestine

The third major step in the worldwide recognition of the Jewish legal right to Palestine under international law, and perhaps the most important of all, was the confirmation by the League of Nations of the instrument known as the British Mandate for Palestine. This legal right, coupled with the universal recognition of the Jewish historical connection with Palestine and the grounds for reconstituting their National Home, was finalized in the Mandate. The Mandate for Palestine became part of international law after being confirmed and approved first by the Council of the League of Nations on July 24th 1922, and later by the entire Assembly.[1] The Mandate instrument was an international treaty concluded between the League of Nations and the Mandatory, namely Great Britain.[2] Its sole object was the establishment of a National Home for the Jewish people, as a whole, in Palestine.[3] The Principal Allied

---

[1] Article 5 of the Covenant of the League of Nations required that any vote in the assembly, as well as in the Council, should be carried out unanimously. See also Grief, op. cit. p. 122; Yoram Dinstein – *The Arab Israeli Conflict from the Perspective of International Law*, 43 U.N.B.L.J. 301, 1994.

[2] Arnold McNair, in his separate judgment in the South West Africa case, stated emphatically that a mandate, which embodies international obligations, belongs to the category of treaty or convention. He then asserted that in the judgment of the Permanent Court of International Justice in the *Mavrommatis Palestine Concessions (Jurisdiction)* case, Series A, No. 2, p. 35, 'the Palestine Mandate was referred to as an "international agreement"; and I have endeavored to show that the agreement between the Mandatory and other Members of the League embodied in the Mandate is still "in force".' See McNair's separate opinion in the case of the *International Status of South West Africa*, ICJ Rep. 1950, [hereinafter referred to as *South West Africa case*], p. 158.

[3] It is common knowledge among international lawyers that treaties are a source of international law. The Statute of the Permanent Court of International Justice recognized this expressly in stating in Article 38 that the Court shall apply as a first source of international law 'international Conventions,

Powers agreed that the Mandatory *should be responsible* for putting into effect the Balfour Declaration. This was the raison d'être of the Mandate for Palestine. The indecisive wording in the Declaration, namely that the British Government 'will use their best endeavours to facilitate the achievement of this object' was used no more. Instead, a clear wording was introduced, making the Mandatory responsible for the establishment of the Jewish National Home. In fact, the Principal Allied Powers made it a condition on the Mandatory that it should be responsible to implement the Balfour Declaration in favor of the establishment in Palestine of a National Home for the Jewish people.

Britain had undertaken and committed itself to accomplishing this objective in conformity with the provisions of the Mandate. As such, this objective was binding on the British Government. But the commitment was also binding on the League of Nations as an international institution. For the League had given its approval to the Mandate, and was duty-bound to supervise the Mandatory in its endeavor to achieve that purpose as well as inspect annual reports and render the Mandatory answerable to any violations of the treaty. Britain had, in fact, undertaken to exercise the Mandate 'on behalf of the League of Nations' subjecting itself to its supervision. As will be observed, no such commitment was made in favor of the non-Jewish communities or Arabs in Palestine.

Universal recognition of the Mandate was further enhanced by the bilateral convention signed on December 3rd 1924 between the United States and Great Britain 'in respect to rights in Palestine'.[4]

---

whether general or particular, establishing rules expressly recognized by the contesting states', Oppenheim-Lauterpacht, Vol. I, op. cit., pp. 25, 26; see also J.L. Brierly – *The Law of Nations*, 4th ed. The Clarendon Press, Oxford 1950, p. 57; 'the subjects of international law include not only States but also international institutions such as the United Nations'; and J.G. Starke – *An Introduction to International Law*, 5th ed. Butterworths, 1963, p.460. In the same category was the League of Nations, which had entered into a treaty with Great Britain regarding the Mandate for Palestine.

4   http//:www.alliedpowersholocaust.org/wp-content/uploads/2015/03/1924-Anglo-American-Convention.pdf; Known as *the Anglo-American Convention* 1924. Its ratification was advised by the Senate on February 20th 1925, it was ratified by the President of the United States on March 2nd 1925, later ratified by Great Britain on March 18th 1925. Exchange of ratifications

This convention proved necessary since the United States was not a Member of the League of Nations and, therefore, was not bound by the Mandate instrument. The Convention embodied the Palestine Mandate verbatim, and the United States confirmed it by signing and ratifying the Convention. The United States consented to the British administration of Palestine pursuant to the provisions of the Mandate embodied in the Convention.[5]

The Mandate was the culmination of a series of interrelated international agreements designed for the sole purpose of establishing a Jewish National Home in Palestine. This began with the Balfour Declaration, proceeded to the San Remo agreement, continued to the Treaty of Sèvres, and ended with the confirmation of the Mandate instrument by the League of Nations. Each step increased and intensified the international recognition of the right of the Jewish people to a National Home in Palestine. The Balfour Declaration was a commitment made by the British Government and was only subsequently approved by the Principal Allied Powers. In the San Remo Resolution, the Principal Allied Powers unanimously decided on its terms and adopted it as signatories. The Treaty of Sèvres was not only signed by the Principal Allied Powers,[6] but also by the ten High Contracting Parties mentioned in the Treaty. The Mandate for Palestine was confirmed and approved by the League of Nations, which then comprised 51 states members, and was further approved by the United States. As Prof. Dinstein put it: 'It follows that virtually the whole international community, as it existed in the era between the two world wars, was legally committed to the Mandate for Palestine, which included the obligation to establish

---

occurred in London on December 3rd 1925. See Cmd. 2559, 1925.

5 Ibid. Article 1. On December 5th 1925, Calvin Coolidge, President of the United States, added an emphatic proclamation at the close of the Convention [which, as noted, embodied the Mandate for Palestine] to the effect that the Convention was to be made public to serve the purpose that 'every article and clause thereof may be observed and fulfilled with good faith by the United States and the citizens thereof'.

6 In the Treaty of Sèvres the British Empire alone comprised six signatories: Great Britain, Canada, Australia, New Zealand, South Africa and India, adding up to 19 signatories altogether.

in Palestine a National Home for the Jewish people.'[7]

The Mandate System – Article 22 of the Covenant of the League of Nations

The Mandate System was newly introduced by the Principal Allied Powers at the end of the First World War to replace annexation. Until then the customary method for victorious nations, at the end of major armed conflicts, was to apply sovereignty over territories which formerly belonged to the defeated. After the Fourteen Points speech delivered by President Wilson to Congress on January 8th 1918, it was decided by the Allies to abandon the concept of annexation and to adopt a different method to deal with territories occupied during the Great War. This accorded with President Wilson's fifth point, which advocated for the 'strict observance of the principle that in determining all such questions of sovereignty, the interests of the populations concerned have equal weight with the equitable claims of the Government whose title is to be determined'.[8]

Three options were discussed at the Peace Conference: (a) internationalization, (b) the Mandate System, and (c) annexation.[9] Internationalization was ruled out as a method that never succeeded wherever it was applied. Lloyd George condemned the first option and the French Colonial Minister, M. Simon, seconded him by noting that 'Similar experiments tried in the past had failed ignominiously'.[10] The British were in

---

[7] Dinstein, op. cit. p. 305.

[8] Lloyd George, op. cit., Vol. I, p. 529. In the Peel Report, op. cit., p. 40, it was stated: 'The Mandate system was mainly the outcome of American ideas. From the moment that the United States entered the War President Wilson made it clear that in his view such territorial readjustments as might result from victory should be made on different principles from those which had been followed at the close of previous wars. There were to be "no annexations" against the wishes of the people concerned. The principle of "national self determination" should be applied as far as possible.' But in this context the Peel Commission admitted that Palestine was unique and different from the other ex-Turkish provinces. The Arabs did not have the same claim to possess Palestine as they had to possess Syria or Mesopotamia.

[9] Lloyd George, ibid., Vol. I, pp. 516-17, 525-27.

[10] Lloyd George, ibid., Vol. I, p. 525.

favor of the Mandate system, but the French were hostile to this idea and preferred annexation. Annexation, enunciated by the French Minister for the Colonies, was the only system that would accomplish both objectives of a colonial government, namely the development of the country and the effective protection and progress of its natives.[11] However, the Mandate system took preference over all other options and was finally adopted by the Principal Allied Powers for deciding the future of the territories detached from Turkey and Germany after the First World War.

The scheme to replace annexation with the Mandate system was initially put forward by General Jan Smuts of South Africa, a statesman and soldier. Smuts submitted a memorandum entitled *The League of Nations – a Practical Suggestion* in which he proposed a new concept of a Power, administering a country as a Mandatory on behalf of the international community and under the supervision of an international body.[12] This concept was substantially different from annexation, since the Mandatory was not granted sovereignty and, therefore, could not act within those territories freely, except under the terms of the Mandate. The Mandate system was in fact alien to the concept of sovereignty, and the doctrine of sovereignty had no application to the new system of mandates.[13] In Oppenheim-Lauterpacht's opinion, the fact that 'Germany and Turkey divested themselves of all rights of ownership in the mandated areas was clear. That the mandatories had not acquired all of those rights was equally clear'.[14] On this assumption, the divested sovereignty of the vanquished lies with the Principal Allied Powers, who, under the Convention of San Remo and the Mandate for Palestine, did not confer it upon the Mandatory.[15]

---

[11] Ibid., p. 527.

[12] Norman Bentwich, *The Mandates System*, Longmans, Green & Co., London 1930, p.2.

[13] Arnold McNair's separate opinion in the South West Africa Case, ICJ, op. cit., p. 150.

[14] Oppenheim-Lauterpacht, Vol. I, op. cit., p. 193.

[15] Oppenheim-Lauterpacht remarked that there existed widely differing views on the question of where sovereignty in respect of the mandated areas

Power of the Allies to Dispose of Territories Captured from the Ottoman Empire

As Sovereignty over Middle East territories was transferred from Turkey to the Principal Allied Powers, the latter acquired the right to dispose of them in any way they agreed on.[16] Thus, it was agreed that territories captured from the Turkish Empire during the First World War should be divided between the Arab Nation as a whole and the Jewish people as a whole, and put under Mandatory administration until they were fit to stand alone. To those two peoples, the Allies, and particularly the British, made commitments during the War, namely 'to recognize and support the independence of the Arabs'[17] in the territories specified in the McMahon-Hussein correspondence, and to secure the establishment of a National Home for the Jewish people in Palestine, with the view that it would ultimately emerge as a Jewish State. When made, these two commitments did not seem

---

resides. Some authorities point at the Mandatory, others point at the Principal Allied Powers or at the League of Nations – the Mandatory acting with the consent of the Council of the League, yet others point at the inhabitants of the mandated area, being temporarily in suspense. See Oppenheim-Lauterpacht, Vol. I, ibid., notes at pp. 202-03. *Cf.* James Crawford – *The Creation of States in International Law*, Clarendon Press, Oxford, 2nd ed. 2006, p. 568. In an article entitled *Israel in Fieri*, Charles Henry Alexander, of Lincoln's Inn, barrister-at-Law, expressed the view that under the Treaty of Lausanne, sovereignty was transferred to the Principal Allied Powers, and that neither the League of Nations nor the Mandatory Powers acquired sovereignty. 4 Int'l L. Q. 423, 424, 1951.

[16] This view was put into practice by Britain and France at the instance of the decision of the Damascus Congress on March 8th 1920 to crown Emir Feisal King of Syria and his brother Emir Abdullah King of Mesopotamia. Lord Curzon as Foreign Secretary, in conjunction with the French Government, repudiated those actions and emphasized the position that the future of the territories in the Middle East, namely Syria, Mesopotamia and Palestine 'could be determined only by the Allied Powers...*in whose hands lay the construction of the Peace Treaty with Turkey and the settlement of the future of the areas belonging to the old Turkish Empire, which it had been decided to sever therefrom*'. [Italics added]. DBFP, op. cit., Vol. XIII, pp. 225, 226-7.

[17] Hurewitz, op. cit., p. 50. The Correspondence included a pledge made by the British Government through Sir Henry McMahon to Hussein, Sherif of Mecca, October 24th 1915. See further pp. 354 et seq., infra.

contradictory, but complementary.[18]

It should be emphasized that at the time these commitments were made, the Arabs formed one nation represented by Hussein, the Sherif of Mecca, later King of Hedjaz, and his son Emir Feisal. There were no Iraqi, Jordanian or Palestinian Arabs then as separate national entities. The commitments were made to the Arab Nation as a whole, including the Arabs of Palestine, through the Sherif of Mecca, on the one hand, and to the Jewish people as a whole, through the Zionist Federation, on the other hand. Both were made in consideration for wartime services to the Allies. No separate commitment was made to the Arab inhabitants of Palestine who, in fact, fought with the Turks against the Allies.

The Mandate system was eventually incorporated into Article 22 of the Covenant of the League of Nations, the latter forming the first part of each of the Treaties signed between the victors and the vanquished after the War.[19] Under the Mandate system, the territories detached from Turkey were not under the ownership of any Mandatory, but were entrusted for administration on behalf of the League of Nations on conditions laid down in written agreements between the Mandatory and the League.[20] This was a self-imposed limitation exercised by the Allied and Associated Powers regarding the sovereignty they acquired as conquerors over conquered territories. This was, as Balfour put it, 'in the interests of what they conceived to be the general welfare of mankind; and they have asked the League of Nations to assist them in seeing that this policy should be carried into effect. But

---

[18] For contradicting views see Gilbert Clayton – *An Arabian Diary*, University of California Press, 1969, p. 10. In Clayton's view, the following three commitments, namely the McMahon pledge, the Sykes-Picot agreement and the Balfour Declaration, which was embodied in the Mandate, were 'completely contradictory'.

[19] For the Treaties referred to see p. 188, n. 23 supra. As mentioned earlier, the Treaty of Sèvres was not ratified. However, in the Treaty of Lausanne, which was ratified, Turkey recognized the full force of the treaties referred to above, in which the Covenant was incorporated as an integral part thereof. Thus, Turkey acknowledged, in fact, the binding effect of Article 22 of the Covenant which applied the Mandate system to territories formerly belonging to her.

[20] Oppenheim-Lauterpacht, op. cit., Vol. I, pp. 192-93.

the League of Nations is not the author of the policy, but its instrument'.[21]

In a legal sense, Article 22 of the Covenant provided the constitutional authority under which the Mandate system functioned. Its origin was in a draft resolution submitted by Lloyd George in reference to Mandatories, which provided the basis on which Article 22 was formed.[22] Article 22 stated:

> To those colonies and territories which as a consequence of the late war have ceased to be under the sovereignty of the States which formerly governed them and which are inhabited by peoples not yet able to stand by themselves under the strenuous conditions of the modern world, there should be applied the principle that the well-being and development of such peoples form a sacred trust of civilisation and that securities for the performance of this trust should be embodied in this Covenant.
>
> The best method of giving practical effect to this principle is that the tutelage of such peoples should be entrusted to advanced nations who by reason of their resources, their experience or their geographical position can best undertake this responsibility, and who are willing to accept it, and that this tutelage should be exercised by them as Mandatories on behalf of the League.
>
> The character of the mandate must differ according to the stage of the development of the people, the geographical situation of the territory, its economic conditions and other similar circumstances.
>
> Certain communities formerly belonging to the Turkish Empire have reached a stage of development where their existence as independent nations can be provisionally recognized subject to the rendering of administrative advice and assistance by a Mandatory

---

[21] C.P. 3998, May 17th 1922, Balfour addressing the Council of the League of Nations at a public sitting in Geneva.

[22] Lloyd George, op. cit., Vol. I, pp. 538-41.

until such time as they are able to stand alone. The wishes of these communities must be a principal consideration in the selection of the Mandatory. [*Referred to as 'A' Mandate*].

Other peoples, especially those of Central Africa, are at such a stage that the Mandatory must be responsible for the administration of the territory under conditions which will guarantee freedom of conscience and religion, subject only to the maintenance of public order and morals... [*Referred to as 'B' Mandate*].

There are territories, such as South-West Africa and certain of the South Pacific Islands... which can be best administered under the laws of the Mandatory as integral portions of its territory, subject to the safeguards above mentioned in the interests of the indigenous population. [*Referred to as 'C' Mandate*].

In every case of mandate, the Mandatory shall render to the Council an annual report in reference to the territory committed to its charge.

The degree of authority, control, or administration to be exercised by the Mandatory shall, if not previously agreed upon by the Members of the League, be explicitly defined in each case by the Council.

A permanent Commission shall be constituted to receive and examine the annual reports of the Mandatories and to advise the Council on all matters relating to the observance of the mandates.

The use of the phrase 'a sacred trust of civilisation' in the first paragraph of Article 22, and the term 'trust' in the second, was influenced by the concept of trust in English and American Law. In Brierly's view 'the governing principle of the Mandates System is to be found in the trust.'[23] McNair added that 'the English courts have for many centuries pursued a vigorous policy

---

[23] J.L. Brierly, *British Year Book of International Law*, Oxford University Press,1929, pp. 217-19, quoted by McNair in the South West Africa Case, op. cit., p. 148-49; See also Bentwich, op. cit., pp. 7-8.

in the administration and enforcement of trusts'.[24]

In nearly every legal system, the institution of trust is based on three general principles: (a) The trustee's power over entrusted property was limited. He was not the owner of the entrusted property, and was not allowed to administer the property for his own benefit, as an owner would be entitled to do. (b) The trustee was under a legal obligation to carry out the trust for the benefit of the beneficiary. (c) Any attempt by the trustee to take hold of the property entrusted to him and treat it as his own would be considered illegal. These principles are akin to the Mandate system. In a nutshell, a trust confers upon the trustee obligations only, and upon the beneficiary rights only, while the trustee is precluded from deriving any personal benefit from the trust.[25]

These principles were applied in several court decisions: In *Rex v. Christian* [1924], before the Supreme Court of South Africa, it was stated that the territory transferred to the Mandatory does not give the latter full title over that territory, but is held by him in the same manner as 'a trustee is in possession of the property of the *cestui que trust* or a guardian of the property of his ward. The former has the administration and control of the property but the property has to be administered exclusively in the interests of the latter'.[26] Again, in the Australian case of *Frost v. Stevenson* (1937), it was stated that 'the mandatory as a kind of international trustee, receives the territory subject to the provisions of the mandate which limit the exercise of the governmental powers of the mandatory'.[27] The idea of the Mandate system was to achieve a transfer of a territory without putting that territory in the ownership of the mandatory. In McNair's view, the new Mandate regime established in pursuance of the principle that the well-being and development of such peoples form a sacred

---

[24] McNair, ibid., p. 149.

[25] McNair in the South West Africa Case, ibid.; Bentwich op. cit. pp. 7-8.

[26] *Rex v. Christian*, South African Law Reports [1924] Appellate Division, p. 121, J. de Villiers, Judge of Appeal, quoted by McNair in the South West Africa Case, op. cit. pp. 150-51.

[27] *Frost v. Stevenson* (1937), 58 Commonwealth Law Reports 528, Annual Digest and Reports of Public International Law Cases 1935-1937, case No. 29, in the High Court of Australia, on appeal from the Supreme Court of New South Wales, quoted in the *South West Africa case*, p. 152.

trust of civilization 'has more than a purely contractual basis, and the territories subjected to it are impressed with a special legal status'.[28]

Article 22 divided the mandates into three categories, often referred to as: 'A', 'B', and 'C', in descending order of development of the benefitting inhabitants, and their ability to stand alone 'under the strenuous conditions of the modern world'. Category 'A' comprised the territories of Syria, Lebanon, Mesopotamia and Palestine, who formerly belonged to the Turkish Empire and whose communities have reached a degree of development which may make them, under certain conditions, eligible to be provisionally recognized as independent States. Those conditions are 'the rendering of administrative advice and assistance by a mandatory' until such time as they are able to govern themselves. Category 'B' comprised mainly the less developed peoples of Central Africa, who required guidance and were as of yet far from able to achieve independence. Category 'C' comprised the under developed people of South West Africa and certain Pacific Islands.

The general aim of the Mandate system was the tutelage of the inhabitants and their development towards self-governance or independence. The fulfillment of this purpose was aimed at particularly in respect of the 'A' Mandate, even though it was not expressly mentioned in Article 22 of the Covenant. The intention was that the mandate 'should come to an end when the infant nation has reached a stage at which it may be able to stand alone. The purpose of the Mandate would then be fulfilled, and the minor would be emancipated and recognized by the Society as an independent State.'[29]

Analysis of the Palestine Mandate

The sole purpose of the British Mandate for Palestine was the establishment of a National Home for the Jewish people, an eventual Jewish State. All other provisions of the Mandate had subsidiary connotations. This could be easily inferred from the

---

[28] South West Africa case, ibid., p. 154.

[29] Crawford, op. cit., p. 566; Bentwich, op. cit., pp. 16-17.

Mandate instrument itself and from other related documentation.

Recitals two and three in the Preamble of the Palestine Mandate stated:

> Whereas the Principal Allied Powers have also agreed that the Mandatory should be responsible for putting into effect the declaration originally made on November 2nd 1917, by the Government of His Britannic Majesty, and adopted by the said Powers, in favor of the establishment in Palestine of a National Home for the Jewish people, it being clearly understood that nothing should be done which might prejudice the civil and religious rights of existing non-Jewish communities in Palestine, or the rights and political status enjoyed by Jews in any other country; and…

> Whereas recognition has thereby been given to the historical connection of the Jewish people with Palestine and to the grounds for reconstituting their National Home in that country…

The gist of the Mandate system in accordance with Article 22 of the Covenant was to entrust the tutelage of the inhabitants of the occupied territories to a Mandatory whose responsibility would ultimately be to prepare them through guidance and development for self-rule or independence. This was the outcome in Syria, Lebanon and Mesopotamia. However, in Palestine the situation was different. There was no intention on the part of the Principal Allied Powers of promoting Palestine to become another Arab State. The main plan, if not the sole one, was the creation in Palestine of a National Home for the Jewish people, and for no other. 'Unquestionably … the primary purpose of the Mandate, *as expressed in its preamble and its articles*, is to promote the establishment of the Jewish National Home' [italics in the original].[30]

As mentioned earlier, after conquering the Middle East from

---

[30] Peel Report, op. cit. p. 39.

the Turks, the Principal Allied Powers agreed to divide the entire area between the Arab nation and the Jewish people. The overwhelming majority of the area was allotted to the Arabs (i.e., Syria, Lebanon, and Mesopotamia), while Palestine was allotted, in conformity with the Balfour Declaration, to the Jewish people.

However, the Jewish people were then scattered all over the globe, and only a fraction inhabited Palestine. Under these circumstances it was not feasible to grant the Jewish people independence in a territory with inhabitants comprised mainly of non-Jews – even though there were clear signs that the Jewish minority in Palestine had reached the stage of development adequate to stand by itself within the meaning of Article 22 of the Covenant.[31] Evidently, it was obvious to the Principal Allied Powers that for the sake of securing the establishment of the Jewish National Home in Palestine, development in stages under the protection of a mighty power was required. During this time the Jews in Palestine would become a majority and take over the country.

Yet, transforming the Jews in Palestine from a significant minority into a clear majority was not an easy task. This could not be achieved unless the Mandatory acted one-sidedly in favor of the Jewish people – without taking any action which might prejudice the civil and religious rights of the existing non-Jewish communities in Palestine. The Mandatory of Palestine was therefore expected to take all necessary measures in favor of the Jewish people to secure the establishment of the Jewish National Home. In particular, it needed to facilitate Jewish immigration, encourage close settlement by Jews on the land, allow acquisition of Palestinian citizenship by Jews, and enable Jews to purchase land for development. It is evident that the Mandate for Palestine had provided everything necessary to achieve this goal. No similar political commitments were made in favor of the non-Jewish communities in Palestine. In Akzin's view, 'The confirmation of the Palestine Mandate by the Council of the League must be considered as an authoritative affirmation

---

[31] Peel Report, ibid., pp. 47-50.

of its consistency with Article 22 of the Pact'.[32]

There was, therefore, a fundamental dissimilarity between the Mandate for Palestine on the one hand and the Mandates for Syria, Lebanon and Mesopotamia on the other hand:

> The Mandate [for Palestine] is of a different type from the Mandate for Syria and the Lebanon and the draft Mandate for Iraq…the acceptance by the Allied Powers and the United States of the Policy of the Balfour Declaration made it clear from the beginning that Palestine would have to be treated differently from Syria and Iraq, and that this difference of treatment was confirmed by the Supreme Council in the Treaty of Sèvres and by the Council of the League in sanctioning the Mandate.[33]

In the Palestine Mandate, the main theme was the implementation of the Balfour Declaration in favor of the establishment of a National Home for the Jewish people – even though they were not then the majority inhabitants of Palestine. On the other hand, the theme in the Mandates for Mesopotamia, Syria and Lebanon was the framing of an organic law in consultation or in agreement with the native authorities. This would take into account the rights, interests and wishes of all the populations inhabiting those territories for the purpose of facilitating their progressive development as independent states. On February 19th 1919, Balfour wrote to Lloyd George:

> Our justification for our policy is that we regard Palestine as being absolutely exceptional; that we consider the question of the Jews outside Palestine as one of world importance, and that we conceive the Jews to have an historic claim to a home in their ancient land; provided that home can be given them without either dispossessing or oppressing the present

---

[32] Akzin, Benjamin – *The Palestine Mandate in Practice*, 25 Iowa L. R. 32, 1939-1940, p. 49.

[33] The Peel Report, op. cit., p. 38.

inhabitants.[34]

It was through the initiative of the Allied and Associated Powers to subject the Mandates to the supervision of the League of Nations. This was done 'in the interests of what they conceived to be the general welfare of mankind'.[35] Balfour, addressing the Council as a League Member, commented on the League's role in the implementation of the Mandate system:

> The mandates are not our creation. The mandates are neither made by the League nor can be altered by the League. Our duties are of two kinds. It is our business in the first place to see that the specific and detailed terms of the mandates are in accordance with the decisions come to be by the Allied and Associated Powers in Article 22 of the Treaty of Versailles, and, in the second place, to see that, in carrying out those mandates, the mandatory Power shall be under the supervision – not the control, but the supervision – of the League of Nations, which possesses an admirable organization through which it can obtain the fullest information as to the method in which each mandatory Power fulfils the duties which are entrusted to it.[36]

The subjection of the Mandatory to the supervision of the League was incorporated into the mandate instrument. Thus, the British Mandate for Palestine was proclaimed under the auspices of the League of Nations. Like other mandates, it was submitted to the Council of the League for approval, and the Council confirmed the Mandate subject to its terms and provisions. The Mandate was to be exercised on behalf of the League of Nations and Britain undertook to do so in conformity with its provisions.[37] It was also stipulated that in accordance

---

[34] F.O. 371/4179/2117, quoted in Friedman, op. cit. p. 325

[35] C.P. 3998, May 17th 1922, op. cit. pp. 3-4.

[36] Ibid., p. 3.

[37] Preamble of the Palestine Mandate, 6th Recital; the phrase 'On behalf of the League' should not be interpreted to mean a relationship between principal

with paragraph 8 of Article 22 of the Covenant, any degree of authority, control or administration that had not been previously specified with Members of the League should be explicitly defined by the Council of the League of Nations. The power and authority conferred upon the Mandatory were therefore limited to those which had been specified in the Mandate instrument. Any deviation had to receive the consent of the Council of the League.[38]

Moreover, it was obligatory upon the Mandatory to submit to the Council of the League an annual report. This report had to receive the approval of the Council, the latter having full authority to reject a superficial report or one not up to the standards of the Council. The report was required to enumerate and specify 'the measures taken during the year to carry out the provisions of the mandate'.[39] Copies of all laws and regulations promulgated during the year had to be attached to the report. The submission of all laws and regulations for the inspection of the Commission could result in a decrease in the Mandatory's full powers of legislation under Article 1. The British Mandatory assumed full responsibility and was responsible solely to the League of Nations for the Holy Places. It also possessed full authority to appoint a special Commission, however, 'the method of nomination, the composition and the functions of this Commission shall be submitted to the Council of the League for its approval, and the Commission shall not be appointed or enter upon its functions without the approval of the Council'.[40]

In the Palestine Mandate, 'the Consent of the Council of the

---

and agent, but rather as that between a trustee and a tribunal to whom the former has a duty to render an account of his administration. Bentwich, op. cit. p. 7; see Rex v. Christian [1924] South African Law Reports, p. 148 (Innes C.J., McNair J. concurring).

[38] Preamble of the Palestine Mandate, 7th Recital. This provided another indication that sovereignty over Palestine was not transferred to Great Britain as Mandatory. Britain was granted in Article 1 of the Mandate full powers to legislate and administer Palestine, but only in conformity with the provisions of the Mandate.

[39] The Mandate for Palestine, Cmd. 1785, HMSO, London, December 1922, Article 24.

[40] Ibid., Articles 13 and 14.

League of Nations is required for any modification of the terms of this mandate'.[41] The Mandatory had to adhere to any general international conventions 'which may be concluded hereafter with the approval of the League of Nations respecting the slave traffic etc...'[42] The Mandatory also had to cooperate any common policy adopted by the League of Nations for preventing and combating disease.[43] In the event of the termination of the Mandate, the Council had to make arrangements to safeguard in perpetuity the rights regarding the Holy Places as well as the rights of public servants to pensions or gratuities.[44]

As mentioned, the establishment of the National Home for the Jewish people was the main theme of the Palestine Mandate. In the Preamble, the character and foundation of the Mandate was formed and defined. This was mainly in asserting the right of the Jewish people to a national home in Palestine and the will of the Principal Allied Powers to realize this objective. The Council of the League of Nations recognized the authority of the Principal Allied Powers to entrust to the Mandatory the administration of the territory of Palestine, fix its boundaries, and confer on it the responsibility for putting into effect the Balfour Declaration. The establishment of a Jewish National Home in Palestine would take into consideration 'the historical connection of the Jewish people with Palestine and to the grounds for reconstituting their

---

[41] Ibid., Article 27. At the 12th Meeting of the Council of the League of Nations, July 22nd 1922, where all members were present, it was decided that alterations in 'A' mandates, as in 'B' and 'C' mandates, required unanimity, and could not be effected by a majority, C.P. 4125, July 25th 1922, p. 140. At first sight, Article 27 may seem to contradict the words of Balfour in his address to the Council on May 17th 1922, stating that 'the mandates are neither made by the League nor can be altered by the League.' [See p. 204, n. 36, supra.] However, this seemingly discrepancy could be explained by the claim that although modification of *the terms* of the Mandate was possible subject to the consent of the Council, altering the substance of the Mandate was not within the power of the Council since sovereignty of those territories remained vested in the Principal Allied Powers. Therefore, as Balfour asserted, the Mandate concept for Palestine could not be altered or modified, not even with the consent of the Council of the League.

[42] Ibid., Article 19.

[43] Ibid., Article 20.

[44] Ibid., Article 28.

National Home in that country.'[45]

Recognition of the 'historical connection' implied the acknowledgement by the Principal Allied Powers and the League of Nations of the validity and legality of the Jewish association with Palestine, signifying that the establishment of a Jewish homeland in that country was not a colonial project. It was, in fact, a sign of an ancient people returning to their homeland. As Feinberg put it: 'In so far as it [the Palestine Mandate] grants the Jewish people the right to return to Palestine and reconstitute there its National Home – thus recognizing the Jewish people as a subject of international law – the Mandate is constitutive of that right and therefore law-making'.[46] This meant recognizing the reasons, basis and justification of the Jewish people to reconstitute their national home in Palestine, distinguishing the Palestine Mandate from the others. While the Mandates for Syria, Lebanon, and Mesopotamia were established to bring about Arab States in those territories for the first time, the Mandate for Palestine was designed to reconstitute a Jewish homeland on the remnants of a Jewish State that had already existed in that area, a Jewish connection that had never ceased during the eighteen centuries of the Diaspora.

This was well-observed in the Peel Report:

> While the Jews had thus been dispersed over the world, *they had never forgotten Palestine…* Judaism and its ritual are rooted in those memories. Among countless illustrations it is enough to cite the fact that Jews, wherever they may be, still pray for rain at the season it is needed in Palestine. And the same devotion to the land of Israel, *Eretz Israel*, the same sense of exile from it, permeates Jewish secular thought. Some of the finest Hebrew poetry written

---

[45] Preamble of the Palestine Mandate, 3ʳᵈ Recital. The recognition given to the right of the Jewish people to reconstitute its national home in Palestine was a big step forward towards recognition of the return of the Jews to their homeland as a right and not on sufferance.

[46] Nathan Feinberg – *The recognition of the Jewish people in International Law*, 1 Jewish Y.B. Int'l L. pp. 16-17, 1948.

in the Diaspora has been inspired like the psalms of the Captivity by *the longing to return to Zion.* [Italics added].

Nor has the link been merely spiritual or intellectual. Always or almost always since the fall of the Jewish State some Jews have been living in Palestine…But, small though their numbers were, the continued existence of those Jews in Palestine meant much to all Jewry. Multitudes of poor and ignorant Jews in the ghettos of Eastern Europe felt themselves represented, as it were, by this remnant of their race who were keeping a foothold in the land against the day of the coming of the Messiah.

This belief in the divine promise of eventual return to Palestine largely accounts for the steadfastness with which the Jews of the Diaspora clung to their faith and endured persecution.[47]

The Mandate comprised three categories of provisions:

1) those in favor of the Jewish people designed to secure the establishment of the Jewish National Home;

2) those in favor of the existing non-Jewish Communities of Palestine for the purpose of safeguarding their civil and religious rights;

3) those applying equally to the whole population of Palestine devoid of any discrimination on the grounds of race, religion or language.

Provisions in the Palestine Mandate Designed to Secure the Establishment of the Jewish National Home

In addition to Recitals 2 and 3 in the Preamble, the following provisions may be regarded as pertinent:

---

[47] The Peel Report, op. cit. pp. 11-12; See also Gribetz, op. cit. p. 10, reaffirming that love of Palestine and a desire for the restoration therein of a Jewish Commonwealth predominated the eighteen centuries of Jewish dispersion. The more the Jew suffered from hostility and persecution the more he clung to his desire for the reconstitution of his National Home.

Article 2

The Mandatory shall be responsible for placing the country under such political, administrative and economic conditions as will secure the establishment of the Jewish national home, as laid down in the preamble, and the development of self-governing institutions, and also for safeguarding the civil and religious rights of all the inhabitants of Palestine, irrespective of race and religion.

Article 4

An appropriate Jewish agency shall be recognised as a public body for the purpose of advising and co-operating with the Administration of Palestine in such economic, social and other matters as may affect the establishment of the Jewish national home and the interests of the Jewish population in Palestine, and, subject always to the control of the Administration to assist and take part in the development of the country.

The Zionist organization, so long as its organisation and constitution are in the opinion of the Mandatory appropriate, shall be recognised as such agency. It shall take steps in consultation with His Britannic Majesty's Government to secure the co-operation of all Jews who are willing to assist in the establishment of the Jewish national home.

Article 6

The Administration of Palestine, while ensuring that the rights and position of other sections of the population are not prejudiced, shall facilitate Jewish immigration under suitable conditions and shall encourage, in co-operation with the Jewish agency referred to in Article 4, close settlement by Jews on the land, including State lands and waste lands not required for public purposes.

Article 7

The Administration of Palestine shall be responsible for enacting a nationality law. There shall be included in this law provisions framed so as to facilitate the acquisition of Palestinian citizenship by Jews who take up their permanent residence in Palestine.

Article 11

The Administration may arrange with the Jewish agency mentioned in Article 4 to construct or operate, upon fair and equitable terms, any public works, services and utilities, and to develop any of the natural resources of the country, in so far as these matters are not directly undertaken by the Administration. Any such arrangements shall provide that no profits distributed by such agency, directly or indirectly, shall exceed a reasonable rate of interest on the capital, and any further profits shall be utilised by it for the benefit of the country in a manner approved by the Administration.

Article 22

English, Arabic and Hebrew shall be the official languages of Palestine. Any statement or inscription in Arabic on stamps or money in Palestine shall be repeated in Hebrew and any statement or inscription in Hebrew shall be repeated in Arabic.

A most important provision to supplement the wording of Recitals 2 and 3 in the Preamble was Article 2 of the Mandate. This made it the responsibility and duty of the British Government to place the whole country of Palestine, without excluding any part of it, under political, administrative and economic conditions necessary to secure – not just facilitate – the establishment of *the* Jewish National Home as laid down in the Preamble. For the first time the definite article was used, with a specifying and particularizing effect, as opposed to the indefinite article (establishment of *a* Jewish National Home) used in the Balfour Declaration, San Remo Resolution, and Treaty of Sèvres.

It was, therefore, incumbent on the British Government to prepare the country politically, administratively and economically for the purpose of bringing about the reconstruction of the Jewish National Home. An example of political conditions might be laying the foundations for the involvement of the Jewish Agency, or the Jewish inhabitants of Palestine, in governmental and public affairs, and the development of self-governing institutions. Moreover, British policy in Palestine should have been clearly defined in accordance with the Mandate by incorporating the Mandate into the law of the land as its constitution to make it binding on the Administration and its civil servants. Civil servants were to receive direct instructions in this regard and chosen to fulfill the aim embodied in the Mandate. The Mandatory was also required to place the country under such economic conditions so as to be able to absorb mass Jewish immigration and settle them in the land, allowing and encouraging the development of industry, commerce and agriculture. Article 2 furthermore charged the Mandatory with the duty to secure the development of self-governing institutions which could be regarded as a necessity for achieving self-rule.[48] As will be seen, most of these requirements were not met.

More specifically, the Mandatory was required to work closely with the Jewish Agency as a public body representing the Jewish people. This would act in an official capacity as an advisory body to the Administration of Palestine in all matters – economic, social or other. The Peel Commission remarked that no similar body was envisaged for dealing with Arab interests.[49] The Jewish Agency was also given the preferential position of constructing or operating public works, services and utilities, and developing the natural resources of the country. It was further open to all Jews, wherever they might be, to cooperate and assist in the establishment of their national home. Moreover, the Jewish Agency was also acknowledged as representing the interests of the individual Jewish inhabitants of Palestine.[50]

The building up in Palestine of Jewish immigration was the primary tool for Jewish national aspirations. Their absorption was

[48] *Cf.* Aktzin, op. cit., pp. 57-58.
[49] Peel Report, op. cit., para. 42(5), p. 39.
[50] Articles 4 and 11 of the Palestine Mandate.

key for the purpose of transforming the Jewish population from an insignificant minority to a significant majority. Allowing Jewish immigration was essential to the British commitment to establish the Jewish National Home. The Palestine Administration was therefore required, under 'suitable conditions' to facilitate Jewish immigration and encourage close settlement of Jews in the land. These included lands in possession of the Administration as 'state lands and waste lands not required for public purposes'.[51] No similar provision was made facilitating immigration of non-Jews from Arab countries or encouraging their settlement in Palestine. In fact, the Mandatory had no commitment to non-Jews living outside Palestine.

The British Administration also had to enact a nationality law, with provisions designed 'to facilitate the acquisition of Palestinian citizenship by Jews who take up their permanent residence in Palestine'.[52] No similar provision was made to facilitate the acquisition of Palestinian citizenship by non-Jews.

Hebrew, in conjunction with English and Arabic, was recognized as an official language in Palestine.[53]

The Mandatory of Palestine was thus charged with multiple obligations: Jewish immigration, Jewish settlement of the land, Jewish concessions, and facilities offered to Jews for the acquisition of Palestinian citizenship. In addition, the safeguarding of the civil and religious rights of the non-Jewish communities in Palestine was to be guaranteed. Taken as a whole, the purpose of the Mandate was to change the ratio between Jews and non-Jews in Palestine, transforming the former into a majority. As such, the latter would then receive safeguards for their protection if proven necessary. It should be remembered that the ratio between Jews and non-Jews at the beginning of the Mandate was 1:10 in favor of the non-Jewish population. Of course, safeguarding provisions were not meant to protect the non-Jewish population in Palestine

---

[51] Article 6 of the Palestine mandate. In Akzin's view 'under suitable conditions' must be understood to mean the application of 'such generally reasonable and suitable conditions as passports, visas, health examinations, and similar methods of reasonable supervision.' Akzin, op. cit. p. 61.

[52] Article 7 of the Palestine Mandate.

[53] Article 22 of the Palestine Mandate.

if they were to remain a significant majority.[54]

In Temperley's view, the Mandate granted nearly all that Zionist representatives asked for at the Paris Peace Conference in 1919, namely, that the Principal Allied powers recognize the historical connection of the Jewish people with Palestine, and their right to reconstitute their National Home in that country; that Britain should become the Mandatory on behalf of the League of Nations; that the Mandatory should be responsible for the creation of such political, administrative and economic conditions that would eventually lead to an autonomous commonwealth. They also asked that Britain should promote Jewish immigration and close settlement on land; that the Mandatory should co-operate in economic matters with the Jewish Agency as representing the Jews of Palestine and the world, and accept the right of the Jewish people to maintain their own schools and conduct their own education in their own language; and that 'the Mandatory should confer the widest possible measures of self-government upon localities.'[55] However, as we shall see, much of the Mandate original provisions have been diluted after Balfour.[56]

Provisions in the Palestine Mandate Designed to Safeguard Civil and Religious Rights of Non-Jewish Communities

Provisions of the second category, namely those designed to safeguard the rights of non-Jewish communities in Palestine, were subsidiary to the purpose of the Mandate. As mentioned above, implementation of the Balfour Declaration was the purpose of the Palestine Mandate, which included protecting the rights of non-Jewish communities living then in Palestine. However, these were confined to civil and religious rights, but not national/ political rights. National/political rights were granted to the Jewish people alone. Safeguarding the rights of the non-Jewish population would be necessary only if the establishment of the

---

[54] See Aktzin, op. cit., p. 54.

[55] Temperley, Vol. VI, op. cit. pp. 175-76.

[56] See pp. 216 et seq., infra.

Jewish National Home was planned. Therefore, 'it being clearly understood that nothing should be done which might prejudice the civil and religious rights of existing non-Jewish communities in Palestine…' (in the second Recital of the Preamble) is only relevant in as much as the establishment of the Jewish National Home in Palestine was the Mandate's primary objective.

Similarly, the Administration of Palestine would not have been required in Article 6 to ensure 'that the rights and position of other sections of the population are not prejudiced' if not for its obligation to facilitate Jewish immigration under suitable conditions and to encourage close settlement of Jews in the land.

Only on two occasions did the Mandate specifically refer to the protection of Islam in Palestine. In Article 9, it stated: 'In particular, the control and administration of Wakfs[57] shall be exercised in accordance with religious law and the dispositions of the founders'. And in Article 13 it was provided 'that nothing in this mandate shall be construed as conferring upon the Mandatory authority to interfere with the fabric or the management of purely Moslem sacred shrines, the immunities of which are guaranteed.'

The rights of the non-Jewish communities in Palestine (predominantly Arabs) as enumerated in the Mandate were found to be meticulously safeguarded, and on these terms the Mandate was unanimously approved. As Balfour put it, addressing the Council of the League of Nations prior to the approval of the Mandate:

> It had been represented that the interests of the Arabs were not sufficiently safeguarded, but the most anxious attention had been paid to the position and interests of the Arab populations by the British Government, and there was no wish or intention that the provision of a Jewish home in Palestine should in any way injure the best interests of the Arabs. Every precaution had been taken that the provision of a

---

[57] 'In Arabic, the term *Wakf* implies a religious endowment fund made by a Muslim, which renders a property unalienable, incapable of being surrendered or transferred.' See definition by Lexico, Oxford Dictionaries, https://www.lexico.com/en/definition/waqf

Jewish home should not encroach upon the interests or susceptibilities of any section of the population.[58]

The Mandate instrument provides the best indication of its main purpose. In fact, the Palestine Mandatory was charged with two sets of duties: those towards the Jewish people and those towards the existing non-Jewish communities in Palestine. The first demanded positive action: the establishment of the National Home and what it entailed in the form of immigration, settlement in the land, and economic growth. However, the second was mainly passive in character: refraining from taking any action that might prejudice minority civil and religious rights. These two sets of duties can only be reasonably construed as meaning that any conditions newly introduced by the Mandatory in favor of the establishment or development of the Jewish national home should not prejudice the civil and religious rights of existing non-Jewish communities in Palestine.[59]

Most of the remaining provisions of the Mandate for Palestine belong to a third category, which applies equally to the whole population of Palestine devoid of any discrimination on the ground of race, religion or language.

Provisions in the Palestine Mandate Applying Equally to the Entire Population

As noted, the Mandatory's primary obligation was to secure the establishment of a National Home for the Jews in Palestine, granting them national/political rights. In addition, the Mandatory had the responsibility to safeguard the civil and religious rights of all the inhabitants of Palestine, irrespective of race or religion.[60]

---

[58] C.P. 4125, July 25th 1922, pp. 145-46. The Council obviously found no contradiction between the establishment of the Jewish National Home and the protection of the civil and religious rights of non-Jewish communities in Palestine. Contradiction arose only when there was a change of heart in British policy, with Arab interests given wider significance compared to the establishment of the Jewish National Home. See pp. 290 et seq., infra.

[59] *Cf.* Akzin, op. cit., p. 58.

[60] The Palestine Mandate, op. cit., Article 2.

Therefore, in civil and religious matters the Jews of Palestine did not enjoy any privileges that their non-Jewish counterparts did not enjoy. The Mandatory had to encourage local autonomy for all,[61] applying the judicial system to foreigners and natives alike to completely guarantee their rights.[62] It had to respect the personal status of the various peoples and communities and their religious interests.[63] It had to safeguard all community interests in the development of the country, introducing a land system appropriate to its needs.[64] It had to take responsibility for the freedom to worship – providing free access to religious sites and free exercise of religion.[65] It had to guarantee complete freedom of conscience to all[66] and the right of each community to maintain its own schools for the education of its own members in its own language.[67] It had to refrain from interfering with or obstructing, subject to general supervision, the activities of religious or eleemosynary bodies of all faiths in Palestine and discriminating against any member of them on grounds of religion or nationality.[68] Finally, it had to recognize the holy days of the respective communities in Palestine as legal days of rest for all members of these communities.[69]

Steps Taken to Dilute the Palestine Mandate

Two stages can be observed in the course of drafting the Palestine Mandate. The first was during the time Balfour held the office of Secretary of State and the second was after Balfour left office on October 23rd 1919. Balfour was superseded by

---

[61] Ibid., Article 3. See Temperley, Vol. VI, op. cit., p. 176: 'While establishing the conditions necessary for the creation of the National Home for the Jewish People, it accords no rights to individual Jews as citizens that it does not equally accord to individuals of any other race or faith'.

[62] Ibid., Article 9.

[63] Ibid.

[64] Ibid., Article 11.

[65] Ibid., Article 13.

[66] Ibid., Article 15.

[67] Ibid.

[68] Ibid., Article 16.

[69] Ibid., Article 23.

Curzon, and during the latter's period in office many efforts were made to dilute the Mandate by altering its main provisions, particularly those concerned, directly or indirectly, with the establishment of the Jewish National Home. In a memorandum submitted on November 30th 1920,[70] Curzon made no secret of this fact. He admitted that the Palestine Mandate 'passed through several revises and was largely rewritten'. Curzon blamed those revises on the French and Italian Governments, who, in Curzon's words, 'at once excited their vehement criticisms on the ground of its almost exclusively Zionist complexion and of the manner in which the interests and rights of the Arab majority (amounting to about nine-tenths of the population) were ignored.'[71] According to Curzon, the Mandate was largely rewritten to receive their consent. This explanation does not hold water. The French and Italian Governments were aware of the meaning and amplifications of the Jewish National Home ever since they approved the Balfour Declaration. These were thoroughly debated at the Supreme Council Conference at San Remo, and it was Curzon, while acting for Balfour, who strived for the approval of the Jewish National Home.[72]

One of the most important revisions affecting the future rights of the Jewish people in Palestine was the exclusion of any insinuation that might indicate the eventual creation of a Jewish State or Commonwealth. The Draft of December 11th 1919, to which the British Government gave their consent, stated:

> The Mandatory shall be responsible for placing Palestine under such political, administrative and economic conditions as will secure the establishment of the Jewish National Home and *the development of a self-Governing Commonwealth*, it being clearly understood etc.[73] [Italics added].

---

[70] CAB. 24/115, C.P. 2197: Memorandum by the Secretary of State for Foreign Affairs, Mandates 'A'.

[71] Ibid.

[72] See pp. 149-55, supra.

[73] DBFP, op. cit., Vol. IV, p. 571, No. 397, Article 3, December 11th 1919, Draft Mandate for Palestine: Draft provisionally agreed upon between Zionist Organization and British Delegation.

The words in italics were omitted from subsequent drafts, thus the original vision of Balfour and other members of the British Cabinet that the Jewish National Home would eventually develop into an independent state was abolished. The idea behind the italicized phrase was first introduced in the Zionist proposals to members of the British delegation to the Peace Conference for the purpose of including them in the Mandate. Balfour commented on these proposals and approved the following statement: 'It [the Mandatory] shall aim at ultimate creation in Palestine of an 'autonomous Commonwealth''.[74] Later this was substituted for 'self-governing Commonwealth' by the British Delegation. The aim of the Mandatory to secure the ultimate creation in Palestine of a self-governing commonwealth reappeared in the Draft Treaty of Peace between Turkey and the Allied Governments[75] and also in further drafts until Balfour vacated his office.[76] Draft Mandates submitted by Curzon as Secretary of State failed to include this phrase in any way.

Another important revision was the attempt to delete from the draft Mandate the recognition given by the High Contracting Parties to the historical connection of the Jewish people with Palestine and the claim which this gives them to reconstitute Palestine as their National Home. In this context, the term Palestine was coupled with the term *Eretz Israel*, meaning 'the Land of Israel', as an indication of the true substance of Palestine. This term, as part of the Preamble, was meant to be approved by the League of Nations. The 'historical connection' was also first introduced by the Zionist Organization, but immediately adopted by Balfour and the British Government with the following alteration italicized: 'The High Contracting Parties recognise the historic connection of the Jewish people with Palestine *and*

---

[74] Rise of Israel: *Tension in Palestine – Peacemaking in Paris 1919*, Vol. 10, Garland Publishing Inc., New York & London, 1987, Doc. 60, p. 222, F.O. 608/99, March 24th 1919: Amendments to the Zionist proposals made by members of the British Delegation to the Peace Conference.

[75] Rise of Israel, Vol. 10, ibid., Doc. 81, p. 312, Art. 3, F.O. 371/4231/100141, July 9th 1919.

[76] Rise of Israel, Vol. 10, ibid.; see also DBFP, op. cit., Vol. IV. p.431. Appendix to Doc. 299, Memorandum by E.G. Forbes Adam, September 26th 1919,

the claim which this gives them to find a National Home in that country'.[77] In a subsequent draft, the British were prepared to adopt the full version by the Zionist Organization in the preamble to the Mandate providing:

> The High Contracting Parties: Recognising the historical connection of the Jewish people with Palestine and the claim which this gives them to reconstitute Palestine as their national home (Eretz Israel)...[78]

However, in the following draft Mandates of June 10th [79] and September 25th 1920,[80] which were submitted by Curzon as Foreign Secretary to the Cabinet for consideration, the provision recognizing the Jewish connection to Palestine was entirely erased from the text. Curzon explained why. In his memorandum dating November 30th 1920, he told the Cabinet that there were, in the course of the discussions, strong objections to this recognition, based on the following arguments:

> It was pointed out (1) that, while the Powers had unquestionably recognised the historical connection of the Jews with Palestine by their formal acceptance of the Balfour Declaration and their textual incorporation of it in the Turkish Peace Treaty drafted at San Remo, this was far from constituting anything in the nature of a legal claim, and that the use of

---

[77] Rise of Israel, Vol. 10, ibid., Doc. 60, p. 221, Amendments to the Zionist Proposals etc. Article 1; Rise of Israel, Vol. 10. Ibid., Doc. 81, p. 312, first Recital; DBFP, op. cit., Vol. IV, p. 429, Memorandum by Forbes Adam, Appendix, first Recital, September 26th 1919.

[78] DBFP, ibid., Vol. IV, p. 571, December 11th 1919, first Recital. Although Balfour was replaced by Curzon on October 24th 1919, the latter became active in the drafting of the Mandate only in mid-March 1920. Soon Curzon tried to water down the Zionist character of the document, see Grief, op. cit. p. 120.

[79] CAB 24/107, C.P. 1470, June 10th 1920, Inter-Departmental Conference on Middle Eastern Affairs: draft Mandate for Palestine.

[80] CAB 24/111, C.P. 1896, September 25th 1920, Declaration Constituting the Mandate for Palestine.

such words might be, and was, indeed, certain to be, used as a basis of all sorts of political claims by the Zionists for the control of Palestinian administration in the future, and (2) that, while Mr. Balfour's Declaration had provided for the establishment of a Jewish National Home in Palestine, this was not the same thing as the reconstitution of Palestine as a Jewish National Home – an extension of the phrase for which there was no justification, and which was certain to be employed in the future as the basis for claims of the character to which I have referred.[81]

According to Curzon, Balfour 'admitted ... the force of the above contentions' and suggested the following alternative:

> And whereas recognition has thereby (i.e., by the Treaty of Sèvres) been given to the historical connection of the Jewish people with Palestine, and to the grounds for reconstituting their National Home in that country.[82]

There could be little doubt that the San Remo agreement embraced a legal commitment by the Principal Allied Powers in favor of the establishment in Palestine of a National Home for the Jewish people. The argumentation presented by Curzon was based on shallow reasoning. The Zionist Organization showed no interest in controlling Palestinian administration. This was clearly stated by the British Government itself in their White Paper of June 3rd 1922, also known as the Churchill White Paper:

> The Palestine Zionist Executive, has not desired to possess, and does not possess, any share in the general administration of the country. Nor does the special position assigned to the Zionist Organization in Article IV of the Draft Mandate for Palestine imply

---

[81] CAB 24/115, C.P. 2197, November 30th 1920, Memorandum by the Secretary of State for Foreign Affairs (Curzon).

[82] Ibid.

any such functions.[83]

Nevertheless, Curzon's insistence on the alteration had serious repercussions.[84] It paved the way for the detachment of what was later known as Trans-Jordan from Palestine, and fortified the distinction that was drawn between 'establishing the Jewish National Home *in* Palestine' and 'reconstituting Palestine as the Jewish National Home'. It was later contended by British officials that 'in Palestine' did not necessarily imply the establishment of the Jewish National Home in the whole of Palestine, but in part of Palestine. [85]

In the same way, immigration moved a long way from the original version accepted by the British under Balfour. Article 6 of the final draft of the Palestine Mandate now stated: 'The Administration of Palestine, while ensuring that the rights and position of other sections of the population are not prejudiced, shall facilitate Jewish immigration under suitable conditions'.[86] Thus, the terms 'British Government' or 'Mandatory' in the original version were substituted for 'Administration of Palestine'. The phrase 'shall promote Jewish immigration' was substituted

---

[83] The Avalon Project, 4th para. http://avalon.law.yale.edu/20th_century/brwh1922.asp

[84] It should be noted that recognition of the historical connection of the Jewish people to Palestine and the right to reconstitute Palestine as their National Home *did not* constitute part of the Balfour Declaration. However, they were acknowledged by the Foreign Office, by E.G. Forbes Adam and the British Delegation to the Paris Peace Talks and incorporated into the Draft of December 11th 1919, before the intervention of Curzon, see p. 219, supra.

[85] See for example the White Paper of June 3rd 1922, Cmd. 1700, regarding British policy in Palestine, op. cit., asserting that 'Jewish National Home in Palestine' did not mean 'that Palestine as a whole should be converted into a Jewish National Home, but that such a Home should be founded 'in Palestine', and Winston Churchill commented years later in a parliamentary debate that 'I entirely accept the distinction between making a Jewish National Home in Palestine and making Palestine a Jewish National Home. I think I was one of the first to draw that distinction.' Parliamentary Debates, H.C. Vol. 347, cc. 2172, May 23rd 1939. See also Akzin, op. cit. p. 55.

[86] Comparison was made mainly between the Mandate draft of December 11th 1919, before Curzon's involvement in the matter, and subsequent drafts which were prepared under the guidance of Curzon as Foreign Secretary.

for the phrase 'shall facilitate Jewish immigration under suitable conditions' and the words 'established rights' were substituted for 'rights and position' in the final draft. Thus was introduced for the first time, the obscure terminology of 'position', which was not defined.[87]

The substitution of 'Mandatory' in the former versions, for 'Administration' in the later ones, with regard to immigration, could not have been accidental. Immigration was the core of the Mandate for Palestine. It was the responsibility of the British Government to carry it through. It had international connotations since it affected Jews all over the world. It was not an internal affair of the Administration of Palestine alone. By this change, immigration was minimized in importance to become an internal affair of Palestine rather than an affair with worldwide repercussions.

In the same Article, the commitment to 'promote' Jewish immigration was watered down to a commitment to 'facilitate' Jewish immigration, and that would be carried out only 'under suitable conditions'. The latter term was later used as a pretext to minimize and later bring to a halt Jewish immigration on the reasoning that immigration required the safeguarding of the 'economic absorptive capacity' of the country. The foundation of this expression was first laid down in the 1922 White Paper[88] advocating that immigration of Jews to Palestine could not 'exceed whatever may be the economic capacity of the country at the time to absorb new arrivals'. This was later adopted by the British Government as an excuse to reduce immigration to a minimum. Thus, in the White Paper of May 17th 1939, the British Government, in forming its policy in Palestine, reiterated that, in practice, from the 1922 White Paper onwards '*the economic absorptive capacity* of the country has been treated as the sole limiting factor' with regard to Jewish immigration. Following that, the British Government proclaimed its decision that-

---

[87] 'The expression [i.e., position] is one which corresponds to no exact legal meaning', see Akzin, op. cit. p. 61.

[88] White Paper of June 3rd 1922, Cmd. 1700.

> Jewish immigration during the next five years will be at a rate which, if *economic absorptive capacity* permits, will bring the Jewish population up to approximately one-third of the total population of the country… After the period of five years, no further Jewish immigration will be permitted unless the Arabs of Palestine are prepared to acquiesce in it.[89] [Italics added].

Also, in Article 6, the replacement of 'established rights' for 'rights and position' introduced vagueness and ambiguity into the Article, which might have then coincided with British interests. While 'established rights' could be interpreted as civil and religious rights mentioned in the Balfour Declaration and in subsequent international documents, the terminology of 'rights and position' had no clear meaning and was open to various interpretations.

More revisions were made in the draft Mandate, mostly prejudicial to the Jewish cause. For example, Article 6, with respect to settlement by Jews of the land, was altered from commitment to 'promote' the construction of such settlements to a requirement merely to 'facilitate' or 'encourage' their construction.[90] Moreover, In Article 5 of the draft dated December 11th 1919, the Jewish Agency was recognized as a public body with power to advise and cooperate with the Palestine Administration, and have a preferential right to construct or operate public works, services and utilities and to develop the natural resources of the country. In later drafts, this power has been taken away and so too the

---

[89] Cmd. 6019, *Palestine Statement of Policy*, May 17th 1939 [the MacDonald White Paper]; also published in League of Nations – *Statement of Policy on Palestine Issued by His Majesty's Government in the United Kingdom on May 17th 1939*, 20 League of Nations Official Journal (O.J.) 363, 1939.

[90] Compare the Draft of December 11th 1919, DBFP, Vol. IV, op. cit. p. 572, with later Drafts prepared under Curzon as Foreign Secretary, i.e., the drafts of June 10th 1920, CAB. 24/107; September 25th 1920, CAB 24/111; November 30th 1920, CAB 24/115; December 7th 1920, Cmd. 1176, *Draft Mandates for Mesopotamia and Palestine*, Miscellaneous No. 3, HMSO, London, 1921; and Cmd. 1785, the final draft approved by the League of Nations, July 24th 1922.

said preferential right. In his Memorandum of November 30th 1920, Curzon pointed out that 'it was felt unanimously, and was agreed by Mr. Balfour, that there was no ground for making this concession, which ought to be refused', but he did not explain the rationale behind this change.

However, on the issue of nationality law, and the obligation to facilitate the acquisition of Palestinian citizenship by Jews, there was very little change. It is interesting to note that in an informal meeting held on March 22nd 1919 between British representatives, among whom were Miss Gertrude Bell, Colonel T.E. Lawrence, Commander David Hogarth, Robert Vansittart and Eric Forbes Adam, and members of the Zionist Organization, an emigration scheme was discussed to arrange for Arab Palestinian peasantry to emigrate to Syria and Egypt in conjunction with the immigration of Jews into Palestine. To this 'Miss Bell and Colonel Lawrence agreed and Miss Bell added that there was scope in Mesopotamia for such emigrants. It was pointed out that it was not impossible to move Arab peasantry from their lands as had been shown when the original Zionist colonies were established.'[91]

Finally, it should be emphasized that at no time during the negotiations and discussions for the establishment of the Jewish National Home was there any attempt by the Zionist Organization or the Jewish Agency to jeopardize the civil and religious rights of the non-Jewish communities in Palestine. For this reason, provisions that were never contested or revised were those concerning non-Jewish rights, particularly the first proviso in the Balfour Declaration, which was repeated verbatim in the San Remo Resolution, the Treaty of Sèvres, and the British Mandate for Palestine.

---

[91] F.O. 608/99, Minutes of March 24th 1919, Rise of Israel, Vol. 10, op. cit., Doc. 60, p. 221, discussion on Palestinian citizenship pp. 223-24.

Chapter V

The Frontiers of Palestine

From Dan to Beersheba

Nothing was more symbolic than to define the borders of mandated Palestine according to its historical and biblical borders. No other concept was suggested and no other borders were considered. From Foreign Office and Cabinet documentation, it can be safely assumed that this attitude was adopted in order to remain in conformity with the establishment of the National Home for the Jewish people which might eventually develop into a Jewish State. As mentioned earlier, in the Ottoman period 'there is no such place or country as Palestine'.[1] Palestine was regarded as part of Syria, the southern region of which comprised the *Sanjaq* [District] of Jerusalem and the northern region formed part of the *Vilayets* [Provinces] of Syria and Beirut. After the military occupation of the Middle East by the Allied Forces and the decision to establish mandates in the territories of Palestine, Mesopotamia, Syria and Lebanon, it was found necessary to define their borders.

The keynote definition of the borders of Palestine was first proclaimed by British Prime Minister Lloyd George. It was not an accurate definition, but a meaningful one. At the Peace Conference, during the discussions on boundaries, 'when asked what he considered the boundaries of Palestine, Lloyd George always answered *"Biblical Palestine, from Dan to Beersheba"*' [Italics in the original].[2] Meinertzhagen reported in his Diary that with all the confusion that existed around the definition of Palestine in the Paris Peace Conference, he questioned the Prime Minister as to his views on the meaning of Palestine. Lloyd George's reply was: 'The area occupied by the twelve tribes, from Dan to Beersheba'. When confronted by other options,

---

[1]   Lloyd George, op. cit., Vol. II, p. 1126.

[2]   Meinertzhagen, op. cit., p. 63.

he rejected them and 'stuck to his Dan to Beersheba'.[3] In fact, Lloyd George used various versions to express his idea of what the frontiers of Palestine should be, all pointing to the biblical era. On top of the above-mentioned versions, Lloyd George insisted on the 'traditional boundaries of Dan and Beersheba', defined as 'original traditional Palestine'.[4] In the First Conference of London, he reiterated that Britain would only accept a mandate for 'a real Palestine, the Palestine of ancient history.'[5] In his memoirs, Lloyd George referred to Palestine as the 'old scriptural Palestine, extending from Dan to Beersheba, i.e., from Banias to Bir Saba... a country of less than 10,000 square miles, including 4,000 square miles to the east of the Jordan.'[6]

In consequence, the biblical phrase *from Dan to Beersheba* formed the foundation upon which the borders of Palestine were to be decided. This definition was adopted by British Cabinet Ministers and by high ranking Government officials. It was eventually also accepted by the French Government. As early as December 18th 1918, a month after the end of the War, Curzon suggested in the War Cabinet Eastern Committee that 'We must recover for Palestine its old boundaries. The old phrase 'Dan to Beersheba' still prevails'.[7] Later, Curzon quoted the Prime Minister on various occasions on the phrase Dan to Beersheba.[8]

---

[3] Ibid., Epilogue, p. 355.

[4] CAB 23/46, Notes of a Cabinet meeting at 10 Downing Street, November 13th 1919, p. 15.

[5] DBFP, op. cit., Vol. VII, p. 104, February 17th 1920.

[6] Lloyd George, op. cit., Vol. II, p. 1126.

[7] Lloyd George, ibid., Vol. II, p. 1144.

[8] Thus, for example, in discussing the boundaries between the spheres of British and French occupation in Palestine and Syria, Curzon based his arguments on an *aide-memoir* presented by Lloyd George to Clemenceau in which the former alluded to Palestine 'in accordance with its ancient boundaries of Dan to Beersheba.' DBFP, op. cit., Vol. IV, p. 589, December 17th 1919. On another occasion, in his capacity as Foreign Secretary, Curzon emphasized to M. Berthelot of France that 'The Prime Minister had publicly committed himself on more than one occasion to *the formula of including in Palestine all the ancient territories from Dan to Beersheba. He could not recede from this attitude'. [Italics added]. DBFP, op. cit., Vol. IV, p. 599, December 23rd 1919. Again, in the Conference of London, February 18th 1920, Curzon repeated to M. Berthelot that 'Mr. Lloyd George had often referred to Palestine as extending from Dan to Beersheba.' DBFP, op. cit., Vol. VII, p. 114.

But what did the British Cabinet, and particularly Lloyd George, mean by the phrase 'Dan to Beersheba'? Often, as seen above, the phrase was used in conjunction with other telling words such as: 'biblical Palestine', 'the area occupied by the twelve tribes', 'ancient boundaries', and 'traditional boundaries'. Lloyd George did not go into any detail to specify what boundaries of Palestine he had in mind, but he referred to a treatise written by Rev. George Adam Smith, namely the *Atlas of the Historical Geography of the Holy Land*[9] as a premise for fixing the boundaries between Palestine and its neighboring countries. The treatise included maps showing the frontiers of Palestine and various towns in the old ages, and, in the words of Lloyd George, it 'was regarded as the ablest book on Palestine which had ever been written'[10] and 'was so accurate in matters of geography that it had been used by Lord Allenby during his campaign'.[11]

Based on Lloyd George's specifications, Meinertzhagen mapped the area which he regarded as biblical Palestine: 'This was bounded on the north by the Litani River and the whole of the catchment area of the River Jordan from the southern slopes of Hermon south through Moab to the head of the gulf of Aqaba and thence along the Egyptian-Turkish frontier to Gaza.'[12] According to Meinertzhagen, both Lloyd George and Balfour agreed to this boundary: 'The Litani River and the inclusion of the Jordan catchment-area became known as the *Meinertzhagen Line*.'[13] [Italics in the original].

This biblical formula, *from Dan to Beersheba*, was mentioned

---

[9]   Published by Hodder and Stoughton, London 1915. George Adam Smith was a Scottish theological professor, Principal of the University of Aberdeen. The research work began in 1894 and was concluded in 1915.

[10] DBFP, op. cit., Vol. VIII, p. 175, at the San Remo conference, April 24th 1920; Lloyd George, op. cit., Vol. II, p. 1180.

[11] DBFP, ibid., Vol. VII, p. 115, February 18th 1920, in the Conference of London; Lloyd George, ibid., Vol. II, p. 1176.

[12] Meinertzhagen, op. cit., p. 355.

[13] Ibid., pp. 63-65.

several times in the Old Testament.[14] It did not aim at specific boundaries but was rather recognized as a concept to allude to the whole of the Land of Israel. The phrase was not meant to be construed literally, to mean verbatim from the towns of Dan in the north to Beersheba in the south.[15] This conclusion could also be derived from the text and maps in George Adam Smith's treatise. The most relevant texts and maps in the treatise relate to three periods: 1) the period of the twelve tribes and the Judges – before 1050 B.C. (Map No. 32); 2) the period of King Saul – about 1020 B.C. (Map No. 33); and 3) the period of the Kingdoms of David and Solomon – 1015-930 B.C. (Map No. 34). Adam Smith was cautious enough to admit that the map of the twelve tribes gave only approximately the disposition of the Tribes of Israel, while the Frontiers of the Kingdom of Saul as indicated on Map 33 were 'of course only approximate'.[16]

There could be no doubt that the above-mentioned maps were inaccurate. But even so, Adam Smith's maps were revealing in showing that the frontiers of the Tribe of Naphtali went as far north as the sources of the Jordan River and the Litani bend (now in Lebanon). In the east, the tribes of Reuben, Gad and half the

---

[14] In fact, the phrase *from Dan to Beersheba* was mentioned on at least nine occasions: Judges 20:1; I Samuel 3:20; II Samuel 3:10; II Samuel 17:11; II Samuel 24:2; II Samuel 24:15; I Kings 4:25; I Chronicles 21:2; II Chronicles 30:5. See also Gabriel G. Tabarani – *Israeli-Palestinian Conflict*, Arthur House Press, Bloomington, U.S.A., 2008, p. 4; Esther Gwan – *Spiritual Watchers Over the Nations*, West Bow Press, Bloomington, U.S.A., 2010, pp. 21-22.

[15] Thus, for example, in II Samuel 24: 2-9, it was told that King David ordered Joab, Minister of the Army, to go through all the land of the tribes of Israel from Dan to Beersheba to conduct a census of the people of Israel. To carry out the King's orders, Joab and his officers crossed the Jordan eastwards to Aroer and to the Gilead, then to Tyre and around Sidon, the latter situated north of the town of Dan, then to the Negev Judah which lies partly south of Beersheba. In any case, the land of the twelve tribes stretched beyond Dan in the north, Beersheba in the south, and the Jordan River in the East.

[16] George Adam Smith, op. cit., p. XVII. Smith based his inexact assertion on 'the song of Deborah (circa 1100 B.C.) with qualifications from the other sources.' With regard to the Kingdom of Saul, Smith remarked, p. XVIII, that the inexact description of the frontiers was particularly true 'of the Israelite extension over Galilee, the East of Jordan, and southwards into the Negeb'. See maps 32, 33 and 34 on next pages.

**Palestine
Period of Israel's Settlement
And of the Judges
Before 1050 B.C.**

GREAT

SEA

Map No. 2: From George Adam Smith – Atlas of the Historical Geography of the Holy Land, map 32.

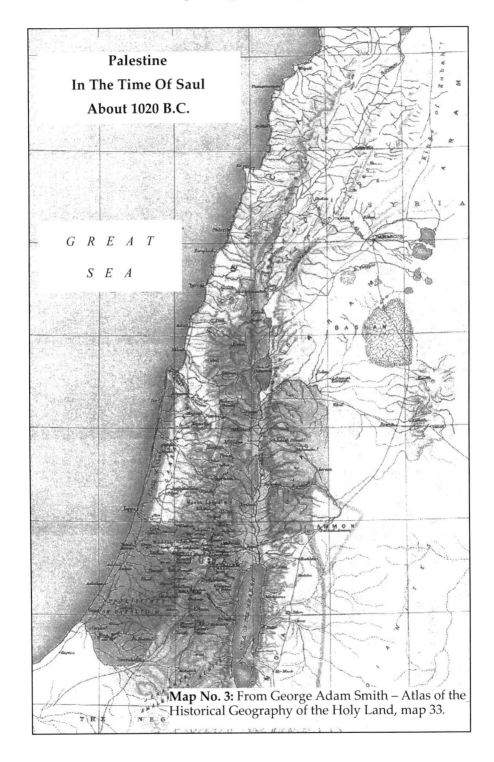

Palestine
In The Time Of Saul
About 1020 B.C.

GREAT SEA

Map No. 3: From George Adam Smith – Atlas of the Historical Geography of the Holy Land, map 33.

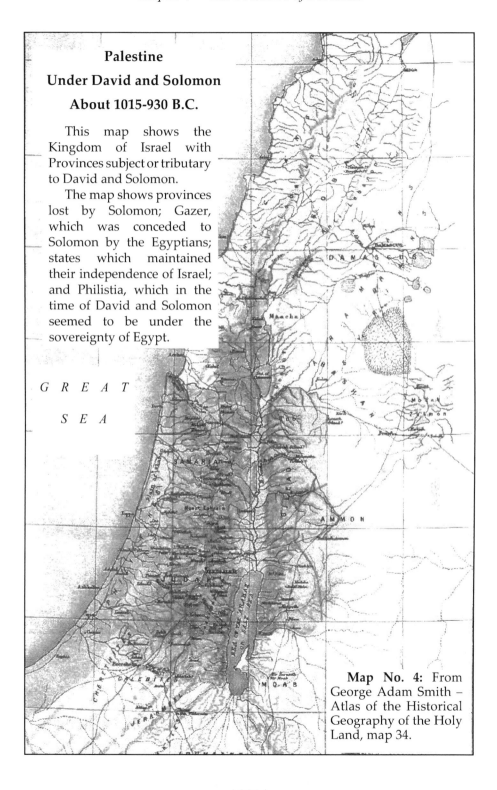

Palestine

Under David and Solomon

About 1015-930 B.C.

This map shows the Kingdom of Israel with Provinces subject or tributary to David and Solomon.

The map shows provinces lost by Solomon; Gazer, which was conceded to Solomon by the Egyptians; states which maintained their independence of Israel; and Philistia, which in the time of David and Solomon seemed to be under the sovereignty of Egypt.

G R E A T

S E A

Map No. 4: From George Adam Smith – Atlas of the Historical Geography of the Holy Land, map 34.

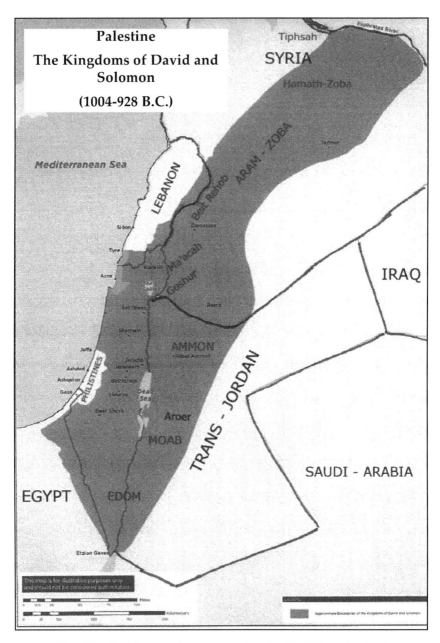

Map No. 5: Adapted from a map by the IDF Mapping Unit.
(This map is for illustrative purposes only.)

tribe of Manasseh occupied the Gilead and other areas east of the Jordan, as far as Busra (now in Syria), over 50 miles [about 85 km] east of the Jordan River. And in the south, the Tribe of Simon occupied territories further south from Beersheba. In the map of the twelve tribes, the location and frontiers of the tribe of Asher were missing. Consequently, Smith noted that the tribe of Asher should be added across the region west of Naphtali, but refrained from specifying the borders of this tribe. However, the Old Testament was generally quite clear about the borders of the tribe of Asher: It bordered in the east with Naphtali, in the west with the Mediterranean, in the south-east with the tribe of Zebulun, and in the north stretched as far as Greater Sidon, including the stronghold of Tyre.[17] Sidon lay north of the Litani River.

During the kingdoms of David and Solomon, the frontiers of Palestine[18] stretched much further north, east and south. In the Palestine Royal Commission Report, it had been stated that the Kingdoms of David and Solomon (1010-930 B.C.) extended 'not only over all Palestine but over most of the territory north and south that lay between the rival empires of Egypt and Assyria'.[19] In *the Historical Geography of the Holy Land*, the borders of the territories under the rule of David and Solomon were marked on Map 34, with an explanatory text by Smith that could be summarized as follows:[20]

> David ruled all Israel (including Judah). During his reign he extended the borders of Palestine on all fronts. In the North he defeated Aram Beth-Rehob,

---

[17] Joshua, 19:28-29.

[18] The term Palestine in this connection is a misnomer. The territory now designated as Palestine was known in the past, from around 1050 B.C. till 70 A.D., as the Land of Israel. The name Palestine was given to the Land of Israel by the Romans after the destruction of the Second Temple and the exile of most of its inhabitants, in order to extinguish any connection between the Jews and their homeland. However, for convenience purposes, I have referred to this Biblical territory as Palestine.

[19] Peel Report, op. cit., p. 3.

[20] George Adam Smith, op. cit., p. XIX, map 34.

allies of the Amonites, probably the district round the present Rihab, and Aram Zoba, probably in the Lebanon and Ma'acah in Golan and crushed a subsequent Aramean (Syrian) confederacy at Helam east of the Jordan. The phrase Arameans beyond the river, mentioned in II Samuel 8:3, implied that all the Arameans south of the Euphrates were engaged against David. It was also said that he put garrisons in Damascus and received tribute from Hamath Zoba. Then, from the Yarmuk across the Jordan up to what the text gives as the land of Tahtim-hodshi, to be read either as the land under Hermon or less probably land of the Hittites towards Kadesh… and then turns towards Sidon and the fortress of Tyre… In the East he ruled the Gilead and the Geshurites (Ashurites, Hebrew text). He conquered Moab to the Arnon and overthrew the Ammonites with their capital. In the South he subdued the Amalekites and smote Edom and made Edom tributary. The Old Testament gives the extent of his kingdom: from Aroer north of Arnon across Gilead to the Yarmouk, with an extension, perhaps, into Bashan, but exclusive of Geshur in Aram and Ma'acah both of which remained independent. In the West 'he gradually drove the Philistines off the Judean highlands, and broke their power by the capture of Gath'.[21]

King Solomon extended the borders even further to the South. After suppressing the revolt in Edom he kept this road open as far as Ezion Geber beside Elath on the Red Sea, from which he sent ships to Ophir. 'He thus controlled all the trade between Damascus (with Mesopotamia beyond) and Egypt, and between Arabia and Gaza'.[22]

Smith based his research on a meticulous study of the

---

[21] George Adam Smith, ibid, see for example II Samuel, Caps. 8, 10, and I Chronicles Caps. 18-20.

[22] Ibid.

Scriptures. He thought that the ascription of power to David up to the Euphrates was doubtful. However, in the Scriptures there was ample evidence that the Kingdoms of David and Solomon stretched from the border with Egypt to the Euphrates:

> **Old Testament, II Samuel, 8:1-4**: David subdued the Philistines and the Moabites, smote the king of Zobah at the river *Euphrates*, and subdued the *Syrians of Damascus*. **8:5-6**: And when the Syrians of Damascus came to succour Hadadezer king of Zoba, David slew of the Syrians two and twenty thousand men. Then David put garrisons in Syria of Damascus and the Syrians became servants to David. **8:12**: David dedicated to God all the gold and silver he got from the nations he subdued: Syria, Moab, Ammon, the Philistines, Amalek, Zobah. **8:14** and he put garrisons in Edom and all they of Edom became David's servants. [Italics added].

> **Old Testament, I Kings 5:1**: And Solomon reigned over all kingdoms from the river unto the land of the Philistines, and unto the border of Egypt; they brought presents and served Solomon all the days of his life. **5: 3**: For he had dominion over all the region on this side of the river, from Tiphsah[23] to Gaza, over all the kings on this side of the river…

> **Old Testament, II Chronicles, 8:3-6**: And Solomon went to Hamath-Zoba and prevailed against it. And he built Tadmor in the wilderness and all the store cities he built in Hamath… and all that Solomon desired to build in Jerusalem, and in the Lebanon, and throughout all the land of his dominion.

It had been suggested that the inhabitants of the territories forming the dominion of David and Solomon be divided into

---

[23] Tiphsah lay on the Euphrates, see map No. 5 on p. 232 supra; see also Yohanan Aharoni – Carta's Atlas of the Bible, p. 68, map 105, 2nd ed. Jerusalem, 1974.

three categories. The first comprised the Israelites who inhabited the territories allocated to the twelve tribes. The second formed the subdued nations such as the people of Edom, Moab, Aram Damascus, and Aram Zoba. In some of these areas, such as Edom and Damascus, David appointed Israeli Governors. The third category comprised the inhabitants of Kingdoms subjected to Israel, who accepted its sovereignty, such as Philistia, Geshur and Hamath.[24] To recapitulate: there was little doubt that according to the Scriptures, the borders of the land of Israel, here referred to as Palestine, during the reign of David and Solomon, stretched from the Euphrates in the North-East to Gaza and the border of Egypt in the South-West, including the cities of Damascus and Tadmor.

It is therefore quite evident, from the description presented by Smith, that the Kingdoms of David and Solomon controlled territories in Syria and Lebanon, also in east of the Jordan and the Negeb as far south as Ezion-geber, situated beside Elath on the Red Sea. More relevant to Allied discussions is Map 34, which clearly shows that the boundary in the North exceeded the Litani bend and the water heads of the Jordan River, while in the east, the territories of Gilead, Ammon, and the northern part of Moab formed part of the Kingdom of David and Solomon. Within those boundaries a strenuous discussion erupted between the British and the French during the Paris Peace Conference, the London Conference, and the San Remo Convention on the water supply for Palestine.

British Stand Regarding the Frontiers of Palestine

The British Government pressed for a viable Palestine within its biblical borders of Dan to Beersheba, which would include the waters of the Jordan, Yarmuk, and Litani Rivers for agricultural and industrial purposes. Lloyd George demanded that the sources of the Jordan River be included within the borders of Palestine. At the London Conference of February 27th 1920, he emphasized that 'the waters of Palestine were essential to its existence.

---

24 Yohanan Aharoni, ibid., p. 68, map 104.

Without these waters, Palestine would be a wilderness.'[25] In fact, economic considerations took a major part in the discussions on Palestine boundaries.

The British insistence on a viable Palestine with a self-supporting economy was not instigated solely by the notion that the country would then be easier to rule. It was no less motivated by the desire to enable Jewish immigration and settlement of the land, as a prelude to the establishment of the Jewish National Home. On June 26th 1919, Balfour, as Foreign Secretary, advised Lloyd George:

> In determining the Palestinian frontiers, the main thing to keep in mind is to make a Zionist policy possible by giving the fullest scope to economic development in Palestine. Thus the Northern frontier should give to Palestine a full command of the water power which geographically belongs to Palestine and not to Syria; while the eastern frontier should be so drawn as to give the widest scope to agricultural development on the left bank of the Jordan, consistent with leaving the Hedjaz railway completely in Arab possession.[26]

In another Memorandum submitted two months later, Balfour reiterated his conviction that 'Palestine must be made available for the largest number of Jewish immigrants'.[27] It should command the water sources of Palestine which naturally belong to it, and for the same reason should stretch into the lands lying east of the Jordan as far as the Hedjaz Railway.

Again, in a meeting in Paris on June 19th 1919, Balfour agreed with Brandeis that 'there must be economic elbow room for a Jewish Palestine; self sufficiency for a healthy social life. That

---

[25] DBFP, op. cit., Vol. VII, p. 104, February 17th 1920.

[26] DBFP, op. cit., Vol. IV, p. 302, Memorandum by Balfour in Paris addressed to Lloyd George on the subject of the disposal of Turkish Territories, copy sent to Curzon.

[27] DBFP, op. cit., Vol. IV, p. 347, Memorandum *Respecting Syria Palestine and Mesopotamia* of August 11th 1919

meant adequate boundaries, not merely a small garden within Palestine. On the North that meant the control of the waters.'[28] In the east, Balfour seemed to have agreed that the border should include territories east of the Jordan as far as the Hedjaz Railroad, and was of the opinion that Feisal would not oppose having the eastern boundary of Palestine go up to that line.

A year later, after Curzon succeeded Balfour as Foreign Secretary, the British Government continued for a while to hold the same view. Curzon instructed Vansittart in Paris to inform the French that the British Government 'are not prepared to conclude any arrangement which does not contain due provision for the future utilization by Palestine of the waters of the Yarmuk and the Litani, which may well prove vital to the economic development of the country *and the creation of a national home for the Jews* '[29] [Italics added]. He also emphasized that the question of the waters of the Yarmuk and the Litani was one to which the British Government attached great importance.

This, therefore, was the policy upon which the British stand in the negotiations on the Palestine borders was based. High ranking officials in the Foreign Office made efforts to implement this policy particularly vis-à-vis the French, but with little success because of strong French opposition. Jewish immigration and colonization was an important consideration in this policy. In their efforts to achieve considerable rectification of the Sykes-Picot line in favor of the Zionists in Palestine, Forbes Adam and Vansittart of the Foreign Office asserted in their comments to a French Memorandum by Berthelot: 'The Allied pledge of a national home involves gradual Jewish immigration into – and colonisation of – Palestine, and, if the present native population is not to be abruptly dislodged, the territory available for Jewish

---

[28] DBFP, ibid., Vol. IV, pp. 1276-78, Report by Felix Frankfurter of a meeting in Balfour's apartment in Paris in the presence of Lord Eustace Percy. It was noted that 'no British record of this interview has been traced in Foreign Office archives.' This was not unusual, for on several occasions the editors of the DBFP indicated that they were unable to trace records of documents referred to in Foreign Office Archives.

[29] DBFP, op. cit., Vol. XIII, p. 382, November 9th 1920, Dispatch from Curzon to Vansittart in Paris.

immigrants must be much developed and made as far as possible self-supporting'.[30] For the same reason, they advocated the inclusion into Palestine of a strip of fertile territory east of the Jordan but west of the Hedjaz Railway, adding that 'the French, who are equally pledged to *the policy of the national home*, should find it difficult to argue that Syria will suffer by this scheme to an extent which would outweigh the advantages to Palestine and *Zionism*'[31] [italics added]. They also rejected the idea of Palestine being internationalized in accordance with the Sykes-Picot agreement 'since the Zionists... are known to be strongly opposed to it'.[32]

In another Foreign Office document,[33] Forbes Adam made a more forceful argument regarding the need for a wider Palestine. This was based on the fact that the British Government by supporting Zionism had accepted the Zionist implications of the Balfour Declaration meaning 'an attempt to make Palestine a state in its natural and geographical and historic frontiers and by gradual immigration and special economic facilities to turn this state into a Jewish state.'[34] Thus, concluded Forbes Adam, behind British policy lay the recognition of the principle of Jewish nationality, which is the essence of Zionism. For this purpose, Palestine should acquire the natural economic facilities to allow Jewish immigration and their settlement of the land. Curzon minuted Adam Forbes' memorandum with the following words: 'I would not give way on the Palestine Frontier points, when Clemenceau said to the P.M. You may have Palestine he meant a reasonable and feasible Palestine'.[35]

Among British high ranking officials and experts, there was

---

[30] DBFP, ibid., Vol. IV, p. 580, Assertions made by Forbes Adam and Vansittart in their comments to a French Memorandum by Berthelot, December 18th 1919.

[31] Ibid., p. 581.

[32] Ibid., p. 585.

[33] Ibid., p. 608, Memorandum by Forbes Adam on France and the Northern Frontier of Palestine, December 30th 1919.

[34] Ibid.

[35] Ibid. p. 610.

a consensus that the borders of Palestine should include the Litani River and the sources of the Jordan River in the north, and territories lying east of the Jordan River in the east. In any case, the Jordan River was not contemplated as a potential eastern border of Palestine. As early as August 22nd 1918, before the end of the war, Ormsby-Gore put forward a proposal for discussion that the borders of Palestine should be drawn in the north on the line of the Litani River and in the east they should include the whole of the Jordan Valley and the lower eastern slopes of the Jordan River.[36] For the Paris Peace Conference, Major O. Elbynne of the British Delegation, Geographical Section, prepared a memorandum on the boundaries of Palestine: in the north running along the thalweg of the Litani from the Mediterranean eastwards to the top of Mount Hermon, and in the east running in a general southerly direction from the top of Mount Hermon down to the Yarmuk River, including part of the Golan Heights, and from there along a line 5-10 miles east of the Jordan River and parallel to it.[37] Meinertzhagen was more realistic. He suggested that the northern border of Palestine should pass north of the Litani so as to include both banks of the Litani within Palestine, rejecting the idea of a border running along the Litani thalweg which could only lead to disputes. He also recommended that the border should include the Hermon waters and the sources of the Jordan. In the east, he suggested that the boundary should pass east of the Jordan River, some 25 to 30 kilometers west of the Hedjaz Railway.[38]

Similar views were entertained by President Wilson. Just before the commencement of the London Conference, he sent

---

[36] *The Zionist Movement and the Foundation of Israel*, op. cit., p. 751 [hereinafter ZMFI], Report by Ormsby-Gore, Political Officer in charge of the Zionist commission, on *The Existing Political situation in Palestine and Contiguous Areas*; see also ZMFI, ibid., p. 757, Ormsby-Gore addressing in similar words the London Zionist Committee on August 16th 1918.

[37] Rise of Israel, op. cit., Vol. 10, Doc. 78, pp. 303-04, F.O. 608/98, April 9th 1919

[38] DBFP, op. cit., Vol. IV, pp. 533-34; Meinertzhagen, op. cit., pp. 61-62; Rise of Israel, ibid., Vol. 10, Doc. 86, pp. 342-43; Dispatch from Meinertzhagen to Curzon on the boundaries of Palestine, November 17th 1919.

a message through the State Department to the British and French Governments urging that 'Palestine should have rational boundaries in the North and East (the Litany River, the watershed of the Hermon and the Haulon and Yaulon [sic] valleys).'[39] He also 'hoped that the French and British Governments were not carrying out the Sykes-Picot Agreement to the detriment of Balfour's Declaration as to the Palestine of the future'.[40] Such also were the recommendations made by the Intelligence Section of the American Delegation to the Paris Peace Conference, who recommended a year earlier, on the assumption that Palestine would eventually become a Jewish State, that 'the new state would control its own source of water power and irrigation, on Mount Hermon in the east of the Jordan, a feature of great importance, since the success of the new state would depend upon the possibilities of agricultural development'.[41] It was also the recommendation of the Middle Eastern Sections of the British and American Delegations that the southern boundary of Lebanon with Palestine should be the Litani.[42]

Zionist Involvement in Determining the Frontiers of Palestine

Zionist involvement in carving the borders of Palestine was intensive and incessant. Zionist leaders often addressed the British Government on the future borders of Palestine and put forward their proposals before British officials in their negotiations with other Allied Powers, particularly France. They also appeared before the Paris Peace Conference on this issue. Zionist views were usually taken into consideration as coming from a recognized body, which had the right to make them. At

---

[39] Meaning, so it seems, the Hauran and the Yarmouk valley. See DBFP, Vol. IV, p. 634, February 10th 1920. Information given by Sir G. Graham to Curzon.

[40] Ibid.

[41] David Hunter Miller – *My Diary at the Conference of Paris*, op. cit., Vol. IV, pp. 263-64, January 21st 1919.

[42] Rise of Israel, op. cit., Vol. 10, Doc. 79, p. 307, F.O. 608/98, April 9th 1919, Draft Joint Recommendations of Middle Eastern Sections of British and American delegations (no date specified).

times, British negotiators made efforts to put the Zionist case forward. The Zionists acted and pursued their demands as the true beneficiaries of the Mandate in accordance with the Balfour Declaration. There was no similar involvement by the Arabs of Palestine, and there was hardly any concern on their part as to how eventually the borders would be fixed.[43]

At the Paris Peace Conference, the Zionist Organization presented their desiderata as to the future frontiers of Palestine, which could be summed up as follows: In the north: Starting at a point on the Mediterranean close to and south of Sidon including the watersheds of the Lebanon and the slopes of Mount Hermon, thence eastward stretching almost as far as the Hedjaz Railway. In the east: Close to and west of the Hedjaz Railway southwards terminating in the Gulf of Aqaba. In the south: The frontier to be agreed upon with the Egyptian Government. In the west: The Mediterranean. Details would be settled by a special Commission, on which there shall be a Jewish representative.[44]

These proposals were put to British officials on several occasions by Weizmann. During talks with Meinertzhagen, Weizmann made it clear that the Zionist aim was Sidon in the north, Hedjaz Railway in the east till Aqaba, and the southern border to be negotiated with the Egyptian Government.[45] On the eastern boundary, he communicated to Field Marshall Henry Wilson, member of the War Cabinet and of the British delegation on the eve of the Peace talks in Paris, that it 'is absolutely essential for the economic development of Palestine that this [the eastern] line be so drawn as to include the territories east of the Jordan

---

[43] There might have been scant reports of negligible Arab involvement regarding the settlement of the boundaries of Palestine. On one occasion, it was reported that two Arabs, one Muslim and one Christian, supported by a few Palestinian Jews and others, initiated a resolution calling for the inclusion of the Litani and the eastern tributaries of the Jordan within the boundaries of Palestine. Herbert Samuel forwarded this resolution to the Cabinet to indicate that 'Palestine spoke with one voice'. See CAB 24/156 British Empire Report, November 24th 1920.

[44] DBFP, op. cit., Vol. IV, pp. 161-62, February 27th 1919 – Statement of the Zionist Organization at the Peace Conference on Palestine frontiers; Also in Hurewitz, op. cit., p.138.

[45] Meinertzhagen, op. cit., pp. 13-14, January 30th 1919.

which are capable of receiving and maintaining large Jewish mass settlements',[46] proposing that they should extend as far east as the Hedjaz Railway.

Later, when it was brought to the attention of Weizmann that a settlement was forthcoming between Britain and France on the northern and north-eastern boundaries of Palestine detrimental to the interests of the Jewish National Home, he hastened to caution Lloyd George,[47] and Curzon on different occasions, against undertaking any settlement which would cut off Palestine from the Litani and deny her the head-waters of the Jordan, the eastern shore of the Sea of Galilee, and the Yarmuk Valley north of the Sykes-Picot line. He added to Curzon: 'I am sure that your Lordship is fully aware how disastrous to the future of the country and the project of the National Home such a settlement would be.'[48] Weizmann referred to the rights to utilize the waters of the Upper Jordan and the Yarmuk as 'our rights' and insisted that it would be impossible to utilize these waters by agreement that did not demand their inclusion within the boundary of Palestine. Weizmann gave practical examples of the difficulties that the National Home would incur from such a settlement.[49]

Graver concern was expressed by Weizmann in his letter to Churchill as Colonial Secretary on March 1st 1921, after Britain had succumbed to French frontier demands. As a consequence, Palestine was deprived of the waters of the Litani and the sources of the Jordan and from the Yarmuk and the fertile plains on the north eastern-shores of the Sea of Galilee. Now that these advantages had vanished, Weizmann pleaded with Churchill to extend the borders of Palestine as far east as the desert, including

---

[46] Rise of Israel, op. cit., Vol. 10, Doc. 75, p. 290, February 4th 1919.

[47] Rise of Israel, ibid., Vol. 10, Doc. 87, pp. 347-49, in Weizmann's detailed letter to Lloyd George on December 29th 1919, sent during the final negotiations with the French.

[48] DBFP, op. cit., Vol. XIII, p. 374, October 30th 1920. Weizmann was updated by Vansittart who was one of the main negotiators with the French.

[49] For example, the Rutenberg project – A scheme for hydro-electric and irrigation undertakings in the Jordan valley constructed by Mr. P. Rutenberg, a Russian Jewish engineer, would be seriously compromised if the eastern part of Lake Tiberias would be severed from Palestine. DBFP, op. cit., Vol. XIII, p. 375, n. 3.

the Hedjaz Railway, subject to providing safeguards for Muslim interests. Weizmann could not have made these pleas to Lloyd George, Curzon, and Churchill unless he was speaking with authority on behalf of the Zionist Organization to whom the pledge for a Jewish National Home in Palestine was made: 'The economic progress of Cis-Jordania itself is dependent upon the development of these Trans-Jordanian plains, for they form the natural granary of all Palestine and without them Palestine can never become a self-sustaining economic unit and a real National Home.'[50] Little did he know then that Churchill had already made up his mind to detach all territories east of the Jordan River from Palestine in order to establish therein another Arab political entity later known as Trans-Jordan.[51]

The Northern and North-Eastern Frontiers of Palestine:
The British-French Dispute

The fiercest discussions on mapping the borders of Palestine took place between the British and the French, and the main theme of these discussions was the Jewish National Home which was to be established in Palestine. The British Government endeavored to include the waters of the Litani, the sources of the Jordan and the Yarmuk valley within the borders of Palestine. However, the French Government insisted on maintaining the Sykes-Picot border line, stretching from north of Acre eastwards to the northern tip of the Sea of Galilee, and crossing the Yarmuk Valley to a point just south of Dar'aa. This would leave in the French zone all the water resources mentioned. Weizmann noted that the French tended to regard Palestine as 'Southern Syria', and Syria as a whole as a French sphere of influence. They resented any attempt to modify the northern frontier. For them, as for the Italians, 'Zionism was nothing more than a camouflage for British imperialism.'[52]

There could be no doubt that the conflict between the British

---

[50] Rise of Israel, op. cit., Vol. 13, pp. 87-88.

[51] On the creation of Trans-Jordan see pp. 266 et seq., infra.

[52] Weizmann, op. cit., p. 289.

and French on the frontiers of Palestine revolved mainly around the realization of the Jewish National Home in that country. The long discussions between the two Powers emanated from contradicting interpretations of the Jewish National Home in the Balfour Declaration. In the words of Forbes Adam:

> From the general tenour of these discussions it seems obvious that the French and British conflict of opinion on this matter fundamentally arises from their different interpretations of the declaration as to the national home for the Jews, to which both Governments, in company with the Italian and U.S. Governments, have subscribed. The French Government interpret this declaration as a promise to protect and somewhat extend the *existing* Zionist colonies', but nothing further, while behind British policy 'is the recognition of the principle of Jewish nationality, which is the essence of Zionism and the intention to lay in the Turkish Peace Settlement the foundation for the *reconstruction of a Jewish Palestine*, as of an Armenia for the Armenians. [Italics added].[53]

Prior to the official meetings of the Supreme Council in London and later in San Remo, both, the British and French prepared memorandums to express their stand on the borders of Palestine. The French refused to make any concessions that did not coincide with the Sykes-Picot line with regard to the northern and north-eastern borders 'for the benefit of the Zionists'. And they declined to 'abandon all the waters of Damascus to the Jewish colonies,' but they were prepared 'to assure the Zionist colonies of an important proportion of the waters which they demand'.[54]

---

[53] DBFP, op. cit., Vol. IV, p. 607-08, Foreign Office Memorandum prepared by Forbes Adam on France and the northern frontier of Palestine, December 30th 1919.

[54] CAB 24/95, C.P. 391, French note by Berthelot communicated to Curzon, December 12th 1919.

The British Government, however, were not satisfied with the French position. In reaction to the French, the Political Section of the British Peace Delegation commented that Britain should make efforts to achieve 'considerable rectification of the Sykes-Picot line in Palestine in favour of the Zionists'.[55] They explained that 'the Allied pledge of a National Home involves gradual Jewish immigration into – and colonization of – Palestine, and, if the present native population is not to be abruptly dislodged, the territory available for Jewish immigrants must be much developed and made as far as possible self-supporting'.[56] The British delegation emphasized Zionist plans designed to cover an extensive scheme of irrigation and electric power development, involving the carrying and conservation of waters of the Litani, the Hasbani, and those flowing from Mount Hermon into the Jordan River. They hoped that the French would not object to a compromise on the Sykes-Picot line in this connection.[57]

Following the Memorandums, two Anglo-French meetings were held in London on December 23rd 1919 to discuss more closely the northern and north-eastern borders of Palestine.[58] The discussions ended in a deadlock, with the French adamant on maintaining the Sykes-Picot border line. In their view, two concessions had already been made by them, namely the cession of Mosul, and their consent to the British Mandate in Palestine instead of internationalization under the Sykes-Picot agreement. The French were prepared to make one last concession: to allot to the Zionists 33 per cent of the water-power of the waters flowing from Mount Hermon subject to an economic arrangement with France. While the French were mainly concerned with the needs of the *existing* Zionist colonies for water-power, the British had in view immigration and colonization on the way to the

---

[55] DBFP, op. cit., Vol. IV, p. 580, Comments on Berthelot's note of December 12th 1919 prepared by Forbes Adam and Vansittart on behalf of the Political Section of the British Peace Delegation, December 18th 1919. These comments were not communicated to Berthelot.

[56] Ibid.

[57] Ibid., p. 581.

[58] DBFP, ibid., Vol. IV, pp. 595-98, and pp. 599-602.

establishment of the Jewish National Home. All attempts made by the British delegation to explain that the French offer would be insufficient to execute this policy fell on deaf ears. At this stage, Curzon erupted that he could not understand why the French insisted on the Sykes-Picot line 'even in places it had been drawn regardless of political, geographical or economic facts'.[59] Curzon insisted that the British Prime Minister was not prepared to give way on this point, and Berthelot replied neither would the French Prime Minister. The meetings were therefore adjourned devoid of any resolution.

This debate resumed at the conference of London on February 17th-21st 1920.[60] At first, the French proposed to arrange that the Zionists should have sufficient water for irrigation purposes, without conceding any territory that would include the Litani, the watersheds of the Hermon, and the catchment of the Yarmuk. Berthelot declared that 'so far as the Zionists were concerned the French were prepared to give them all the water-power that they needed'.[61] The British, however, were not entirely convinced. Lloyd George demanded a real Palestine, a Palestine of ancient history, from Dan to Beersheba, with waters which were essential to its very existence, without which Palestine would be a wilderness. In putting forward his arguments, Lloyd George quoted Jewish claims to that effect.[62] On the other hand, Lloyd George argued that those same waters were of no use to anyone holding Syria. He, therefore, asked the French to be more flexible on this matter. In fact, the French at this stage were prepared to go partway towards the British position. Berthelot stated without making any commitments on territorial concessions that some arrangement could be made for the protection of the waters of Palestine.[63]

---

[59] Ibid., p. 598.

[60] DBFP, op. cit., Vol. VII, pp. 99 et seq., February 17th 1920; pp. 112 et seq., February 18th 1920; pp. 120 et seq., February 18th 1920; pp. 173 et seq., February 21st 1920.

[61] Ibid., p. 103.

[62] Ibid., p. 104.

[63] Ibid., p. 107.

However, a fundamental change in Lloyd George's attitude to the French on the northern and north-eastern borders of Palestine occurred towards the end of the Conference. Perhaps he was misled or thought it futile to carry on endless debates with the French while the latter showed no signs of compromise. On the last day of the Conference, Lloyd George took the stand to assert that 'the historical boundaries of Palestine to the north and south were limited by Dan and Beersheba, and the British had no intention of claiming any extension beyond *these towns*'[64] [italics added]. As for water supply from the Litani and sources of the Jordan, he left that to the populations themselves to make special arrangements with France as the Mandatory for Syria. After consulting with Lord Allenby and 'other authorities', he was convinced by Berthelot, who based his views on the maps of George Adam Smith that 'this work clearly showed that the historic boundaries of Palestine had never extended beyond Dan and Beersheba.'[65] At this stage, the British and French were at one on the boundaries of Dan to Beersheba – with the exclusion of the Litani, the watersheds of the Hermon, and the waters of the Yarmuk.

During these discussions, a telegram sent by Judge Brandeis of the United States Supreme Court addressed to Weizmann to be conveyed to Lloyd George was read out to the assembly. Brandeis, on behalf of the Zionist Organization of America, called for borders in the north of Palestine that 'must include Litany River, watersheds of Hermon on east, must include plain of Jaulan Hauran; if Balfour Declaration, subscribed to by France as well as other Allied and Associated Powers, is to be made effective, these boundaries must be conceded to Palestine. Less than this would produce mutilation promised Home'.[66] Both Lloyd George and Berthelot dismissed those demands as being extravagant and unsubstantiated. Berthelot recognized as legitimate the use of waters south of Dan only, but to show good faith, France was prepared to show generosity in the supply

---

[64] Ibid., p. 183.

[65] Ibid., p. 184.

[66] Ibid., pp. 183-84. Telegram dating February 16th 1920.

of water to *the Zionist population*.[67] It seems, from Lloyd George's memoirs, that the French did not limit themselves to making provisional arrangements for water supply. Rather, they gave guarantees, which the British Government accepted, that this supply would not be interfered with by France as the Syrian Mandatory.[68]

Two months later in San Remo, on the day the Mandates for Palestine, Mesopotamia, and Syria were confirmed, Lloyd George made every effort to reach an understanding with the French on the northern and north-eastern borders of Palestine. He was in a jubilant mood ready to state that all difficulties that had previously arisen between the two Governments had vanished. He again dismissed Zionist claims to the whole of the country up to the Litani River, including Tyre and Sidon, because these 'had never been included in history in the boundaries of Palestine.'[69] Berthelot rejoiced at hearing those words coming from Lloyd George. Perhaps this understanding paved the way to a quicker conclusion of the San Remo Agreement.

Notwithstanding Lloyd George's apparent understanding with the French on the northern and north-eastern boundaries of Palestine, negotiations between both parties recommenced soon after the San Remo Conference. On June 21st 1920, Vansittart reported that he was trying to obtain concessions from the French on the north-eastern borders and the division of the Litani water in favor of the Jewish settlers. He was hoping to succeed: 'If I don't, the Jews will have to lump it. We can give them the Meinertzhagen line south of the Sykes-Picot line, and if I can't move the French, they must be content with that.'[70] As for the

---

[67] The waters were designated to answer immigration and colonization by Jews. The French proposal for the supply of waters was therefore aimed at the Jewish settlers. The Arab population, which was stable in numbers, to whom immigration and colonization did not apply, was not part of the deal.

[68] Lloyd George, op. cit., Vol. II, p. 1179-80.

[69] DBFP, op. cit., Vol. VIII, pp. 174-75. Meeting of the Supreme Council held in San Remo, April 25th 1920.

[70] DBFP, op. cit., Vol. XIII, p. 291, Vansittart, temporarily head of the Political Section of the British Peace Delegation, was then engaged in working on the delimitation of the borders of Syria and Palestine. He made his report in a letter addressed to Major Young.

distribution of the Litani waters, Vansittart said he envisaged a great struggle. The French maintained that the line sketched by Berthelot was never a definite offer as it was subject to the approval of Prime Minister Millerand, which was never given. They later put forward a distinctly less satisfactory line, although it included Banias and Metullah. Vansittart regretted that he did not strike sooner after San Remo, when he could have managed to get the whole Berthelot line in the north and the Meinertzhagen line in the east. Vansittart was, in fact, acting for the Zionist Organization in his negotiations with the French: 'I have communicated the Zionist desideratum to the French and put it in the most favourable light possible'.[71] He updated Major Young and did so, doubtful whether the Zionist proposals would be at all accepted: 'I am continuing to press the Zionist claim as best I can'.[72]

It became clear to the British that the French would not be moved to make any further concessions in relation to the northern and north-eastern frontiers of Palestine. Talks were resumed and an Inter-Departmental Committee was erected at the British Foreign Office to consolidate British interests on this issue. It was assumed that if the French were not willing to be flexible on territory, special emphasis should be placed on safeguarding the water supply of Palestine. Consequently, Curzon instructed Vansittart 'to press for a readjustment which would give to Palestine a fuller control over the head-waters of the Jordan, and

---

[71] DBFP, ibid., Vol. XIII, p. 300. On June 29th 1920, the Zionist desideratum on water supply from Syrian territory was communicated to the French by Vansittart, requiring that the northern boundary of Palestine as defined in the Treaty should be made subject to the following conditions: that Palestine could share the waters of the Litani River with Syria in proportion to the needs of the respective countries; that the administration of this right should be vested in a Commission; and that the right conferred upon Palestine should include permission to divert water from the Litani to Palestine and also to make use of the waters of the Jordan and its tributaries. For this purpose Palestine would be entitled to acquire land and carry out works. (See enclosure 2 in Vansittart's report to major Young, No. 272, June 29th 1920, DBFP, ibid., Vol. XIII, pp. 304-05).

[72] DBFP, ibid., Vol. XIII, p. 300.

especially of the Yarmouk, which is its principal feeder'.[73] He was also instructed to push forward Zionist desiderata on the northern waters as mentioned in his enclosure to Major Young of June 29th 1920.[74] He was to use his best endeavors to secure the frontier based on the Meinertzhagen line, namely: 'A line running east of Ras-el-nakura on the coast to the hills about 5 miles west of Lake Hule, thence north along the divide between the Litani and the Nahr Hasbani to El Bire, thence along the 'Meinertzhagen line' to the Yarmouk River.'[75] This would include much of the water reservoirs of the north and north east of Palestine.

The French refused to meet the minimum British requirements. They even went back on their commitment to conclude a formal agreement on Palestine utilization of the Yarmuk, North Jordan and Litani waters. The British Government was aware that the territory east of the Sea of Galilee and north of the Yarmuk Valley, which the French refused to concede, was 'vital to the practical operations of the Zionist engineering plans.'[76] Curzon conveyed to Vansittart during his negotiations with the French that 'His Majesty's Government are not prepared to conclude any arrangement which does not include due provision for the future utilisation by Palestine of the waters of the Yarmuk and the Litani, which may well prove vital to the economic development of the country and *the creation of a national home for the Jews*'[77] [Italics added]. Therefore, it was decided by the British Government to temporarily suspend any agreement on borders with the French Government and to expunge border definitions from the Mandates.[78]

However, Vansittart managed to persuade Curzon that

---

[73] DBFP, ibid., Vol. XIII, p. 349.

[74] Enclosure 2 in Vansittart's report to major Young, No. 272, June 29th 1920, see n. 62, supra.

[75] DBFP, op. cit., Vol. XIII, No. 322, p. 350, September 30th 1920.

[76] DBFP, ibid., p. 381, November 8th 1920.

[77] DBFP, ibid., No. 334, p. 382, November 9th 1920.

[78] DBFP, ibid., No. 332, p. 378, November 6th 1920; and No. 333, pp. 381-82, November 8th 1920.

deferring the conclusion of an agreement with France on the northern and north-eastern borders of Palestine would be detrimental to British interests and would provide no advantage to the Zionist cause. In the absence of a convention between the two countries, the Sykes-Picot line would then prevail and the Zionists would be unable to take up any territory beyond that line. Again, a major issue in the discussions was whether the proposed agreement would meet Zionist requirements. While the British believed the French proposition fell far short of the Zionist requirements, the French thought that the Zionists went far beyond the formula of Dan to Beersheba – to which both the British and the French adhered. Vansittart conceded that in his prolonged discussions he 'could achieve no modification of the French attitude in regard to frontiers and water supply'.[79]

In consequence, the British decided to give in to the French on both matters. On December 23rd 1920, a Franco-British Convention was signed to settle the boundaries between the territories under the French Mandate of Syria and Lebanon, on the one hand, and the British Mandates of Mesopotamia and Palestine, on the other.[80] Article 1 of the Convention defined the boundaries between Syria, Lebanon and Palestine. By this Convention, the French did, in fact, agree to make adjustments along the Sykes-Picot line so as to include within Palestine the areas of Safed, the waters of Lake Huleh, and the Jordan sources as far north as Metullah and Banias, the latter known as the site of biblical Dan. The French Government, however, made no concessions regarding the north-eastern frontier of Palestine which was inconsistent with the Sykes-Picot Agreement, whether in the north of the Yarmuk Valley or east of the Sea of Galilee. Moreover, the French refused to enter any formal agreement allowing utilization by Palestine of the waters of the Yarmuk,

---

[79] DBFP, ibid., Vol. XIII, No. 337, pp. 385-87, November 13th 1920.

[80] Cmd. 1195, op. cit. (1921); CAB 24/126, C.P. 3123, Appendix 31, Annexure 1, pp. 197-200; the American Journal of International Law, Vol. 16, No. 3, Supplement: Official Documents (July 1922) pp. 122-26. Convention on Certain Points Connected with the Mandates for Syria and the Lebanon, Palestine and Mesopotamia.

North Jordan, or the Litani.[81] Under Article 2 of the Convention, a Commission was established to demarcate on the spot the border line between Syria and Palestine. The Commission concluded its mission on March 7th 1923 and the boundary line between Syria and Palestine from the Mediterranean to El-Hamme was finally fixed.[82]

The Southern Frontier of Palestine

The southern boundary was the first Palestine Mandate boundary on which agreement was reached, although it did not then achieve international recognition. Merely an administrative boundary, the borderline between Egypt and Palestine did not become an official international boundary during the three decades of the British Mandate. The British Government regarded the delimitation of the borders between Palestine and Egypt as an internal affair,[83] with no need for outside intervention, since Egypt and Palestine were both subject to British administration. After the establishment of the State of Israel, the status of the border line between Israel and Egypt remained unchanged: It was not recognized as an international boundary, but as a cease-fire line. It only became an international boundary after the conclusion of the peace treaty with Egypt in 1979 (the Camp David Accords).[84]

---

[81] DBFP, op. cit., Vol. XIII, p. 381, November 8th 1920. Letter from Tilley on behalf of Curzon addressed to Weizmann. However, Article 8 of the Convention stipulated that experts on both sides would, within six months, examine whether there was any surplus of waters from the Upper Jordan, the Yarmuk and their tributaries, after the needs of territories under the French Mandate were met, and if so, France would act liberally to supply the surplus waters to Palestine.

[82] League of Nations-Treaty Series, No. 565: *Exchange of Notes Constituting an Agreement Between the British and French Governments Respecting the Boundary Line Between Syria and Palestine from the Mediterranean to El Hamme.* March 7th 1923. http://www.assidmer.net/doc/British-French_ Boundary_Agreement,_1923.pdf

[83] DBFP, op. cit., Vol. IV, p. 1277, Balfour's assent to Justice Brandeis assumption, See Memorandum by Frankfurter, June 24th 1919.

[84] Gideon Biger, *The Boundaries of Modern Palestine 1840-1947*, Routledge Curzon (Taylor & Francis Group), London and New York, 2004, p. 80.

At first, there was much confusion and uncertainty regarding the delimitation of the southern border of Palestine. The British Government accepted the formula of Dan to Beersheba. So did the French. The question was whether this formula went as far south as the Gulf of Aqaba and the Red Sea. On August 16th 1918, while the war was still waging, Ormsby-Gore presented his views on the future borders of Palestine in the interest of the British Empire and Zionism. Speaking of the southern border, he suggested that the line should go from the southern tip of the Dead Sea in the east, across the south of Beersheba, and thence to Raffah in the West, leaving out the whole Negev desert as far south as Aqaba. 'With regard to Aqaba', he added, 'the demand for this would lead to great political complications'.[85] In a later Report, he explained that the Negev was a Bedouin country which was more akin to the province of Sinai than to Palestine.[86] These were also the views submitted by Major O. Elbynne of the Geographical section to the British Delegation to the Peace Conference in Paris on April 9th 1919.

In 1918, uncertainty prevailed in the British Cabinet too. At a meeting of the War Cabinet Eastern Committee, in a discussion regarding the southern boundary of Palestine, Curzon alluded to the prevailing arguments. That is, on the one hand the productive lands south of Gaza should be included in Palestine because they were necessary to the development of the country, while, on the other hand, bringing into Palestine the Bedouins of the Negev Desert would only complicate matters since they belong in Sinai and they should not be associated with Palestine at all.[87] Curzon urged the Committee to come to a decision with respect to this boundary before attending the Peace Conference.

The Zionists were also active in putting forward their claims

---

[85] ZMFI, op. cit., p. 757. Address by Ormsby-Gore at a meeting with the London Zionist Political Committee, Annex 2 to a Report on the existing political situation in Palestine, submitted on August 27th 1918.

[86] ZMFI, ibid., p. 751, August 27th 1918; Report by W. Ormsby-Gore on the existing *Political Situation in Palestine and Contiguous Areas*, by the political officer in charge of the Zionist Commission.

[87] Lloyd George, op. cit., Vol. II, p. 1145.

with regard to the delimitation of the southern border. These comprised two main elements: the desire to bring about the inclusion of (a) the Negev triangle within the borders of Palestine and (b) the fertile areas east of El Arish in the delimitation of the border line with Egypt. The Zionists asked that the Negev triangle, namely from the Dead Sea in the east, via the Gulf of Aqaba in the south, to the outskirts of, but not including, El-Arish, in the west, be embodied in Palestine, leaving the details of the border line to be agreed upon with the British controlled Egyptian Government. This last requirement was submitted by the Zionist Delegation to the Council of Ten at the Peace Conference on February 27th 1919.[88] The Political Section of the British Delegation to the Peace Conference supported the Zionist demands as a compromise between the Zionists and the Egyptian Government. These were 'to include an enclave of the fertile territory west of the present Palestine-Egyptian frontier up to, but not including, El Arish, as well as the triangle of territory between the present Egyptian frontier and the Wadi Araba down to the Gulf of Akaba.'[89]

Meinertzhagen, based on Lloyd George's formula of 'Dan to Beersheba', mapped the area which he regarded as biblical Palestine. He discovered that the territory of Palestine in biblical times included the Negev triangle from Moab [the Dead Sea] in the east, to the head of the Gulf of Aqaba in the South, and thence along the Egyptian-Turkish administrative frontier to Gaza in the West. Interestingly, 'both Lloyd George and Balfour agreed to this boundary'.[90] On another occasion, Meinertzhagen briefed Curzon on the Palestine frontiers, recommending that the southern boundary should remain the old Turkish-Egyptian boundary from the Gulf of Aqaba to Raffah.[91]

Weizmann made no secret of the Zionist ambition to incorporate

---

[88] DBFP, op. cit., Vol. IV, pp. 161-62.

[89] Rise of Israel, op. cit., Vol. 10, Doc. 80, p. 309-10, F.O. 608/98, Memorandum by the Political Section of the British Delegation on Palestine Frontiers, May 6th 1919.

[90] Meinertzhagen, op. cit., p. 355.

[91] DBFP, op. cit., Vol. IV, p. 535, November 17th 1919.

the Negev desert with an outlet to the Red Sea into the frontiers of Palestine. He made that clear at a meeting with Meinertzhagen[92] and later addressed Churchill as Colonial Secretary on this matter. The justification for this desire had historical and economical roots. It was proven that in biblical Palestine, King Solomon had access to the Red Sea. It was also argued that this outlet was vital to the economic future of Palestine, where the Jewish National Home was to be established. Weizmann preferred to base his arguments mainly on economic grounds and on the significance of the Negev and the Red Sea to Palestine and to the Jewish National Home.[93]

It is noteworthy that the incorporation of the Negev triangle within the boundaries of Palestine contradicted the Sykes-Picot Agreement, but on this occasion the French showed very little, if any, opposition. In contrast to the north and north-eastern boundary of Palestine, which had to contend with French interests in Syria and Lebanon, France had no interest in the Negev, which, in any event, was designated to be part of area B, under British influence. Regardless, the British considered the Sykes-Picot Agreement to be a 'foolish document'[94] and they referred to it as an 'unfortunate agreement',[95] and that, anyway, it perished in the fire of the war flames. The French, during the premiership of Clemenceau, treated it, according to Lloyd George, as a document that had been scrapped. The Zionists opposed it vehemently and so did the Arabs.[96] Therefore, there could be no opposition to a British move to make the Negev part of Palestine.

The delimitation of the southern border with Egypt was conducted as an internal British affair. Discussions on this matter took place between the British Administration of Palestine and the British Administration of Egypt, without the intervention of the other Allied Powers and without the involvement of the

---

[92] Meinertzhagen, op. cit., p. 13, January 30th 1919.

[93] Rise of Israel, op. cit., Vol. 13, p. 89, March 1st 1921.

[94] Lloyd George, op. cit., Vol. II, p. 1025, see also p. 1116.

[95] Ibid., p. 1292.

[96] Ibid., p. 1037-38; Weizmann, op. cit., p. 191; George Antonius – *The Arab Awakening*, Allegro Editions, 1939, p. 248.

Zionists in the negotiations. The question was whether to keep the administrative border line that was agreed upon on October 1st 1906 between the Ottoman Empire, who then ruled the provinces of Jerusalem and Hedjaz, and Great Britain, who controlled Egypt, or to make any changes therein. The 1906 border line was a straight line connecting Raffah on the Mediterranean with the northern tip of the Gulf of Aqaba, and was imposed by the British on the Ottomans through gun-boat diplomacy. In 1906, the British insisted on this line for the purpose of keeping the Ottomans as far away as possible from the Suez Canal, a vital British route to India and the Far East.[97]

A change in this state of affairs occurred when Britain occupied Palestine. Thus, what used to be a British-Ottoman boundary extending from Raffah to the Gulf of Aqaba became a dividing line between two territories controlled by the same Power – Britain. After discussions held within the British Political Delegation on these matters and a memorandum prepared on May 9th 1919, it was decided to cling to the 1906 line and adopt it as the boundary between Egypt and Palestine. It came as a compromise between various proposals. This decision, which lasted until 1979, was not followed by any official announcement either from the British Administration in Palestine or that in Egypt. [98]

The Eastern Frontier of Palestine

The Eastern frontier was the most complicated and last to be determined.[99] The Mandate comprised territories on both

---

[97] The Ottomans insisted on an administratively designated boundary, since in their view Egypt was nominally still under the authority of the Ottoman Empire, and the concept was that the dividing line between Sinai and the provinces of Jerusalem and Hedjaz did not form an international boundary, but an internal administrative one. See c– "The Evolution of the Egypt-Israel Boundary: From Colonial Foundations to Peaceful Borders", in *International Boundaries Research Unit: Boundary and Territory Briefing*, Clive Schofield ed., University of Durham, U.K. 1995. Vol. I No. 8, pp. 5, 8.

[98] Biger, op. cit., p. 96.

[99] The Eastern Boundary in this context means the boundary south of the Yarmuk Valley and south of the Sykes-Picot line. The eastern boundary north of the Yarmuk, namely the North-Eastern boundary discussed above, was settled through the Franco-British Convention of December 23rd 1920. See pp. 244 et seq., supra, on the British-French Dispute.

sides of the River Jordan, from the Mediterranean in the west to Mesopotamia in the east. The border between these two countries was to be determined by the Principal Allied Powers, as stipulated in the San Remo Resolution and Mandate instrument. However, this border was determined by the British alone, without any outside intervention, after having illegally established in the eastern part of Palestine a separate political entity by the name of Trans-Jordan in total breach of the Mandate.[100] Ample evidence exists that Mesopotamia and Palestine were to be coterminous.[101] The Principal Allied Powers conferred three mandates in the Middle East on two Mandatories: the Mandate for Syria, including Lebanon, to France and the Mandates for Mesopotamia and Palestine to Britain. No mandate was established for Trans-Jordan, which did not then exist. How far east the Mandate for Palestine would extend was indeterminate until after Trans-Jordan was created. As a result, it became necessary to fix the border between Palestine and Trans-Jordan rather than between Palestine and Mesopotamia.

At no time before the creation of Trans-Jordan was the Jordan River contemplated to form the eastern boundary of Palestine.

---

[100] See pp. 266 et seq., infra.

[101] See for example Curzon's statement to Vansittart on September 30th 1920 that 'the mandates for Palestine and Mesopotamia as originally drafted assumed that the two areas were coterminous', DBFP, op. cit., Vol. XIII, p. 351; See also Balfour's memorandum on Syria, Palestine and Mesopotamia, August 11th 1919, in which he regards Syria, Palestine and Mesopotamia as coterminous areas, DBFP, op. cit., Vol. IV, p. 347; see again John Tilley's minutes on Major Young's Memorandum of November 6th 1920, in which he spoke of a mutual frontier between Palestine and Mesopotamia, making no mention of Trans-Jordan. He suggested that a decision in this regard 'should be deferred as long as possible owing to innumerable difficulties raised in regard to the western frontier of Mesopotamia'. DBFP, op. cit., Vol. XIII, p. 380. [John A.C. Tilley served as British Assistant Secretary for Foreign Affairs]. See, following, minutes by Curzon in which he stated that he would like to clear off 'A' Mandates, specifically referring to the Mandates for Syria, Palestine and Mesopotamia. Again, there was no mention of Trans-Jordan. Ibid. In *Recommendations of the Prime Minister's Interdepartmental committee on the Creation of a Middle East Department in the Colonial Office*, of January 31st 1921, the Committee referred to the boundaries of Mesopotamia and Palestine as unsettled coterminous boundaries, no mention being made to Trans-Jordan, Hurewitz, op. cit., No. 57, p. 232; CAB 21/186, C.P. 2545, February 7th 1921.

Weizmann asserted that at the time of the Declaration, November 1917: 'The eastern boundary of Palestine went as far as the Hedjaz Railway and included Trans-Jordan'[102] – the Hedjaz Railway ran 40-60 km east and parallel to the Jordan River. Furthermore, the British Government brought about the insertion of Article 25 into the Mandate in order to create Trans-Jordan as a political entity on the eastern part of Palestine. This read:

> In the territories lying *between the Jordan and the eastern boundary of Palestine as ultimately determined,* the Mandatory shall be entitled ...to postpone or withhold application of such provisions of this mandate as he may consider inapplicable...[103] [Italics added]

Obviously, the Jordan did not mark the eastern boundary of Palestine. Lloyd George's formula *from Dan to Beersheba, the area occupied by the twelve tribes,* which was also adopted by the French, suggested the inclusion, within the boundaries of Palestine, of the Gilead, Ammon and Moab territories, which were occupied in the biblical era by the tribes of Manasseh, Gad and Reuben, all situated on the east side of the Jordan,

Balfour, in his role as Foreign Secretary, proclaimed on various occasions that Palestine comprised territories on both sides of the Jordan. In a Memorandum addressed to Lloyd George, with a copy sent to Curzon, he stated that 'the eastern frontier should be so drawn as to give the widest scope to agricultural development *on the left bank of the Jordan,* consistent with leaving the Hedjaz railway completely in Arab possession'[104] [Italics added]. On another occasion, he prepared a detailed Memorandum on the situation respecting Syria, Palestine and Mesopotamia, in which he stated firmly that 'Palestine is essentially the valley of the Jordan, with the adjacent coast and plains' – a reality he claimed

---

[102] Weizmann, op. cit., p. 180.

[103] http://avalon.law.yale.edu/20th_century/palmanda.asp; The British Mandate, The Avalon Project, Yale Law School, Lilian Goldman Library.

[104] DBFP, op. cit., Vol. IV, p. 302, June 26th 1919.

was disputed by no one. He emphasized that *Palestine should extend into the lands lying east of the Jordan,*[105] to be made available to the largest number of Jewish immigrants. In an interview with Justice Brandeis, Balfour expressed optimism that Feisal, representing Hedjaz's interests, would agree 'to having an eastern boundary of Palestine go up to the Hedjaz railroad.'[106]

Meinertzhagen's map, based on Lloyd George's formula from Dan to Beersheba, advocated that the eastern border of Palestine should run 25-30 km west of the Hedjaz Railway, and thus encompass the fertile areas east of the Jordan River and take full control of the Jordan valley and the Dead Sea as a whole. This line became known as the Meinertzhagen line and it was suggested by Meinertzhagen to Curzon on November 17th 1919 as the future eastern boundary of Palestine.[107] However, less than a year later, Curzon was having second thoughts on the future of the territories east of the Jordan River.[108]

The concept that Palestine should extend to the east of the Jordan River was shared by other British professional officials apart from Meinertzhagen. Thus, Ormsby-Gore suggested in August 1918, while the war for the conquest of Palestine was still waging, that Palestine should command the whole of the Jordan valley and its lower eastern slopes, excluding the plateau of Ajlun and the mountains of Moab.[109] Similarly, Major O. Elbynne of the Geographical Section, British Delegation to the

---

[105] DBFP, ibid., Vol. IV, p. 347, August 11th 1919.

[106] DBFP, ibid., Vol. IV, p. 1277, June 24th 1919.

[107] Meinertzhagen, op. cit., p. 62; DBFP, ibid., Vol. IV, p. 533; Rise of Israel, Vol. 10, Doc. 86, pp.342-43, November 17th 1919.

[108] Curzon instructed Herbert Samuel, after the latter assumed position as High Commissioner, that the eastern boundary of Palestine, south of the Sykes-Picot line, would be fixed 'by agreement between us and local authorities'. DBFP, op. cit., Vol. XIII, p. 331, August 6th 1920. For further details see pp. 266 et seq., infra.

[109] ZMFI, op. cit., p. 757, Ormsby-Gore laying down his proposals for the future borders of Palestine in a meeting with the London Political Committee of the Zionist Organization on August 16th 1918; and again in a thorough report on the existing political situation in Palestine and contiguous areas. ZMFI, ibid. p. 751, August 27th 1918.

Peace Conference, proposed that in the east the boundary should generally run from point 2794 on the top of Mount Hermon (Djebel Esh Sheikh) southwards to the Yarmuk and then via Um Keiss, Wadi Zerka to Wadi El Jadeia 10 km east of the eastern shore of the Dead Sea, all locations situated east of the Jordan River.[110] The main objection to a further extension of the border line to the east was that it would further increase the Muslim and Arab population of Palestine.[111]

The American Administration did not lag far behind. On February 10th 1920, just before the Conference of London convened, a message was received from President Wilson addressed to France and Britain. It urged that 'Palestine should have rational boundaries in the North and East', specifically referring to the Litani River and watershed of the Hermon in the north, and presumably to the Hauran and the Yarmuk valleys in the east, hoping that 'the French and British Governments were not carrying out the Sykes-Picot Agreement to the detriment of Mr. Balfour's Declaration as to the Palestine of the future'.[112] It was also the recommendation of the Intelligence Section of the American Delegation to the Peace Conference that Palestine should control its own water sources 'on Mount Hermon in the east to the Jordan'.[113]

The Zionist claim to the eastern boundary of Palestine shifted from the Hedjaz Railway to the Syrian Desert, particularly after Britain succumbed to the French regarding the northern frontier and gave up demands to the waters of the Litani and the sources of the Jordan and the Yarmuk. At first, the Zionists refrained from asking for an eastern frontier that would go beyond the Hedjaz Railway because this was thought to be an Arab domain.

---

[110] Rise of Israel, op. cit., Vol. 10, Doc. 78, pp 303-04, Memorandum on the Proposed Boundaries of Palestine, April 9th 1919.

[111] Rise of Israel, ibid., Vol. 10, Doc. 80, p. 308, Memorandum by the Political Section of the British Delegation on *Palestine Frontiers*, May 6th 1919 (F.O. 608/98).

[112] DBFP, op. cit., Vol. IV, p. 634.

[113] David Hunter Miller – *My Diary at the Conference of Paris*, op. cit., Vol. IV, Doc. 246 (para. 26 on Palestine), p. 263. January 21st 1919.

However, when economic sources were cut off from Palestine in the north, the Zionists saw no alternative but to insist on a frontier in the east that would go as far as the desert, subject to guarantees being given to safeguard Arab interests with regard to the Hedjaz Railway.

Thus, in early conversations with British Officials, Weizmann openly showed satisfaction with an eastern boundary adjacent to the Hedjaz Railway. This was what he transmitted to Meinertzhagen,[114] and later to Field Marshall Henry Wilson, member of the War Cabinet stating: 'It is absolutely essential for the economic development of Palestine that the eastern line be so drawn as to include the territories east of the Jordan which are capable of receiving and maintaining large Jewish mass settlements', clarifying that 'Trans-Jordania as far as the Hedjaz Railway would afford the requisite opportunities for such development.'[115] This was also the official requirement which was presented by the Zionist Delegation to the Paris Peace Conference on February 27th 1919.[116] Herbert Samuel, then Chairman of the Advisory Committee on the Economic Development of Palestine, whose advice was sought by Sir W. Tyrell, advocated strongly for the incorporation within the borders of Palestine of the fertile territory east of the Jordan as a necessary component for the maintenance of its inhabitants and the establishment of a modern state.[117]

Jewish claims were generally taken into consideration by the British negotiators in the early stages. In a Memorandum prepared on May 6th 1919 by the Political Section of the British Delegation to the Peace Conference, note was taken of Zionist demands for Palestine frontiers based on three categories: maximum, intermediate and minimum. It was taken into account that maximal Jewish demands were the incorporation within the borders of Palestine of the 'fertile country East of the Jordan and

---

[114] Meinertzhagen, op. cit., pp. 13-14, January 30th 1919.

[115] Rise of Israel, op. cit., Vol. 10, Doc. 75, p. 290, February 4th 1919.

[116] DBFP, op. cit., Vol. IV, pp. 161-62; Hurewitz, op. cit., p. 138.

[117] DBFP, ibid., Vol. IV, (Enclosure 3 in No. 197), p. 285, June 5th 1919.

in the Nahr Yarmuk valley'.[118]

However, Zionist contentment with the Hedjaz Railway forming the eastern border of Palestine changed into deep concern when it came to be known that the British had given in to French demands regarding the northern boundary. This would deprive Palestine of territories stretching up to the Litani and of the water resources of the Jordan and the Yarmuk Rivers. It became obvious to the Zionists that the only territories for survival were those in the east, and they pleaded to extend the eastern frontier as far as the desert subject to safeguarding Arab interests in the Hedjaz Railway. On March 1st 1921, Weizmann addressed Churchill on what he referred to as 'a matter of vital importance to the economic future of Palestine and the upbuilding of the Jewish National Home'[119] and appealed to Churchill 'to draw no definite eastern frontier short of the desert'.[120] Weizmann based his appeal not only on economic but also on historical grounds, stating that the territories east of the Jordan were in biblical times inhabited by Jews, namely by the tribes of Gad, Reuben and Manasseh. Weizmann barely knew that at the time he pleaded with Churchill, the latter had already made up his mind to detach the whole area east of the Jordan from Palestine, and to construct a new Arab political entity by the name of Trans-Jordan, in total breach of the Mandate instrument and the convention of San Remo, as will be discussed in the next chapter.

---

[118] Rise of Israel, op. cit., Vol. 10, Doc. 80, pp. 308-09, F.O. 608/98.

[119] Rise of Israel, ibid., Vol. 13, Doc. 10, p. 86.

[120] Ibid., p. 87.

Part III

Breach of Trust

Chapter I

The Creation of Trans-Jordan and the First Partition of Palestine

By the end of 1920, a change in British foreign policy on Palestine could be observed. This was due to a multitude of factors: the conclusion of Balfour's office as Foreign Secretary, Arab violence, the reluctance of the British Administration in Palestine to implement the provisions of the Mandate in furtherance of the establishment of the Jewish National Home, and the creation of the Middle East Department in the Colonial Office and the appointment of Winston Churchill as Colonial Secretary. This change was sensed by Herbert Samuel, who soon after taking office as High Commissioner warned Foreign Secretary Curzon of 'making a grave error of policy if we do not include Trans-Jordania in Palestine. It will certainly result in anarchy or French control across the border'.[1] Curzon did not agree with Samuel. He replied that the British Government was opposed to the immediate inclusion of Trans-Jordan under the Palestine administration, but to avoid the danger of the area relapsing into a state of anarchy, he suggested the dispatch of a few British political officers as advisers to major towns such as Salt and Kerak for the purpose of assisting in the formation of local self-government in those areas.[2] Curzon was anxious to convey to Samuel that the British Government had no intention at that stage of extending their responsibilities in Trans-Jordan and insisted upon Samuel to abide strictly by this policy.[3]

Under Curzon's instructions, Samuel proceeded to Salt on August 20th 1920, where he informed deputations from local towns, villages, and tribes that the organization of Trans-Jordan

---

[1] *Documents on British Foreign Policy 1919-1939*, ed. Rohan Butler & J.P.T. Bury, First Series, HMSO, London 1958, [hereinafter DBFP], Vol. XIII, No. 302, p. 334. Warning by Samuel in a private telegram to Curzon sent on August 7th 1920 and marked *very urgent*.

[2] DBFP, Ibid., Vol. XIII. pp. 337-38, telegram No. 80 of August 11th 1920.

[3] DBFP, Ibid., Vol. XIII, p. 344, telegram No. 110 of August 26th 1920. See also CAB 24/156 British Empire Report, No. 25, September 1st 1920, pp. 5-6.

would not form part of the Palestine administration, but would be ruled by self-governing bodies assisted by British officers serving as political advisers.[4]

A month later, it became obvious that the British were pondering the separation of Trans-Jordan from the territory of the Jewish National Home. This move followed considerations made by an Inter-Departmental Committee at the British Foreign Office on the question of the frontiers between the French and British mandatory areas. Curzon was well aware of the fact, as he put it, that 'the mandates for Palestine and Mesopotamia as originally drafted assumed that the two areas were coterminous'.[5] Although there could be no doubt that the territory of Trans-Jordan as far east as Mesopotamia formed part of the Mandate for Palestine, Curzon instructed Vansittart in continuance of negotiations with the French that the British Government is 'already treating 'Trans-Jordania' as separate from the Damascus State, while at the same time avoiding any definite connection between it and Palestine, thus leaving the way open for the establishment there, should it become advisable, of some form of independent Arab Government, perhaps by arrangement with King Hussein or other Arab chiefs concerned'.[6] For this reason, Curzon instructed Vansittart to leave the eastern boundary of Palestine and the south-western boundary of Mesopotamia to later determination.

This shift in British foreign policy became more conspicuous when late in December 1920, Curzon mentioned a frontier between Palestine and Trans-Jordan, rather than between Palestine and Mesopotamia, and directed Samuel to inform Feisal that fixing this frontier was a matter for the British Government to decide in consultation with the local inhabitants.[7]

---

[4] DBFP, Ibid., Vol. XIII, p. 343, August 22nd 1920.

[5] DBFP, Ibid., Vol. XIII, p. 351. September 30th 1920; J.C. Hurewitz, ed. – *The Middle East and North Africa in World Politics: A Documentary Record,* 2nd Edition, Yale University Press, New Haven & London, 1979. Doc. 92, p. 392; Norman Bentwich, *Mandates System*, Longmans, Green & Co., London, 1930, p. 22.

[6] Ibid.

[7] DBFP, ibid., Vol. XIII, p. 421, December 23rd 1920.

At that particular time, the Colonial Office entered into the picture with its newly created department: The Middle East Department. This department was formed after recommendations to create it were made by an Inter-Departmental Committee appointed at the start of 1921 by the Prime Minister. These recommendations were endorsed by the Cabinet on February 14th 1921, and following that Churchill replaced Lord Milner as Colonial Secretary. In their report of January 31st 1920, the Committee did not seem to be on the same page as the Foreign Office on two major points. Firstly, they stated that they understood Palestine to cover Trans-Jordan and secondly, that the boundary in the east was to run between Palestine and Mesopotamia, making no mention of Trans-Jordan.[8] As a result of the creation of the new department that took over from the Foreign Office and the appointment of a new Colonial Secretary, the Cabinet authorized Churchill to hold a conference in Cairo for consultations, meetings, and discussions with British Authorities on the scene. According to Colonel T.E. Lawrence, who took part in the preliminary preparations made in London for the conference:

> The decisions of the Cairo Conference were prepared by us in London…it was decided to include Trans-Jordan in Palestine, to make it indistinguishable from Palestine and to open it to Jewish immigration. Every point was decided at Cairo, as originally settled in London, except the one about Transjordan. When the Conference met, Abdullah was marching from the Hedjaz to Transjordan with a view to attacking the French in Syria. To stop him would have required troops and money. It was decided to negotiate with him.[9]

---

8   Hurewitz, op. cit., Doc. 57, p. 232; CAB 21/186, C.P. 2545.

9   From Sir Lewis Bernstein Namier's notes of conversations with T.E. Lawrence made on July 19th 1930. Namier stated that he put down in a minute a summary of what he heard from Lawrence and published later in the Manchester Guardian on May 20th 1935, the day of Lawrence's funeral. Namier held a position in the Political Intelligence Department of the Foreign Office.

In fact, the British position on Trans-Jordan crystallized when Emir Abdullah appeared on the scene from the Hedjaz threatening to attack the French for expelling his brother Feisal from the throne in Syria. Abdullah regarded Emir Feisal as King of Syria, including Trans-Jordan with its capital in Damascus and sent messages to all the Sheiks to unite them against the French. It was also announced that for this purpose he joined Sherif Mohammed Ali and formed an alliance with Mustapha Kemal of Turkey. Urgent alerts to this effect were dispatched to Curzon by Samuel as early as December 1920,[10] concluding 'I should be remiss if I did not call attention to the seriousness of the situation which may be now developing'.[11] Alerts continued in the following months. For example, in February 1921 Samuel criticized British inactivity, pointing out that 'there had been no interruption either in the preparations for an attack on the French or in the Sherifian propaganda'.[12] He stressed that Sherifian influence was on the increase, and that an attempt was made to sabotage the railway north of Dar'aa in the French zone.[13]

In his memoirs, Samuel explained the gravity of the situation which he termed 'critical'. He indicated that when news arrived that Emir Abdullah was marching from the south into Transjordan at the head of a large force of Arabs,[14] with the declared intention of attacking the French in Damascus, the British had to make a

---

[10] DBFP, op. cit., Vol. XIII, pp. 408, 411, 413. Urgent telegraph warnings of Abdullah's arrival in Ma'an were sent by Samuel to Curzon on December 3rd 1920; on December 6th; and on December 12th. Again on February 22nd 1921 to warn of Abdullah's arrival with his men in Amman, CAB 24/156, British Empire Report, No. 38, March 2nd 1921.

[11] DBFP, ibid., Vol. XIII, p. 413, December 12th 1920.

[12] CAB 24/156, British Empire Report, No. 37, February 16th 1921, reporting of telegraphs sent by Herbert Samuel on February 1st and 10th 1921.

[13] Ibid.

[14] In his report to Amery as Colonial Secretary, on April 22nd 1925, Samuel stated that Emir Abdullah arrived in Trans-Jordan from Hedjaz "with a small force". See Rise of Israel, op. cit., Vol. 13, Doc. 35, 493, p. 544, *Report of the High Commissioner on the Administration of Palestine 1920-1925*. It seems that the British Government exaggerated the force that accompanied Abdullah and wrongly attributed to him military capabilities that he did not have, this being known only later.

stand. On the one hand, they could not allow their mandatory area to be used as a base for an attack on their French neighbors. On the other hand, the British had no force available to stop them and neither did they wish to be in direct conflict with the Arabs whom they regarded as friends. It was also feared that an Arab attack on the French from Trans-Jordan might give the French an excuse to invade Trans-Jordan south of the Sykes-Picot line and entangle the British in a conflict they would do their utmost to avoid.[15] The solution was found in the appeasement of Emir Abdullah by the creation of Trans-Jordan as an Arab territory east of the river Jordan and appointing him ruler of that territory.[16]

The persistent dispatches received from Samuel caused much anxiety in the Cabinet. Curzon hastened to approach Feisal, while the latter was in London, to warn him, as representative of the Hashemite family and the King of Hedjaz, against taking any action that would be detrimental to French interests in Syria.[17] Promises were made and assurances given by Feisal that Abdullah would cause no trouble, but information kept coming that Arab attack on French installations in Syria was imminent. To combat the situation, British policy with regard to the area of Trans-Jordan was reshaped. Soon after the creation of the Middle East department on February 14th 1921 and before the departure of Churchill and his entourage to the Cairo Conference on March 1st, Churchill was furnished with a memorandum drawn up in London by the Middle East Department. This was presumably carried out under his instructions, which brought about a complete change in the British position on Trans-Jordan from the one described by Colonel Lawrence. The Memorandum was drafted with the view of ultimately separating Trans-Jordan from Palestine, the former to be treated as Arab territory. As a justification for this change, the McMahon pledge was brought up which promised the establishment of an independent Arab State in portions of the Turkish Vilayet of Damascus, and since

---

[15] Paul L. Hanna – *British Policy in Palestine*, Public Affairs Press, Washington D.C. 1942, p. 76; Hurewitz, op. cit., doc. 92, p. 392.

[16] Herbert Samuel – *Memoirs*, The Cresset Press, London, 1945, p. 160.

[17] DBFP, op. cit., Vol. XIII, p. 412, December 8th 1920.

the western border of this Vilayet was the River Jordan, Trans-Jordan was not to be included in Palestine. In virtue of this logic, it was then contended, Palestine and Trans-Jordan did not stand on the same footing,[18]

The main cause for separating Trans-Jordan from the rest of Palestine was to restrain Emir Abdullah, who was believed to contemplate an attack on the French in Syria, from carrying out his scheme. However, the British were aware that the separation of Trans-Jordan from the rest of Palestine would constitute an illegal act and a total violation of the Mandate, since the British Mandatory derived its legal authority in Palestine from the Mandate instrument, and it would be acting illegally if all its terms, particularly those referring to the Jewish National Home, were not literally applied to the whole territory of Palestine. The Colonial Secretary sought the advice of the Middle East Department, but that too was given on the basis that the Mandate for Palestine stretched on both sides of the River Jordan. The Department pointed out that if the British Government 'wish to assert their claim to Trans-Jordan and to avoid raising with other Powers the legal status of that area, they can only do so by proceeding upon the assumption that Trans-Jordan forms part of the area covered by the Palestine Mandate. In default of this assumption Trans-Jordan would be left, under article 132 of the Treaty of Sèvres, to the disposal of the Principal Allied Powers.'[19]

However, Britain did not wish to bring the matter again before the Principal Allied Powers. Therefore, the Middle East Department made efforts to find legal measures to reconcile the

---

[18] See Memorandum Drawn up in London by the Middle East Department prior to the Cairo Conference, CAB 24/126, C.P. 3123, Appendix 2, p. 30; Rise of Israel, op. cit., Vol. 13, Doc. 26, p. 199; in his *Middle East Diary*, op. cit., p. 355, Meinertzhagen asserted that after Lloyd George and Balfour had agreed to the borders of Palestine within the Meinertzhagen line, this territory shrinked further so as to include the region from Dan to Beersheba and the Transjordan catchment area of the Jordan valley only. 'This was further whittled down in 1921 when Mr. Churchill presented the Emir Abdullah with Transjordan, *thus depriving the Jews of a valuable expansion area.*' [Italics added].

[19] CAB 24/126, C.P. 3123, Appendix 2, p. 30; Rise of Israel, op. cit., Vol. 13, Doc. 26, p.199.

Mandate as it was defined with a recognition and support of an Arab State east of the Jordan River. After much deliberation, the Department thought it found the answer in both the second Preamble and Article 3 of the Mandate:

> In the first place, the preamble provides that nothing shall be done which may prejudice the civil and religious rights of existing non-Jewish communities. In the second place, article 3 obliges the Mandatory to encourage the widest measure of self-Government for localities consistent with the prevailing conditions. We consider that these two clauses, taken in conjunction, afford adequate justification for setting up in Trans-Jordan a political system somewhat different from that in force on the other side of the river.

However, this interpretation could not hold water and was clearly invalid. The main theme of the Mandate, as we have seen, was based on the Balfour Declaration, the San Remo Resolution and the wording of the Treaty of Sèvres. Under these international documents, it was Britain's first and foremost responsibility and commitment to establish in Palestine on both sides of the Jordan a National Home for the Jewish people. This commitment was made amid the recognition that had already been given 'to the historical connection of the Jewish people with Palestine and to the grounds for reconstituting their national home in that country'. No such recognition was given by the international community to any other nation or community. Yet, this commitment was coupled with a clear understanding that the establishment of the Jewish National Home would not prejudice the civil and religious rights – not national rights – of existing non-Jewish communities in Palestine. Safeguarding the rights of the existing non-Jewish population in Palestine came, therefore, only as a subsidiary to the main theme. In this context, British compliance with the Balfour Declaration could in no way form a basis for the establishment of an independent Arab entity in the territory pledged by the Principal Allied Powers, and confirmed by the League of Nations, to be the National Home for the Jewish people.

By the same token, the interpretation given by the Middle East Department to Article 3 of the Mandate was exaggerated and unreasonable. Article 3 provided that 'the Mandatory shall, *so far as circumstances permit*, encourage local autonomy'. [Italics added]. This could not have given the Mandatory the power to split Palestine into two parts, creating on a substantial part of it a new political entity, separated from Palestine, with a view to becoming later a State. Furthermore, there was nothing in Article 3 to suggest that the phrase *so far as circumstances permit* meant that the Mandatory was obliged to encourage the *widest measure* of self-Government. What's more, the interpretation given to 'local autonomy' as a legal basis for creating a new political entity was far-fetched and hardly corresponded with its true meaning.

The justification the Department wished to find in both the Preamble and Article 3 contradicted its earlier observation that all Mandate terms should be literally applied to the whole territory of Palestine, for which the British Government accepted responsibility. If the British justification would be accepted, it could turn the Mandate into a farce leaving the Mandatory with full power to decide on the prevailing conditions and their application. Thus, the Mandatory would be *prima facie* given power to split Palestine into small independent colonies, referred to as local autonomies, making a sham of the Balfour Declaration and the establishment of the Jewish National Home.

Churchill was a powerful and pragmatic leader. He had just then taken office as Colonial Secretary. He departed for the Middle East on a fact-finding mission. With his "boots on the ground", Churchill was supposedly better informed than his colleagues in London. His main aim was to reduce expenditure and security forces. He, therefore, approached the Prime Minister and the Cabinet with a one way solution: to placate Emir Abdullah and the Hashemite family, who provided the main danger to peace and tranquility in the region, by separating Trans-Jordan from

Palestine and changing its character in a way that the terms regarding the establishment of the Jewish National Home would not apply. Abdullah was to be appointed as the ruler of that territory fortified by British troops who would also restrain him. Churchill advocated the immediate occupation of Trans-Jordan by British forces based on the above scheme to appease Abdullah as the best way to stop intrigue against the French. In a telegram to Lloyd George, Churchill concluded: 'There is no alternative to this policy as we cannot contemplate hostilities with Abdullah in any circumstances. We must therefore proceed in co-operation and accord with him.'[20]

Churchill requested to be given authority to settle with Emir Abdullah on those terms. Lloyd George expressed the Cabinet's 'considerable misgivings' with regard to Churchill's proposals on Trans-Jordan. To that Churchill replied: 'Abdullah has power to do a great deal of harm particularly against French in Trans-Jordan and if he became actively hostile we should have no means of coping with him'.[21] Churchill's insistence seemed to have convinced the Cabinet and the Prime Minister that there was no alternative to the policy suggested by Churchill,

---

[20] CAB 24/121, C.P. 2751, telegram from the Secretary of State for the Colonies Cairo to the Prime Minister in London. March 18th 1921.

[21] Rise of Israel, op. cit., Vol. 13, Doc. 12, pp. 99-100, F.O. 371/6342, March 23rd 1921; CAB 24/121, C.P. 2770, March 22nd-23rd 1921. This was the view of others too at the Cairo Conference. Samuel agreed that Trans-Jordan should be regarded as a territory to be administered on different lines from Palestine; Major Somerset expressed the view that if Abdullah was not appointed it would be impossible to get rid of him; and Colonel Lawrence said that Abdullah by reason of his position and lineage, possessed very considerable power for good or harm over the tribesmen. See CAB 24/126, C.P. 3123, pp. 97, 99, for internal debate by British officials at the Cairo Conference, March 17th 1921. Col. Lawrence was also reported to have told Sir Lewis B. Namier, who held a position in the Political Intelligence Department of the Foreign Office 1918-1920, that 'as the Cabinet were absolutely opposed to British troops being sent across the Jordan and money being spent on operations... Abdullah could ... be stopped by persuasion only. Had he gone against Syria, the French, after having dealt with them there, could not have been stopped from occupying Transjordan, which had been used as a base against them. Therefore, the best solution was to have a 'British Abdullah' in Transjordan. The situation which had arisen in the spring of 1921 left no other choice'. The Manchester Guardian, May 20th 1935.

and therefore they approved it. It was agreed that Trans-Jordan should be treated henceforth as an Arab province or adjunct of Palestine, while preserving its Arab character and administration. Consequently, Churchill was given the 'go-ahead' to pursue the matter with Abdullah.

For the purpose of meeting with Abdullah, Churchill left Cairo for Jerusalem. The first meeting took place on March 28th 1921. At this meeting, Churchill offered Abdullah to rule Trans-Jordan either directly or through an Arab Governor selected by him and appointed by the High Commissioner of Palestine. Churchill stressed that although economically and geographically the area of Trans-Jordan should go with Palestine, the British Government was prepared to propose that it be constituted as an Arab province under an Arab Governor responsible to the High Commissioner of Palestine. Churchill then referred to the necessity of determining the eastern border between Trans-Jordan and Mesopotamia and the southern border with the Hedjaz. In this context, Palestine was not again mentioned as being coterminous with those two states. In return, Abdullah was to guarantee that he would repress and refrain from causing any agitation or violence to the French from or within Trans-Jordan. This was the key issue in the transaction. Churchill admitted openly to Abdullah that the British Government was 'only concerned to see that the French were not annoyed from Trans-Jordania'.[22] Churchill went on to explain the substance of the offer to prove to Abdullah that it was real and meaningful:

> Trans-Jordania would not be included in the present administrative system of Palestine, and therefore the Zionist clauses of the mandate would not apply. Hebrew would not be made an official language in Trans-Jordania, and the local Government would not be expected to adopt any measure to promote Jewish immigration and colonisation. [23]

---

[22] CAB 24/126, C.P. 3123, Report on Middle East Conference, Appendix 19- Trans-Jordania, p. 112, March 28th 1921.

[23] Ibid., p. 110.

In his conversations with Abdullah, Churchill was clearly referring to the Mandate of Palestine as including territories on both sides of the Jordan, which Abdullah accepted as a fact and so did the other participants. Churchill made a deliberate distinction between Palestine west of the Jordan and the rest of Palestine east of the Jordan and demanded that Abdullah would accept British policy in western Palestine and would not interfere in its application. Abdullah admitted that he came to Trans-Jordan to preserve the remnant of his brother's kingdom of Syria. This was his original intention. But eventually he promised to abide by the terms of the British offer and gave his word of honor that he would keep Trans-Jordan quiet and take no action against the French.

Accordingly, Abdullah was informally appointed to head the newly established Government of Trans-Jordan, albeit under British superintendence and control. This arrangement was to last for six months. He would then be replaced by an Arab Governor who would be selected jointly by Abdullah and the High Commissioner of Palestine and appointed by the latter. The ultimate arrangement contemplated for Trans-Jordan was that the territory should be regarded as an Arab province of Mandatory Palestine, a country extending on both sides of the Jordan River under the High Commissioner for Palestine, 'but not administered by the same methods as has been the case during the last six months or eight months'.[24] The last quotation from Samuel, addressing a meeting assembled at Government House in Jerusalem on March 31st 1921 for the implementation of the agreement with Abdullah, pointed to the fact that for eight months since the appointment of Herbert Samuel on July 1st 1920 as High Commissioner, Palestine east of the Jordan was administered in the same manner as Palestine west of the Jordan with the view to becoming the National Home for the Jewish people, and was, therefore, open to Jewish immigration and settlement. The agreement with Abdullah brought that right to an end.

Under these circumstances, the British Government wished to

---

[24] Ibid, Appendix 21, pp. 126-27.

detach Trans-Jordan from the rest of Palestine, and to establish therein a new Arab political entity in place of a National Home for the Jewish people. However, Churchill was aware of the legal difficulty Britain would be in if such a plan was implemented. Therefore, the goal was to be achieved in stages. The first stage was to preserve Trans-Jordan as part of the Palestine Mandate, but under a different administration. For this purpose,

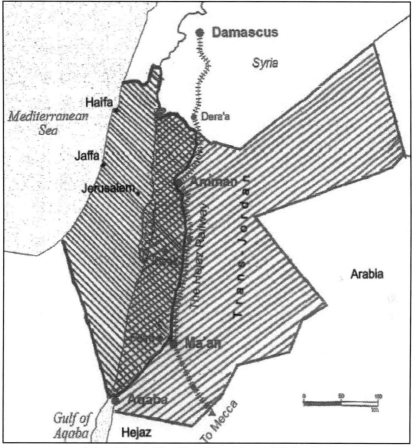

Map No. 6: The First Partition of Palestine
and the Creation of Trans-Jordan.

The land promised as a National Home for the Jewish people.

The creation of Trans-Jordan, first as an Emirate for Emir Abdullah of Hedjaz.

The detached area from the National Home in favor of the Arab Nation; constituting the first partition of Palestine.

he consulted with legal advisers of the Colonial Office and the Foreign Office. He enquired whether the establishment of a local administration in Trans-Jordan under the authority of the High Commissioner of Palestine 'on somewhat different lines from those to be established in Palestine' required modification of the Mandate. Churchill also wished to know whether Britain could have a free hand in interpreting the Mandate and applying its terms as it thought fit to local conditions in specified areas, by adding a general clause to that effect.[25] At that point, Churchill did not ask for advice on the legality of the detachment of Trans-Jordan from the rest of Palestine, but only on the construction of a different administration regarding a specified territory within Palestine. In that context, the answer was that it would be extremely undesirable for the British Government at such a late juncture to propose any alterations to the Mandate.[26] However, if an alteration was necessary, the insertion of the following clause was recommended to come soon after Article 24:

> In the territories lying between the Jordan and the eastern boundary of Palestine as ultimately determined, the mandatory shall be entitled to postpone or withhold application of such provisions of this mandate as he may consider inapplicable to the existing local conditions, and to make such provision for the administration of the territories as he may consider suitable to those conditions, provided no action shall be taken which is inconsistent with the provisions of articles 15, 16 and 18.[27]

This clause was later designated as Article 25, after being modified by adding the words 'with the consent of the Council

---

[25] CAB 24/126, C.P. 3123, Appendix 31, pp. 207-08, Annexure 3(a), paraphrase of telegram from Mr. Churchill to Colonial Office, March 21st 1921.

[26] On December 7th 1920 Britain submitted its final draft of the Mandate for Palestine to the Council of the League of Nations for approval. Cmd.1176, published by HMSO 1921.

[27] CAB 24/126, C.P. 3123, Appendix 31, op. cit., p. 208, Annexure 3(b), paraphrase of telegram from Colonial Office to Churchill , March 25th 1921.

of the League of Nations' after the phrase 'the mandatory shall be entitled'. That is, the consent of the Council of the League of Nations was required for exercising the authority given to Britain to 'postpone or withhold' the application of certain provisions of the Mandate. In consequence, the British Government presented to the Council of the League of Nations a Memorandum on September 16th 1922 asking for the Council's approval of Article 25. The Memorandum was approved subject to the July 24th 1922 decision on the coming into force of the Palestine and Syrian mandates, and was circulated to the other members of the League by the Secretary General.

Article 25 did not provide Britain with the authority to separate Trans-Jordan from the rest of Palestine for the purpose of creating a new political entity. The legal advisers were not asked to examine the legal consequences of such a separation and evidently, they pronounced no opinion on this matter. Though the recommended text was vague and extremely wide as Churchill requested, it did not, and never aimed to, provide him with any legal basis for the divorce of Trans-Jordan from Palestine. In fact, the proviso of Article 25 is a witness to this assumption. It preserved Articles 15, 16, and 18 of the Mandate, which focused on promoting equality and preventing discrimination among inhabitants, foreign nationals, and religious bodies in Palestine. Their preservation, as applying to Palestine rather than to Trans-Jordan, provided proof to the assumption that Trans-Jordan was at that stage still politically regarded as an integral part of Palestine.

The second stage occurred when the British Government submitted their request to the Council to pass a resolution confirming that all terms of the Palestine Mandate concerned with the establishment of the Jewish National Home would not apply to Trans-Jordan, the frontiers of which were defined as comprising –

> all territory lying to the east of a line drawn from a point two miles west of the town of Akaba on the Gulf of that name up the center of the Wady Araba,

Dead Sea and River Jordan to its Junction with River Yarmuk, thence up the center of that river to the Syrian Frontier.[28]

The British seem to have been confident that their request would be met, since a month earlier they had already given constitutional recognition to the administrative separation of Trans-Jordan from Palestine. This was effected through H.M. Order in Council of August 10th 1922, which provided in Article 86 that 'this Order in Council shall not apply to such parts of the territory comprised in Palestine to the east of the Jordan and the Dead Sea as shall be defined by order of the High Commissioner'.[29]

More particularly, the provisions of the Palestine Mandate that were not to apply to Trans-Jordan according to the said British scheme were:[30]

> **Recital 2 of the Preamble** – regarding the responsibility laid on the Mandatory, on Britain, to put into effect the Balfour Declaration in favor of the establishment in Palestine of a National Home for the Jewish people, coupled with a clear understanding that it would not jeopardize civil or religious rights of non-Jewish Communities;

> **Recital 3 of the Preamble** – regarding the recognition given to the historical connection of the Jewish people with Palestine and to the grounds for reconstituting their national home in that country;

> **Article 2** – Making the Mandatory responsible for placing the country under such political,

---

[28] Cmd. 1785, Presented to the British Parliament, December 1922, relating to its Application to the Territory known as Trans-Jordan, under the provisions of Article 25.

[29] https://content.ecf.org.il/files/M00929_PalestineOrderInCouncil1922English.pdf.

[30] Ibid.

administrative and economic conditions as will secure the establishment of the Jewish National Home, as laid down in the preamble;

Article 4 – Regarding the recognition given to the Jewish Agency as a public body for the purpose of advising and co-operating with the Administration of Palestine in such economic, social and other matters as may affect the establishment of the Jewish National Home and the interests of the Jewish population in Palestine;

Article 6 – Regarding the commitment of the Palestine Administration to facilitate Jewish immigration under suitable conditions, and to encourage close settlement by Jews on the land;

Article 7 – Regarding the commitment to facilitate the acquisition of Palestinian citizenship by Jews who take up their permanent residence in Palestine;

Article 11 – Regarding the Administration's authority to arrange with the Jewish Agency to construct or operate, upon fair and equitable terms, any public works, services and utilities, and to develop any of the natural resources of the country, in so far as these matters were not directly undertaken by the Administration;

Article 13 – Regarding responsibility of the Mandatory in connection with the holy places and religious buildings or sites in Palestine;

Article 14 – Regarding the appointment of a special commission to study, define and determine the rights and claims relating to the Holy places and to the different religious communities in Palestine;

Article 22 – Regarding the three official languages in Palestine namely: English, Arabic and Hebrew. The main purpose for adding this Article to the list was aimed at abolishing Hebrew as one of the official languages in Trans-Jordan.

Article 23 – Regarding the obligation of the Palestine Administration to recognize the holy days of the respective communities in Palestine as legal days of rest. Since, so it seems, it was not contemplated that Jews would live in Trans-Jordan, the recognition of the Sabbath as a holy day for the Jews in that area was abolished.

To remain then within the Mandate framework, the British Government declared that it accepted full responsibility as Mandatory for Trans-Jordan and that the Administration of Trans-Jordan would operate under the general supervision of the Mandatory for Palestine. However, this did not last for long.

The third stage took place when Samuel as High Commissioner and representative of the British Government was authorized in April 1923 to go to Amman, which was declared the capital of Trans-Jordan, to make the following public statement:

Subject to the approval of the League of Nations, His Majesty's Government will recognize the existence of an ***independent Government in Trans-Jordan*** *under the rule of his Highness the Amir*[31] ***Abdullah***, provided that such Government is constitutional and places His Britannic Majesty's Government in a position to fulfil its international obligations in respect of the territory by means of an agreement to be concluded between the *two Governments.*[32] [Italics and emphasis added].

---

[31] Amir in Arabic means prince. In English it is often pronounced Emir.

[32] Rise of Israel, op. cit., Vol. 13, Doc. 35, pp. 544-45, April 22nd 1925, Report of the High Commissioner [Sir Herbert Samuel] on the Administration of Palestine 1920-1925.

Likewise, Emir Abdullah, later King Abdullah, asserted in his Memoirs that 'on May 15th 1923 the independence of Transjordan was declared at an official reception attended by Members of the Government and delegations from Palestine. The High Commissioner, Sir Herbert Samuel, came from Jerusalem accompanied by General Clayton.'[33] However, the agreement mentioned in Samuel's address was not concluded until 1928, but in the meantime the Government of the Emir continued to receive recognition and support.[34] In practice, Jews of any nationality were not allowed to enter, settle or acquire citizenship in Trans-Jordan, in complete violation of Article 18 of the Mandate which specifically remained in force.[35] This practice went far beyond the aim of the Council's Resolution. It was criticized by the Permanent Mandates Commission, but persisted under the tacit support of the British Government.[36]

The Agreement of February 20th 1928[37] was the fourth

---

[33] *Memoirs of King Abdullah of Trans-Jordan*, ed. Philip Graves, Jonathan Cape publishers, London 1950, under the heading "We Win Trans-Jordan", chapter 17, p. 207, also published in Rise of Israel, ibid., Vol. 13, Doc. 9, p. 81.

[34] See report by Herbert Samuel at the end of his term of office, April 22nd 1925, entitled: *Report of the High Commissioner on the Administration of Palestine 1920-1925*, p. 54, published in Rise of Israel, ibid., Vol. 13, Doc. 35, p. 545.

[35] Article 18 was aimed at safeguarding equality and preventing discrimination in Palestine against the nationals of any State Member of the League of Nations. Therefore, 'Jews nationals of a State Member of the League could invoke Article 18 to enter Transjordan. They must therefore be treated in exactly the same way as the nationals of any other State Member of the League'. See comments by M. Van Rees in Minutes of the Permanent Mandates Commission, 15th Session, 7th Meeting, Minute 842, June 15th 1928.

[36] The British representative to the Permanent Mandates Commission admitted that 'the policy of the mandatory Power was to leave it to the government of Transjordan to decide whether or not it would admit Jews coming from Palestine. In view of its pledges, the mandatory Power could not bring any pressure to bear on the Government of Transjordan to allow them to enter'. See League of Nations, Permanent Mandates Commission, Minutes of the 15th Session, 7th Meeting, Minute 842, June 15th 1928. See also Akzin, op. cit. p. 39, relying on Minutes of the Permanent Mandates Commission in a number of cases.

[37] Cmd. 3069, Trans-Jordan: Agreement between the United Kingdom and Trans-Jordan, HMSO, London, 1928, published also in Rise of Israel, op. cit., Vol. 13, Doc. 17, pp. 119-25; Bentwich, op. cit., Appendix I, pp. 188-94; Hurewitz, op. cit., Doc. 92, pp. 392-96.

stage in the scheme to bring about the total separation of Trans-Jordan from Palestine and pave the way for the establishment of a new political entity detached from Palestine. It deprived the Jewish National Home, in favor of the Arabs, of a large portion of Palestine, in complete violation of the Mandate and of British commitments to the Zionist Organization and to the Jewish people as a whole. The Agreement was put into effect without having been presented to the Council of the League of Nations for approval, a fact which was strongly criticized by the Permanent Mandates Commission, who finally accepted it due to great pressure from the British Government.[38] The Agreement further stated in Article 20 that it 'shall come into force so soon as it shall have been ratified by the High Contracting Parties after its acceptance by the constitutional government to be set up under Article 2'. However, it seems that the Agreement had never been ratified.[39]

The Agreement included major steps towards the complete detachment of the eastern part of Palestine from its western part. In the Preamble, it was provided that 'His Britannic Majesty is prepared to recognize the existence of an *independent Government* in Trans-Jordan under the rule of His Highness the Amir of Trans-Jordan' – not yet, however, an independent State [italics added]. In the Agreement, Abdullah was already referred to as the 'Amir of Trans-Jordan' and his Administration mentioned as an existing fact. A High Commissioner was appointed for Trans-Jordan as the sole representative of the British Government in that territory, independent of the High Commissioner for Palestine. The powers of legislation and administration entrusted to the Mandatory for Palestine were delegated for the area of Trans-Jordan to Emir Abdullah. An Organic Law came into effect for Trans-Jordan asserting that 'its provisions shall apply to the whole *independent country of Transjordan*'[40] [italics added],

---

[38] Minutes of the Permanent Mandates Commission, 13th Session, pp. 42 *et seq*, quoted in Akzin, op. cit., pp. 39-40.

[39] Rise of Israel, op. cit., Vol. 13, Doc. 17, p. 125, published in 1987, wherein it was stipulated that the 1928 Agreement "had not yet been ratified". If ratification did not occur as late as 1987, it is unlikely to have occurred later on.

[40] See Organic Law of Transjordan, Official Gazette, No. 188, April 19th 1928, Article 1.

within defined frontiers with Syria in the north, Mesopotamia in the east, Hedjaz in the south, and Palestine in the west.[41] In 1934, a supplement was added to the 1928 Agreement allowing Emir Abdullah to conduct limited foreign policy in the form of appointing consular representatives in neighboring Arab States.[42]

Trans-Jordan was later recognized by Britain as a fully independent state, and Emir Abdullah as its sovereign in the Treaty of Alliance Between His Majesty in Respect of the United Kingdom and His Highness the Amir of Trans-Jordan, signed in London on March 22nd 1946.[43] For this purpose Britain did not seek any confirmation from the Principal Allied Powers nor from the Council of the League of Nations, apart from a notification given by the British Foreign Secretary Ernest Bevin to the General Assembly on January 17th 1946 regarding the future of Trans-Jordan: 'It is the intention of His Majesty's Government in the United Kingdom to take steps in the near future for establishing this territory as a sovereign independent State and for recognizing its status as such'.[44] In the last Assembly of the League of Nations held in Geneva on April 8th 1946, a general resolution was passed that 'welcomes the termination of the mandated status of Syria, Lebanon and Transjordan, which have, since the last session of the Assembly, become independent members of the world community'.[45] However, the General Assembly had no authority to confirm or approve the establishment of a new state within fixed boundaries. This was vested in the Principal Allied Powers with the approval of the Council of the League,

---

[41] Ibid., Article 20.

[42] Cmd. 4661 of June 2nd 1934: *Agreement Between His Britannic Majesty and His Highness the Amir of Trans-Jordan Supplementary to the Agreement Signed on 20th February 1928.* Rise of Israel, op. cit., Vol. 13, Doc. 19, pp. 130-32, Article 1.

[43] United Nations, Treaty Series, 1947, No. 74, Article 1, p. 144; Cmd. 6779, March 22nd 1946.

[44] United Nations, Official Records of the General Assembly, First Session, First Part, Plenary Meetings, p. 167.

[45] United States Department of State/ Foreign Relations of the United States, 1946, The Near East and Africa, Vol. VII, Trans-Jordan, quoted in an Aide-Memoire from the British Embassy in Washington to the State Department dated June 10th 1946. pp. 799-800. The League of Nations ceased to exist on April 20th 1946.

and these do not seem to have been given.

Conclusions

The British Government thus led to the partition of Palestine depriving the Jewish people, to whom the pledge embodied in the Balfour Declaration was made, from immigrating, settling and building their National Home in the eastern part of the country.[46] By this, Britain created another Arab State, in addition to the Arab States of Syria, Lebanon and Mesopotamia, on an area promised as a National Home for the Jewish people. This invalid action constituted a breach of the trust conferred upon Britain by the Principal Allied Powers.

Britain was entrusted with the administration, not the sovereignty, of Palestine and was granted full powers of legislation and administration. Britain, therefore, derived its legal power in Palestine from the Mandate. Her authority was confined to what was prescribed in the terms of the Mandate: 'Any degree of authority, control or administration to be exercised by the Mandatory, not having been previously agreed upon by the members of the League, shall be explicitly defined by the Council of the League of Nations.'[47] Britain's solemn acceptance of the responsibility for establishing the Jewish National Home was subject to implementing Article 22 of the Covenant of the League of Nations, which established the right to self-determination. In Palestine, this right, in contrast to all other mandates, was not conferred on the local population, but on the Jewish people worldwide. In comparing the text of the Mandate for Palestine, on the one hand, with those for Mesopotamia or Syria, this discrepancy is immediately visible. Particularly, this discrepancy is evident from comparing the second and third Preambles and Article 2 of the Palestine Mandate with the Preambles and the first articles of the Mandates for Syria and Mesopotamia.

---

[46] This partition was later followed by a second partition of the remainder of Palestine, i.e. of western Palestine, for the purpose of establishing yet another Arab State dividing the territory west of the Jordan between Jewish people and the existing local Arabs. See Chapter II, infra.

[47] British Mandate for Palestine, 7th Recital of the Preamble.

As outlined, Britain took upon itself the responsibility for putting into effect the Balfour Declaration in favor of the establishment of a Jewish National Home in Palestine, within such boundaries as may be fixed by the Principal Allied Powers. Even though the boundaries of Palestine were not yet fixed, there was no doubt that the territory lying east of the Jordan formed an integral part of Palestine. Article 25 of the Mandate clearly considered 'the territories lying between the Jordan and the eastern boundary of Palestine' as territory of Palestine. In fact, there would have been no necessity to add Article 25 to the Mandate if Trans-Jordan had not been regarded as part of Palestine. The British commitment was to establish the Jewish National Home in Palestine, not in a part of Palestine. For Britain to limit its commitment to cover only part of Palestine it needed the consent of the Principal Allied Powers. This consent was never given and the British Government was reluctant to bring the matter again before the Principal Allied Powers to seek their consent. In those circumstances, the decision of Britain to add Article 25 into the Mandate was carried out without authority. The Council of the League was asked by Britain to approve its major violation of the Mandate, and the Council had no legal power to do so without the explicit consent of the Principal Allied Powers. Therefore, the approval of the Council of the League was invalid.

More specifically, the League's Council acted in violation of the duty it assumed under the Mandate, namely, to see that the Mandate was executed in conformity with its provisions. As stipulated in the Mandate, its execution by the Mandatory was to be carried out on behalf of the League of Nations, and the Council of the League was to supervise the Mandatory's actions. For this reason, the Mandatory was required to 'make to the Council of the League of Nations an annual report to the satisfaction of the Council as to the measures taken during the year to carry out the provisions of the mandate,'[48] with a Permanent Mandates Commission established to supervise those reports. It was, therefore, the duty and obligation of the Council

---

[48] Mandate for Palestine, Article 24; The Covenant of the League of Nations, Article 22, 7th and 9th paragraph.

to see that the Mandatory was implementing the establishment of the Jewish National Home in Palestine, not in a part of Palestine. The Council's approval of the administrative separation of Trans-Jordan from the rest of Palestine was in violation of this duty.

This was all the more so since the inclusion of Article 25 was not a minor amendment. Withholding the establishment of the Jewish National Home in the territory of Trans-Jordan brought about a total deviation in the entire concept of the Mandate for Palestine. As mentioned above, Jews were not allowed to enter Trans-Jordan, let alone to settle there. It abandoned the raison d'être of the Palestine Mandate in that territory. It was a breach of British commitments based on the Balfour Declaration, the San Remo Convention and the Mandate for Palestine. In reality, it created a new Mandate and referred to it as the Mandate for Trans-Jordan, appointing a separate High Commissioner, namely, the High Commissioner for Trans-Jordan, independent of the High Commissioner of Palestine – all of which had no legal foundation. In fact, if there was an entity that had the power to make any such modifications in the Mandate it was only the Principal Allied Powers, in whose favor Turkey renounced all her rights and title over Palestine. Article 27 of the Palestine Mandate provided that any modification of the terms of the Mandate required the consent of the League's Council. The Council was, therefore, authorized to confirm the inclusion of Article 25 if initiated or decided on by the Principal Allied Powers. However, the Council per se had no authority to initiate or decide on any modifications in the Mandate. Since Britain was not competent to decide on the inclusion of Article 25, the approval of this decision by the Council did not carry any legal weight. In any event, it is doubtful whether a total deviation of this kind could be considered a *modification* in any meaningful sense of the term.

Furthermore, it is highly questionable whether the Principal Allied Powers, Britain or the League of Nations could morally renege on their promise to the Jewish people, as third party beneficiaries, to give effect to the Balfour Declaration in favor of the establishment of a Jewish National Home in Palestine.

In fact, several iterations of this promise had been repeated in international documents that were made public, thus creating expectations for its fulfillment.[49]

The ultimate goal of Britain to establish a new independent state on the eastern part of Palestine had, therefore, no legal foundation. The gradual formation of this new state in stages could not alter this conclusion. Article 25 did not, and was never aimed to, provide any legal foundation for the political separation of Trans-Jordan from Palestine. Neither did it supply any foundation for its administrative separation. Be that as it may, it is noteworthy that Britain did not again seek or receive any approval from the Council or from the Principal Allied Powers for her later treaties of 1928 and 1946 with Emir Abdullah. In fact, these treaties were illegal and invalid because they violated international law. According to Oppenheim-Lauterpacht, international law imposes a duty on states to refrain from concluding treaties inconsistent with the obligations of former treaties: 'The conclusion of such treaties is an illegal act which cannot produce legal results beneficial to the law-breaker'.[50] The creation of Trans-Jordan as an independent state in a part of Palestine was fundamentally inconsistent with the terms of the Mandate for Palestine, with Britain further unilaterally determining its frontiers. These were decided after its creation, without having any authority to do so, as the authority was retained by the Principal Allied Powers, as clearly stipulated in the first Preamble of the Mandate for Palestine.

---

[49] Legally, the doctrine of third party beneficiaries was not yet adopted in English Law: see *Tweddle v. Atkinson* (1861) 1 B. & S. 393, 397, quoted in Cheshire and Fifoot's Law of Contract 8th edition, Butterworths London, 1972, p. 431; see also J.G. Starke, op. cit., p. 328 'As a general rule a treaty may not impose obligations or confer rights on third parties, and many treaties expressly declare that they are to be binding only on the parties.'

[50] Oppenheim-Lauterpacht, Vol. II, op. cit., p. 805; see also J.G. Starke, op. cit., p.353.

Chapter II

Change of Heart Leading to the Second Partition of Palestine

It should be noted that it was the British Government who produced the declaration in favor of the establishment in Palestine of a National Home for the Jewish people. It was they who pushed forward its implementation and argued intensively in its favor at the Paris Peace Conference. They later demanded its inclusion in the San Remo Resolution, the Treaty of Sèvres and finally the Mandate. Britain withstood opposition from France, Italy, and the Vatican. However, those were the days of Balfour as Foreign Secretary and Lloyd George as Prime Minister. But a few years later, the British attitude gradually drifted from promoting the National Home according to the true meaning and object of the Declaration, i.e., in favor of the establishment of a Jewish National Home that might eventually lead to the creation of a Jewish State. Instead, it took a different course – into making Palestine another Arab State with the Jews remaining an insignificant minority, similar to the way they lived in any other country since the dispersion. In this manner, the British Government after Balfour whittled down the Mandate into a meaningless document.[1]

This change of heart had many reasons: Balfour, the champion of the National Home, was no longer in office. On February 1921, Churchill was appointed Colonial Secretary in direct charge of Palestine. His influence on Lloyd George proved to be very effective. Churchill was the author of the first partition of Palestine and he laid the foundations for the second

---

[1] A comprehensive study of the period beginning with the approval of the British Mandate by the Council of the League of Nations on July 24th 1922 till its end on May 15th 1948 is beyond the scope of this work. For the purpose of this analysis, it suffices to show major turning points in British policy and the change of heart of the British government from one intended to establish a Jewish National Home in Palestine, which, if the experiment succeeded, would eventually lead to a Jewish State, to an entirely different one intended to establish another Arab State in the western part of Palestine.

partition, which was adopted later. Secondly, Arab opposition became manifest through violent demonstrations, riots, and acts of terror inflicted on the Jewish community and sometimes on British military forces. Thirdly, the British Administration and high ranking officials were, almost without exception, anti-Zionists who not only turned a blind eye to Arab terrorism and destruction, but systematically and intentionally encouraged them to commit attacks for the sake of destroying the idea of the Jewish National Home. The Arabs of Palestine thus believed, or were led to believe, that they could alter the Zionist policy by acts of terror and intimidation. Fourthly, the promulgation of the Balfour Declaration was not followed by any clear policy which would instruct the Administration in how to act decisively.

It was not until roughly the middle of 1920 that the British Government began to have second thoughts regarding the Jewish National Home. Since the Balfour Declaration in November 1917, it was devoted to the establishment of a National Home for the Jewish people in conformity with the true meaning of the Mandate. However, the local Administration in Palestine acted in total contradiction to the intentions and policy of the British Government. Nevertheless, a few years later, British policy gradually began to shift from what was required under the Mandate to promoting the establishment of an Arab State in Palestine. Thus, within a few years, the official policy of the British Government matched that of the local Administration in Palestine.

Arab riots and acts of terror were a major factor in bringing about this change. Nevertheless, the British could not openly repudiate the Declaration or dissolve the Mandate since it was already an international document confirmed by the Principal Allied Powers and approved by the League of Nations. The only way they could effect a policy change was through false interpretations of the Mandate to fit their new intentions, an interpretative distortion ad absurdum. Gone was establishing a National Home for the Jewish people in Palestine, which might eventually lead to a Jewish State, it being clearly understood that the civil and religious rights of the non-Jewish communities in

Palestine would be safeguarded. In its place was the construction of another Arab State with a Jewish minority – one not to exceed at any time a third of the non-Jewish population of the country, leaving this minority with no apparent safeguards.

During the first stages of the British occupation of Palestine, there was a wide gap between the avowed policy of the British Government regarding the establishment in Palestine of the Jewish National Home on the one hand and its execution by the local Administration on the other hand. During 1919 and 1920, the British Government made notable endeavors at promoting the establishment of the Jewish National Home in the Paris Peace Talks, in the San Remo Resolution, in the treaty of Sèvres and in the Mandate. Simultaneously, the British Administration in Palestine was acting in total contradiction to this policy. This caused much concern within the Zionist leadership. On June 5th 1919, Herbert Samuel, as Chairman of the Advisory Committee on the Economic Development of Palestine, complained to Sir William Tyrell of the Foreign Office that the Palestine Administration was not acting in harmony with the British Government's policy. Furthermore, in its relations with the Arabs, it was not applying a policy consistent with the Balfour Declaration.[2]

A month later, Samuel and Weizmann complained to Sir R. Graham in the Foreign Office that the British Military Authorities in Palestine 'took every opportunity of injuring Zionist interests'. They showed a marked hostility to Jews, and were spreading the idea that the British Government had no real intention of carrying out their commitments in accordance with the Balfour Declaration.[3] Samuel noted that this would inevitably lead the Arabs of Palestine to believe that the establishment of the Jewish National Home was not a closed case, encouraging Arab

---

[2]   DBFP, op. cit., Vol. IV, pp. 284-85, letter from Samuel to Tyrell, forming enclosure 3 to Doc. 197 which was transmitted to Balfour. Samuel was not then acting in any official capacity. He was appointed High Commissioner for Palestine only a year later, on July 1st 1920.

[3]   DBFP, ibid., Vol. IV, pp. 307-08, July 2nd 1919: Note by Sir R. Graham of the Foreign Office re conversations he had separately that afternoon with Samuel and Weizmann.

violence and agitation in order to compel the British Government to abandon the Balfour Declaration altogether. Samuel thus urged the Government to send a clear message to the local Administration with definite instructions that the matter was a *chose jugée*, and that continued agitation would lead to futile results.[4]

These complaints were echoed by Meinertzhagen, Chief Political Officer for Syria and Palestine, as being perfectly true.[5] Similarly, at a meeting with the Zionist organization in London, General Clayton expressed his views that what was needed was a clear statement of policy and a declaration that the Mandate was a fait-accompli, one that would have to be accepted by 75% of the Arab population. At the present time, some still thought there was hope of reversing the policy, perhaps through violence.[6]

In consequence, Curzon sent a telegraphic message on August 4th 1919 to Col. French in Cairo to the effect that:

> Terms of Mandate will embody substance of declaration of November 2, 1917... American and French Governments are equally pledged to support establishment in Palestine of Jewish national home. This should be emphasised to Arab leaders at every opportunity and it should be impressed on them that the matter is a *'chose jujée'* and continued agitation would be useless and detrimental.[7]

The telegram was also aimed at putting the Arabs of Palestine at ease by stating that they would not be deprived of their land nor required to leave the country, that there was no question of

---

4   DBFP, ibid., Vol. IV, letter from Samuel to Tyrell, forming enclosure 3 to Doc. 197 which was transmitted to Balfour.

5   Meinertzhagen, op. cit., p. 22, June 14th 1919: relying on evidence confirmed by Col. Stirling of General Clayton's staff, Meinertzhagen wrote in his Diary that the Administration in Palestine 'are encouraging the Arabs to oppose Zionism, that the Arabs are being granted privileges denied to the Jews, that the police are corrupt and that the Jews regard the Administration as half-hearted regarding the National Home'.

6   DBFP, op. cit., Vol. IV, p. 332-33, July 9th 1919.

7   DBFP, ibid., Vol. IV, p. 329.

the majority being subjected to the rule of the minority, and that all denominations in Palestine would enjoy religious liberty.

Despite the telegram, tensions in Palestine did not subside. A month later, Meinertzhagen briefed Curzon that there was strong opposition to Zionism in Syria and Palestine, which was being voiced by nearly all communities and classes, and also by official circles. This situation was aggravated by French, Italian, and Arab propaganda. The Vatican did not lag behind in expressing violent opposition to Zionism. Though some high ranking officials tried to conceal their personal views, their anti-Zionist inclinations in Palestine were plain.[8]

In October 1919, as a result of continued Arab agitation, it was again found necessary for the British Government to make a clear statement on its policy in Palestine. At Meinertzhagen's suggestion, and based mainly on a draft he prepared, the Foreign Office issued a revised declaration stating that the establishment of a National Home for the Jews was a settled policy of the British Government and its Allies. No amount of agitation would influence British adherence to the Balfour Declaration which had been endorsed by the Principal Allied and Associated Powers. On the other hand, the draft was concerned with allaying Arab misapprehension. It stated that there would be no interference in the custody of the Holy Places of Muslims and Christians, no flooding of Palestine with Jewish immigrants, and no eviction of Arab landowners, reaffirming that the majority would not be ruled by the minority.[9] However, the foregoing statement of policy did not bring peace.

On March 8th 1920, Feisal was proclaimed by the Syrian National Congress as King of Syria and Palestine. This was preceded by anti-Zionist demonstrations in Jerusalem, instigated and directed mainly by the French, calling for a united Syria

---

8   Meinertzhagen, op. cit., pp. 50-51; DBFP, ibid., Vol. IV, pp. 425-26, September 26th 1919: Letter from Meinertzhagen to Curzon briefing him on the state of Zionism in Palestine; See also DBFP, Vol. IV, p. 525, November 10th 1919 and Meinertzhagen, pp. 58-59.

9   DBFP, ibid., Vol. IV, p. 472, October 14th 1919, and pp. 507-08, November 7th 1919.

and Palestine under a French Mandate.[10] In Meinertzhagen's words: 'This period has been marked by an increased political agitation against Zionism, and in anti-Zionist demonstrations'. He remarked that 'anti-Zionist feeling is passing out of control'.[11] By April 1920, anti-Zionist sentiment was translated into major riots and acts of terror that broke out in Jerusalem.

It was not difficult to perceive that British policy in Palestine followed a certain pattern. After each major Arab attack, described as 'disturbances' in most of the British official Reports, a Royal or Official Commission was set up to look into the causes of the 'disturbances'. In most cases, the Commissions found that the Arabs were the initiators of these attacks, and that these attacks were predominantly aimed at Jewish communities and settlements, causing destruction to property and loss of life. Yet the Commissions invariably put the blame for the riots on the Jewish population. The recommendations embodied in the Commission's report were soon followed by a White Paper proposing a renewed British policy for Palestine, which would jeopardize the most essential provisions of the Mandate; namely, those concerned with immigration, land settlement, and land purchase for development. This cycle repeated itself in the major riots that occurred in Palestine during 1920, 1921, 1929, 1933, and 1936.

The Riots of 1920

Arab agitation and anti-Jewish propaganda culminated in a major riot that occurred in Jerusalem on April 4-7, 1920. This coincided with the Western Christian Easter, the Jewish Passover, and the Muslim Nebi Musa festival. It took place just a couple of weeks before the Conference of San Remo, hoping to disrupt its outcome.[12] The details of the riot were described by the Palin Commission that was set up to investigate the

---

[10] DBFP, ibid., Vol. XIII, pp. 219-20, Meinertzhagen, op. cit., p. 70, dispatch from Meinertzhagen to Curzon March 2nd 1920.

[11] Meinertzhagen, ibid., pp. 72-73, April 1st 1920.

[12] Weizmann, op. cit., p. 257.

causes and circumstances of this upheaval.[13] At the end of their investigation, the Commission came to the conclusion that the Arabs were the instigators of the aggression, and apart from a few exceptions, 'the Jews were the sufferers, and were, moreover, the victims of a peculiarly brutal and cowardly attack, the majority of the casualties being old men, women and children.'[14] The Palin Report noted: 'In front of the Grand Hotel several Jews were beaten and at least one stabbed... The crowd then passed down into the city looting Jewish shops and assaulting Jews and one Jew at least was shot about this time.'[15] There were attempts to fix the responsibility on the Jews, but the evidence was inconclusive and unreliable.[16] In fact, there was definite evidence that the police at times even gave active assistance to looters. Several Arabs arrested during the riots for offenses and Arab policemen charged with misconduct seem to have escaped without prosecution.[17] The Report concluded: 'The Jews of the City [of Jerusalem], as could be expected, were in a condition of complete panic'.[18]

To facilitate these attacks, British troops were removed from the central quarters of the walled city of Jerusalem in spite of specific warnings that further trouble was to be expected the next day.[19] There was an attempt to lynch a Jewish prisoner who was alleged to have been shooting Arabs from his home. Various cases of looting occurred, even after martial law was declared, the most important being the Talmudic College.[20] The Court of inquiry found that the heaviest sufferers were the Jews who

---

[13] A Commission set up on April 12th 1920 by the Commander in Chief of the British Military Forces in Palestine, as a Court of Inquiry, headed by Major-General Sir Philip C. Palin, to record, inter alia, 'the evidence as to the circumstances which gave rise to the disturbances which took place at and near Jerusalem on the occasion of the Nebi Musa Pilgrimage on 4th April and following days.'

[14] Report of the Palin Court of Inquiry, F.O. 371/5121, April 12th 1920, para. 58.

[15] Ibid., para. 57.

[16] Ibid., paras. 56, 57.

[17] Ibid., para. 59.

[18] Ibid., para. 60

[19] Ibid., para. 62.

[20] Ibid., paras. 63, 65.

sustained 216 casualties and the Muslims only 25. The Court further stated:

> From these figures it is clear that the incidence of the attack was against the Jews and that the attack against them was made in customary mob fashion with sticks, stones and knives. All the evidence goes to show that these attacks were of a cowardly and treacherous description, mostly against old men, women and children and frequently in the back. The total retaliatory efforts of the Jews and the military authorities resulted in only 25 recorded casualties... The attack was entirely directed against the Jews. [21]

The Commission also found that practically all the losses caused by looting and damage to goods were experienced by the Jewish Community.[22]

However, the Commission put the blame squarely on the Zionist leadership, stating that 'the Zionist Commission and the official Zionists by their impatience, indiscretion and attempts to force the hands of the Administration, are largely responsible for the present crisis' even though the Commission had arrived at a conclusion that 'the Military Governorate of Jerusalem failed to make adequate preparations for a possible disturbance at the Nebi Musa pilgrimage in spite of the receipt of warnings and ample knowledge of the situation.'[23] The Palin Commission thus placed the responsibility for the Arab upheaval on the victims.

---

[21] Ibid., para. 66. This was echoed in the Peel Report asserting that 'a serious outbreak of rioting and looting occurred in April 1920, in Jerusalem. *Savage attacks were made by Arabs on Jews*, and firm action of the troops was required to restore order'. [Italics added].

[22] Ibid., para. 67. Major Hedog-Jones of the British Army testified before the Commission saying: 'I personally saw many houses which had been cleared of everything, even the cupboards being torn out of the walls and the woodwork of partitions, doors and cupboards and windows completely removed. Some very pitiful cases were encountered where whole families had been bereft of everything, and young couples just starting life had lost all they had collected for their homes.'

[23] Ibid., paras. 69 (2), 69 (7).

The Commission stated:

> On the one hand we are faced with a native population thoroughly exasperated by a sense of injustice and disappointed hope, panic stricken as to their future… On the other hand, we have the Zionists whose impatience to achieve their ultimate goal and indiscretion are largely responsible for this unhappy state of feeling… They are ready to use their powerful foreign and home influence to force the hand of this or any future Administration. If not carefully checked, they may easily precipitate a catastrophe, the end of which it is difficult to forecast.[24]

The Peel Commission summarized the causes of Arab grievances as follows:

1. The Arabs' disappointment at the non-fulfillment of the promises of independence which they believe to have been given them in the war;
2. The Arabs' belief that the Balfour Declaration implied a denial of the right of self-determination, and their fear that the establishment of the National Home would mean a great increase of Jewish immigration and would lead to their economic and political subjection to the Jews;
3. The aggravation of these sentiments on the one hand by propaganda from outside Palestine associated with the proclamation of the Emir Feisal as King of a re-united Syria and with the growth of Pan-Arab and Pan-Muslim ideas and on the other hand by the activities of the Zionist Commission, supported by the resources and influence of Jews in the world at large.[25]

In arriving at its conclusions, the Palin Commission was further motivated by the assumption that ninety percent of the

---

[24] Ibid., para. 68.
[25] Peel Report, op. cit., p. 50.

Arabs of Palestine became, as a consequence of British policy, bitterly hostile to the Administration. Arab plans to rise up in revolt against the British might engulf the whole of Islam in the Near East. The Commission asserted: 'The signs and warnings openly displayed cannot safely be ignored'.

As for the riots of April 1920, Meinertzhagen recorded from first-hand information, that he had ample warning that they would occur, that Arab elements in Jerusalem were stirred up by Haj Amin El-Husseini, an Arab leader and later the Mufti of Jerusalem. He was encouraged and guided by Colonel Waters-Taylor, the Chief of Staff, and officers of the Administration, who were, almost without exception, anti-Zionists.[26] Meinertzhagen further reported:

> Waters-Taylor saw Haj al Amin [Haj Amin El-Husseini] on Wednesday before Easter and told him that he had a great opportunity at Easter to show the world that the Arabs of Palestine would not tolerate Jewish domination in Palestine; that Zionism was unpopular not only with the Palestine Administration but in Whitehall and if disturbances of sufficient violence occurred in Jerusalem at Easter, both General Bols [Chief Administrator] and General Allenby would advocate the abandonment of the Jewish Home. Waters-Taylor explained that freedom could only be attained through violence.[27]

On the withdrawal of British troops from the Old City of Jerusalem, as reported by the Palin Commission, Meinertzhagen commented that Colonel Waters-Taylor intentionally absented himself in Jericho and left Jerusalem without military protection for the purpose of giving the Arabs 'a fine opportunity' to destroy Jewish elements in Jerusalem. He discovered soon after his arrival in Palestine as Chief Political Officer that all British Officials were working against Zionism, hoping to crush it at its

---

[26] Meinertzhagen, op. cit., p. 79, April 9th 1920.

[27] Ibid., p. 82, April 26th 1920.

birth, some openly and some clandestinely: 'It gave me a shock when I found that officers of the British Administration were actively implicated and plotting against their own Government'.[28] The Arabs were thus encouraged by British officers to believe that by acts of violence they could sabotage Zionism.

Likewise, Weizmann testified to the fact that even though incitement and animosity were widely spread among the Arab population, there was no evidence that the local Administration was making any effort to avert trouble. As noted, officials in the British hierarchy were encouraging the agitators. For example, Meinertzhagen reported that John Shuckburgh, head of the Middle East Department, was deeply anti-Zionist and saturated with *hebraphobia*.[29] The Jews were apprehensive and warned the Administration, with Weizmann confronting General Allenby and General Bols with information regarding an imminent upheaval, which they dismissed as unfeasible. Weizmann wrote later: 'This pogrom might have been averted had proper steps been taken in time to check the agitation, had the attitude of the administration been different.'[30]

Churchill's Visit to Jerusalem, March 1921

A major turning point in British policy came during Churchill's visit to Jerusalem in March 1921 as Colonial Secretary. In a spirit of appeasement and impartiality, Churchill addressed Arab Deputies, members of the Executive Committee of the Haifa Congress, who confronted him with their complaints. Churchill responded that the British Government would not repudiate the Balfour Declaration nor stop immigration of Jews to Palestine, pointing out that National Home inevitably involved immigration. Churchill also reiterated that the Balfour Declaration had

---

[28] Ibid., p. 81, April 26th 1920. It is noteworthy that Meinertzhagen warned both Allenby and Bols of the coming trouble but none of them paid much attention. See also p. 89, June 2nd 1920.

[29] Meinertzhagen, ibid., p. 96, April 24th 1921.

[30] Weizmann, op. cit., pp. 254, 256. Meinertzhagen who witnessed a pogrom in Odessa years ago said about the 1920 riots that they 'were an exact replica in miniature of a pogrom'. Meinertzhagen, ibid., p. 80.

been ratified and approved and was internationally accepted and therefore not susceptible to change. It was on the basis of establishing the Jewish National Home that the Mandate had been undertaken. He also made clear that the historical connection of the Jews to Palestine was officially recognized, as was their right to build up their National Home in that country.

Churchill then turned to what he referred to as the second part of the Balfour Declaration 'which solemnly and explicitly promises to the inhabitants of Palestine the fullest protection of their civil and political rights.' He went on to say, 'If the one promise stands, so does the other.' Addressing Britain's position in Palestine as trustee, Churchill proclaimed that the British Government would strive to be loyal to the promises it had given both Arab and Jewish peoples. However, none of the international documents preceding the Mandate show that Britain had made any promises to the Arabs of Palestine, nor were any *political* rights offered, and in any case the safeguards did not carry the same weight as the pledges to the Jewish people. Churchill was clearly attempting to placate the Arab population of Palestine by a show of impartiality. He then added:

> [Balfour] spoke of the 'establishment in Palestine of a National Home for the Jews'. He did not say he would make Palestine *the* National Home for the Jews [italics in the original]. There is a difference between the two which is of great importance. The fact that Palestine shall contain a National Home for the Jews does not mean that it will cease to be the national home of other people, or that a Jewish Government will be set up to dominate the Arab people. On the contrary, the British Government is well disposed towards the Arabs in Palestine, and, indeed, cherish a strong friendship and desire for co-operation with the Arab race as a whole.[31]

In this little passage, Churchill laid down the foundations

---

[31] CAB 24/126, C.P. 3123, p. 151, March 28th 1921.

for a second partition of Palestine. These foundations, in fact, became a reality less than two decades later, in the Peel Commission's Report of 1937, the outcome of which was a strong recommendation to detach another part of Palestine from the territory allotted to the Jewish National Home for the creation of an additional Arab State. The assertion made by Churchill that Palestine had been until then 'the national home of other people' and would not cease to be so was a revolutionary idea in utter disregard of the Mandate instrument.[32] It had never been contemplated that the Jewish National home had been established in a country which was already the national home of another people. No international document adopted such an idea. The non-Jewish communities in Palestine never regarded themselves as a people standing on their own. They repeatedly self-identified as part of the Syrian people, or were considered by Feisal as part of the large Arab nation to whom the McMahon pledge was addressed.

In addition, Churchill radically re-interpreted the Declaration. By the phrase, the 'establishment in Palestine of a National Home for the Jews', he claimed Balfour did not mean to say Palestine would be '*the* National Home for the Jews' [italics in the original]. However, this was clearly a politically motivated rhetorical sleight of hand rather than an observation based on any accuracy. In all international documents from the Balfour Declaration to the San Remo Resolution, the Treaty of Sèvres, and Mandate, Palestine was promised to the Jewish people for the establishment of their National Home. It would have been unnecessary to add to the Declaration civil and religious safeguards for the protection of the non-Jewish communities unless it was envisaged that eventually the existing Arabs in Palestine would become a minority, in which case constitutional protection would be required. If it were contemplated that two separate nations were to occupy Palestine, the Mandate and all preceding international documents would have explicitly said so. Moreover, if that was the case, the international documents

---

[32] The Mandate draft had already been presented by Balfour to the Council of the League of Nations for approval on December 7th 1920.

would have stipulated civil and religious safeguards for the Jews living in the territories presumed to become the National Home of the Arabs of Palestine in the same manner they were added to protect non-Jewish communities in a Jewish National Home.

The fact that the Balfour Declaration applied an indefinite rather than a definite article in reference to 'National Home for the Jewish people' resulted from a mishap that in no way involved the Arabs of Palestine. As mentioned,[33] it was due to strong opposition from Lord Edwin Montagu, the only Jewish Minister in the British Government at the time. The change in phrasing was not aimed at the substance or the purpose of the Declaration; it was mainly for satisfying those anti-Zionist Jews of Britain opposed to the Declaration.[34]

Churchill thus pandered to the Arab Delegation. He recognized their 'national ideals' on the same footing as the Jewish national ideals.[35] He promised restrictions on Jewish immigration, making it contingent on providing means of support. And as for Arab fear of Jewish domination, he promised that 'the present form of government will continue for many years, and step by step we shall develop representative institutions leading up to full self-government. All of us here today will have passed away from the earth and also our children and our children's children before it is fully achieved'.[36] Thus, any visible prospect of Jewish independence in Palestine was left out, placing responsibility for the establishment of the Jewish National Home entirely on the Jewish people. As such, Churchill was exonerating the British Government from any obligation to facilitate or to bring about in any way the achievement of this goal. If the Jews fail, Churchill

---

[33] See pp. 69 et seq., supra.

[34] See pp. 70-71, supra. In August 1917, the original draft of the Declaration was approved by the British Government announcing that 'Palestine should be reconstituted as the national home of the Jewish people'. This version received beforehand the explicit approval of Lloyd George, Balfour, and the Foreign Office.

[35] CAB 24/126, C.P. 3123, p. 151. 'We cannot tolerate the expropriation of one set of people by another or the violent trampling down of one set of national ideals for the sake of erecting another.'

[36] Ibid., p. 152.

asserted, that would be the end of the experiment. Again, in the House of Commons, Churchill emphatically put the responsibility for Arab agitation on the Zionists, declaring that 'the cause of unrest in Palestine, and the only cause, arises from the Zionist movement, and from our promises and pledges in regard to it'.[37]

The Riots of 1921

Soon after Churchill's appeasing words in Jerusalem, Palestine was the scene of another Arab upheaval. It began on May 1st 1921 in Jaffa and soon spread to other Jewish colonies such as Petach Tikva, Khedera, Kfar Saba, Ain Hai and Rehoboth. A detailed account of the riots was given by a Commission of Inquiry appointed on May 23rd 1921 by the High Commissioner, under the chairmanship of Sir Thomas Haycraft, Chief Justice for Palestine.[38] The Commission reported that serious acts of violence had occurred in Jaffa on May 1st on two successive days, which escalated into vicious local attacks on Jewish agricultural colonies on May 4th-6th. There also occurred in Jaffa in June and July 1921 sporadic anti-Jewish manifestations.

The May 1st Jewish workers' procession in Jaffa provided a pretext for the outburst of violence in that area and in other parts of the country. The most violent was the Arab attack on the Immigration House in Jaffa, which was used as a shelter for newly arrived Jewish immigrants. Those who fled from the building to save their lives were beaten to death by the mob in the streets. The Jaffa riots resulted in 13 Jews killed and 24 wounded, 1 Arab killed and 4 wounded.[39] In Khedera, the Arab attackers 'burned, ransacked, destroyed and looted at will'.[40] The lives

---

[37] Rise of Israel, op. cit., Vol. 13, Doc. 30, p. 262, June 14th 1921.

[38] The Commission's terms of reference were to 'inquire into and report upon the recent disturbances in the town and neighbourhood of Jaffa, to extend their inquiries and report further upon recent disturbances which have taken place in any part of the District of Jaffa or elsewhere in Palestine.' Cmd. 1540, *Palestine, Disturbances in May 1921: Reports of the Commission of Inquiry with Correspondence Relating Thereto*, HMSO, London, October 1921, pp. 3-4. [Haycraft Report].

[39] Haycraft Report, ibid., pp.26-27.

[40] Ibid., p. 10.

of the Khedera colonists were in great peril. If the raid would not have been interrupted by the British Army, there could be no doubt in the Commission's mind that Khedera would have been destroyed. There was much looting in Jewish quarters, and the Commission commented that 'the looting and wreckage of furniture and household effects were appalling in its savage thoroughness'.[41] Similar attacks were waged on Kfar Saba and Ain Hai. The colony of Ain Hai was totally destroyed.[42] Attacks were also conducted against the Jewish colonies of Petach Tikvah and Rehoboth.[43]

In its final conclusion, the Commission of Inquiry asserted that the riot of May 1921 was no ordinary riot:

> The disturbance raged for several days with intensity wherever Arabs came into contact with Jews, and spread into the surrounding country, where Jewish colonies, having nothing to do with Bolshevism, were attacked with ferocity... We have no doubt that the Arabs were the first to turn this quarrel into a race conflict. They behaved with a savagery that cannot be condoned... The killing was accompanied and followed by an orgy of pillage which was a disgrace to a civilized community.[44]

The Commission further stated that the Jews retaliated with equal savagery 'but they had much to revenge'.[45] The looters were almost exclusively Arabs, the victims almost exclusively Jews. Well stocked shops in Suk el-Deir and Ajami were forcibly entered and stripped of their contents.[46]

Yet in the Commission's view, the Jews were mainly to blame for the unrest, even though the Arabs were generally the

---

[41] Ibid., p. 11.
[42] Ibid., pp. 37-38.
[43] Ibid., pp. 38, 41.
[44] Ibid., pp. 43-44.
[45] Ibid.
[46] Ibid., p. 46.

aggressors causing most of the casualties. In their opinion, the Jews should have been more conciliatory towards the Arabs. Zionist publications and articles should have been less provocative. Dr. Eder, acting chairman of the Zionist Commission, stated that there could only be one National Home in Palestine and no equality in the partnership between Jews and Arabs, but a Jewish predominance as soon as the Jews become majority. The Commission found that such claims were at the root of the 1921 unrest and one of the irritant causes of Arab discontent.[47] The fundamental cause of the Jaffa riots was a feeling among the Arabs of discontent with the Jews due to political and economic causes, connected with immigration and with their conception of Zionist policy. The Commission also put the blame on the local police that lacked proper training, and who in many cases were indifferent and sometimes even took part in the violence or encouraged it.[48]

On June 3rd 1921, Herbert Samuel reaffirmed, in a speech delivered in Jerusalem, that British policy in Palestine was to restrict Jewish immigration so as to be proportional to the employment available in the country, and that the employment should be new work and work of a permanent character. He ruled out mass immigration, and due to Arab agitation suspended immigration 'pending a review of the situation'.[49] In his speech, Samuel gave a more conciliatory interpretation to the Balfour Declaration, referring to the Arabs as the 'people of Palestine' whose welfare was entrusted to Britain under the Mandate. He further promised that the British Government 'would never impose upon them a policy which that people [the people of Palestine] *had reason to think* was contrary to their religious,

---

[47] Ibid., pp. 55-57.

[48] Ibid., Appendix A, p. 59.

[49] Rise of Israel, op. cit., Vol. 13, Doc. 29, p. 260. Speech delivered on the occasion of King George V's birthday. Meinertzhagen commented that Samuel had shown weakness by stopping immigration and discussing elective assemblies while the Arabs deserved punishment for breaking the peace and killing Jews. Meinertzhagen, op. cit., p. 102.

their political, and their economic interests'.[50] [Italics added]. This interpretation was quite remote from the intentions of the initiators of the Balfour Declaration, who confined the safeguards of the non-Jewish Communities in Palestine to civil and religious rights only.[51]

The Churchill White Paper, June 1922.

The appeasing words of Samuel backfired at the Administration. They did not reduce Arab agitation. On the contrary, they increased Arab unrest and violence. They spread doubt as to the determination of the British Administration to actually see the implementation of the Balfour Declaration through: 'So long as this doubt exists the Arabs will continue to try to influence His Majesty's Government, will certainly promote violence, and will make a great effort to convince the world that Zionist policy is impossible'.[52] In consequence, Samuel urged that another declaration on British policy in Palestine should be made public. This precipitated the promulgation of the first White Paper on Palestine, also known as the 'Churchill White Paper' on June 3rd 1922.[53] The Churchill White paper was drafted after consultation with Herbert Samuel, and was aimed mainly to

---

[50] Ibid., p. 261. Meinertzhagen remarked that Samuel defined the Balfour Declaration in language which watered that document down to such an extent as to make it meaningless. In consequence, the Muslims were encouraged to demand the complete abandonment of the Zionist policy. Meinertzhagen, ibid., p. 109.

[51] In a meeting held with Lloyd George, Balfour and Churchill, Weizmann expressed anxiety over Samuel's speech. In his opinion, the speech was a negation of the Balfour Declaration. 'The Declaration meant an ultimate Jewish majority, and this speech would never permit such a majority to eventuate'. To this, both Lloyd George and Balfour replied 'that by the Declaration they always meant an eventual Jewish State.' Lloyd George spoke of Samuel's weakness and both Churchill and himself were opposed to giving representative Government to Palestine. In Churchill's view, the difficulty in Palestine arose from the fact that the Declaration 'was opposed by the Arabs, nine-tenths of the British officials on the spot, and some of the Jews in Palestine'. See notes by Meinertzhagen with regard to a conversation held at Balfour's house on July 22nd 1921. ibid., p. 104.

[52] Meinertzhagen, ibid., p. 110. November 16th 1921.

[53] Cmd. 1700, HMSO 1922, pp. 17-21.

placate the Arabs.[54] Although it was a serious whittling down of the Balfour Declaration, it only added to the confusion and uncertainty of British policy in Palestine, thus calling for further Arab demands. The White Paper lacked clarity and consistency, trying to please the Arab population while adhering to the Balfour Declaration. This gave the Declaration an awkward and distorted interpretation that could not be reconciled with its true meaning and original aims.

The White Paper began with a statement expressing the very earnest desire of the Colonial Secretary to settle the outstanding questions which caused uncertainty and unrest among the Arab population. It was clear to the British Government that it was impossible at this stage to repudiate or change the Balfour Declaration.[55] They, therefore, reaffirmed it but gave it a distorted and misleading interpretation to suit their pro-Arab appeasing policy. Churchill assured the Arab population that there was no intention to create a 'wholly Jewish Palestine', that Palestine

---

[54] According to Weizmann, the main memorandum of the Churchill White paper was probably drawn up by Samuel with the intention to appease the Arabs as far as possible. Weizmann, op. cit., p. 290.

[55] In the British Cabinet, it was stated that 'it is no longer pertinent to discuss the policy of the original Declaration of 1917. There are some of our number who think that that Declaration was both unnecessary and unwise, and who hold that our subsequent troubles have sprung in the main from its adoption. But that was nearly six years ago. We cannot ignore the fact that ever since it has been the accepted policy of His Majesty's Government, that it was also accepted, not indeed without some reluctance, by the whole of our Allies, that it met with special favour in America, that it was officially endorsed at San Remo, that it figured in the original Treaty of Sèvres, and that it was textually reproduced in the Mandate for Palestine, which was officially submitted and approved by the Council of the League of Nations in July 1922. Further, it has been the basis upon which Zionist co-operation in the development of Palestine has been freely given and upon which very large sums of Jewish money have since been subscribed. Whether this policy has been wise or unwise, the above considerations, which cannot be disputed, possess a cumulative weight from which it is well-nigh impossible for any Government to extricate itself without a substantial sacrifice of consistency and self-respect, if not of honour'. See Report on *The Future of Palestine* prepared by a special Cabinet Committee that was appointed by the Prime Minister to advise the Cabinet as to the policy to be adopted by the Government in regard to Palestine. CAB 24/161, C.P. 351 (23), July 27th 1923, p. 3.

would never become 'as Jewish as England is English', nor was the subordination of the Arab population ever contemplated in Palestine. He then went on to dwindle the Jewish National Home so as to have it established only in part of Palestine, or what was left of it, after having detached Trans-Jordan from its original territory. The White Paper stated:

> Attention should be drawn to the fact that the terms of the Declaration referred to do not contemplate that Palestine as a whole should be converted into a Jewish National Home, but that such a Home should be founded *in Palestine*. [Italics in the original].

Thus, the White Paper introduced a new interpretation of the Balfour Declaration, one irreconcilable with the aims of its initiators. As noted, it also laid down the foundations for a second Partition of Palestine and the creation of another Arab state in addition to Trans-Jordan. Although similar ideas had already been put forward by Churchill to the Executive Committee of the Haifa Congress in March 1921, it was the first time the British Government made this interpretation of the Balfour Declaration its official policy. This interpretation had no legal basis, contradicted the literal meaning and aims of the Mandate, and violated British commitments based on it. *In Palestine* did not mean, and could never have meant, in part of Palestine.[56] This was also evident from the Peel Commission's Report in asserting that 'The field in which the Jewish National Home was to be established was understood, at the time of the Balfour Declaration, to be the whole of historic Palestine, and the Zionists were seriously disappointed when Trans-Jordan was cut away from that field under Article 25'.[57] The particle '*in*' was given a distorted interpretation so as to mean that the Jewish National Home was intended to be established not in Palestine as a whole, but only in part of it. However, any comparison between

---

[56] For the meaning of Jewish National Home in Palestine, see further pp. 81 et seq., supra.

[57] The Peel Report, op. cit., p. 38.

the use of the term *in Palestine* in this connection and the use of the same term in other connections in the Mandate was sufficient to reveal the absurdity of this contention.[58]

The White Paper then proceeded to provide its interpretation for the phrase 'National Home for the Jewish people' in the Declaration:

> When it is asked what is meant by the development of the Jewish National Home in Palestine, it may be answered that it is not the imposition of a Jewish nationality upon the inhabitants of Palestine as a whole, but the further development of the existing Jewish community, with the assistance of Jews in other parts of the world, in order that it may become a center in which the Jewish people as a whole may take, on grounds of religion and race, an interest and pride.
>
> But in order that this community should have the best prospect of free development and provide a full opportunity for the Jewish people to display its capacities, it is essential that it should know that it is in Palestine as of right and not on sufferance. That is the reason why it is necessary that the existence of a Jewish National home in Palestine should be internationally guaranteed and that it should be formally recognized to rest upon ancient historic connection.

---

58 In his article *The Palestine Mandate in Practice*, op. cit., pp. 55-56, Akzin accumulated comparable provisions from the Mandate to prove that the term *in Palestine* was used in the Mandate to mean in the whole of Palestine. e.g. 'Nothing should be done which might prejudice the civil and religious rights of existing non-Jewish communities *in Palestine*'. [2nd preamble]; 'permanent residence *in Palestine*'. [Article 7]; 'the privileges and immunities of foreigners… shall not be applicable *in Palestine*.' [Article 8]; 'The Mandatory shall be responsible for seeing that the judicial system established *in Palestine* shall assure to foreigners, as well as to natives, a complete guarantee of their rights'. [Article 9]; 'All responsibility in connection with the Holy Places and religious buildings or sites *in Palestine*…is assumed by the Mandatory'. [Article 13]; 'no discrimination *in Palestine* against nationals of any State member of the League of Nations'. [Article 18]; 'any statement or inscription in Arabic on stamps or money *in Palestine* shall be repeated in Hebrew' [Article 22]; 'the Administration of Palestine shall recognize the holy days of the respective communities *in Palestine*' [Article 23]. [All italics added].

It is remarkable that the assurance to be in Palestine 'as of right and not on sufferance' was extended in the above paragraph to the 'existing Jewish Community' alone and not to the entire Jewish people whom the Balfour Declaration and the Mandate referred to. This disparity was significant. Jews living in Palestine already enjoyed this right to go home. It was the Jewish people in the Diaspora who needed that right, and that right was not given to them. Yet Jewish immigration would be allowed only as long as it did not exceed 'whatever may be the economic capacity of the country at the time to absorb new arrivals'.[59] Palestine was, therefore, no longer regarded as the land in which the Jewish people as a whole could establish their National Home. Instead, it would be a place wherein the Jewish inhabitants of Palestine, a minority of some 80,000 people, could develop a center in which the Jews of the world could take pride and interest.[60]

Notably, the sanctioning of a Jewish center in Palestine, allowing it to develop by the 'existing Jewish community', was no match to the pledge made by the British Government in the Balfour Declaration to confer upon the Jewish people as a whole a National Home in Palestine and to use its best endeavors to facilitate the achievement of this objective. In the White Paper, Britain assumed a passive role. In fact, it retreated from its commitment and responsibility to put into effect the Balfour Declaration. With this interpretation, the British Government altered the aim and purpose of the Mandate without bothering to obtain the consent of the Principal Allied Powers and the Council of the League of Nations. The establishment of a Jewish center

---

[59] Cmd. 1700, op. cit., p. 19, June 3rd 1922. The 'economic capacity' test was used as a safety valve to stop or reduce Jewish immigration to Palestine whenever the Mandatory or the Administration in Palestine thought it was necessary to do so for political reasons.

[60] It is of interest that the Executive of the Zionist Organization, whether willfully or mistakenly, ignored this disparity. In their letter to the Colonial Office of June 18th 1922, accepting the White Paper, they expressed satisfaction from the fact that the British Government 'lay it down as a matter of international concern that *the Jewish people* should know that it is in Palestine as of right', and that in consequence of this right *the Jews* would be allowed to increase their numbers in Palestine through immigration. [Italics added]. Cmd. 1700, op. cit., Doc. 7, p. 29.

in Palestine, which would cause the Jewish people to feel interest and pride on grounds of religion or race, was no different from other Jewish centers in other parts of the world.

But then Churchill proposed the establishment of a legislative Council containing members elected on a wide franchise. The legislative Council would consist of 11 officials, including the High Commissioner in the Chair, and twelve elective members, 10 Arabs and 2 Jews. The idea, according to the White Paper, was to 'foster the establishment of a full measure of self-government in Palestine'. The legislative Council was intended to form a major step in this direction. And if all went well, it was envisaged that a further measure of self-government would be extended to Palestine. The Assembly which seemed to form the parliamentary body for the whole of Palestine would be placed in control over the executive, and a larger share of authority would be extended to the elected representatives of the people.

In view of the above, the status of the Jewish National Home was far from clear. The proposition to hold elections on a wide franchise was aimed to cover the whole of Palestine, yet the Jewish National Home was planned according to the White Paper to cover only part of Palestine. In Palestine, the Arabs then constituted a significant majority and their ratio in the contemplated legislative Council was 10:2 in their favor. Under these circumstances, the Jews as a minority had to be protected from the non-Jewish majority – yet the Balfour Declaration included safeguards for the Arabs and not for the Jews. It could, therefore, be easily observed that the White Paper turned the substance of the Balfour Declaration on its head, in total contradiction to its original aims and purpose even as the White Paper solemnly declared that they were not susceptible of change.

The White Paper supported Jewish immigration on the one hand, albeit subject to the economic absorptive capacity of the country. On the other hand, it proposed that a special committee should be established, consisting entirely of members of the new legislative Council elected by the people to advise the Administration on matters concerning the regulation of immigration. It could well be anticipated that the Arab majority in that committee would do their utmost to hamper Jewish immigration in total opposition to the Mandate. In conclusion, under the White Paper there was practically no chance the Jewish National Home would ever develop into an independent entity.[61]

Prior to its publication, the Zionist Organization was specifically required by the Colonial Secretary to approve the White Paper and to make known its approval among the people of Palestine, the British public, and the world at large. The Zionist Organization was further required to do everything in its power to resolve any misunderstandings and misconceptions of the White Paper, and to make sure its declared aims and intentions were consistent with the policy of the British Government. In addition, Churchill required from the Zionist Organization 'a formal assurance that your Organization accepts the policy as set out in the enclosed statement [draft of the White Paper] and is prepared to conduct its own activities in conformity therewith'.[62]

Notwithstanding the serious whittling down of the Balfour Declaration, the Zionist Organization had no alternative but to approve the Churchill White Paper. The Mandate was not yet approved by the Council of the League of Nations and there was genuine anxiety among the Zionist leaders that the British Government might stall its approval. Weizmann recalled that 'it was made clear to us that confirmation of the Mandate would be conditional on our acceptance of the policy as interpreted in the White Paper, and my colleagues and I therefore had to

---

[61] Many years later, Churchill gave evidence before the Peel Commission stating that there was nothing in the definition of the National Home to prohibit the ultimate establishment of a Jewish State. See the Peel Report of 1937, op. cit., p. 33. It was also reported by the Peel Commission that in 1920 Churchill 'spoke or wrote in terms that could only mean that [he] contemplated the eventual establishment of a Jewish State'. The Peel Report, ibid., p. 25.

[62] Cmd. 1700, op. cit., p. 17, letter from the Colonial Office, signed J.E. Shuckburgh, to the Zionist Organization in London, June 3rd 1922. In Meinertzhagen's view, Shuckburgh was an anti-Semite in charge of the Middle East Department at the Colonial Office, who was responsible for deliberately sabotaging the National Home. See Meinertzhagen, op. cit., p. 116, entry June 14th 1922.

accept it, which we did, though not without qualms'.[63] There was also some optimism among the Zionist leadership that 'the White Paper, if carried out honestly and conscientiously, would still afford us a framework for building up a Jewish majority in Palestine, and for the eventual emergence of a Jewish state'.[64] On June 18th 1922, the executive of the Zionist Organization passed a resolution which assured the British Government that its activities would be conducted in conformity with the policy set forth in the White Paper.[65]

On June 22nd 1922, there was a vote in the House of Lords, which rejected the Mandate by a majority of 60 votes. On July 4th, however, there was a debate in the House of Commons that approved the Mandate by 232 to 35 votes. Hence, on July 24th 1922, the Palestine Mandate was approved by the League of Nations.[66]

The Riots of 1929

The British Administration went out of its way to please the Arabs of Palestine, fearing that Arab agitation would increase and spiral out of control. In fact, the Administration had made three successive proposals to the Arabs, placing them on equal terms with the Jews. As noted, the Administration offered them the establishment of a legislative Council in which they would form a significant majority of the elected members. The Arabs rejected this offer. The Administration then offered them the reconstruction of an Advisory Council so as to secure effective Arab representation. This offer was again rejected. A further

---

[63] Weizmann, op. cit., p. 290. The confirmation of the Mandate for Palestine by the Council of the League of Nations took place on Saturday July 24th 1922, amid last minute efforts to postpone it which failed, Weizmann, pp. 292-93.

[64] Weizmann, ibid., p. 291. This optimism was first expressed by V. Jabotinsky, at that time a member of the Zionist Executive and a hard liner, who agreed to add his signature to the Resolution.

[65] Cmd. 1700, op. cit., pp. 28-29.

[66] Meinertzhagen, op. cit., pp. 118-19. On the vote in the House of Lords, Meinertzhagen commented: 'The power of the modern House of Lords is the power of an air bubble... It was, of course a purely artificial expression of opinion, and is at root an anti-Semite vote'. Ibid.

proposal was made for the recognition of an Arab Agency on the same footing as the Jewish Agency, which was also rejected.[67] In consequence, Lord Devonshire, the Colonial Secretary, informed the Cabinet that the very generous offers which have been made to the Arabs were rejected. 'There can be little doubt that their action has been influenced by encouragement received at this end. They believe, and they have been encouraged to believe, that if only they hold out they can get much better terms from us.'[68] Strengthened by this belief, the riots of 1929 were deadlier than ever before.

Under the pretext of two Arabs killed by Jews, which after thorough investigation was proven to be totally false, the Arabs commenced attacks against the Jewish community in Palestine. These began in Jerusalem on Friday August 23rd 1929, and continued for a few days soon spreading to other parts of Palestine where Jewish villages and settlements were in existence. The Shaw Commission which was appointed to investigate those riots stated categorically that 'the outbreak in Jerusalem on the 23rd of August was from the beginning an attack by Arabs on Jews for which no excuse in the form of earlier murders by Jews has been established.'[69]Arab attacks were launched on Jewish villages around Jerusalem, then extended to Beisan, Safed, Haifa, Nablus, Hebron and other Jewish communities. On the riots of Hebron, the Shaw Commission reported:

> About 9 o'clock on the morning of the 24th of August, Arabs in Hebron made a most ferocious attack on the Jewish ghetto and on isolated Jewish houses lying outside the crowded quarters of the town. More than 60 Jews, including many women and children, were murdered and more than 50 were wounded. This savage attack, of which no condemnation

---

[67] CAB 24/162, C.P. 433(23), Appendix No. 5 of a Memorandum by the Secretary of State for the Colonies to the Cabinet, October 27th 1923.

[68] Ibid., see statement by the Colonial Secretary on p. 1 of the Memorandum.

[69] Report of the Commission on the Palestine Disturbances of August 1929, Cmd. 3530, HMSO, 1930, chaired by Sir Walter Shaw, [hereinafter The Shaw Commission Report].

could be too severe, was accompanied by wanton destruction and looting. Jewish Synagogues were desecrated, a Jewish hospital, which had provided treatment for Arabs, was attacked and ransacked, and only the exceptional personal courage displayed by Mr. Cafferata, the one British Police Officer in town, prevented the outbreak from developing into a general massacre of the Jews in Hebron.[70]

There was also some sporadic Jewish retaliation. The Shaw Commission found that 'In a few instances, Jews attacked Arabs and destroyed Arab property. These attacks though inexcusable, were in most cases in retaliation for wrongs already committed by Arabs in the neighbourhood in which the Jewish attacks occurred'.[71]

During the riots, the High Commissioner for Palestine was on leave in the United Kingdom. Upon his return to Palestine on August 29th 1929, finding the country in a state of disorder and unlawful violence, he announced the following proclamation:

> I have learned with horror of the atrocious acts committed by bodies of ruthless and blood-thirsty evil-doers, of savage murders perpetrated upon defenceless members of the Jewish population regardless of age and sex, accompanied, as in Hebron, by acts of unspeakable savagery, of the burning of farms and houses in town and country and of the looting and destruction of property. These crimes have brought upon their authors the execration of all civilized peoples throughout the world.[72]

It was reported that during these riots 133 Jews were killed and 339 wounded, with 87 Arabs killed and 181 wounded. Many of the Arab casualties and possibly some of the Jewish casualties were caused by military or police fire.[73]

---

[70] Shaw Commission Report, ibid., p. 64

[71] Ibid., p. 158.

[72] Ibid., p. 68. The Proclamation was announced on September 1st 1929.

[73] Shaw Commission Report, ibid., p. 65.

The Shaw Commission of Enquiry

As a result, on September 13[74] 1929, the Colonial Secretary, Lord Passfield,[74] appointed a Commission of Enquiry headed by Sir Walter Shaw to 'enquire into the immediate causes which led to the recent outbreak in Palestine and to make recommendations as to the steps necessary to avoid a recurrence.'[75] At the end of their enquiry, the Commission laid the responsibility for the causes of the riots mainly on the Jews. Their recommendations to prevent a recurrence of violence were designed predominantly to lay more restrictions on Jewish immigration as well as land settlement and purchase of land by Jews. The Commission found these to be the immediate causes for the 1929 Arab riots in Palestine. The failure of the British Administration to provide adequate protection for the attacked Jewish communities was hardly investigated and those responsible for this oversight were never tracked down. The Commission failed to examine the lack of preventive measures to avert the riots, the warnings the British High Command in Palestine received before the riots, and why they failed to heed these warnings.[76] No less important, the Commission refrained from making any recommendations to prevent recurrences of future deadly riots.[77] In fact,

---

[74] Sidney Webb.

[75] Shaw Commission Report, ibid., p. 3.

[76] In the Shaw Commission Report, it was stated that on the eve of the outbreak, Jewish representatives warned the Administration that trouble was to be expected the following day, and expressed anxiety over security precautions not being adequately taken, but the British authorities brushed it aside. See Shaw Commission Report, ibid., p. 59. Meinertzhagen commented emphatically that 'the Administration was in fact in possession of evidence showing that an outbreak was not only brewing but was almost inevitable. There can be no question that the recent outbreak was preventable'. Meinertzhagen, op. cit. p. 143, entry September 1st 1929.

[77] In a letter sent to Lord Passfield on August 29th 1929, Meinertzhagen urged the Colonial Secretary to hold a full and impartial enquiry 'not on the causes of the outbreak, for these are well known, but on the responsibility of the Administration. Why were warnings unheeded? Why was protection inadequate? Why did the Administration fail in its first duty, security?' Meinertzhagen felt he had a right to address the matter as a British officer who served in Palestine in 1919 and was familiar with the military and political situation there. See Meinertzhagen, ibid.

notwithstanding the High Commissioner's proclamation in which he described the country as being in shambles and total disorder, the Commission praised the British police in Palestine: 'They acted up to the finest tradition of British service, and when faced with circumstances of great danger, displayed signal personal courage.'[78] The responsibility for poor performance was attributed solely to the Palestine local police, who were unable to confront the riots efficiently.

The investigation concentrated on Arab resentment toward Jewish immigration, Jewish land settlement, and land transactions involving Jews. In fact the immediate causes were found by the Commission to be Arab objection to the Balfour Declaration, Mandate, and establishment of a National Home for the Jewish people in Palestine. The Commission expressed its complete understanding with these objections. Consequently, their recommendations centered on the prevention of these causes, with a view to appease the Arabs and ultimately gain some quiet in the Holy Land.

According to the Commission, what first sparked the riots in August 1929 was the result of long-simmering tension between Jews and Muslim Arabs concerning the exercise of worship at the Wailing Wall in Jerusalem. On the eve of September 23rd 1928, the Jewish Day of Atonement, a screen used in Jewish tradition to separate men from women had been affixed to the pavement adjoining the Wall. The Muslims demanded its removal and this demand was met by the Administration.[79] As the Commission reported: 'During the next six months the Moslem religious authorities, encouraged perhaps by this success, exercised to the full those rights in the neighbourhood of the Wall by which they could annoy the Jews and at the same time emphasize

---

[78] Shaw Commission Report, op. cit., p. 146. There can be no doubt that the British Authorities in Palestine acted negligently or indifferently in protecting Jewish life and property. The Commission admitted that if the Arabs would have conducted a revolt against the British Authority in Palestine it would have entailed 'consequences far more serious than any which can be said to have followed from the events of August last'. Ibid., p. 150.

[79] Cmd. 3229, Memorandum by the Secretary of State for the Colonies: The Western or Wailing Wall in Jerusalem, HMSO November 1928.

their ownership of the Wall, the pavement, and the surrounding property'.[80] In addition, the Administration decided to issue building permits to the Arabs with the effect of converting the pavement in front of the Wall into a thoroughfare. In protest, the Jews held a demonstration in Tel Aviv on August 14th 1929, with another demonstration at the Wailing Wall the following day. The Muslims held a counter demonstration on August 16th. Not surprisingly, the Commission found that of all incidents connected with the Wailing Wall, the Jewish demonstration at the Wailing Wall on August 15th was the immediate cause of the outbreak.[81]

The Commission also found a cause for the 1929 riot in Arab disappointment with the Balfour Declaration. Their leaders felt 'threatened by the advent of a new and powerful element composed of a capable and progressive people'.[82] They also feared the Jew as an economic competitor. Those fears were intensified by resolutions taken up by the 16th Zionist Congress held that year in Zurich with statements to enhance immigration and land settlement, as a result of which 'the Arabs have come to see in the Jewish immigrant not only a menace to their livelihood but a possible overlord of the future'.[83] Jewish immigration, land purchases, and enterprise served to intensify early Arab fears based on the belief that eventually they would be deprived of their land and livelihood and that they would ultimately come under the domination of the Jews. The Jews were thus found responsible by the Commission for this situation by their eager desire to see their hopes fulfilled: 'Had some modification been made in the full Zionist programme… the opposition of the Arab people might never have been fully roused or, if roused, might have been overcome.'[84]

As a result, the Commission came to the conclusion that

---

80 Shaw Commission Report, op. cit., p. 154.

81 Ibid., p. 155.

82 Ibid., p. 151.

83 Ibid.

84 Ibid., p. 152

'racial animosity on the part of the Arabs, consequent upon the disappointment of their political and national aspirations and fear for their economic future, was the fundamental cause of the outbreak of August last'.[85] The outbreak of violence was thus caused by Arab resentment against the Balfour Declaration, the establishment of the Jewish National Home in Palestine, and the British commitment to put it into effect. The only way the British Government could appease the Arab population in its effort to prevent further unrest was through an interpretation of the Balfour Declaration and the Mandate which differed completely from the aims and purpose of their founders.

Faithful to the new British approach to the Balfour Declaration, the Commission stated that the Declaration could be construed in two ways:

> Upon one construction... the maintenance of the religious and civil rights of the existing non-Jewish communities in Palestine is an over-riding condition, on the absolute fulfilment of which every active step in the creative aspect of the policy is to be contingent. But upon another construction the first aspect of the policy takes precedence; there would be a binding obligation on His Majesty's Government to pave and prepare the way for the establishment of a Jewish National Home in Palestine and the second aspect of the policy would be a minor consideration.[86]

Judging by their recommendations, it is clear that the Commission adopted the first construction.

The first recommendation, which was considered by the Commission to be of 'the highest importance', advised the British Government to issue a clear statement of policy aimed at shifting the balance from the first part of the Declaration to the second; i.e., from the establishment of a National Home for the Jewish people to the safeguarding of the religious and civil

---

85 Ibid., p. 150.
86 Ibid., p. 137.

rights of the non-Jewish communities in Palestine. It was also advised in this context that that statement should contain more explicit directives on such vital issues as land and immigration.[87] On the question of Jewish immigration, the British Government was advised to issue a clear and definite declaration of policy applying severer regulations and control. They were also advised to reaffirm the Churchill White Paper, and to adopt a policy designed to prevent the repetition of excessive immigration as occurred in 1925-1926. It was further recommended to devise a mechanism whereby non-Jewish interests in Palestine could be consulted upon matters concerning the regulation of immigration, the ultimate purpose being subjection of the character and qualifications of the immigrants to the most rigid scrutiny under the control of the Administration.[88]

On the question of land transfer to Jews, rigid restrictions were recommended. It would seem that the Commission extended the terms 'civil and religious rights', which were conferred upon the non-Jewish communities in Palestine so as to apply to their economic welfare too, which in the Commission's view should be protected. The Commission found that Jews acquired land from Arabs at exorbitant prices and that the cost of future purchases were likely to be even higher.[89] Nevertheless, they were perturbed lest these sellers, to whom they referred as 'displaced' people, remain without land to cultivate. The Commission was positive that 'a continuation, or still more an acceleration, of a process which results in the creation of a large discontented and landless class is fraught with serious danger to the country', and, therefore, 'it is clear that further protection of the present cultivators and some restriction on the alienation of land are inevitable'.[90] One way to achieve that was 'by restriction on the transfer of land now in Arab hands to others than Arabs',[91] but it was suggested that this, and other means, needed to be further

---

[87] Ibid., pp. 139, 142, 165.

[88] Ibid., p. 112.

[89] Ibid., p. 141.

[90] Ibid., p. 124.

[91] Ibid.

examined by advisers of the Palestine Government.

A newly devised cause for applying further restrictions on immigration, land settlement, and land purchase by Jews in Palestine was the natural increase of the local rural population, which had to be taken into account. It was estimated that within thirty years the local population might increase by some 300,000, who would be looking for land to provide them with a living. The Commission thus came to the conclusion that the point of absorption had reached its limits, and that there was no further land available which could be occupied by new Jewish immigrants without displacing Arab cultivators.[92] This conclusion, in actual fact, would have the effect of bringing immigration, land settlement, and land purchase by Jews to an almost standstill, in flagrant violation of the Mandate.

The Shaw Commission perceived the role of Britain in Palestine as a task designed to administer a policy of a dual nature. This was based on the Churchill White Paper, which defined the primary duty of the British Administration as one of holding the balance between the two parties – Arab and Jewish. According to the Commission, the Administration was not given clear directions to assist either party in the fulfillment of their aspirations. Therefore, no flaw was found in the conduct of the Administration, who acted successfully in steering the middle course between the conflicting lines of policy, and managed to maintain a neutral and impartial attitude.[93] However, this attitude contradicted the very essence of the Mandate, which required that the Jews be 'placed in the position of "most-favoured-nation" in Palestine' provided, of course, that Arab civil and religious rights were not prejudiced.[94] In fact, British policy in Palestine

---

[92] Ibid., p. 123.

[93] Ibid., pp. 143, 160-61.

[94] Meinertzhagen, op. cit., p. 141, entry September 1st 1929. Meinertzhagen in a letter addressed to Lord Passfield, the Colonial Secretary, on August 29th 1929. On July 30th 1919, Balfour was quoted by Meinertzhagen, upon the appointment of the latter as Chief Political Officer in Palestine, that 'All development, industrial schemes of all kinds, and financial assistance must be based on the principle that Jews are the most-favoured nation in Palestine.' Brig. General Clayton to Foreign Secretary Balfour: Any real development

was far from being balanced and impartial. At that stage, the tide was predominantly in favor of the non-Jewish population of Palestine.[95]

Finally, the Commission emphatically rejected the Zionist complaint that British officials in Palestine were unsympathetic to the Jewish cause, and that they allowed their official judgment to be influenced by their personal feelings. They termed the complaint by its very nature a 'distasteful one'. According to the Commission, a similar complaint was made by the Arabs. However, while the Arab complaint was baseless, the Zionist complaint was well-founded. There was ample evidence that British officers in Palestine were acting to sabotage the Mandate and the Balfour Declaration. The Shaw Commission, by rejecting the Zionist complaint, either acted *mala fide* or in total ignorance of the facts.[96]

---

of the ideas of Zionism in Palestine must 'entail extending a measure of preferential treatment to the Jews in Palestine'; see The Zionist Movement and the Foundation of Israel 1839-1972, editor: Beitullah Destani, Vol. 2, 1917-1918, Archive Editions 2004 [hereinafter ZMFI], Doc. 131, p. 719, June 16th 1918.

[95] Meinertzhagen to Lord Passfield: 'British sympathy is with the Arab and not with the Jew.' Meinertzhagen, ibid., p. 141, entry September 1st 1929. On July 6th 1923, he quoted Shuckburgh telling him that 'the policy of H.M.G. is favourable to the Arabs and that the Balfour Declaration is too meaningless to mean anything', ibid., p. 132. On July 5th 1921, he wrote: 'Powerful forces are working against Zionism both in England and in Palestine', ibid., p. 101. On July 23rd 1921, he noted that both Arab opinion and British military advice in Palestine had been steadily working against Zionism and would, if they could, destroy it, ibid., p. 103.

[96] Churchill, in a meeting with Lloyd George, Balfour, and Weizmann among others, stated that the Balfour Declaration was opposed by nine-tenths of the British officials in Palestine. See Meinertzhagen p. 104, entry July 23rd 1921. On June 21st 1921 Meinertzhagen wrote in his Diary that 'the atmosphere in the Colonial Office is definitely hebraphobe, the worst offender being Shuckburgh who is head of the Middle East Department. Hubert Young and little Lawrence do their utmost to conceal their dislike and mistrust of the Jews but both strongly support the official pro-Arab policy of Whitehall', ibid., p. 99. And on November 16th he wrote that British officials acting against their Government's policy in England and in Palestine and advising the Arabs on what actions to take was no less than political sabotage of the worst kind, ibid., p. 112. Meinertzhagen also pointed out that since 1920, British policy in Palestine had been whittled down to exasperating limits,

The Shaw Commission recommendations were mainly aimed at appeasing the Arab population on such vital issues as immigration, close settlement on land and land purchase by Jews, on the belief that appeasement would reduce or prevent further Arab riots and acts of terror. Yet in the Arab line of reasoning, riots and violence paid off and made a difference. Through them, they achieved significant and meaningful results, which evidently encouraged them to continue this type of protest. The yielding of British authorities to Arab demands was thus the main cause of Arab violence. The Shaw Commission was aware of this fact. In their Report, they highlighted their observation that the most important causal factor in the 1929 upheaval was Arab belief that the British Government and Administration would be influenced by Arab violence. The Commission had no hesitation in ascertaining that this belief –

> played a part in many of the events which led immediately up to the disturbances and was the direct cause of others. By some at least among those who… organized demonstrations at the Wailing Wall or in other ways challenged the Administration it was thought that through these means the decisions of the Government might be influenced.[97]

In these circumstances, the Shaw Commission recommendations, which were clearly influenced by Arab agitation and terror, were bizarre and incomprehensible. They had no chance of achieving quiet. On the contrary, adherence to these recommendations did not result in preventing or ending future violence.

The Passfield White Paper, October 1930

The Shaw Commission Report led to another Statement of Policy announced by the British Government, often referred

---

while obstruction to Zionism was carried out by 'unsympathetic officials in both Palestine and Downing Street' who proved greater enemies to Zionism than economic or political obstacles. Letter to the Times, November 19th 1930, ibid., p. 145.

[97] Shaw Commission Report, op. cit., p. 157.

to as the Passfield White Paper. This White Paper went one step further to whittle down the Mandate. In fact, it promoted Arab nationalism in Palestine and created conditions that would finally lead to a bi-national community with an Arab majority in that country. British policy in this respect was abundant with contradictions and lack of feasibility. On the one hand, it was recognized that the interests and aims of the Arabs and the Jews were diverse and conflicting. On the other hand, the British Government adopted the concept that 'a double undertaking is involved, to the Jewish people on the one hand and to the non-Jewish population on the other'.[98] However, this concept was unrealistic and could never lead to a solution to the problem as later historical events proved, since the Jewish people endeavored to bring about the implementation of the Mandate as originally contemplated. In juxtaposition, the Arabs made every effort to have it discarded or nullified, while simultaneously demanding the fulfillment of their own aspirations. These two objectives were irreconcilable and the fact that the British Government stated otherwise undermined their credibility to both sides.

A striking proof of the failure of the Mandatory to fulfill its obligations under the Mandate is the fact that it succumbed to Arab riots and acts of terror instead of putting into effect the Balfour Declaration and implementing the Mandate. In this context, it is quite revealing that the Shaw Commission, and thence the Passfield White Paper, claimed that before the Zionist advent to Palestine there were no hostilities between Arabs and Jews, and they lived in harmony.[99] The Passfield White Paper went even further to emphasize the difference in this matter between

---

[98] Cmd. 3692: *Statement of Policy by His Majesty's Government in the United Kingdom*, HMSO, October 1930, [the Passfield White Paper], para. 3.

[99] Shaw Commission Report, op. cit., p. 150: 'In less than ten years three serious attacks have been made by Arabs on Jews. For eighty years before the first of these attacks there is no recorded instance of any similar incidents. It is obvious then that the relations between the two races during the past decade must have differed in some material respect from those which previously obtained... before the War the Jews and Arabs lived side by side if not in amity, at least with tolerance, a quality which to-day is almost unknown in Palestine'.

the colonies established by P.I.C.A.[100] and those established by the Zionists. The contention was that hostilities began only due to the Zionist advent in Palestine on the basis of the Balfour Declaration. The Arabs were, therefore, hostile to that same Declaration that the British Government pledged to implement and put into effect. These hostilities against the implementation of the Declaration were the very reason why Britain decided to whittle it down in violation of the Mandate.

As mentioned, the Mandate was conferred upon Britain for the purpose of putting into effect the Balfour Declaration in favor of the establishment in Palestine of a National Home for the Jewish people. Britain pledged to carry out this task and prepare the country politically, administratively, and economically. No similar pledge was made to the existing Arab population of Palestine. The understanding between the British Government and the Zionist Federation with regard to safeguarding the civil and religious rights of existing non-Jewish Communities in Palestine assumed that someday in the future the Arab majority would turn into a minority and might need protection. To make the National Home possible, the British Government undertook to facilitate Jewish immigration as well as land purchase and settlement as a right, not on sufferance. Without these three privileges, there was no chance of establishing a Jewish National Home in Palestine, as conceived by the Balfour Declaration and the Mandate.

However, by adopting a double undertaking the British Government took the interpretation of the Balfour Declaration and the Mandate too far from their original meaning. The Mandatory flatly rejected the claim that 'the principal feature of the Mandate is the passages regarding the Jewish National Home, and that the passages designed to safeguard the rights of the non-Jewish community are merely secondary considerations qualifying to some extent, what is claimed to be the primary object for which the Mandate has been framed'.[101] It deviously stated that it was a

---

[100] Passfield White Paper, op. cit., p. 17. P.I.C.A. stands for *The Palestine Jewish Colonization Association* which was not funded by the Zionist Organization.

[101] Ibid., para. 8.

conception that had *always* been regarded as 'totally erroneous'. [Italics added]. The British furthermore managed to secure the approval of the Permanent Mandates Commission to their double undertaking proposition, in consequence of which the latter made the following pronouncement: '(1) that the obligations laid down by the Mandate in regard to the two sections of the population are of equal weight; (2) that the two obligations laid down by the Mandatory are in no sense irreconcilable'.[102] The White Paper indicated with satisfaction the fact that these two assertions received the authorization of the Council of the League of Nations.

The White Paper went on to build the future structure of Palestine on the basis of a bi-national community in a situation in which the Arabs constituted a significant majority. The British Government aimed now at applying the Mandate to the existing Jews of Palestine alone, leaving out the Jewish people as a whole to whom the pledge was actually made. The White Paper, therefore, made reference to *the people of Palestine* as a whole even though no such people were then in existence. In an effort to appease the local Arabs, the British Government decided, in the first place, to grant the people of Palestine 'a measure of self-government in Palestine, in the interests of the community as a whole'.[103] At the same time, they would defer immigration, impose restrictions on land settlement, and diminish the authority of the Jewish Agency.

For the purpose of establishing self-government in Palestine, the British decided to set up a legislative Council for the *people of Palestine*, which would consist of the High Commissioner in the chair, 10 official appointed members, and 12 unofficial elected members, who were to be elected by primary and secondary elections. This was a revival of the Legislative Council proposed

---

[102] Ibid. While the British Government was in full accord with the Permanent Mandates Commission's assertion that the two obligations were 'in no sense irreconcilable', the White Paper nevertheless recognized the difficult and delicate task of carrying out a policy to reconcile two obligations which involved conflicting interests.

[103] Ibid., p. 18.

in the Churchill White Paper of 1922 for elections to be conducted on a wide franchise.[104] With a population at the time of 147,000 Jews as opposed to 700,000 Arabs, and a hostile Administration, the future of the Jewish National Home in Palestine was in jeopardy.[105] In the Peel Report, it was realized that 'an advance towards real self-government meant an advance towards the subjection of the National Home to an Arab majority'.[106] The Legislative Council, according to the Palestine Order in Council of 1922, was to determine all impending questions by a majority of the votes of members present. Due to the number of official and non-Jewish members in the Legislative Council, the Jewish representatives would always form a minority.[107]

On immigration and land settlement, the White Paper adopted the Shaw Commission recommendations by stating that 'at the present time and with the present methods of Arab cultivation there remains no margin of land available for agricultural settlement by new immigrants'.[108] The White Paper expressed

---

[104] The validity to establish a Legislative Council for the entire people of Palestine may be called into question. The White Paper based this authority on Article 2 of the Mandate which stated:

The Mandatory shall be responsible for placing the country under such political, administrative and economic conditions as will secure the establishment of the Jewish national home, as laid down in the preamble, and the development of self-governing institutions, and also for safeguarding the civil and religious rights of all the inhabitants of Palestine, irrespective of race and religion.

However, from the structure of this Article, it is doubtful whether the phrase 'development of self-governing institutions' related to the whole inhabitants of Palestine. It is more likely that it related to the Jewish National Home as a step or measure for securing the establishment of that National Home. The phrase 'and also for safeguarding, etc.' that follows indicates that the first two sentences are linked and should be interpreted as one. The White Paper, however, interpreted Article 2 as conferring upon the Mandatory an obligation 'to place the country under such political, administrative and economic conditions as will secure the development of self-governing institutions'. (See the Passfield White Paper, Cmd. 3692, ibid., p.14, para. 12).

[105] Weizmann, op. cit., p. 334.

[106] The Peel Report, op. cit., p. 91.

[107] The Palestine Order in Council, August 10th 1922, Part III, Article 32.

[108] The Passfield White Paper, op. cit., p. 16; see also the Hope-Simpson Report, *Palestine Report on Immigration, Land Settlement and Development,* Cmd. 3686, HMSO, London, 1930, p. 105.

concern first and foremost over 'displaced Arabs' who 'lost their land' and became 'landless'. This concern was apparently for those Arab land-owners who sold their land willingly to Jews at exorbitant prices.[109] The gain Arab sellers made in these transactions was ignored. The White Paper regarded them as displaced Arabs who were entitled to available land as a matter of priority. This attitude enhanced the already prevalent policy of curtailing Jewish immigration and land settlement, and had little to do with safeguarding Arab civil or religious rights. The Administration refused to allow Jewish settlements on state lands and waste lands in conformity with the Mandate because these were designated for 'Arab cultivators who are now landless'.[110]

Another justification brought up by the White Paper for the purpose of restricting Jewish immigration and land settlement was attributed under Article 6 of the Mandate to unemployment. This Article states the following:

> The Administration of Palestine, while ensuring that the rights and position of other sections of the population are not prejudiced, shall facilitate Jewish immigration under suitable conditions and shall encourage... close settlement by Jews on the land, including State lands and waste lands not required for public purposes.

The White Paper argued that before allowing Jewish immigration and land settlement, the Administration had to ensure that the rights and position of other sections of the population were not prejudiced. The Mandatory made use of Article 6 to justify their restrictions on Jewish immigration and close settlement on land. In their view, the economic absorptive capacity of Palestine should take into consideration both Arab and Jewish unemployment:

---

[109] Shaw Commission Report, op. cit., p. 141: 'Land for Jewish settlement in Palestine is acquired only at a high cost and the cost of further purchases is likely to be even higher'.

[110] The Passfield White Paper, op. cit., p. 16.

Clearly, if immigration of Jews results in preventing the Arab population from obtaining the work necessary for its maintenance, or if Jewish unemployment unfavourably affects the general labour position, it is the duty of the Mandatory Power under the Mandate to reduce, or, if necessary, to suspend, such immigration until the unemployed portion of the 'other sections' is in a position to obtain work.[111]

However, this argument was, in fact, baseless. The Peel Commission found that Jewish immigration increased 'the economic absorptive capacity' of the Land, rather than decreased it:

'The more immigrants came in, the more work they created for local industries to meet their needs, especially in building: and more work meant more room for immigrants under the labour schedule.'[112]

And concluded:

'With almost mathematical precision the betterment of the economic situation in Palestine meant the deterioration of the political situation'.[113]

In any event, this policy apparently stood in direct contrast to the previous findings of the White Paper. Based on reports by the Shaw and the Hope-Simpson Commissions,[114] it was evident that while Jewish workers were hardly, if at all, employed in

---

[111] Ibid., p. 21. See also the Hope Simpson Report, op. cit., p. 103.

[112] The Peel Commission Report, op. cit., p. 85.

[113] Ibid., p. 86, See table showing the correlation between the rising figures of immigration on the one hand and the economic absorptive capacity in Palestine, on the other hand.

[114] Following the Report submitted by the Shaw Commission, the British Government appointed a second Commission under the Chairmanship of Sir John Hope-Simpson to enquire into issues regarding land settlement, immigration and development in Palestine, which were the source of acute controversy. The Hope-Simpson Report was published on October 1st 1930 and provided some findings upon which the White Paper was based.

Arab villages, many Arab workers were in fact employed in Jewish settlements and industries.[115] Therefore, it was unlikely that Jewish immigration might impact Arab unemployment.[116] What is more, the British never saw immigration as a threat to Jewish employment.

The White Paper's harsh assertion on the necessity to suspend immigration until unemployed Arabs were in a position to obtain work was later refuted by a Statement made on February 13th 1931 by the Prime Minister, Ramsey MacDonald. In fact, he asserted that 'His Majesty's Government never proposed to pursue such a policy'.[117] This Statement was addressed to Weizmann and communicated to the House of Commons as an authoritative interpretation of the Passfield White Paper. The Statement reaffirmed that the British commitment under the Mandate was made to the Jewish people as a whole and not only to the Jewish people of Palestine. It also reiterated the British Government's

---

[115] The Passfield White Paper, op. cit., pp. 17-18: It was reported that Jewish businesses endeavored to employ only Jewish workers. In fact, the White Paper criticized the Jewish Agency for strictly forbidding the employment of non-Jewish labor in any works or undertakings carried out or furthered by the Agency. Moreover, in all leases granted by the Jewish National Fund on its holdings, the lessee undertook to execute his farming only with Jewish labor, and these conditions were strictly observed. There was, on the other hand, no incentive for the Jewish worker to be employed in Arab villages because of the lower standard of the Arab fellah, and the desire of the Jewish Agency to safeguard the standard of life of the Jewish laborer. The gap between the two standards of living was remarkable: The Hope-Simpson Commission reported that 'the condition of the Fellah is little if at all superior to what it was under the Turkish regime'. On the other hand, Jewish settlers achieved remarkable progress, by consistently adopting an advanced policy of Agricultural development, 'with every advantage that capital, science and organization could give them'. See the Hope-Simpson Report, ibid., p. 105.

[116] The Hope-Simpson Report held the view that to some extent the Arab labor market had been adversely affected by Jewish immigration. However, it added, Jewish agricultural and industrial development which followed Jewish immigration provided new opportunities for the Arab laborer, and reasoned that 'in many directions Jewish development has meant more work for the Arabs, and it is a fair conclusion that the competition of imported Jewish labour is equalized by those increased opportunities'. Hope-Simpson Report, op. cit., p. 98.

[117] Parliamentary Debates H.C., February 13th 1931, Hansard, Vol. 248, cc 751, para. 15.

positive obligation to facilitate Jewish immigration and to encourage land settlement, assuring the Jewish people that this could be fulfilled without prejudice to the rights and position of the Arab population of Palestine.[118] However, apart from these assertions which were mainly aimed at settling Jewish nerves, there was no revision to the traditional British policy in Palestine.

The Riots of 1933 and 1936

It required five more years, and two additional Arab riots to convince the British Government that their policy in Palestine was irredeemable, illogical, and would never succeed. On October 1933, the Arab Executive declared a general strike which led to demonstrations and riots. As the Peel Commission put it:

> The angry mob was only dispersed after repeated baton charges by the police. In the course of the next few weeks the trouble spread to other parts of Palestine. On the 27th October there was a serious outbreak at Jaffa. So excited and so dangerous was the temper of the Arab rioters that the police were forced to use their firearms before order could be restored. The news of these events quickly reached Nablus where public buildings were attacked and the police stoned, and travelled on to Haifa where that evening and the next day there were similar disturbances. On the 28th and 29th rioting broke out again at Jerusalem. At each of these towns the attacks on the police, though nowhere so grave as at Jaffa, were formidable enough to compel them to fire in self-defence... There was one feature of this last outbreak of Arab violence which was as unprecedented as it was significant. In 1920, 1921 and 1929 the Arabs had attacked the Jews. In 1933 they attacked the Government.[119]

---

[118] Ibid., para. 7.

[119] The Peel Report, op. cit., p. 84. The Peel Commission also noted that in the riots of October 1933 'the Jews were happily not involved', but in December, a gathering affiliated to a minority-group among the Jews, known as the Revisionists, was involved in a clash with the police in Tel Aviv where it was reported that 'nobody was killed, but 11 police and 8 civilians were injured', see p. 85.

The riot of 1933 was in comparison a minor one. A more deadly riot broke out in the spring of 1936. This was preceded by demands presented to the High Commissioner by the Arab leadership in November 1935, of which the main ones were: '(1) the establishment of democratic government, (2) the prohibition of the transfer of Arab lands to Jews, (3) the immediate cessation of Jewish immigration and the formation of a committee to determine the 'absorptive capacity' of the country'.[120] Since those demands were only partly met, tension continued to rise until, in the spring of 1936, more violent unrest broke out. On April 20th 1936, a general strike was declared by the Arab National Committee throughout the country which was aimed to continue until Arab demands of the previous November were met. The strike was accompanied by Arab violence and sabotage. Deliberate attacks were carried out on Jewish colonies and dwellings, with the loss of over 80 Jewish lives, most of whom were murdered, and over 300 wounded. Women and children were not spared.[121] Much destruction was done to Jewish trees and crops and to commercial or industrial property in Jaffa. There was persistent sniping at Jewish colonies. Jews were attacked and stoned in various parts of the country. Arab attacks were also conducted against Government installations causing destruction to railway lines, oil pipelines, roads, and telephone wires, with one bridge blown up.[122]

On the whole, the outbreak of 1936 followed the same pattern as the previous ones except it was more ferocious, better organized, lasted six months and covered the whole country. The 'disturbances' of 1936 overshadowed all their predecessors.[123]

---

[120] Ibid., p. 89.

[121] Ibid., p. 104. The Peel Commission related that 'of many tragic cases we may mention that of Mr. Lewis Billig, Lecturer in Arabic Literature in the Hebrew University, who had devoted his life to Arabic studies and was murdered in his house in the suburbs of Jerusalem'.

[122] Ibid., pp. 97-98, 101.

[123] Ibid., p. 104. For the first time, so it seems, a Commission appointed to investigate riots in Palestine used the term 'disturbances' while in parenthesis, adding that it was a misnomer which gave a misleading impression of what had really happened. Such deadly riots and acts of terror could hardly be referred to as mere disturbances.

It was characterized by the appearance of armed Arab bands and terrorist gangs in the hills of Palestine including volunteers from Syria and Iraq under the command of trained guerilla leaders from outside Palestine. This, in the eyes of the Peel Commission, was the most serious development of the 1936 riots. Arab terrorist gangs were not content with taking Jewish lives and destroying Jewish property alone, but had directed their main assault against the Government of Palestine. In consequence, British forces were imported from Egypt and Malta, and only with this large military force of around 20,000 men was peace restored. Arab casualties were roughly estimated in official reports at 195 Arabs killed and 84 wounded, but in the opinion of the Commission the number of Arabs killed was far higher. They were credibly estimated at 1,000 killed 'mostly in fighting, since very few Arabs were murdered'.[124]

The Palestine Royal Commission 1937
[The Peel Commission]

As a result of the 1936 upheaval, a Royal Commission was appointed on August 7th 1936 headed by William Robert Wellesley, Earl Peel, 'To ascertain the underlying causes of the disturbances which broke out in Palestine in the middle of April... and if the Commission is satisfied that any ... grievances are well founded, to make recommendations for their removal and for the prevention of their recurrence.'[125]

The Peel Report was by far the most thorough and comprehensive Report ever made to investigate the underlying causes of the repeated 'disturbances' in Palestine. Through this investigation the Commission was convinced without any doubt that 'the underlying causes of the disturbances' or the 'rebellion'[126] as the Commission preferred to call it, were: '(a) the desire of the Arabs for national independence and (b) their hatred and

---

[124] Ibid., p. 105.

[125] Ibid., p. IX.

[126] Ibid., p. 363.

fear of the establishment of the Jewish National Home'.[127] The Arab Higher Committee and Palestinian Arab leaders told the Commission in evidence that their grievances were not caused by the way the Mandate had been carried out, but by the actual existence of the Mandate as such. They refused to accept the fact that Palestine was never pledged to the Arabs under the McMahon correspondence.[128] They denied the validity of the Balfour Declaration, and they disputed the right of the Principal Allied Powers to entrust the Mandate to Great Britain. In their view, the Mandate as exercised was incompatible with the Covenant of the League of Nations and with principle of self-determination embodied in the Covenant.[129]

Soon the Peel Commission realized that the two parts of the Declaration if interpreted in a balanced way, giving the safeguards the same weight as the establishment of the National Home, had no chance of being reconciled. It would lead to continuous friction and violence, with no prospect of a solution. The Commission found that the Mandatory Administration had a long record of excessive leniency toward Arab political agitation 'to its furthest possible limit', treating acts of violence and murder with a policy of conciliation: 'After each successive outbreak, punishment was sparing and clemency the rule: there was no real attempt at disarmament, nor any general repression.'[130] But Arab appeasement served no purpose for conciliation like impartiality had failed: 'It has now been tried for 17 years, and at the end the Arabs, taken as a whole, are more hostile to the Jews and much more hostile to the Government than they were at the beginning.'[131] The Commission repudiated all previous attempts made by the Palestine Government to establish a Legislative Council or an enlarged Advisory Council in which Jews and Arabs were supposed to co-operate, or the establishment of a single self-governing Palestine. All these attempts had failed in

---

[127] Ibid., p. 110.

[128] On the McMahon Correspondence see pp. 314 et seq., supra.

[129] Ibid., p. 107.

[130] Ibid., p. 140

[131] Ibid.

the past and proved impracticable.[132]

The Commission also found that the conciliatory policy of the Palestine Government and the placatory attitude of its senior officers convinced the Arabs that the Mandatory was not seriously determined to implement the Balfour Declaration. This factor contributed to the steady growth of the conflict, which was inherent in the situation from the outset. As noted, it was marked by a series of five Arab outbreaks against the Jews, with the last two also directed against the British Authorities.[133] In consequence of this policy, the Commission became convinced that 'peace, order and good government can only be maintained in Palestine for any length of time by a rigorous system of repression.'[134]

The Peel Commission, thorough as it was, failed to interpret the Mandate as was originally conceived by its founders. 'To put it in one sentence', stated the Commission, 'We cannot – in Palestine as it now is – both concede the Arab claim of self-government and secure the establishment of the Jewish National Home.'[135] However, The Mandate never pledged self-government to the Arabs of Palestine. In fact, such a claim lacked any foundation and went contrary to the Mandate. Under these circumstances, there was little wonder that the Commission arrived at the conclusion that the situation in Palestine had reached a deadlock that required a solution, and that the solution should be found in the idea of partition.

The Commission, therefore, recommended that neither the Arabs nor the Jews should rule all Palestine, but there was no reason why each race should not rule part of it. Saying that, the Commission did not ignore the fact that this would be the second partition of Palestine, the first being the severance of Trans-Jordan from historic Palestine, which many thought was bad enough. The Commission seems to have been motivated by the fear of an outbreak of another Arab rebellion: 'If 'disturbances'

---

132 Ibid., pp. 364, 372, 373.

133 Ibid., p. 371.

134 Ibid., p. 373.

135 Ibid., p. 374.

[Parenthesis in the original]… should recur on a similar scale to that of last year's rebellion, the cost of military operations must soon exhaust the revenues of Palestine and ultimately involve the British Treasury to an incalculable extent.'[136] The Commission, therefore, recommended the termination of the existing Mandate and the creation of two sovereign states, a Jewish State and an Arab State, with a new Mandate encompassing the Holy Places, mainly Jerusalem and Bethlehem. It was then suggested that in the new Mandate the policy of the Balfour Declaration should not apply. The aim was to execute a plan which 'must do justice to the Arabs and the Jews.'[137] Justice not on the lines of the Mandate, i.e., the preservation of civil and religious rights of the non-Jewish communities in Palestine, but in creating two national entities in Palestine, which was contrary to the Mandate and its spirit.

Meinertzhagen, who was closely familiar with British politics in Palestine, commented that the Peel Commission had made the Zionist problem infinitely worse than it was when it began work. Their proposal suggested a further whittling down of the area allotted to the Jewish people for their National Home. From a large area pledged to the Jewish people which included Trans-Jordan, it was now proposed to allot to the Jews a much smaller area confined mainly to a strip of coastal Palestine. In Meinertzhagen's opinion, if the British Administration were friendlier to Zionism and would have expressed more determination to crush terrorism with the aid of a strong garrison, and at the same time would have made it abundantly clear that Zionism was there to stay culminating eventually in the creation of a Jewish State, most Arab violence would have been avoided: 'If I had been allowed to do that in 1919, we should have had none of this trouble. It is a hundred times more difficult now but still practical politics.'[138]

This view was supported by Lloyd George, who told

---

[136] Ibid., p. 373.

[137] Ibid., p. 380.

[138] Meinertzhagen, op. cit., p. 166, December 6th 1937. In a letter to *The Times* on February 7th 1937 Meinertzhagen wrote: 'The Peel Commission completely lost sight of the original intention of the British Government to give the Jews their national home in Palestine (not in a little bit of Palestine)'. Ibid., p. 167.

Meinertzhagen on October 12[139] 1938 that the Palestine question 'has been badly mishandled for years, and now has got almost completely out of control... They [The Government] have surrendered in the face of every difficulty.'[139]

The Peel Report was published on July 7th 1937. On the same day, the British Government issued a Statement of Policy in which any land transaction was prohibited and immigration was severely curtailed.[140] In that Statement, the British finally admitted the futility of their policy based on the assumption that their 'obligations' to Arabs and Jews were compatible. They now arrived at a conclusion that the conflict between the aspirations of Arabs and Jews in Palestine was irreconcilable, and therefore a scheme of partition would be the only solution to the deadlock.

The Palestine Partition Commission 1938 [The Woodhead Commission]

For the purpose of demarcating the frontiers of the two new sovereign states and the new Mandate, the British Government appointed a Commission headed by Sir John Woodhead,[141] with the technical functions of ascertaining and considering in detail the practical possibilities of partition.[142] The Arabs rejected the idea of partition outright. The Arab Higher Committee dispatched a memorandum to the Permanent Mandates Commission, expressing unanimous disapproval of the proposal and demanding instead recognition of complete Arab independence in Palestine as well as immediate cessation of Jewish immigration. This uncompromising disapproval was followed by the immediate intensification of Arab violence lasting from July through August and September 1937, during which 'a widespread campaign of

---

[139] Meinertzhagen, ibid., p 172, September 28th 1938. Lloyd George was then not in office as Prime Minister.

[140] Cmd. 5513, *Palestine Statement of Policy*, HMSO, London, July 1937, p. 3.

[141] Cmd. 5634, *Policy in Palestine: Despatch dated 23rd December 1937, from the Secretary of State for the Colonies to the High Commissioner for Palestine*, HMSO, London, January 4th 1938.

[142] Cmd. 5854, *Palestine Partition Commission Report*, HMSO, London, October 1938, [hereinafter referred to as the Woodhead Commission Report].

murder and intimidation cost many Jews and Arabs their lives.'[143] The year 1938 saw no decline in violence: 'almost every day brought its record of murder, intimidation and sabotage'.[144] Amid this atmosphere of racial hostility, the partition scheme was debated in the Twentieth Zionist Congress[145] and rejected. The Congress also rejected the Peel Commission's assertion that the Mandate had proved irreconcilable, and demanded its implementation. Nevertheless, the door for further negotiations was left open for the purpose of discussing the precise terms of the British Government relating to the establishment of the Jewish State.

Be that as it may, after thorough investigation the Woodhead Commission came to the conclusion that partition along the lines suggested by the Peel Commission was not practical. They found that under any plan of partition the budget of the Jewish State was likely to show a substantial surplus, while the budgets of the Arab State including Trans-Jordan and the Mandated Territories were likely to show substantial deficits. For this and other reasons, the Woodhead Commission found itself unable to recommend frontiers that would make possible the establishment of self-supporting Arab and Jewish States. Consequently, the British Government adopted the view that under the circumstances provided by the Woodhead Commission 'the political, administrative and financial difficulties involved in the proposal to create independent Arab and Jewish States inside Palestine are so great that this solution of the problem is impracticable.'[146]

The Malcolm MacDonald White Paper 1939

As a result, the British Government abandoned the scheme of partition, but came up with a new plan embodied in a White Paper presented to Parliament by Malcolm MacDonald, the Colonial

---

[143] Ibid., p. 17.

[144] Ibid., p. 19.

[145] The Twentieth Zionist Congress was held in Zurich on August 3-16, 1937.

[146] Cmd. 5893, *Statement by His Majesty's Government in the United Kingdom*, HMSO, London, November 1938.

Secretary, in May 1939.[147] In this plan, the British Government moved from their obligation to establish a National Home for the Jewish people with a view that it would eventually emerge into a Jewish State should the experiment succeed, to a complete shift towards establishing an Arab-Muslim regime in Palestine where Jews would remain a significant minority. Cynically, the White Paper based this new policy on the very terms of the Mandate itself.

In the first place, the MacDonald White Paper made it abundantly clear that any idea proclaiming that the Jewish National Home meant eventually the establishment of a Jewish State was false and incompatible with British policy in Palestine. It was held that this concept was contrary to British obligations to the Arabs under the Mandate and to assurances given to the latter that they would not be subjected to Jewish domination. The British Authorities were satisfied that their obligations to the Jews under the Mandate were confined to no more than the further development of the existing Jewish Community in Palestine with the assistance of Jews in other parts of the world. Secondly, the Jewish population was to crystallize to form a permanent minority at a rate of one third of the total population of Palestine. Hence, the statement in the Churchill White Paper that the Jewish people was in Palestine 'as of right and not on sufferance' ceased to have any effect.

Jewish immigration to Palestine, which was the very essence of the Mandate, was to stop completely within a period of five years. The terms were that Jewish immigration during the five years following 1939 would be allowed only to a limit that would not exceed one third of the total population of Palestine. During this period immigration would be subject not only to the economic absorptive capacity of the country, but also to a newly introduced undefined political criterion; namely, its damaging or adverse effect on the political or economic position of the country. The White Paper clearly admitted that those changes were the outcome of Arab terror and violence: 'The lamentable

---

[147] Cmd. 6019, *Palestine Statement of Policy*. May 17th 1939, HMSO, London 1939. [The MacDonald White Paper].

disturbances of the past three years are only the latest and most sustained manifestation of this intense Arab apprehension.'[148] The White Paper endeavored to placate the Arabs for the purpose of preventing further violence, which had already caused a serious setback to the economic progress of Palestine, the depletion of its exchequer, and jeopardized the security of the country.

In the five transitional years, some 75,000 Jewish immigrants would be admitted, 10,000 each year, with another 25,000 immigrants to be admitted if proven to have economic means. After the five-year period, no further Jewish immigrants would be permitted without the acquiescence of the Arabs of Palestine. In sum, Jewish immigration into Palestine would be, after a period of five years, subject no more to the economic absorptive capacity and political criterions, but to the approval of the Arab population in Palestine, who were known to have violently resisted it all along. It was obvious to the British as much as to the Jews and Arabs that this decree meant the total cessation of Jewish immigration, subjecting the existing Jewish population to become a permanent minority in the land which was pledged to be their National Home. It is illuminating that such restrictions did not apply to Arab immigration into Palestine.[149]

The British Government, thereafter, did not hesitate to exempt itself from its obligations to facilitate Jewish immigration into Palestine, in flagrant violation of the Mandate:

> His Majesty's Government are satisfied that, when the immigration over five years which is now contemplated has taken place, they will not be justified in facilitating, nor will they be under any obligation to facilitate, the further development of the Jewish National Home by immigration regardless

---

[148] Ibid., p. 9.

[149] On this point Meinertzhagen commented: 'One hears a lot about Jewish immigration into Palestine. One hears little of the unrestricted Arab immigration into Palestine. There has been a steady flow into Palestine, attracted by Jewish prosperity'. See Meinertzhagen, op. cit., p. 199.

of the wishes of the Arab population.[150]

This policy was severely attacked in the British Parliament: 'The whole debate, indeed, went against the Government. The most important figures in the House attacked the White Paper'.[151] Winston Churchill, in particular, the author of the 1922 White Paper, spoke with much force:

> The provision that Jewish immigration can be stopped in five years' time by the decision of an Arab majority… is a plain breach of a solemn obligation… [for] to whom was the pledge of the Balfour Declaration made? It was not made to the Jews of Palestine. It was not made to those who were actually living in Palestine. It was made to world Jewry and in particular to the Zionist associations. It was in consequence of and on the basis of this pledge that we received important help in the War, and that after the War we received from the Allied and Associated Powers the Mandate for Palestine… But what sort of National Home is offered to the Jews of the world when we are asked to declare that in five years' time the door of that home is to be shut and barred in their faces? The idea of home to wanderers is, surely, a place to which they can resort.[152]

As for land transfer and settlement for Jews, restrictions continued to apply. The High Commissioner was given general powers to prohibit and regulate transfers of land in circumstances which, in his opinion, might jeopardize Arab cultivators in maintaining their existing standard of life, or by becoming landless.

The last blow to the Jewish National Home was struck when the

---

[150] Cmd. 6019, op. cit., p. 11, para. 15.

[151] Weizmann, op. cit., p. 411.

[152] Parliamentary Debates H.C., May 23rd 1939, Hansard, cc 2171-73. Weizmann referred to Churchill's speech against the MacDonald White Paper as 'one of the great speeches of his career'.

MacDonald's White Paper announced the British Government's intention to establish within ten years an independent Palestine State, in which the people of Palestine as a whole, with a significant Arab majority, would enjoy the rights of self-government as enjoyed by the people of neighboring countries.[153] In such circumstances of persistent curtailing and then cessation of immigration, ensuring Jewish permanent minority status in Palestine, coupled with a harsh policy of preventing land purchase and settlement by Jews, the establishment of a Jewish National Home was seriously jeopardized. The envisaged concept was instead one of a Palestine State 'in which the two peoples of Palestine, Arabs and Jews, share authority in government in such a way that the essential interests of each are secured',[154] it being understood that the sharing of authority by each side would be conducted in proportion to their respective populations.[155] This declaration was made amid strong animosity prevailing between Jews and Arabs and explicit conclusions made by several British Commissions to the effect that the interests of the two peoples could not be reconciled as their aspirations were totally and completely contradictory. The White Paper gave no indication how in practice the sharing of government was to take place.

The British Government invoked Article 2 of the Mandate, which entrusted them with the obligation to secure the development of self-governing institutions, to justify the creation of a Palestinian State with a permanent Arab majority coupled with a complete cessation of Jewish immigration. The Mandatory considered that a self-governing institution was a preliminary step to the formation of a Government in which Jews and Arabs would share authority on a proportional basis. However, this view contradicted the spirit and literal sense of the

---

[153] A period to be extended if the situation in Palestine was not yet ready for independence.

[154] Cmd. 6019, op. cit., pp. 5-6, para. 8.

[155] See, for example, para. 10(4) of the White Paper: '...the objective being to place Palestinians in charge of all the Departments of Government... Arab and Jewish representatives will be invited to serve as heads of Departments approximately in proportion to their respective populations.' Cmd. 6019, ibid., pp. 6-7.

Mandate. Churchill repudiated it in Parliament by stating that the paramount duty of the British Government was the establishment of the Jewish National Home, with the establishment of self-governing institutions to be subordinated to that pledge. [156]

Other prominent opponents of the MacDonald White Paper included Leopold Amery and Herbert Morrison. Amery, then an M.P., argued that it was a confession of failure, a desperate attempt to appease the Arabs 'at all costs'. It was a direct negation of the principles on which the Administration in Palestine had been based and a repudiation of the pledges upon which Britain was entrusted with the Mandate for Palestine. In fact, the MacDonald White Paper effectively translated into British recognition of Palestine as Arab land. The Jews would then be reduced to a permanent minority under Arab authority, living in Palestine on sufferance – a reality never contemplated by the Balfour Declaration.[157] Morrison, also an M.P., criticized British maneuvering, stating that the Government endeavored 'to twist the Balfour Declaration and the Mandate to fit in with the policy of the White Paper, and then to prove that the White Paper was not out of harmony with the Declaration or the Mandate'. But Morrison made it clear that 'the White Paper is not in harmony with either the Balfour Declaration or the Mandate, is not in harmony with their wording, is not in harmony with their spirit'.[158] He also noted that the Arabs achieved their position in the White Paper not by persuasion, but by terror and violence: 'The White Paper is a complete surrender to disturbance, murder and assassination'.[159]

---

[156] Parliamentary Debates H.C., May 23rd 1939, Hansard, c. 2170.

[157] Parliamentary Debates H.C., May 22nd 1939, Hansard, c. 2012. Leopold Amery served as Colonial Secretary (1924-1929). He was familiar with British policy regarding Palestine. Weizmann referred to him in his memoirs as an open-minded politician of large stature and superior abilities, who 'realized the importance of a Jewish Palestine in the British imperial scheme of things more than anybody else... [and] had much insight into the intrinsic fineness of the Zionist movement'. Weizmann, op. cit. p. 182.

[158] Parliamentary Debates H.C., 23 May 1939, Hansard, Vol. 347, c. 2130.

[159] Ibid., c. 2142. Herbert Morrison was a labor politician and statesman. He held several senior positions in the British Government. He served as Minister of Transport, then Home Secretary. During the Second World War, he served in Churchill's War Cabinet until 1945. Later, he was elected Leader

The MacDonald White Paper received the approval of the House of Commons despite the fact that it was bitterly attacked.[160] It was unanimously rejected by the Zionist Organization without even being discussed. It was declared illegal by the Permanent Mandates Commission who stated explicitly: 'The policy set out in the White Paper is not in accordance with the interpretation which, in agreement with the Mandatory Power and the Council, the Commission has placed upon the Palestine Mandate'.[161] This decision did not come before the Council of the League of Nations for approval because of the outbreak of the Second World War.

During the Second World War, Jews were acutely conflicted. On the one hand, they were eager to immensely contribute to the British war effort. Yet the gates of Palestine were barred to Jewish immigration at a time when the Jewish plight was at its most dire, with hundreds of thousands of refugees – men, women and children – seeking refuge in the promised National Home from a fate of persecution and extermination in Europe. Boats packed with these desperate refugees were moored in the Mediterranean, unable to discharge their homeless passengers.

During the war period, Weizmann met with Churchill a few times to discuss the Jewish National Home and plans for the future. Weizmann found in Churchill a friendly ally and was greatly encouraged by those talks. Thus, in December 17th 1939, Weizmann told Churchill that after the war, the Jews intended to build up a state of 3-4 million Jews in Palestine. Churchill retorted: 'Yes, indeed, I agree with that'.[162] When Churchill heard of the Zionist plan to send 100,000 Jewish immigrants to Palestine every year for 15 years, he did not show any objection but was interested to know if financial aid was necessary.[163] On the whole, he was sympathetic and understanding. In 1942 Churchill assured Weizmann that he had a plan for the Jews,

---

of the House of Commons and Deputy Prime Minister in Clement Attlee's Governments 1945-1951.

[160] Parliamentary Debates H.C., May 23rd 1939, Hansard, Vol. 347, c. 2193. Ayes 281, Noes 181.

[161] Weizmann, op. cit., pp. 413-14.

[162] Weizmann, ibid., p. 419.

[163] Ibid., p. 436.

and that together with Roosevelt he could carry it out, bringing an end to the White Paper and promoting a change for the better in the status of the Jewish National Home. He also assured Weizmann of his desire to settle the Jewish problem in Palestine, and that he managed to secure the co-operation of Roosevelt. On November 4th 1944, at Chequers, Churchill was more specific in his conversation. He spoke of partition and of the inclusion of the Negev in the Jewish territory, but would not take any action until the war was over. [164]

The war ended in May 1945, but there was no change in British policy with regard to Palestine. Churchill informed Weizmann that the implementation of the Jewish National Home would have to be postponed until after the Peace Conference took place. On July 5th 1945, following the general elections in Britain, Churchill lost his post as Prime Minister and the Labor Party took over to form a new Government.[165] Meinertzhagen commented that Churchill had broken his pledge to give the Jews sovereignty over Palestine, due no doubt to fear of the Arabs and any trouble they might cause.[166]

Disillusionment was far greater when the Labor Government came to power. The Labor Party was traditionally pro-Zionist and strongly supported the Jewish National Home. In their Conference of June 1943, the British Labor Party even went beyond Jewish expectations: They supported mass immigration of Jews into Palestine and encouraged local Arabs to move out, subject to compensation, as Jews moved in.[167] Again, during their election campaign in 1945, the Labor Party made repeated promises of assistance to the Zionists. They pledged to reverse the MacDonald White Paper and included that pledge in their election propaganda. Attlee himself wrote in the Daily Herald, before the General Elections of 1945, that during the war 'they associated themselves with the ideal of a National Home in Palestine for the

---

[164] Ibid.

[165] Meinertzhagen, op. cit., pp. 194-95, entry July 3rd 1945.

[166] Ibid., pp. 195-96, entry July 24th 1945.

[167] Weizmann, op. cit., p. 436.

Jewish people and that ever since... have repeatedly affirmed their enthusiastic support of the effort towards its realization.'[168]

However, on November 13th 1945, the Labor Government officially repudiated the pledges of the Labor Party and went back on all its promises regarding the Jewish National Home. On that day, the British Foreign Secretary, Ernest Bevin, promulgated a statement on behalf of the Labor Government in which he advocated that the remnants of the Holocaust, the survivors of torture and extermination on the soil of Europe, should remain in Europe rather than go to Palestine.[169] Bevin's statement repeated the dual pledge formula which was allegedly made to the Arabs on the one hand and to the Jews on the other, treating them with equal weight: 'Both communities lay claim to Palestine, one on the ground of a millennium of occupation and the other on the ground of historic association coupled with the undertaking given in the First World War to establish a Jewish Home'.[170] Meinertzhagen referred to some of Bevin's statements as 'utter rubbish', 'meaning nothing at all' and 'completely unconstructive'. He also found his statements to be 'almost flippant, concealing an insidious emasculation of the whole problem'.[171]

The Labor Government decided to appoint a new Commission of Inquiry instead of abrogating the MacDonald White Paper, the latter being a pledge repeatedly made by the Labor party.[172] For this purpose, they invited the United States Government to set up a joint Anglo-American Committee of Inquiry to examine the question of European Jewry and to make a further review of

---

[168] Meinertzhagen, op. cit., p. 198, entry September 28th 1945.

[169] Statement on Palestine by British Foreign Secretary Bevin, November 13th 1945. Parliamentary Debates, HC, Vol. 415, cc. 1927-35; Weizmann, op. cit., pp. 439-40.

[170] Ibid., Bevin's reference to Arab occupation allegedly lasting a millennium was grossly exaggerated. The Peel Commission conducted a thorough survey on the history of the Middle East, and they asserted that the Arabs, who emerged from the Arabian desert, invaded Syria, Iraq, Persia and Egypt among other places between A.D. 632 and 713, and occupied them for not more than three centuries. See the Peel Report, op. cit., p. 5.

[171] Meinertzhagen, op. cit., pp. 199-201.

[172] Weizmann, op. cit., p. 439.

the Palestine problem. The Americans concurred. The Anglo-American Report was published on May 1st 1946. During the entire period since the formation of the Labor Government, immigration was allowed at a rate not exceeding fifteen hundred refugees per month. Weizmann commented that Bevin's approach to the Jewish problem was brutal, coarse, and bullying, lacking any understanding of the unfortunate plight of the remnants of the Holocaust.[173]

The Anglo-American Committee recommended that 100,000 certificates be issued immediately, as suggested by U.S. President Truman, for admission of Jewish victims of Nazi and Fascist persecution into Palestine. The Committee made nine more recommendations which had no practical effect and nothing came out of the report. In Weizmann's view 'the whole device had been nothing but a stall'.[174] The White Paper continued to dominate Jewish immigration into Palestine, which was fixed at 1,500 per month.

Considering the consistent negative attitude of the Labor Government regarding the establishment of the Jewish National Home, it should not come as a surprise that while the Anglo-American Committee of Inquiry was deliberating on the fate of Palestine, which until then included Trans-Jordan, Britain took action to formally and completely sever Trans-Jordan from Palestine.[175] Meinertzhagen pointed out:

---

[173] Ibid., p. 440.

[174] Weizmann, ibid., 441.

[175] On January 17th 1946, Foreign Secretary Bevin announced at the General Assembly the intention of the British Government to establish Trans-Jordan as a sovereign independent State and to recognize it as such. See United Nations, Official records of the General Assembly, First Session, First Part, Plenary Meetings, p. 167. Cited in *Trans-Jordan: Attitude of the United States Regarding the Granting of Independence to Trans-Jordan by the United Kingdom*, February 13th 1946, see Volume VII on *Foreign Relations of the United States: Diplomatic Papers, 1946 (the Near East and Africa)*, United States Government Printing Office, Washington 1969, p. 794, n.1. http://images.library.wisc.edu/FRUS/EFacs/1946v07/reference/frus.frus1946v07.i0017.pdf. Later on, in March 1946, a Treaty of Alliance was signed between Britain and Amir Abdullah in which Britain recognized Trans-Jordan as a fully independent State and Amir Abdullah as its sovereign. See Cmd. 6916 of March 22nd 1946, Treaty Series No. 32 (1946), *Treaty of Alliance Between*

In their anxiety to ensure that the Jews would not get Trans-Jordan or that the Commission should even recommend anything about Trans-Jordan, His Majesty's Government, in a hurry, went behind the backs of the Commission and, whilst it was sitting, severed Trans-Jordan from Palestine whereas geographically and in every other sense it is Palestine and always has been.[176]

In consequence of the failure of the Anglo-American Report to produce any results in finding the formula for peace in Palestine, the British Government referred the whole matter to the General Assembly of the United Nations. It soon became evident to the Zionist Organization that the Anglo-American Committee and other mechanisms employed ostensibly by the British Government to solve the Palestine impasse were nothing but delaying devices. In Weizmann's view, referring the issue to the United Nations had no other purpose than to achieve further delay. Bevin did not expect that the outcome would be partition and the creation of a Jewish State.[177]

On May 15th 1947, the General Assembly established the United Nations Special Committee on Palestine (UNSCOP). The Special Committee was given wide powers to record facts, carry out investigations, and make recommendations. It was to report no later than September 1st 1947. The majority of UNSCOP recommended that Palestine should comprise three entities: an Arab State, a Jewish State, and the City of Jerusalem. The Arab and Jewish States were to become independent after a transitional period of two years beginning on September 1st 1947. The City of Jerusalem was to be placed under the international trusteeship system by means of a trusteeship agreement designating the

---

His Majesty in Respect of the United Kingdom and His Highness the Amir of Trans-Jordan, Article 1. All these initiatives, calculated to formally sever Trans-Jordan from Palestine, took place while the Anglo-American Committee of Inquiry was conducting its investigation on the future of Palestine.

[176] Meinertzhagen, op. cit., p. 208.

[177] Weizmann, op. cit., p. 452.

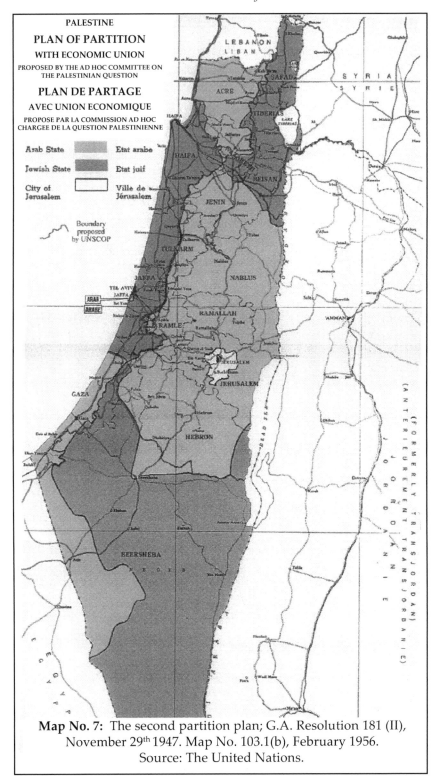

Map No. 7: The second partition plan; G.A. Resolution 181 (II), November 29th 1947. Map No. 103.1(b), February 1956. Source: The United Nations.

United Nations as the Administering Authority.[178] The three entities: The Arab State, Jewish State, and Jerusalem were to be linked in an economic union. The General Assembly further established an ad hoc Committee on the Palestine question composed of all Members. The ad hoc Committee considered reports submitted by Sub-Committees and then recommended to the General Assembly a plan for the partitioning of Palestine, with economic union. On November 29th 1947, the Assembly adopted the Report submitted by the ad hoc Committee by a vote of 33 in favor, 13 against, and 11 abstentions.

The General Assembly, therefore, adopted a partition plan (Resolution 181 (II)).[179] The Resolution provided that the British Mandate over Palestine was to terminate and that British armed forces were to withdraw as soon as possible, but not later than August 1st 1948. Britain, in fact, announced its intention to terminate the Mandate on May 15th 1948. The independent states and the special international regime for Jerusalem were to come into existence two months after British withdrawal was complete but not later than October 1st 1948. The boundaries of the three entities were determined.[180] However, the British Government and its representatives in Palestine were doing their utmost to turn the decision of UNSCOP and the ad hoc Committee against the Jews, basing their endeavors on arguments which had long since been disproved.[181]

The Zionist Organization accepted the General Assembly's Resolution of November 29th 1947. The Arabs of Palestine and the surrounding Arab countries rejected it outright. The period that followed saw a complete deterioration in the security of the Jews in Palestine. During the transitional period preceding British evacuation, while still being responsible for the maintenance of

---

[178] Report of the United Nations Special Committee on Palestine, UNSCOP, September 3rd 1947, Section B, Part I on Partition and Independence, Recommendation No. 1; and Part III on the City of Jerusalem, Recommendation No. 1.

[179] See map No. 7 on p. 344, supra.

[180] Ibid., Part II on Boundaries.

[181] Weizmann, op. cit., p. 455.

law and order, the British did nothing to protect Jews from Arab attacks. Violent riots which could be easily suppressed were permitted to spread. While the Authorities did not protect Jews from violence, they did not allow Jews to carry arms. Jewish convoys were attacked, and the defenders were often searched when they were on duty. The British attitude became openly anti-Jewish. The Mandatory Power refused to comply with the Assembly's recommendation to open a port of immigration, and allowed Government services to disintegrate. Furthermore, it allowed the invasion into Palestine of irregular Arab forces. Thus, Arab attacks multiplied. British policy substantially encouraged the Arab population to resort to violence and agitation in order to gain what they could not achieve through negotiations at the United Nations.[182]

Britain relinquished its Mandate over Palestine on May 15th 1948. Shortly after that, the new State of Israel was proclaimed, which was followed by a concerted military attack on the nascent country by seven Arab armies: those of Egypt, Trans-Jordan, Syria, Iraq, Lebanon, Saudi-Arabia and Yemen. The outcome of the war, however, is beyond the scope of this study.

---

[182] Weizmann, ibid., pp. 470-71.

Part IV

The Arab Stand

The Arabs of Palestine based their national rights over Palestine on two major pillars: On British pledges and on the doctrine of self-determination. The former includes the Hussein-McMahon Correspondence, the Hogarth Message, the Declaration to the Seven, and the Anglo-French Declaration, and these will now be discussed.

Chapter I

The Hussein-McMahon Correspondence [1]

A few months after the beginning of the First World War,[2] Sherif Hussein of Mecca approached Lord Kitchener, the British Foreign Secretary, on behalf of the entire Arab Nation, promising to revolt against the Turks in exchange for Arab independence in the Arab inhabited territories of the Middle East. On July 14th 1915, Hussein sent a letter to Sir Henry McMahon, the British High Commissioner in Cairo, proposing the limits of the territories to receive Arab independence and demanding an answer to his proposal within 30 days:

> England to acknowledge the independence of the Arab countries, bounded on the north by Mersina and Adana up to the 37° of latitude, on which degree fall Birijik, Urfa, Mardin, Midiat, Jezirat (Ibn Umar), Amadia, up to the border with Persia; on the east by the borders of Persia up to the Gulf of Basra; on the south by the Indian Ocean, with the exception of the position of Aden to remain as it is; on the west by the Red Sea, the Mediterranean Sea up to Mersina. England to approve of the proclamation of an Arab Khalifate of Islam.[3]

Hussein's ambitious proposal took the British Government

---

[1] Cmd. 5957, *Correspondence between Sir Henry McMahon, His Majesty's High Commissioner at Cairo, and the Sherif Hussein of Mecca.* Miscellaneous No. 3, HMSO, London, 1939. The Correspondence comprises ten letters exchanged between Hussein and McMahon, from July 14th 1915 to March 10th 1916. The correspondence with Hussein was in Arabic. The English text of the Correspondence is based on the original drafts in English of the letters sent by McMahon before they were translated into Arabic, and on the contemporary translations into English of the letters received from Hussein. See Explanatory Note on Cmd. 5957, p. 2.

[2] The War began on October 30th 1914.

[3] Cmd. 5957, ibid., Doc. No. 1. p. 3.

by surprise. The British Government was then only prepared to recognize the independence of Arabia and the approval of an Arab Khalifate, which was confirmed by McMahon. However, Britain was not ready at this stage to accept recognition of such wide limits of Arab independence. McMahon, therefore, replied that on the question of boundaries, 'it would appear to be premature to consume our time in discussing such details in the heat of war', particularly when Turkey was still in control of large portions of those territories and many of the Arabs were fighting alongside the Turks against the British.[4]

McMahon's reply was received by Hussein with evident disapproval. He insisted on an early decision as to the boundaries of the contemplated Arab State, telling McMahon that his people, and not only himself, were united on this issue. Hussein assured him that the required boundaries did not include places inhabited by foreign races. However, Hussein did not deny McMahon's allegation that many Arabs were fighting alongside the Turks against the British – but he urged him not to use this claim as an excuse to deny the Arabs their demands.[5]

Fearing the loss of Arab cooperation in the war, McMahon made the following statement on October 24th 1915 on behalf of the British Government, the most controversial yet important of the Hussein-McMahon Correspondence:[6]

> The two districts of Mersina and Alexandretta and portions of Syria lying to the west of the districts of Damascus, Homs, Hama, and Aleppo cannot be said to be purely Arab, and should be excluded from the limits demanded.
>
> With the above modification, and without prejudice to our existing treaties with Arab chiefs, we accept those limits. As for those regions lying within those frontiers wherein Great Britain is free to act without detriment to the interests of her ally, France,

---

4 Cmd. 5957, ibid., Doc. No. 2, pp. 4-5, August 30th 1915.

5 Cmd. 5957, ibid., Doc. No. 3, pp.5-7, September 9th 1915.

6 Cmd. 5957, ibid., Doc. No. 4, pp. 7-9, October 24th 1915.

I am empowered in the name of the Government of Great Britain to give the following assurances and make the following reply to your letter:

(1) Subject to the above modifications, Great Britain is prepared to recognize and support the independence of the Arabs in all the regions within the limits demanded by the Sherif of Mecca.

In reference to the above, Hussein stated:

We renounce our insistence on the inclusion of the *vilayets* of Mersina and Adana in the Arab Kingdom. But the two *vilayets* of Aleppo and Beirut and their sea coasts are purely Arab *vilayets,* and there is no difference between a Moslem and a Christian Arab: they are both descendents of one forefather.[7]

To this dispatch McMahon replied:

I am gratified to observe that you agree to the exclusion of the districts of Mersina and Adana (former reading – *vilayets*)[8] from the boundaries of the Arab territories... With regard to the *vilayets* of Aleppo and Beirut... as the interests of our ally, France, are involved in them both, the question will require careful consideration and a further communication on the subject will be addressed to you in due course.[9]

---

7   Cmd. 5957, ibid., Doc. No. 5, pp. 9-11, November 5th 1915.

8   The text has been revised due to criticism that the original draft was not an accurate reproduction of the Arabic used in the actual correspondence. See Explanatory Note, Cmd. 5957, ibid., p. 2.

9   Cmd. 5957, Ibid., Doc. No. 6, 11-12, December 14th 1915. In a Foreign Office Memorandum prepared by W.J. Childs on October 24th 1930, it was noted that 'No such later communication was ever sent: the correspondence has therefore remained incomplete', see British Documents on Foreign Affairs, [hereinafter BDFA], Part II, series B, Vol. 15, Ed. K. Bourne & D.C. watt, University Publications of America, 1989, p. 404.

However, McMahon saw fit to add in his letter a reminder to Hussein urging him not to spare any effort to bring all the Arab peoples to join in the common cause and to refrain from affording any assistance to the enemy.

On the French-British alliance mentioned in McMahon's latest letter, Hussein replied, while referring to those territories as 'the northern parts and their coasts' that he would –

> avoid what may possibly injure the alliance of Great Britain and France and the agreement made between them during the present wars and calamities; yet... at the first opportunity after this war is finished, we shall ask you (what we avert our eyes from today) for what we now leave to France in Beirut and its coasts... It is impossible to allow any derogation that gives France, or any other power, a span of land in those regions.[10]

McMahon in reply, made no mention of Hussein's claim to Beirut and its coasts and simply acknowledged 'with satisfaction' his desire to avoid anything which might injure the British-French alliance.[11]

This correspondence did not lead to any formal agreement or treaty. No map was attached to McMahon's pledge – neither were the limits of the Arab territory specified with any landmark. The correspondence remained inconclusive.[12] There was no offer and acceptance in the contractual sense of the word. Each side, instead of consenting verbatim to the offer of the other side, made a new offer, which again was not specifically accepted. It can hardly be said that a *consensus-ad-idem* existed between the parties.[13] A Foreign Office Memorandum of November

---

[10] Cmd. 5957, ibid., Doc. No. 7, pp. 12-14, January 1st 1916.

[11] Cmd. 5957, ibid., Doc. No. 8, pp. 14-15, January 25th 1916.

[12] Isaiah Friedman – *The Question of Palestine, British-Jewish-Arab Relations 1914-1918*, 2nd Expanded Edition, Transaction Publishers, New Brunswick, U.S.A. 1992, p. 95.

[13] As stated in Cheshire and Fifoot's *Law of Contract*, 8th Edition, Butterworths, London 1972, p. 31: 'the offeree must unreservedly assent to the exact terms

1918, prepared by its Political Intelligence Department, on 'British Commitments to King Hussein' stated unequivocally: 'Our commitments to King Hussein are not embodied in any agreement or treaty signed or even acknowledged by both parties. In this way they differ from those to Russia, France, Italy and certain independent Arab rulers such as the Idrisi and Bin Saud.'[14]

Feisal was aware of the weakness of his argument; namely, that in the Hussein-McMahon Correspondence, Palestine had been included in the Arab designated territories. He, therefore, came up with an allegation that a treaty had in fact been signed between the British Government and Hussein in 1915, which preceded McMahon's letter of October 24th 1915, but that Hussein kept the matter secret and 'never wanted to show the Treaty to anyone else'.[15] Lloyd George, after consulting with Curzon and Allenby, denied any knowledge of a definite sealed treaty on the matter of boundaries and limits between Hussein and the British Government.[16] This point was further stressed by the Colonial Secretary, the Duke of Devonshire, in the British Cabinet:

> Critics of British policy sometimes speak about a 'Treaty' having been concluded with the Arabs in 1915. Nothing of the kind took place. It is true that

---

proposed by the offeror. If, while purporting to accept the offer as a whole, he introduces a new term which the offeror has not had the chance of examining, he is merely making a counter offer. The effect of this in the eyes of the law is to destroy the original offer'. See also *Hyde v. Wrench* (1840) 3 Beav. 334, cited in Cheshire and Fifoot, p. 31.

14 CAB 24/68 G.T. 6185, p. 1 (undated, presumably October or November 1918); also in BDFA, op. cit., Vol. 15, Doc. 16, p. 183. Though the Memorandum was published unsigned, Isaiah Friedman identified the author as Dr. Arnold J. Toynbee, who at that time was attached to the Political Intelligence Department of the Foreign Office, see Friedman, op. cit., pp. 95-96.

15 Documents on British Foreign policy, First Series, Vol. IV, HMSO, London, 1952. ed. E.L. Woodward & R. Butler [hereinafter DBFP], Enclosure to Doc. 283, p. 403, *Notes of a Meeting held at 10 Downing Street, September 19th 1919.*

16 DBFP, ibid., Vol. IV, enclosure to Doc. 283, September 19th 1919, pp. 399, 404.

the Sherif in the first letter of the series (14th July 1915) drew up a list of what he called 'fundamental propositions', which might conceivably be regarded as the first draft of a convention, but no further progress was made in the direction of a formal agreement. What followed was a long and rather inconclusive correspondence which left many points still unsettled when the Sherif actually took the plunge and revolted against the Turks.[17]

To substantiate his argument, on August 28th 1918, Hussein presented to Sir Reginald Wingate, the British High Commissioner in Cairo, a so-called 'agreement come to with the British Government regarding the rising and its foundation'. This agreement which was alleged to have preceded the Hussein-McMahon Correspondence was in direct contradiction with the latter. It is clear that had there been a prior agreement, the McMahon-Hussein Correspondence would have been superfluous. The 'agreement' presented by Hussein was therefore without any foundation.[18] Major Young of the Foreign Office, while referring specifically to that document stated emphatically: 'The fact is that no actual agreement was ever arrived at'.[19]

---

[17] CAB 24/159, C.P. 106 (23), p. 6, *Memorandum by the Secretary of State for the Colonies*, February 17th 1923.

[18] It was well known in British official circles that Hussein had the habit of ignoring or refusing to take note of conditions laid down by the British Government to which he objected, and then carrying on as if the particular question had been settled between him and Britain according to his own desires. See Memorandum on British Commitments to King Hussein, CAB 24/68 G.T. 6185, p. 1.

[19] BDFA, op. cit., Part II, Series I, Vol. 11, p. 276, *Foreign Office Memorandum on Possible Negotiations with the Hedjaz*, November 29th 1920. The so-called agreement, in its most relevant part, stated as follows: 'Great Britain agrees to the formation of an Independent Arab Government in every meaning of the word 'independence' internally and externally, the boundaries of the said Government being, on the east, the Persian Gulf; on the west, the Red Sea, the Egyptian frontier and the Mediterranean; on the north, the northern boundaries of the Vilayet of Aleppo and Mosul up to the river Euphrates and its junction with the Tigris as far as their mouths in the Persian Gulf, but with the exception of the Aden colony, which is excluded from these boundaries'. See Appendix A, August 28th 1918, p. 283.

As noted, the question of whether Palestine had been included or excluded from the area marked for Arab independence was not expressly mentioned in any of the Hussein-McMahon prolonged Correspondence. As we shall observe, British authorities maintained emphatically that Palestine was excluded from this territory, while the Arabs maintained emphatically that it was included.

It is clear that the language and terms used in the Correspondence were loose, indeterminate, and vague. One reason was because the decisive document of October 24th 1915 that contained the pledge was drafted in haste under great pressure. The fact was that after suffering a humiliating debacle at Gallipoli, Britain was deeply concerned about the outcome of the conflict. It was then that Hussein, through his Cairo agent, Mohammed Sherif el-Faroki,[20] presented the British Authorities in Cairo with an ultimatum – that unless the British acknowledge and support Hussein's demands of July 14th 1915, the Arabs would side with Germany and Turkey, who were prepared, according to Arab propaganda which later proved false, to adhere to Hussein's demands. McMahon asked the Foreign Office for instructions and received an urgent telegram from Foreign Secretary Grey on October 20th 1915, instructing him that the most important goal at that time was 'to give an assurance that will prevent the alienation of the Arabs'.[21] With this in mind, McMahon made his pledge on behalf of the British Government subject to certain reservations. He was again urged to apply a policy in which 'to win the Arabs over to our side against the Turks is our vital and foremost object, not the acquisition of a new sphere of influence for ourselves'.[22] McMahon commented that he had to use all

---

[20] BDFA, ibid., Part II, Series B, Vol. 15, p. 396: El-Faroki was a key figure in the negotiations leading to the McMahon-Hussein Correspondence. He was an Arab Nationalist who served in the Ottoman Army but later defected to the British lines at Gallipoli in September 1915. He subsequently acquired the Sherif's confidence, acted as his emissary, and had much influence on British-Sherif negotiations.

[21] BDFA, op. cit., Part II, Series B, Vol. 15, p. 400, October 20th 1915.

[22] Ibid., p. 404, Foreign Office telegram, undated, but in Childs' view the communication would obviously relate to November 5th or 6th 1915.

his wits to compose a reply to Hussein in his letter of October 24th, which would be acceptable to the latter and at the same time leave, as far as possible, a free hand to the British Government in the future.[(23)]

Another reason might have been the fact that the letters were translated from English to Arabic when sent to Hussein and from Arabic to English when received from Hussein. There was much criticism by the Arab delegations to the Conferences on Palestine that the translations were not necessarily accurate and some changes were suggested.[(24)] However, imprecise terms and loose language were used by both parties alike. They were used even by Hussein himself who was supposed to know better the differences of the terms and localities.

For example, in his letter of July 14th 1915, Hussein referred to the cities of Mersina and Adana as forming the northern limits of the area to be allocated to the Arabs. Yet in his reply of October 24th 1915, McMahon did not refer to the *cities* of Mersina and Adana, but to the *districts* of Mersina and Alexandretta and to the *districts* of Damascus, Homs, Hama and Aleppo, stating that the two districts of Mersina and Alexandretta and portions of Syria lying to the west of the districts of Damascus, Homs, Hama, and Aleppo could not be said to be purely Arab, and, therefore, should be excluded from the territories pledged to the Arabs. In his letter of November 5th 1915, Hussein renounced his insistence on the inclusion of the *vilayets* of Mersina and Adana in the territories allocated to the Arabs, this time using the term *vilayet* for them, but opposed the exclusion of the two *vilayets* of Aleppo and Beirut and their sea coasts from territories pledged to the Arabs. In the Correspondence, the terms *vilayet*, district, and region were used interchangeably. For Mersina was a city and not a *vilayet*, and Adana was then invoked as a *vilayet* and not as a city, the latter two being nonidentical. The *vilayet* of Beirut was mentioned. This *vilayet* covers the coastal area of the southern

---

[23] Ibid., p. 401, October 26th 1915.

[24] Cmd. 5974, *Report of a Committee set up to Consider Certain Correspondence between Sir Henry McMahon and the Sharif of Mecca in 1915 and 1916*, HMSO, London, March 16th 1939, p. 4, para. 5. The Conferences on Palestine were set up to consider the McMahon-Hussein Correspondence.

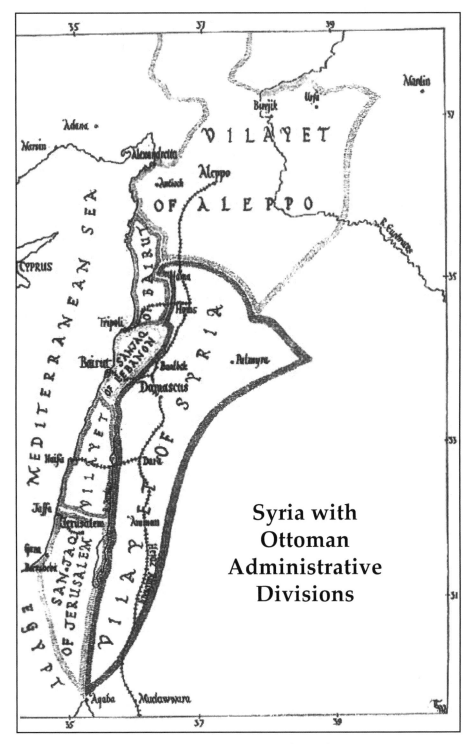

Map No. 8: From George Antonius – *The Arab Awakening*, p. 176.

Mediterranean including parts of Palestine. In McMahon's reply of December 14th 1915, he acknowledged Hussein's consent to the exclusion of the districts of Mersina and Adana, not using the term *vilayet*, but 'with regard to the *vilayets* of Aleppo and Beirut', using this time the term *vilayet*, he would need the consent of the French. This nebulous situation no doubt added to the discrepancy between the British and Arab interpretation of the correspondence.

It should be noted that under Turkish administration the territory under consideration was divided into three administrative areas as shown on map No. 8: the *vilayets* of Aleppo, Syria, and Beirut. The *vilayet* of Syria extended southwards to include parts of the area of Trans-Jordan. The *vilayet* of Beirut extended southwards to include part of Palestine up to a short distance of Jaffa. The rest of Palestine, including Jerusalem was not included in any of the *vilayets*; it was an independent *Sanjak*. None of the parties referred to these *vilayets* in the technical and strict sense of the word.[25]

Hussein's letter to McMahon of July 14th 1915 displayed a growing appetite. He was not satisfied with the independence of the Arabian Peninsula alone, of which the Hedjaz formed only part, but demanded control over all areas inhabited by Arabs. Thus, he drew up a map of an area forming a semi-rectangular shape to include territories later known as Syria, Lebanon, Iraq, Palestine, and Trans-Jordan, in addition to the Arabian Peninsula with the exclusion of the Aden enclave. The British were prepared to adhere to this demand, but only subject to certain reservations concerning the exclusion of the following territories:

(a) The districts of Mersina and Alexandretta;
(b) Those portions of Syria lying to the west of the districts of Damascus, Homs, Hama and Aleppo;
(c) Those regions, lying within the demanded area, wherein Britain was not free to act without detriment to the

---

[25] Cmd. 5479, *Palestine Royal Commission Report*, HMSO, London, July 1937, chaired by Earl Peel, also known as the Peel Commission [hereinafter the Peel Report], p. 19, para. 6.

interests of her ally, France;

(d) Territories within the demanded area which were subject to Treaties with other Arab Chiefs.

Reservations (a) and (d) did not seem to give rise to any opposition. However, reservations (b) and (c) have been the cause of endless controversy over their interpretation of whether they implied that Palestine was part of these reservations and, therefore, excluded from the McMahon pledge, or not. These two reservations were of two categories which complemented each other. One was specific – the exclusion of the districts of Mersina and Alexandretta and portions of Syria lying to the west of the districts of Damascus, Homs, Hama and Aleppo. The other was general – the exclusion from the areas demanded by Hussein of unspecified regions wherein the British were not free to act without detriment to French interests.

As for the specific reservation, the controversy between Britain and the Arabs was over the question of whether the term 'district' coincided with the Turkish term *vilayet*. If it did, the British might be right in claiming that Palestine was excluded from the pledge, since it lay west of the *vilayet* of Damascus, also known as the *vilayet* of Syria, whose inhabitants were not purely Arabs. As mentioned earlier, the *vilayet* of Syria stretched as far south as to include parts of the territory today known as Trans-Jordan, and there could be no doubt that Palestine lay west of Trans-Jordan.[26] On the other hand, the Arabs contended

---

[26] Prof. Isaiah Friedman, who investigated the McMahon-Hussein Correspondence thoroughly, indicated that he managed to track down the Arabic version of McMahon's letter of October 24th 1915 at the Public Records Office in London, which was thought to have been lost, and its retranslation which was carried out at the British Residency in Cairo in November 19th 1919. He clarified: 'By juxtaposing these two documents and comparing them to McMahon's original letter of October 24th 1915, it becomes crystal clear that the Arab term *wilaya*, the Ottoman *vilayet*, and the English 'district' were identical in meaning, and so it was understood at the time by the contemporary *dramatis personae*, both British and Arab. The District of Damascus covered the whole area, which later became Trans-Jordan, down to Ma'an and Akaba'. See Isaiah Friedman – *Palestine: A Twice Promised Land?* Vol. 1 (1915-1920), Transaction Publishers, New Brunswick & London, 2000.

that according to the borders drawn by Hussein in his letter of July 14th 1915, with the Mediterranean as its western border, there could be no doubt that Palestine had been included in the territories demanded by Hussein. If Palestine was meant to be excluded from the demanded territory, this intention should have been mentioned specifically. And, since Palestine had not been specifically excluded, it was therefore included. The Arabs rejected the equation that the term 'district' applied by McMahon was equivalent to *vilayet*.[27]

The general reservation was aimed at excluding territories from within the area allocated for Arab independence in which France had special interest. The British argued that since France displayed special interest in Palestine over the years, and particularly at a time relevant to the making of the pledge, it was included in this reservation, even though not mentioned by name.

This was substantiated by the fact that French ambitions with regard to Syria and Palestine were well known at the time to all parties concerned. They go back to a time antecedent to the McMahon Correspondence. In fact, they go back many centuries. Some argue that these interests originated in the Crusades and the subsequent Latin Kingdoms in Syria and Palestine.[28] During the centuries these interests developed into a tradition that France was entitled to a special privileged position in those regions. These interests were not only sentimental. They were historical, political, religious, cultural, and economic, supported by a succession of French governments up to the contemporary period of the Correspondence.[29] In 1912, the British had already declared that they had no political aims in Syria, which then included Palestine, subject to economic interests which had to remain intact, and recognized the rights of France in those

---

[27] Cmd. 5974, op. cit., p. 14, February 23rd 1939, Memorandum by George Antonius, Secretary-General of the Arab delegations to the Conference.

[28] BDFA, op. cit., Part II, Series B, Vol. 15. p. 388.

[29] BDFA, ibid., Part II, Series B, Vol. 15, p. 386. Chapter II holds a survey showing French involvement in Syria, which then included Palestine, pp. 388-90.

territories.[30] Lloyd George affirmed in his memoirs that 'the British Government had through the whole of the negotiations emphasized the fact that the French had a traditional interest in Syria'.[31]

As the war proceeded, France, in anticipation of victory for the Allies and the subsequent dismemberment of the Ottoman Empire, made a formal claim to her Allies in March 1915, following a Russian claim for Constantinople and the Dardanelles, demanding the possession of Cilicia and Syria, which included Palestine and the Christian Holy Places. With these claims at her doorstep, the British Government appointed the De Bunsen Committee to outline British desiderata in the region.[32] The De Bunsen Report was announced on June 30th 1915, a fortnight before the commencement of the McMahon-Hussein Correspondence and four months before McMahon's letter of October 24th 1915. The Committee took note of French demands for Syria including Palestine and the Christian Holy Places, but recommended that Palestine should be treated differently: 'Palestine must be recognized as a country whose destiny must be the subject of special negotiations, in which both belligerents and neutrals are alike interested'.[33] Based on the above, the British Government could not have ignored French claims to Syria and Palestine, whether prior to or during the McMahon-Hussein Correspondence, and would not have been in a position to assign these two countries unreservedly to Hussein without detriment to her ally, France.[34] According to the Peel Commission, the general reservation in McMahon's

---

[30] DBFP, op. cit., vol. V, p. 2 – The Council of Four at the Paris Peace Conference, per M. Pichon the French Minister for Foreign Affairs, March 20th 1919; see also BDFA, ibid., Part II, Series B, Vol. 15, p. 386.

[31] Lloyd George, op. cit., p. 1034.

[32] The De Bunsen Committee was an interdepartmental 'Committee on Asiatic Turkey' appointed by Prime Minister Herbert Asquith on April 8th 1915 and chaired by Sir Maurice De Bunsen, Assistant Undersecretary of State at the Foreign Office. More on the De Bunsen Committee see p. 138, supra.

[33] J.C. Hurewitz ed. *The Middle East and North Africa in World Politics: A Documentary Record*, 2nd ed., Vol. 2, p. 28, para. 4; p. 33, par. 34; and p. 45, para. 96. See also the Peel Report, op. cit., p. 17.

[34] BDFA, op. cit., Part II , Series B, Vol. 15, p. 393;

letter of October 24[35] 1915 was the direct result of the French formal claim of March 1915 to the control of the whole of Syria including Palestine.[35]

Again, in November 1915, soon after McMahon sent the British undertaking of October 24th 1915 to Hussein, during negotiations held in London with Georges-Picot, the French clung to their claim for the control of the whole of Syria down to the Egyptian frontier. Later, they would compromise to having the Syrian interior managed by Arabs under French influence. These negotiations led to the Sykes-Picot Agreement in May 1916. In this agreement, Palestine was to be separated from Syria and subjected to a special regime, which would not be Arab, but would be determined by agreement between Russia, France and Britain.[36]

As late as March 1919, at the Paris Peace Conference, France still insisted on control over Syria, including Palestine.[37] The French asked for recognition of their historic and traditional roots in the area. They pointed out that no government had invested as much over the years in these territories as France, arguing that its involvement in Syria was defined by the establishment of Lebanon, operating a large number of hospitals in Syria, and founding a great many primary and secondary schools in which thousands of students received a French education. Moreover, the railway system of Syria was French. Beirut was entirely a French port. The gas and electricity works were French, and so was the lighting along the coast. France established many factories in Syria, and took pains to improve the agricultural system there. In conclusion, with all the French effort and work invested over the years in the development of Syria, including Palestine, France could not abandon her rights in those areas.[38]

A turning point in French claims to Palestine and the Holy

---

[35] Peel Report, op. cit., p. 19.

[36] Ibid., p. 21.

[37] BDFA, op. cit., Part II, Series B, Vol. 15, notes on pp. 400, 430; Cmd. 5974, op. cit., p. 12.

[38] DBFP, op. cit., Vol. V, p. 4, March 20th 1919, Minutes of a meeting of the Council of Four, per M. Pichon, French Foreign Minister.

Places did not occur until December 1918, when Clemenceau, the French Prime Minister, agreed to relinquish French rights over Palestine and Mosul in favor of Great Britain. At a meeting in London, he was asked by Lloyd George to do so in exchange for British recognition of French domination of Cilicia and Syria.[39] Yet at the Peace talks in March 1919, Pichon, the French Foreign Minister, nevertheless tried to reverse the situation. He strongly protested against any idea of dividing Syria as he claimed that Syria had a geographical and historical unity. He pleaded that the whole Syrian region should be treated as one unit and that France should become the Mandatory of the entire region on behalf of the League of Nations.[40]

Four dispatches that were sent during October 30th and November 5th 1915 by Foreign Secretary Grey to McMahon show that the French were consulted extensively on the boundaries of Arab independence, particularly with regard to Syria, including Palestine, and that the French were in contact with the Arabs on this issue.[41]

It is discernible that Hussein and his followers were aware of French interests in Syria and Palestine during the correspondence with McMahon. In his pledge to Hussein of October 24th 1915, McMahon did not exclude Palestine by name, neither did he exclude specifically the *vilayet* of Beirut which extended to Palestine as far south as Jaffa, bordering with the *Sanjak* of Jerusalem.[42] Hussein must have understood that McMahon was referring also to Palestine as a territory excluded from the pledge, for it was he who, in his reply of November 5th 1915, brought up for the first time the *vilayet* of Beirut, the exclusion of which he strongly opposed. Hussein insisted that the two *vilayets* of Aleppo and Beirut and their seacoasts were purely Arab *vilayets*,

---

[39] Ibid., p. 3; see also pp.807-08, reply by Clemenceau May 21st 1919.

[40] Ibid., p. 4. Pichon further stated that the French Government would have preferred Palestine to be the responsibility of an international administration, but in the context of his speech, it seems that the statement was no more than paying lip service to this idea.

[41] BDFA, op. cit., Part II, Series B, Vol. 15, pp. 402-03.

[42] George Antonius – *The Arab Awakening*, Allegro Editions Publishers, U.S.A., 1939, see map opposite p. 176.

and therefore should be included in the territory allocated for Arab independence. McMahon responded that with regard to the *vilayets* of Aleppo and Beirut the French would have to be consulted since their interests were involved, a matter that would require careful consideration.[43] In his reply of January 1st 1916, Hussein did not deny the fact that French interests were involved in those parts of Syria and Palestine, and further stated that he had no desire to injure the alliance between Britain and France on this issue.[44]

Arab cognizance of French interests in Syria and Palestine was further confirmed by the Arab delegation to the Palestine Conference on February 23rd 1939. In a Memorandum presented by George Antonius, Secretary General of the Arab Delegations, it was asserted, without any reservation, that in the pre-war days, France did put forward claims to special rights in Syria, which then included Palestine.[45] Those claims were recognized by Britain, and a formal declaration to that effect was made by Foreign Secretary Grey, which was openly disclosed in the French Senate on December 21st 1912 by the French Prime Minister. The Arab delegation admitted that as early as 1912 Britain had already accepted the view that Syria was politically a French preserve.[46]

Also, around November 5th 1915, El-Faroki had talks with

---

[43] BDFA, op. cit., p. 404. In McMahon's reply to Hussein of December 18th 1915.

[44] Ibid., p. 405. However, Hussein added that 'at the first opportunity after the war we shall ask for what we now leave to France in Beirut and its coasts.' It is noticeable that Hussein's addition did not refer to the *vilayet* of Beirut, which included part of Palestine, but to Beirut *per se* and its coasts.

[45] By Palestine, the Arab delegation meant the whole of Palestine, and not part of it, as might have been understood from the Sykes-Picot Agreement or from the definition of the *vilayet* of Beirut. The Arab delegation pointed out in its Memorandum that 'the term Syria in those days was generally used to denote the whole of geographical and historic Syria... It included that part of the country which was afterwards detached from it to form the mandated territory of Palestine'. By 'mandated territory' they meant Palestine as far south as the Red Sea and the Egyptian frontier. That was the extent of French claims to Palestine.

[46] Cmd. 5974, op. cit. p. 12, para. 1-4.

Mark Sykes for the purpose of providing France with economic preferences in Syria and Palestine, and the employment of French advisers in the administration of these regions. Such an attitude was due to Arab acknowledgement of French interests in Syria and Palestine. El-Faroki assured Sykes that the Arabs would negotiate an agreement to allow a French monopoly of all enterprises in Palestine and Syria.[47]

Herbert Samuel, as High Commissioner for Palestine, asserted in a memorandum circulated in the British Cabinet, what had already been common knowledge: 'It is well known…that the French have long had ambitions with regard to Palestine. The disappointment in France, when Palestine was separated from Syria after the war, and the mandate for Syria alone was allotted to her, was freely expressed'.[48]

British authorities, therefore, based their argument that Palestine was excluded from McMahon's pledge on these two reservations. The specific reservation was applied in the Churchill White Paper of June 1922, which stated emphatically that the promise by McMahon to Hussein, in his letter of October 24th 1915, was made subject to a reservation which excluded from its scope territories lying to the west of the Districts of Aleppo, Homs, Hama and Damascus. 'This reservation has always been regarded by His Majesty's Government as covering the *vilayet* of Beirut and the independent *Sanjak* of Jerusalem. The whole of Palestine west of the Jordan was thus excluded from McMahon's pledge'.[49] In addition, the British argued that Palestine, in any event, was excluded from the area allocated for Arab independence on the basis of the general reservation that Britain could not act freely in territories, within the limits specified by Hussein, which might be detrimental to French interests.[50]

---

[47] BDFA, op. cit., Part II, Series B, Vol. 15, p. 189.

[48] CAB 24/165, C.P. 136 (24), January 25th 1924, p. 4.

[49] http://avalon.law.yale.edu/20th_century/brwh1922.asp June 3rd 1922, para. 11; Peel Report, op. cit., p. 20.

[50] See also BDFA, op. cit., Part II, Series B, Vol. 15, p. 440, per Childs: 'If it be held that Palestine is covered by the specific reservation (as His Majesty's Government hold that it is), the general reservation does not apply to Palestine.

This interpretation was contested by the Arabs on several occasions. They argued that both reservations did not apply to Palestine. As for the specific reservation, the Arab delegation to the Conferences on Palestine submitted that

> The word *districts* in McMahon's phrase could not have been intended as the equivalent of *vilayets*, because there were no such things as the '*Vilayet* of Damascus', the '*Vilayet* of Homs' and the '*Vilayet* of Hama'. There was one single Vilayet of Syria of which Damascus was its capital and two small administrative divisions of which Homs and Hama were the principal towns. McMahon's phrase can only make sense if we take his *districts* as meaning 'districts' in the current use of the word, that is to say, the regions adjacent to the four cities, and his reservation as applying to that part of Syria – roughly from Sidon to Alexandretta – which lies to the west of the continuous line formed by those four cities and the districts immediately adjoining them.[51]

For the sake of clarity, the Arab delegation explained that the Turkish term *vilayet* originated from the Arabic term *wilaya* but the two did not necessarily have the same meaning. *Wilaya* in Arabic meant a district without any specific administration, while the Turkish term *vilayet* was used to denote a determined administrative unit headed by a Vali. Now, the Arabs maintained that having the letters written in Arabic the term used was *wilaya*, which corresponded to the English term 'district' in general and

---

But if it be contended (as the Arabs contend) that Palestine does not come within the scope of the specific reservation, then the general reservation has full force there.'

[51] Cmd. 5974, op. cit., p. 15, para. 13, Memorandum signed by George Antonius, Secretary-General of the Arab Delegations to the Conferences on Palestine, February 23rd 1939. See arguments on the same line presented by another Palestine Arab delegation to the Colonial Secretary, Winston Churchill, in London on February 21st 1922, Cmd. 1700, *Correspondence with the Palestine Arab Delegation and the Zionist Organisation*, June 1922, p. 26.

not to the term *vilayet*. The controversy between the British approach and the Arab one was, therefore, in the interpretation of the terms 'district' and *vilayet* used in the Correspondence. The British maintained that the District of Damascus used by McMahon meant the *vilayet* of Syria, with Damascus as its capital, stretching southwards to include the area of Trans-Jordan as far south as Ma'an and the Red Sea. Any territory west of this line, meaning the whole of Palestine, was, therefore, excluded from the Arab envisaged state. The Arabs rejected this interpretation and argued that the sentence used by McMahon could only make sense if the term 'district' was interpreted in its ordinary sense. And, therefore, only the territory lying west of a straight line stretching from Aleppo in the north via Homs and Hama to Damascus in the south was excluded. The excluded area was roughly the Syrian littoral and Lebanon, but not Palestine which did not lie west of the Aleppo-Damascus line.

Sir Michael McDonnell, former Chief Justice for Palestine, who represented the Arab case, posed the question:

> Why for example, speak of the districts of Damascus, Homs, Hama and Aleppo, not one of which is east of Palestine, and all of which go northward in that order away of Palestine?…Why not, if Palestine was to be described, speak of Lake Huleh, the River Jordan, the Lake Tiberias and the Dead Sea as the eastern boundary?'[52]

On this point McMahon explained why he confined himself to the specific mention of Damascus, Homs, Hama and Aleppo: because these were places the Arabs were familiar with, because these were the terms used by El-Faroki in his negotiations with the British, and because at the time there was no place further south of any significance he could think of for the purpose of defining the excluded area. He then said:

> I did not make use of the Jordan to define the

---

[52] Cmd. 5974, ibid., p. 32, February 28th 1939.

limits of the southern area, because I thought it might possibly be considered desirable at some later stage of negotiations to endeavour to find some more suitable frontier line east of the Jordan and between that river and the Hejaz Railway. At that moment, moreover, very detailed definitions did not seem called for. [53]

McMahon's words in the last quotation bore a solid foundation, since the British Government did regard Palestine at the time as extending east of the Jordan and west of the Hedjaz Railway, and it is plausible that this fact prevented McMahon from mentioning landmarks of any importance south of Damascus to define the excluded area of Palestine.

With regard to the general reservation, the Arabs did not seem to deny French interests in Palestine at the time the reservation was made, and, therefore, its consequent exclusion from the pledge. However, they contended that after Clemenceau had conceded Palestine to Britain in the wake of the war, this reservation lost its justification and force, and had no more validity. They maintained that 'that portion of Syria which was no longer destined to be included in the sphere of French interests – as was eventually the case with Palestine – must in default of any specific agreement to the contrary, necessarily remain within the area of Arab independence proposed by the Sharif and accepted by Great Britain.'[54] This argument had been rejected by Britain. Lord Maugham, the Lord Chancellor of England, representing the case for Britain at the Conferences on Palestine asserted in reply that the pledge given to recognize and support Arab independence was attributed to a region as defined on October 24th 1915, from which Palestine was excluded. Any subsequent modification of this region emanating from the fact that France waived her rights over Palestine in favor of Britain in the wake

---

[53] BDFA, op. cit., Part II, Series B, Vol. 15, Letter from McMahon to Sir John Shuckburgh of the Colonial Office, March 12th 1922, providing explanations respecting his letter to Hussein of October 24th 1915.

[54] Cmd. 5974, op. cit., Annex A, p. 16, para. 15, per George Antonius, February 23rd 1939.

of the First World War could have no bearing on the extent of the area to which the pledge originally applied.[55]

Important corroborating evidence includes the agreement signed on January 3rd 1919 by Feisal, representing and acting on behalf of the Arab Kingdom of Hedjaz, on the one hand, and Weizmann, representing and acting on behalf of the Zionist Organization, on the other hand. Referred to as the Feisal-Weizmann Agreement, it made a clear distinction between the Arab State and Palestine, regarding them as two separate political entities.[56] The Agreement provided solid proof that neither Feisal nor Hussein, in whose name Feisal acted, regarded Palestine then as part of an Arab State. In the Preamble, both parties aimed at 'the consummation of their national aspirations' and 'the development of the Arab State and Palestine' as two separate entities. Further, in the Agreement it was stipulated that Palestine and the Arab State shall each appoint duly accredited agents to act in *their respective territories*;[57] that the Arab State and Palestine will determine '*the definite boundaries*' between them;[58] that all measures shall be adopted to guarantee the *carrying into effect in Palestine of the Balfour Declaration* [all italics added];[59] and to encourage and stimulate mass immigration of Jews into Palestine and promote their rapid settlement of the land.[60] The Agreement further announced the intention of the Zionist Organization to send to Palestine a Commission of experts to survey the economic capabilities of Palestine. The Zionist Organization promised to place the Commission at the disposal of the Arabs for the purpose of conducting a similar survey in the Arab State.[61] All these commitments lead to the inevitable conclusion that

---

[55] Ibid., February 24th 1939, p. 27

[56] George Antonius, op. cit., Appendix F, p. 437; https://mfa.gov.il/mfa/foreignpolicy/peace/mfadocuments/pages/the%20weizmann-feisal%20agreement%203-jan-1919.aspx

[57] Ibid., Article I.

[58] Ibid., Article II.

[59] Ibid., Article III.

[60] Ibid., Article IV.

[61] Ibid., Article VII.

Palestine and the Arab State were accepted by Hussein and Feisal as two separate political entities. Feisal and Hussein conceded to Weizmann almost all that was promised to the Jewish people in the Balfour Declaration, the San Remo Convention, and the British Mandate for Palestine.

The Agreement was written in English, but at the bottom of the document Feisal added in his own handwriting a reservation in Arabic stating: 'If the Arabs are established as I have asked in my manifesto of 4 January, addressed to the British Secretary of State for Foreign Affairs, I will carry out what is written in this agreement. If changes are made, I cannot be answerable for failing to carry out this agreement'.[62] It has been argued that since not all Arab demands were met the Agreement did not go into effect. This argument was contested by Weizmann in his appearance before the United Nations Special Committee on Palestine (UNSCOP) in 1947.[63] Be that as it may, the alleged invalidity of the Agreement has no consequences on the question under consideration, i.e., whether Feisal, in concluding this agreement in the name of his father with Weizmann, clearly admitted and accepted the fact that Palestine did not form part of the territories pledged to the Arabs in the McMahon correspondence.

---

[62] According to George Antonius, the above quoted translation of the reservation was made by T.E. Lawrence at the time, which was, in his opinion, no more than 'a rough summary in English of Feisal's stipulation'. Antonius suggested in 1939 a different translation which he thought was more accurate: 'Provided the Arabs obtain their independence as demanded in my Memorandum dated the 4th of January 1919, to the Foreign Office of the Government of Great Britain, I shall concur in the above articles. But if the slightest modification or departure were to be made [sc. In relation to the demands in the Memorandum] I shall not then be bound by a single word of the present Agreement which shall be deemed void and of no account or validity, and I shall not be answerable in any way whatsoever'. See George Antonius, op. cit., Appendix F, pp. 437-39; The Peel Commission, however, adopted Lawrence's translation, see the Peel Report, op. cit., p. 27.

[63] General Assembly, Official Records, 2nd Session, Supplement 11, UNSCOP, Vol. III, Annex A, Oral Evidence Presented at the 21st Public Meeting, July 8th 1947, p. 13: Weizmann stated that since all Arab demands as stipulated in Feisal's reservation had been realized, and all Arab countries became independent, the condition upon which depended the fulfillment of the Agreement was fulfilled, and 'therefore, this treaty, to all intents and purposes, should today be a valid document'.

More corroborating evidence could be found in Feisal's presentation at the Paris Peace Conference on February 6th 1919 stating the Arab case. Lloyd George, who was present at the Conference, noted that 'when [Feisal] came to deal with Palestine, he admitted that it was on a different footing to the countries that were traditionally Arab'.[64] Feisal's attitude was expressed in the Minutes of the Conference as follows:

> Palestine, in consequence of its universal character, he left on one side for the consideration of all parties interested. With this exception, he asked for the independence of the Arab areas enumerated in his memorandum.[65]

In his Memorandum, Feisal enumerated the provinces of Arab Asia as being: Syria, Iraq, Jezira, Hedjaz, Nejd and the Yemen, making no reference to Palestine.[66] At the Peace Conference in Paris, Feisal 'was persuaded not merely to accept but to welcome the policy of the Balfour Declaration.'[67] Notably, Feisal made no mention of his father's correspondence with McMahon when presenting the Arab case. In a conciliatory tone, he asserted that though 'in Palestine the enormous majority of the people are Arabs, the Jews are very close to the Arabs in blood, and there is no conflict of character between the two races. In principles we are absolutely at one'.[68]

After the Zionists submitted their proposals regarding Palestine at the Peace Conference, Feisal wrote to Felix Frankfurter, on March 5th 1919, saying:

> Our deputation here in Paris is fully acquainted

---

[64] Lloyd George, op. cit., Vol. II, p. 1042.

[65] BDFA, op. cit., Part II, Series I, Vol. 2, p. 110, Minutes of the Paris Peace Conference of 1919; see also Lloyd George, ibid., pp. 1042-43, 1155-56.

[66] Hurewitz, op. cit., Doc. 33, pp. 130-31.

[67] Peel Report, op. cit., p. 26, para. 25.

[68] David Hunter Miller – *My Diary at the Conference of Paris*, Vol. IV, Doc. 250, Memorandum by the Emir Feisal, p. 298; see also Hurewitz, op. cit., Doc. 33, p. 131-32, Emir Feisal's Memorandum to the Supreme Council at the Paris Peace Conference, January 1st 1919.

with the proposal submitted yesterday by the Zionist Organization to the Peace Conference, and we regard them as moderate and proper. We will do our best, in so far as we are concerned, to help them through: we will wish the Jews a most hearty welcome home.

Feisal ended his letter stating: 'I look forward, and my people with me look forward, to a future in which we will help you and you will help us, so that *the countries* in which we are mutually interested may once again take their places in the community of civilized peoples of the world'.[69] [Italics added]. The same attitude was echoed by Emir Abdullah, Hussein's second son. In a meeting between Churchill as Colonial Secretary and himself, during the Middle East Conference held in Jerusalem on March 28th 1921, the latter declared openly that he accepted the fact that Britain could not act freely to surrender Palestine west of the Jordan to the Arabs, due to the peace settlement and promises made to third parties.[70] In a detailed report dated August 22nd 1918 on the Existing Political Situation in Palestine and Contiguous Areas, Ormsby-Gore stated: 'I am quite satisfied that neither he [King of Hedjaz] nor Sherif Feisal are seriously upset by the Zionist movement, nor have they any desire to include cis-Jordan Palestine in their dominions'.[71]

In addition, Lloyd George reported in his memoirs that the Arab leaders never offered any objections to the Balfour Declaration so long as the rights of the Arab population in Palestine were

---

[69] Also quoted in Israel Cohen – *The Zionist Movement*, edited and revised by Bernard Richards, Zionist Organization of America, New York, 1946, p. 126. Felix Frankfurter was then a member of the Zionist delegation to the Peace Conference and later judge of the United States Supreme Court. See https://www.jewishvirtuallibrary.org/feisal-frankfurter-correspondence-march-1919

[70] CAB 24/126, C.P. 3123, p. 108, Report on the Middle East Conference held in Cairo and Jerusalem, March 12th to 30th 1921.

[71] *The Zionist Movement and the Foundation of Israel 1839-1972*, editor: Beitullah Destani, Vol. 2 (1917-1918), Archives Editions 2004, [hereinafter ZMFI], pp. 745, 751: Secret report by W. Ormsby-Gore, Political Officer in charge of the Zionist Commission.

respected.[72] In fact, 'the Arabs' special concern was for Irak and Syria... Palestine did not seem to give them much anxiety. For reasons which were quite obvious to them, they realized that there were genuine international interests in Palestine which placed it in a totally different category'.[73] This was substantiated by Blanche Dugdale in her biography of Balfour:

> Balfour was never called to defend the Declaration against Arab opposition because no hostility had been evinced by Hussein or his sons – then acknowledged representatives of Arab Nationalism – when they became aware of the Balfour pledge. They had no objection to the policy in itself, as was proved at the Peace Conference, nor did they claim it was a breach of any promise to themselves, for Palestine was excluded from the Arab area in the McMahon correspondence.[74]

Forbes Adam indicated in his Memorandum of December 30th 1919 that 'the Zionists have several times received satisfactory assurances from Feisal personally as to his attitude towards their general programme'.[75] In fact, Feisal knew by then, through Lawrence, that the Arabs were to have control over the whole of Syria including Lebanon, but excluding Palestine.[76] Curzon recorded on March 30th 1920 that Feisal had already recognized the pledges of the British Government to the Jewish people in Palestine.[77] After meeting with Weizmann on June 4th 1918 in his camp in Aqaba, Feisal became convinced of the benefits which the National Home would bring to Palestine as a whole.

---

[72] Lloyd George, op. cit., Vol. II, p. 1142.

[73] Ibid., p. 1032.

[74] Blanche Dugdale – *Arthur James Balfour 1906-1930*, Putnam's Sons, New York 1937, pp. 159-60.

[75] DBFP, op. cit., Vol. IV, Doc. 409, p. 608, para. 3.

[76] Friedman, *The Question of Palestine*, op. cit., p. 92, quoting Allenby Papers, October 3rd 1918.

[77] DBFP, op. cit., Vol. XIII, Doc. 232, p. 238.

Following that, Clayton cabled Miss Gertrude Bell that 'the main ambition of the Sherifian Arab lies (at any rate of Sherif Feisal) in Syria... [and] he is quite prepared to leave Palestine alone provided he can secure what he wants in Syria'.[78] Similarly, Col. C.E. Vickery, an expert on Arab affairs, who was sent to Jeddah to investigate the original Arabic text of the Correspondence and found that Palestine was not included in McMahon's pledges to Hussein, stated later in 1939:

> I can say most definitely that the whole of the King's demands were centered around Syria, and only around Syria... He stated most emphatically that he did not concern himself at all with Palestine and had no desire to have suzerainty over it for himself or his successors.[79]

The Sherif of Mecca – Sole Spokesman for the Arab Nation

In their negotiations with the British Government and throughout the McMahon-Hussein Correspondence, Hussein and Feisal made it abundantly clear that they were not acting on their own behalf nor on behalf of the Hedjaz alone, but were acting on behalf of the whole of the Arab nation, and in that capacity were acknowledged by Britain.[80] In his letter to McMahon of July 14th 1915, and in the letters that followed, Hussein made claims on territories far beyond the Hedjaz, extending from Mersina and Adana in the north, down to the Indian Ocean in the south, Persia and the Persian Gulf in the east and the Red Sea and the Mediterranean in the west, thus engulfing the

---

78 Peel Report, op. cit., p. 26, para. 25; Friedman, *The Question of Palestine*, op. cit., pp. 91-92 citing Clayton Papers, private collection, June 17th 1918.

79 Friedman, ibid., p. 91, quoting from letter to *The Times*, February 21st 1939; reproduced in *Documents Relating to the McMahon Letters,* pp. 18-19, and in *Documents Relating to the Palestine Problem*, p. 25, both pamphlets published by the Jewish Agency for Palestine, London, 1939 and 1945 respectively. See also Leonard Stein –*The Balfour Declaration*, Simon and Schuster, New York, 1961, pp. 268-69.

80 BDFA, Part II, Series B, Vol. 15, op. cit., pp. 193, 194.

vast territories of Syria, Iraq, Lebanon, Palestine, the Arabian Peninsula, and Yemen with the exclusion of Aden.[81] On the question of the boundaries of Arab independence, Hussein made efforts to show that he was not putting forward his own personal demands but was acting in the name of the Arab inhabitants of the territories under consideration. So did Abdullah, Hussein's second son, when hosted in Jerusalem by Churchill to discuss the Arab question. He underlined to his host that 'the Sherifian family did not regard the Arab question merely as a personal one. They regarded themselves more in the light of spokesmen for the whole of the Arab nation'.[82] Within the Arab peoples themselves, Hussein 'was recognized as the principal leader of the Arab national movement, and his family were generally considered the natural heads of any combination of Arab States which the future might bring forth.'[83]

On various occasions the Sherifian family made use of their position as spokesmen for the Arab people. Thus, Feisal made a formal protest *in the name of the Arab nation* against any changes in the form of government in Syria.[84] On other occasions Feisal expressed the gratitude of his father and himself *in the name of the Arab nation* for all that Britain had done for the Arabs, and discussed questions 'on which the whole future of the Arab nation depended'.[85] Hussein's position as 'spokesman of the Arab people' was also acknowledged in Cabinet meetings of the

---

[81] Cmd. 5957, op. cit., Doc. 1, p. 3.

[82] CAB 24/126, C.P. 3123, *Report on the Middle East Conference held in Cairo and Jerusalem,* p. 108, March 12th to 30th 1921.

[83] CAB 24/165, C.P. 136 (24), Memorandum by Herbert Samuel, High Commissioner for Palestine, to the Colonial Secretary, p. 4, January 25th 1924, stating that even though King Hussein was regarded by many as incompetent as a Bedouin King of a Bedouin State, he was nevertheless recognized as the principal leader of the Arab national movement.

[84] DBFP, op. cit., Vol. IV, Appendix A, Doc. 318, pp. 461-62, Dispatch from Feisal to the British Prime Minister, October 11th 1919.

[85] DBFP, Vol. IV, ibid., Doc. 283, p. 398. At a meeting with the British Prime Minister at No. 10 Downing Street, on September 19th 1919; see also Doc. 293, p. 417, September 23rd 1919.

British Government.[86]

Besides British recognition, France, Russia, the Paris Peace Conference, and the Conference of London all acknowledged and recognized the Sherifian family as speaking on behalf of the entire Arab nation. In a note communicated to Curzon on December 12th 1919, Berthelot confirmed that Feisal was presented by the British Government to the Peace Conference as representative of the Arab people, and that the Conference accepted this fact, with the consent of France.[87] Similarly, the Conference of London decided to confer upon Feisal an official standing and to regard him as the qualified representative of the Arabs, a move that was approved by France, who subsequently treated Feisal as such in her negotiations with him.[88] It was accepted by the vast majority of Arabs in Syria, Mesopotamia, Palestine, and Arabia including Hedjaz that Hussein and his family were representing them in their talks with Britain and the Allied Powers regarding their independence. It would be, therefore, safe to conclude that all commitments, understandings, and agreements arrived at between Britain, France, and the Supreme Council, on the one hand, and Hussein and the Sherifian family, on the other, respecting the question of Arab independence and its frontiers, affected Arabs in all the territories in question – including the Arabs of Palestine.

However, within a few months after Feisal's presentation at the Peace Conference and the conclusion of his agreement with Weizmann, the Sherifian family, and particularly Feisal, did a dramatic *volte face* on the Palestine question. Due to his intention to be crowned King of Syria, and because of growing Arab opposition, Feisal was anxious to repudiate his agreement with Weizmann[89] and to deny any acceptance or even

---

86 DBFP, Vol. IV, ibid., Doc. 293, p. 414, para. 4., see, for example, Minutes of a meeting held between the British Prime Minister and other members of the Cabinet and Feisal, September 23rd 1919.

87 CAB 24/95, C.P. 391, p. 11.

88 DBFP, op. cit., Vol. VII, Doc. 13, p. 117, Notes of an Allied Conference held at No. 10 Downing Street, February 18th 1920; See also Lloyd George, op. cit. Vol. II, p. 1106.

89 DBFP, ibid., Vol. IV, Doc. 258, p. 370, September 3rd 1919, dispatch from Col. Meinertzhagen, Chief Political Officer in Cairo, to Curzon, indicating

acquiescence regarding the separation of Palestine from Syria for the establishment of the Jewish National Home. On July 3ʳᵈ 1919 Feisal announced that 'no partition of Syria from Palestine would be acceptable as they were nationally one'.[90] On another occasion he declared that 'unity of Syria was a vital issue defining the area as from Gaza to the Taurus Mountains'.[91]

Around March 7ᵗʰ 1920, Feisal was crowned by a self-constituted Congress at Damascus as King of Syria, Palestine, and Mosul.[92] He survived in this post for almost five months until he was ousted from office by the French on July 24ᵗʰ 1920. During this time, Feisal opposed vehemently any separation of Palestine from Syria. In his correspondence with Allenby, he stressed that 'Palestine, geographically, ethnographically, traditionally, economically and from point of view of language and national desire can in no way be separated from Syria'.[93] He then invoked the British pledge in McMahon's letter of October 24ᵗʰ 1915, contending that Britain 'recognized Palestine to be within the Arab Empire whose limits as therein defined are accepted by the British Government'.[94] This was argued by Feisal even though

---

that Feisal's move was motivated by fear that his Agreement with Weizmann might be construed as acquiescence in the partition of Syria; in a Memorandum drafted on August 12ᵗʰ 1919 on the Arab Movement and Zionism, Major J.N. Camp, Assistant Political Officer at Jerusalem, advanced an opinion that 'Dr. Weizmann's agreement with Emir Feisal is not worth the paper it is written on or the energy wasted in the conversation to make it'. DBFP, ibid., Vol. IV, Doc. 253 (enclosure), pp. 364-65.

[90] DBFP, ibid., Vol. IV, Doc. 219, p. 312, Feisal's interview with the American Commissioner, reported by Col. French in Cairo to Curzon, July 10th 1919. Feisal, though, admitted in that interview that only a few months earlier he was prepared to accept a certain amount of immigration and extension of the existing Jewish colony in Palestine, but since wider Zionist aspirations had frightened his people, they were determined to oppose Zionism altogether.

[91] DBFP, ibid., Vol. IV, Doc. 272, p. 381, Report made by Meinertzhagen to Curzon, September 11ᵗʰ 1919, of a meeting between himself, Laforcade of the French Foreign Ministry and Feisal, in Damascus, to enhance French-Arab relations, during which time Feisal made his statement.

[92] DBFP, ibid., Vol. XIII, Doc. 221, p. 226, March 13ᵗʰ 1920. Feisal's coronation in Syria was vigorously opposed by Britain and France, who totally rejected this move. DBFP, Vol. XIII, doc. 220, p. 225 and Doc. 221, pp. 226-27.

[93] DBFP, ibid., Vol. IV, Doc. 248, p. 258, May 13ᵗʰ 1920.

[94] Ibid. This statement was made by Feisal almost five years after the conclusion of the Hussein-McMahon Correspondence.

he was reminded by Allenby that he had known all along of the British pledge to create a national home for the Jews in Palestine, and that he acquiesced to this fact. Feisal did not seem to deny his acquiescence but explained that it had been due to 'some misunderstanding'.[95] He then reaffirmed his objection to the establishment of a Jewish National Home in Palestine and stated categorically that 'Syrians will never agree to handing over of this integral part of their country to Jews'.[96]

Dethroned from Syria, with little prospect of being king of any other part of the Arab hemisphere, Feisal concentrated now on Palestine. During negotiations held at the Foreign Office in London in 1920-1921 between Feisal, representing his father, King Hussein, and R.C. Lindsay, representing the Foreign Secretary, Feisal contended that 'with regard to Palestine... nothing in the original correspondence stated that Palestine should be excluded from the Arab boundaries... Palestine did not lie to the west of the four towns [Aleppo, Homs, Hama and Damascus], and was therefore in his opinion, included in the area for which His Majesty's Government had given pledges to his father'.[97] It was later stated by Churchill in the House of Commons that as far as he was aware, this was the first time, five years after the conclusion of the Hussein-McMahon Correspondence, that Feisal had ever suggested that Palestine was to be included in the area designated for Arab independence.[98] Thus, Feisal, in the name of Hussein, committed a dramatic *volte face* from his previous attitude towards the Palestine question. On this, Temperley remarked that 'had the Sherif's son, the Emir Feisal,

---

[95]   Ibid., Doc. 244, p. 253, April 27th 1920, following the San Remo Conference.

[96]   Ibid., Doc. 258, p. 285, June 9th 1920.

[97]   BDFA, op. cit., Part II, Series B, Vol. 15, pp. 435-36. See Childs' Memorandum on *the Exclusion of Palestine from the Area Assigned for Arab Independence by the McMahon-Hussein Correspondence of 1915-1916.* See also Friedman, *The Question of Palestine*, op. cit., p. 94.

[98]   C.P. 106 (23), February 17th 1923, pp. 5-6, July 11th 1922. Churchill's statement in the House of Commons may not have been totally accurate since there is evidence that Feisal invoked the McMahon pledge as a basis for demanding Palestine a few months earlier, in his letter to Allenby on May 13th 1920. Be that as it may, the fact is that Hussein and Feisal's *volte face* occurred four or five years after the conclusion of the Hussein-McMahon Correspondence.

not been ejected from Syria by the French, much less might have been heard of his father's claim to Palestine'.[99]

The British further argued that it was highly inconceivable that McMahon would include Palestine in the area of Arab independence, and that Hussein was, or should have been, aware of this fact.[100] Firstly, this was because British policy was consistent all along to regard Palestine on a different footing than the rest of the Arab world. The De Bunsen Committee recommended in 1915 that Palestine should cease to be part of Syria and be dealt with as a separate question, subject to international control. Then came the Sykes-Picot Agreement in which the core of historical Palestine was to be under 'international administration'.[101] In 1917, Balfour announced the Declaration associated with his name to which the Arabs did not at the time raise any opposition. It was contended that it was inconceivable for Balfour to announce the Declaration had Palestine been pledged to the Arabs. These were followed by the Conferences of San Remo in April 1920 and the Mandate for Palestine in 1922.

Secondly, in the Correspondence, Hussein made it clear that the areas he demanded for Arab independence were within 'limits which include only our race' and insisted that 'within these limits they have not included places inhabited by a foreign race'.[102] And in his letter of October 26th 1915 to the Foreign Secretary, only two days after making his pledge to Hussein, McMahon reported that he was definite in stating to Hussein that Britain will only recognize Arab independence in territories which were purely

---

[99] Harold W.V. Temperley – *A History of the Peace Conference of Paris*, Vol. VI, Henry Frowde and Hodder & Stoughton, London, 1924, p. 175; Friedman, *The Question of Palestine*, op. cit., p. 92.

[100] Prof. Isaiah Friedman, who examined closely British Official Foreign Office records, which were made available by the Public Record Office in London, testified that those records 'fully confirm this conclusion', Friedman, ibid., p. 82.

[101] The Sykes-Picot Agreement stipulates in Article 2 that in Palestine, which is colored brown on the map attached thereto, 'there shall be established an international administration, the form of which is to be decided upon after consultation with Russia, and subsequently in consultation with the other Allies, and the representatives of the Shereef of Mecca'.

[102] See Hussein's letter to McMahon, September 9th 1915, Cmd. 5957, op. cit., p. 6.

Arab, 'this being the main point on which agreement depends'.[103] However, Palestine was not purely Arab: 'Before the First World War it contained a population the highest estimate of which was between 600,000 and 700,000 persons, of which less than one quarter were Jews and the remainder (except for small Christian communities or settlements) Moslems'.[104] Similar proportions were demonstrated in a Report submitted to Sir O'Conner by Consul Blech, stating that in 1907 the Jewish population in Palestine numbered 100,000 out of a total population of 400,000-450,000.[105] Furthermore, save for the Jewish population, Palestine was inhabited by Christians of various denominations such as Greeks, Latins, Maronites, Catholics, and Protestants. Thousands of pilgrims visited the country every year, with churches, institutes, and schools scattered all over. In Bethlehem, for example, almost all inhabitants were Christians. In 1912, the Muslims there numbered 300 out of a population of 11,000, while in Nazareth the Christians numbered 10,000 out of a population of 15,000.[106]

Thirdly, it was inconceivable that Britain, who liberated Palestine from the Ottoman Crescent, would deliver it to the Arab Crescent without conditions to safeguard free access to the Christian shrines in the Holy Land. As the Lord Chancellor of England noted: 'No British official could possibly undertake to assign Palestine to another Moslem State without making the most express reservations with regard to Christian Holy Places'.[107]

---

[103] BDFA, Part II, Series B, Vol. 15, op. cit., p. 401.

[104] Lloyd George, op. cit., Vol. II, p. 1126.

[105] F.O. 371/356 No. 40321(n. 62), Report of November 16th 1907, quoted in Friedman, *The Question of Palestine*, op. cit., p. 84, n. 110.

[106] Cmd. 5974, op. cit., pp. 21-22, para. 6. The Lord Chancellor, Lord Maugham, who made reference to these last figures, highlighted that though the great majority of these Christians were no doubt Arabs by race, 'a large residue of foreign Christians and foreign Christian interests remained'.

[107] Cmd. 5974, ibid., p. 22, para. 8, per Lord Maugham as member of the Committee to consider the Hussein-McMahon Correspondence; Curzon, in a Memorandum submitted to the British Cabinet on December 12th 1917, soon after the capture of Jerusalem, commended the placing of 'the Christian colours once again on the walls of Jerusalem' by British forces, and added that 'the whole world, America included, will wish this to be the last crusade

Curzon thus concluded: 'The fact that the question of guarantees was not even mentioned makes it clear beyond all doubt that Sir Henry McMahon never supposed for a moment that his letter would be read as including Palestine' in the area of Arab independence.[108] In a Memorandum circulated by the Colonial Secretary to the British Cabinet, it was stated that 'it is scarcely conceivable that, having reconquered the Holy Land from the Turks, we could have handed it over to the Arabs. It would have been impossible to justify such a step to the League of Nations or to the civilized world as a whole'.[109] As mentioned above, Arab leaders acquiesced to this notion and accepted it as a fact that was not susceptible to change. In Leonard Stein's words: 'If the question is whether the British Government had committed itself in 1915 to leaving Palestine under Arab control, the answer seems clearly to be that there was no such commitment'.[110]

It had also been argued by Britain as an undisputed fact that since 1915 onwards all British Governments expressed their strong belief that McMahon intended by his correspondence with the Sherif, and particularly in his letter of October 24th 1915, to exclude Palestine from the area of Arab independence.[111] Similarly, British officials who took an active part in drafting the letters to Hussein testified that it had never been their intention to include Palestine in the independent Arab territories. McMahon himself, in an explanatory note dated March 12th 1922 to Sir John Shuckburgh, stated:

> I write you these few lines to place on record the fact that in my letter of 24th October 1915 to the Sherif of Mecca, it was my intention to exclude Palestine

---

for the expulsion of the Ottoman Turk, and the recovery of the Holy Places of Christendom'. Whatever be the future Government in Palestine, he added, it could never be allowed to return to the Turks. Its return would not make possible the establishment of the Jewish National Home in Palestine. CAB 24/4/33, G. 182, December 12th 1917. p. 3.

[108] Ibid.

[109] CAB 24/165, C.P. 121 (24), February 12th 1924.

[110] Stein, *The Balfour Declaration*, op. cit., p. 269.

[111] Cmd. 5974, op. cit., p. 21, para. 3.

from independent Arabia, and I hope that I had so worded the letter as to make this sufficiently clear for all practical purposes... It was as fully my intention to exclude Palestine as it was to exclude the more northern coastal tracts of Syria... I may mention that I have no recollection of ever having anything from the Sherif of Mecca, by letter or message, to make me suppose that he did not also understand Palestine to be excluded from independent Arabia.[112]

Again in 1937, McMahon stated, 'definitely and emphatically, that it was not intended by me in giving the pledge to King Hussein to include Palestine in the area in which Arab independence was promised'.[113] General Gilbert Clayton, who was on McMahon's staff in 1915-1916, and according to his own testimony, was 'in daily touch with McMahon throughout the negotiations with King Hussein, and made the preliminary drafts of all the letters', said in 1923:

It was never the intention that Palestine should be included in the general pledge given to the Sharif; the introductory words of Sir Henry's letter [Sir Henry McMahon] were thought at that time – perhaps erroneously – to cover that point.[114]

Lloyd George who served as Prime Minister in the relevant years of 1916-1922, pointed out very clearly that Britain gave the Arabs as a whole a twofold undertaking in Palestine: 'that the establishment of a Jewish National Home would not in any way, firstly, affect the civil or religious rights of the general population of Palestine; secondly, would not diminish the general prosperity of that population. *These were the only pledges we gave to the Arabs'*.[115] [Italics added].

---

[112] BDFA, Part II, Series B, Vol. 15, op. cit., p. 437.

[113] Cmd. 5974, op. cit., p. 8, para. 13.

[114] Ibid.

[115] Lloyd George, op. cit., Vol. II, p. 1142.

Adhering firmly to its policy, Lloyd George's Government gave Mark Sykes clear instructions on his departure to the East in April 1917 that he was to do nothing which might prejudice the Zionist cause and was to enter into no commitments with the Arabs in regard to Palestine. It was maintained that Hussein could not have been *bona fide* under any impression that the McMahon pledge extended to Palestine.[116] Even so, Hussein was informed by McMahon that the British commitment would not engulf any territory in which Britain was not free to act without detriment to her ally, France. It was up to Hussein to enquire as to what that entailed. However, Hussein made no enquiries, presumably because the existence of French claims to Palestine was common knowledge and was most likely communicated to him through Arab nationalist sources in Syria with whom he had been in close touch, and perhaps through other sources, even before the beginning of the Correspondence.[117]

At any rate, the Arabs of Palestine had no say in the matter. They did not then, in 1915, form a separate nation. The area later known as Palestine formed part of southern Syria. In fact, the Arabs of Palestine considered themselves inhabitants of Greater Syria. Britain did not have separate negotiations with them, nor did it make any commitments to them specifically. They were not one of the signatories of the exchanged letters. They were represented by Hussein as the spokesman for all Arabs, and this representation was accepted by the Principal Allied Powers in the Peace Conferences of Paris and London and particularly by Britain and France. It was emphasized by the British Government that 'the McMahon pledge was given not to the Arabs of Palestine but to Hussein'.[118] On July 11th 1922, Churchill, as Colonial Secretary, asserted in the House of Commons: 'No pledges were made to the Palestine Arabs in 1915. The undertaking was given to the sheriff of Mecca…'.[119] The Arabs of Palestine were not,

---

[116] Stein, *The Balfour Declaration*, op. cit., p. 268.

[117] Cmd. 5974, op. cit., pp. 22-23, paras. 10-11.

[118] CAB 24/165, C.P. 121 (24), February 12th 1924, pp. 2-3, Memorandum circulated by Colonial Secretary Thomas in the Cabinet.

[119] C.P. 106 (23), February 6th 1923, p. 5, in reply to a question raised in the House of Commons.

therefore, in any position, to put forward claims concerning the implementation of the British pledge to Hussein. If anything, it was Hussein alone who could challenge British failure to comply with her commitments, and on this point he was on the debit side.

The Hussein-McMahon Correspondence was a *quid pro quo* bargain. It was not a unilateral British commitment. The pledge was given for a consideration. The deal aimed at promoting an Arab uprising against the Turks while fully participating in the war on the side of the Allies.[120] In return, Britain agreed to support and recognize the independence of the Arabs in territories specified in the correspondence. It was made clear to Hussein that the execution of the McMahon pledge was dependent upon Arab fulfillment of their part in the bargain. Hussein and his entourage knew that the Arabs were under an equal obligation to carry out their part. However, the Arabs as a whole failed to do so. It was only Hussein's own people who revolted against the Turks and did the fighting. As the Peel Report noted: 'The Arabs of Palestine did not rise against the Turks. And while some Palestinian conscripts deserted, others continued fighting in the Turkish Army'.[121] Lloyd George attested in his memoirs that the Arabs of Palestine were 'quiescent and cowering', and that 'right through the war and up to the end there were masses of Arab soldiers from Mesopotamia, Syria and Palestine in the Turkish army fighting against the British'.[122] In fact, most of the Arabs, and definitely the Arabs of Palestine, did not join the British in the fighting. On the contrary, they fought alongside the Turks against the British.

The Arabs of Palestine violated the understanding achieved in the Hussein-McMahon Correspondence and were one of the causes of its frustration. They sided with the enemy and fought the British during the crucial periods of the war. Lloyd George indicated that when the British Government sent messages to

---

[120] CAB 24/165, C.P. 121 (24), op. cit. p. 3; Friedman, *The Question of Palestine*, op. cit., p. 74; Walter Laqueur – *A History of Zionism*, Weidenfeld & Nicolson, London, 1972, p. 190.

[121] Peel Report, op. cit., p. 22, para. 12.

[122] Lloyd George, op. cit., Vol. II, pp. 1026-27.

Hussein and to the Arabs of Palestine informing them of their intention to establish a National Home for the Jews in Palestine, they failed to do so with the latter, since 'We could not get in touch with the Palestinian Arabs as they were fighting against us'.[123] In sum, as Lloyd George noted: 'The Palestinian Arabs fought for Turkish rule'.[124] Under those circumstances the British Government owed the Arabs of Palestine nothing, whether politically, morally or militarily. It is surprising that the British Government did not make use of this argument when confronted by Arab delegations from Palestine with allegations of British infringement of the McMahon pledge.[125]

Besides the Arabs of Palestine, it was the Arab nation as a whole who failed to fully carry out their part in the war. Hussein promised to organize a general uprising of the Arab people with an estimated force of some 250,000 strong. This did not come to pass. The British were greatly taken aback. They could not but arrive at the conclusion that they had been misled. The failure to carry out the original plan for a major Arab uprising against the Turks with a view to joining British forces in the fighting wiped out much of the validity of the Hussein-McMahon understanding. It was Hussein who did not deliver. Neither the Syrians nor the inhabitants of Palestine did anything to assist the Arab cause.[126]

British officials who were involved in British-Arab relations at the time of the Correspondence or had first-hand information of Arab performance during the war confirmed these facts. Philip Graves, a member of the Arab Bureau in Cairo, later served on the Arab section of the General Headquarters of the Expeditionary

---

[123] Ibid., p. 1140.

[124] Ibid., p. 1119.

[125] See for example Cmd. 1700, *Correspondence with the Palestine Arab Delegation and the Zionist Organisation,* HMSO, London, June 1922, Churchill did not make use of this argument so as to dismiss, in the first place, Palestinian Arab allegations of British infringement of the McMahon pledge. See arguments put forward by the Palestine Arab Delegation in London on March 16th 1922, p. 11, and British reply thereto on April 11th 1922, pp. 15-17.

[126] More detailed information in Friedman, *The Question of Palestine*, op. cit., pp. 76-79.

Force in Palestine, attested that though the participation of the Arabs and the Bedouins of Hedjaz in the war was commendable, the Arabs of Syria and Palestine 'remained passive or aided the Turks.'[127] C.S. Jarvis, formerly governor of Sinai, said: 'The Syrians as a people did nothing whatsoever towards assisting the Arab cause... beyond holding secret meetings and talk. The inhabitants of Palestine did rather less'.[128] Charles Webster, a renowned historian, who served during the war in the British Military intelligence, commented that 'a general Arab insurrection was planned [but] it never took place... [it was] mainly the soldiers of Britain, the Commonwealth and India who played a part in the overthrow of Ottoman rule'.[129] Arabs on the whole remained loyal to the Ottoman Empire whom they regarded as a Muslim Power, the destruction of which they refused to support. Lawrence attested that the Syrian-Palestinians preferred to see the Judean Hills stained with British blood rather than fight the Turks for their own freedom. [130]

In fact, early indications of this attitude could be found in the first stages of the Correspondence while the war was still waging. McMahon found it necessary at that stage to warn Hussein that Arabs, in the very parts claimed by the latter for Arab independence, 'far from assisting us, are neglecting this their supreme opportunity and are lending their arms to the German and the Turk, to the new despoiler of the old oppressor'.[131] Hussein did not deny the allegation but insisted, nevertheless, on obtaining the British pledge. However, since no change in Arab attitude occurred even after the pledge of October 24th 1915 was given, McMahon repeated his demand to Hussein in his letter of

---

[127] Philip Graves – *Palestine, the Land of three faiths*, London 1923, pp. 40, 112-13, quoted in Friedman, ibid., p. 79. Graves served as *The Times* correspondent in Constantinople and later as staff officer in eastern theatres of war.

[128] C.S. Jarvis – Three *Deserts*, London 1936, p. 302, quoted in Friedman, ibid.

[129] Charles K. Webster – "British Policy in the Near East", in *The Near East*, Lectures on the Harris Foundation, (Chicago 1942), ed. Ph. W. Ireland, p. 156, quoted in Friedman, ibid., p. 80.

[130] Friedman, *The Question of Palestine*, ibid., p. 330.

[131] Cmd. 5957, op. cit., p. 5, McMahon's letter to Hussein, August 30th 1915.

December 14th 1915: 'It is most essential that you should spare no effort to attach all the Arab peoples to our united cause and urge them to afford no assistance to our enemies.'[132] However, these entreaties were mostly in vain.

Thus, when Hussein and his sons began the Arab uprising in June 1916, the Arabs of Palestine, Syria and Mesopotamia did not join the fighting on the side of the Allies. Hussein was the exception to the rule. Although he was unable to carry out great battles with his camelry and cavalry, he nevertheless managed to cause some disruption to Turkish lines of communication, sabotage the strategic Hedjaz railway, and harass Ottoman troops; but there was a considerable gap between performance and expectations.[133] Nevertheless, the Arabs fared exceedingly well after the war: Turkish rule disappeared from the whole Arabian Peninsula. Hussein became King of an independent Hedjaz; Feisal became King of Iraq, Abdullah of Trans-Jordan. Further south the Imam of the Yemen and the Idrisi of Asir have become rulers of independent States. 'The Arabs as a whole (thanks to Great Britain) have acquired a freedom undreamed of before the war'.[134] Lloyd George commented that no other race, among those freed from oppression in consequence of the War, had fared better than the Arabs in achieving independence, 'although most of the Arab races fought throughout the War for their Turkish oppressors'.[135]

---

[132] Ibid., p. 12.

[133] But at the Peace Conference, in an effort to convince the French to yield the four cities of Damascus, Hama, Homs and Aleppo in favor of the Arabs, Lloyd George emphasized to Pichon that Arab help during the war was 'essential', and Allenby added that it was 'invaluable'. See Lloyd George, Vol. II, op. cit., p. 1063; BDFA, op. cit., Vol. V, p. 8, the Council of Four, Minutes of a meeting held on March 20th 1919 in Paris.

[134] CAB 24/165, C.P. 121 (24), p. 3, Colonial Office statement at the British Cabinet, February 12th 1924.

[135] Lloyd George, op. cit., Vol. II, p. 1119.

Chapter II

Other British Promises to the Arabs

The Hogarth Message, January 1918

A second British undertaking invoked as grounds for Arab sovereignty and independence in Palestine was a message delivered to Hussein by the British Government through Commander David George Hogarth, who visited him in Jeddah for that purpose on January 4th 1918.[1] The Message begins with a promise made on behalf of the Allied Powers to pursue a policy intended to help the Arab people to unite and to be given every opportunity to become a nation again. In the second paragraph the Message turns to Palestine, with the following stipulations: (a) that 'no people shall be subject to another', (b) that with regard to the Holy Places, 'there must be a special regime to deal with these places approved by the world', and (c) that the Mosque of Omar would be considered a Muslim concern alone, not subject to any non-Muslim authority. In its third and last paragraph, the Message went on to say:

> Since the Jewish opinion of the world is in favor of a return of Jews to Palestine and in as much as this opinion must remain a constant factor, and further as His Majesty's Government view with favor the realisation of this aspiration, His Majesty's Government are determined that in so far as is compatible with the freedom of the existing population both economic and political, no obstacle should be put in the way of the realisation of this ideal.[2]

The Message ended by saying that Zionist leaders were

---

[1] George Antonius, op. cit., p. 268-69; Hogarth was 'a scholar and archaeologist, sometime keeper of the Ashmolean Museum, and one of the greatest authorities of his time in Arabian history'. Antonius, ibid., p. 267, n. 1.

[2] Cmd. 5974, op. cit., p. 48, Annex F.

determined to achieve their success through friendship and cooperation with the Arabs, and 'such an offer is not one to be lightly thrown aside'.[3]

Commander Hogarth kept a record of his conversation with Hussein and took notes of the latter's reactions. Hogarth said he read to Hussein each paragraph separately. In response, Hussein praised Britain for the first two paragraphs and 'agreed enthusiastically' to the formula in paragraph 3 (Jewish Settlement in Palestine), for which he seemed quite prepared, 'saying he welcomed Jews to all Arab lands'.[4]

Hogarth's Message was limited in scope and significance. With regard to Palestine, it made reference to Muslim-Arab interests on the one hand and to Jewish interests on the other. On the Muslim-Arab side, the Message was confined to giving full authority to the Muslims over the Mosque of Omar alone. All other Holy Places whether affiliated to Jews, Muslims or Christians were to be dealt with under international auspices. On the Jewish side, the Message seemed to coincide with the Balfour Declaration, and subsequently with the San Remo Convention and the British Mandate for Palestine in the promotion of Jewish, but not Arab, immigration to Palestine. Hussein was told that the British Government was in favor of the realization of those Jewish aspirations and that no obstacle to that end would be tolerated. Notably, the Hogarth Message did not change course from the consistent British policy with regard to Palestine, neither did it make or confirm any pledges that Palestine was to become part of the territory designated for Arab independence. On the contrary, the only authority the Muslim Arabs were given in Palestine through the Hogarth Message was full control of the Mosque of Omar.[5]

The Arabs, in their strong desire to gain Palestine, contended

---

[3] Ibid.

[4] Charles L. Geddes – *A Documentary History of the Arab-Israeli Conflict*, Praeger, New York, 1991, p. 43.

[5] Hogarth's message was delivered to Hussein after Jerusalem had been captured from the Turks on December 9th 1917, but while most of Palestine was still under Turkish rule. Palestine in full was conquered in September 1918.

through the mouthpiece of George Antonius and other Arab representatives, that Hogarth's Message gave Hussein explicit assurances that Jewish settlement in Palestine would not conflict with Arab independence in that territory. This, it was argued, was evident to Hussein from the notes he took down in Arabic after Hogarth had read to him the Message in English. His notes read that 'Jewish settlement in Palestine would only be allowed in so far as would be consistent with *the political and economic freedom of the Arab population.*'[6] [Italics in the original]. This phrase signified, in the eyes of the Arab representatives, a 'fundamental departure' from the text of the Balfour Declaration which undertook to guarantee only the civil and religious rights of the non-Jewish population.

However, the text taken down by Hussein was not an exact translation of the original, and the British representatives to the Conference on Palestine[7] asked, 'for the sake of clarity', to uncover the terms of the whole Message. The English text did not refer specifically to 'Jewish settlement' but rather to Jewish immigration ('a return of Jews to Palestine'); it did not state that no Jewish immigration will be allowed unless it was compatible with 'economic and political freedom' but that in so far as it was compatible with economic and political freedoms, no obstacle should be put in the way to massive Jewish immigration. And, finally, the original text did not allude to the freedom of the *Arab population* but to that of the *existing population*, which included before the war a Jewish population of around 25% of the total population numbering at least 100,000,[8] and inhabitants of other denominations such as Druze, Circassians, and Christians who were not Arabs.

Obviously, the Hogarth Message, in all its paragraphs, did not promise in any way, whether explicitly or implied British recognition of Arab sovereignty or independence in the territory

---

6   Antonius, op. cit., p. 268. The quoted passage represented a rendering by Antonius of the note made by Hussein in Arabic during his conversation with Hogarth. See also Cmd. 5974, op. cit. p. 10, March 16th 1939.

7   Cmd. 5974, ibid.

8   See p. 385, n. 105 supra.

of Palestine. On the contrary, Hussein was specifically informed that 'no people shall be subject to another'. That meant that Arabs would not be subject to Jews, but also that Jews would not be subject to Arabs. This alone had the effect of frustrating any concept Hussein might have had regarding placing Palestine on the same footing as Iraq, Syria or Arabia. Economic and political freedom were mentioned only with regard to Jewish immigration and not in any connection to Arab sovereignty or independence. The British Government continuously contended that the area of Arab independence did not include Palestine. Clearly, the Hogarth Message was not aimed at creating a second Arab State, Palestine, in addition to the greater Arab State, the independence of which the British Government pledged to support.

Evidently, Hussein could not have thought otherwise. Upon his return to Cairo, Hogarth took further notes of his conversation with Hussein. He wrote: 'The king would not accept an independent Jew State in Palestine, nor was I instructed to warn him that such a State was contemplated by Great Britain'. Hussein presumably would not have communicated this phrase to Hogarth if he was assured by the latter that Jewish immigration would not interfere with Arab independence in Palestine, as was suggested by Antonius.

It was also plain, looking at Hogarth's Message, that Britain had no intention of surrendering rule of Palestine to Hussein and the Arabs. Under paragraph 3 of that Message, Jewish immigration to Palestine could only be carried out subject to the supervision and determination of the British Government: 'His Majesty's Government are determined…'.[9] This is hardly consistent with Arab independence or sovereignty. If Britain meant to confer upon Hussein independence in Palestine, the use of this text would have been totally superfluous.[10]

---

[9]   Cmd. 5974, op. cit., Annex F, p. 48, para. 3; Geddes, op. cit. Doc. 7, p. 41.

[10] It is noteworthy that the Hogarth Message, in the form of notes taken down by Hussein in Arabic, was first made public by George Antonius in his treatise *The Arab Awakening* published in 1938. The original English text was not published until March 1939. See Cmd. 5974, ibid.

Declaration to the Seven, June 1918

A third document the Arabs allude to in order to substantiate their claim to Palestine is what later became known as the 'Declaration to the Seven'.[11]

It had been reported by George Antonius, for the first time in 1938,[12] that in the Spring of 1918, seven Syrian Arab notables living in exile in Egypt formed themselves into a political group and called themselves 'The Party of Syrian Unity' (Hizb El-itihad Al-suri). The Seven strived at curtailing Hussein's ambitions in Syria, their main object being saving Syria from falling into the hands of the Hedjaz. They got together and drafted a memorial addressed to the Foreign Office and handed it to Reginald Wingate, the British High Commissioner in Egypt.[13] They asked to remain anonymous. What prompted them to deliver the memorial was uncertainty over British policy in the Middle East. They wished to know whether the Arabs would enjoy complete independence in Arabia. By Arabia they meant the Arabian Peninsula, Syria, Mesopotamia, Mosul and a large part of the province of Diarbeckr. Palestine and Lebanon were not included in the list, apparently not by mistake. They were not part of their desiderata. The background of the memorial and its contents shows that they had very little to do with Palestine or Zionism. Its main theme lay in three paragraphs which supported the claim that Syria should be independent, and by no means inferior to Hedjaz.[14]

The memorial opened in a highly pretentious manner, in which

---

[11] The term 'Declaration to the seven' was used by the Arabs. See Antonius, op. cit. Appendix D p. 433. In fact, the 'Declaration' was no more than a Foreign Office reply to a memorandum drafted by seven private Arabs, Syrian in origin, living in exile in Cairo.

[12] In his book: *The Arab Awakening*, ibid., pp. 270-74 and Appendix D, p. 433.

[13] Sir Reginald Francis Wingate succeeded Sir Henry McMahon as British High Commissioner in Egypt in 1917.

[14] Elie Kedourie – *The Anglo-Arab Labyrinth, the McMahon-Hussein Correspondence and its Interpretation 1914-1939*, Cambridge University Press, 1976, pp. 294, 297; Isaiah Friedman – *Palestine: A Twice Promised Land? The British, the Arabs & Zionism 1915-1920*, Vol. I, Transaction Publishers, New Brunswick, 2000, p. 196.

the signatories declared themselves representatives of various Arab political societies and supporters of the Arab movement. They claimed that they had full power to speak for Syria and that they represented four-fifths or more of the total inhabitants of that country, including those still behind enemy lines. But in actual fact the Party of Syrian Unity was a newly born party, comprising only of a few self-appointed politicians who had no authority or mandate to speak on behalf of any political society in Syria, let alone four-fifths of the total population. [15]

On June 16th 1918, Hogarth delivered to the Seven the British reply to the memorial. The reply was drafted by Mark Sykes with the approval of Lord Hardinge, the essence of which was as follows:

> The areas mentioned in the memorandum fall into four categories:
>
> 1. Areas in Arabia which were free and independent before the outbreak of the war;
> 2. Areas emancipated from Turkish control by the action of the Arabs themselves during the present war;
> 3. Areas formerly under Ottoman dominion, occupied by the Allied forces during the present war;
> 4. Areas still under Turkish control.
>
> In regard to the first two categories, His Majesty's Government recognize the complete and sovereign independence of the Arab inhabiting these areas and support them in their struggle for freedom.
>
> In regard to the areas occupied by the Allied forces... It is the wish and desire of His Majesty's Government that the future government of these regions should be based upon the principle of the consent of the governed...
>
> In regard to the areas mentioned in the fourth

---

15 Kedourie, ibid., p. 293; Friedman, ibid.

category, it is the wish and desire of His Majesty's Government that oppressed peoples of these areas should obtain their freedom and independence...[16]

Antonius held the view that the third category included Palestine from the Egyptian border to a line just north and inclusive of Jerusalem and Jaffa, and commented that the Foreign Office reply 'proved to be extremely important, both for what it contained and for the effect it had'.[17] He went on to say that 'the Declaration to the Seven is by far the most important statement of policy publicly made by Great Britain in connexion with the Arab revolt; and yet, strangely enough, it has remained one of the least known outside the Arab world'. These contentions were founded on gross and groundless exaggerations.[18] In fact, there was nothing strange in the declaration fading into oblivion, since no one at the time, whether in the Arab world or outside it, paid much attention to it, if at all.

The main question remains as to why would any high official of the British Empire in those days bother to reply to a memorial drafted by a handful of private citizens of Syrian origin living in Egypt in exile, with no official position, and no mandate to represent any government or political authority. Furthermore, no indication has been made by Antonius to show that the seven were of Palestinian origin or were in any way authorized to speak on behalf of the Arabs of Palestine. Antonius continues to say that 'in one sense, the Declaration to the Seven was more decisive still than the Hussein-McMahon compact; it was more comprehensive, free from any territorial reservations, and it had the added merit of being a public utterance'.[19] Now, why would the British Foreign Office make a commitment more decisive

---

[16] Cmd. 5974, op. cit., Annex G, p. 49; Antonius, op. cit., Appendix D, pp. 433-34, Antonius discloses for the first time in Appendix D of his book the names of the seven signatories and admits that the English version of the British reply was, 'so far as I am aware', first published in his book in 1938, twenty years after it was made, p. 271.

[17] Antonius, ibid., p. 271

[18] See similar view expressed by Elie Kedourie, op. cit., p. 296.

[19] Antonius, op. cit., p. 273.

than the McMahon pledge to seven private people, who were not in any position to be recipients of such commitments, if only six months earlier the British Government delivered to Hussein the Hogarth Message which added no further commitments to those in the McMahon pledge? Why would the British prefer to make commitments to the Seven rather than to Hussein, who was King of Hedjaz and the acknowledged Sherif of Mecca?

That the British Foreign Office took the trouble to reply to the seven Syrian individuals might be explained by the fact that Wingate, in his covering dispatch, warned the Foreign Office that in the absence of any reply, or in the event the reply proved unsatisfactory, the Seven might 'feel themselves free to modify their pro-Ally inclinations and ultimately… to enter into communications with the enemy'. Wingate, therefore, stressed the idea that it was 'ill-advised' to ignore Arab 'aspirations towards independence and eventual political union', and this advice might have been seriously taken into consideration in London.[20]

However, even if Antonius' argument that Palestine was included in the territories relating to the third category had been valid, there was nothing in the British reply to suggest any commitment on their part. The British reply was phrased in general terms devoid of any obligation to act. The phrase relating to the third category beginning with the words 'it is the wish and desire of His Majesty's Government' conveyed wishful thinking rather than a commitment which required implementation. The statement that followed, namely: 'the future government of these regions should be based upon the principle of the consent of the governed', was nothing more than lip service and diplomatic rhetoric to placate the Arabs rather than expression of a commitment.[21]

The Anglo-French Declaration, November 1918

A fourth document invoked by the Arabs in an attempt to

---

[20] Quotations from Kedourie, op. cit., p. 295.

[21] Kedourie, ibid., p. 296.

substantiate their claim to Palestine was the Declaration made by Britain and France on November 7th 1918, usually referred to as the Anglo-French Declaration. The Declaration stated the following:

> The object aimed at by France and Great Britain in prosecuting in the East the War let loose by the ambition of Germany is the complete and definite emancipation of the peoples so long oppressed by the Turks and the establishment of national governments and administrations deriving their authority from the initiative and free choice of the indigenous populations.
>
> In order to carry out these intentions France and Great Britain are at one in encouraging and assisting the establishment of indigenous Governments and administrations in *Syria and Mesopotamia*, now liberated by the Allies, and in the territories the liberation of which they are engaged in securing and recognising these as soon as they are actually established. [Italics added].
>
> Far from wishing to impose on the populations of these regions any particular institutions they are only concerned to ensure by their support and by adequate assistance the regular working of Governments and administrations freely chosen by the populations themselves. To secure impartial and equal justice for all, to facilitate the economic development of the country by inspiring and encouraging local initiative, to favour the diffusion of education, to put an end to dissensions that have too long been taken advantage of by Turkish policy, such is the policy which the two Allied Governments uphold in the liberated territories.[22]

The Anglo-French Declaration was not concerned with Palestine. This was obvious from the text itself, clearly showing

---

[22] Cmd. 5974, op. cit., pp. 50-51; see a slightly different version in Lloyd George, op. cit., Vol. II, p. 1036.

that it applied only to Syria and Mesopotamia but not to Palestine. The term 'Syria' in the Declaration did not include Palestine, since following the world-wide proclamation of the Balfour Declaration in November 1917, Palestine was considered a separate entity completely detached from Syria, and so it was understood. This was confirmed in the British Cabinet by the Colonial Secretary in his statement that 'the [Anglo-French] Declaration was in effect a promise to promote self-Government in the territories to which it referred. *It will be seen that it did not mention Palestine, and purports explicitly to refer to Syria and Mesopotamia only*'.[Italics added].[23]

The Declaration's disinterest in Palestine could also be ascertained from the circumstances behind the reasons for making it. These were mainly concerned with the execution of French policy in Syria. Lloyd George, who was then Prime Minister, attested that it was to allay growing Arab suspicion and hostility towards the French, caused by grave suspicion that the French intended to annex the four Syrian cities of Damascus, Homs, Hama and Aleppo.[24] Geddes pointed out that the Declaration was announced, and immediately made public in the Arab press, in order to allay Arab fears and suspicion following the institution of military administration in Syria and, particularly, the division of Syria into three zones. The Arabs feared the prospect of the replacement of one colonial Power by two others.[25] Antonius tells us that the initial cause for making the Declaration had been an incident attributed to the hoisting of the Arab flag in Beirut. The French objected to this act and, consequently, Allenby demanded its removal, which nearly provoked an explosion of violence. Thereafter, the Declaration was hurriedly issued. 'It had an instantaneous effect', said Antonius, 'and within a few days the effervescence had died down'.[26] In none of these incidents was Palestine referred to.

---

[23] CAB 24/159, C.P. 106 (23), Memorandum by the Colonial Secretary on Palestine, February 17th 1923, p. 6, para. 12.

[24] Lloyd George, op. cit., Vol. Ii, pp. 1036-37.

[25] Geddes, op. cit., Doc. 10, pp. 57-58.

[26] Antonius, op. cit., p. 274-75.

The Validity of Arab Argumentation under International Law

The Arab stand was based mainly on the four documents mentioned above. However, none of these documents recognized Arab sovereignty over Palestine. True, the language used by McMahon in his letter of October 24th 1915 was ambiguous and could also be interpreted so as to include Palestine in the Arab dominion. However, a succession of British Governments, consistently and emphatically, denied any intention to recognize or support the inclusion of Palestine within the area designated for Arab independence, adding that Hussein and the Sherifian family were aware of this fact. This denial was supported by British attitude and actions, whether taken before or after the Hussein-McMahon Correspondence, showing that Britain never entertained any intention to give up Palestine in favor of the Arabs. This was demonstrated in the De Bunsen Report of March 1915, the Sykes-Picot Agreement of 1916, the Balfour Declaration of 1917, the San Remo Convention of 1920 and the British Mandate of 1922. All these actions were widely publicized, while Hussein and his entourage either accepted them as a fact or acquiesced to them. It was only a few years after the McMahon pledge that Feisal began to oppose the Jewish National Home in Palestine, basing his opposition on the McMahon letter of October 24th 1915.

It is highly significant that the Hogarth Message and the Declaration to the Seven, delivered in 1918, were revealed only twenty years later, in Antonius' book *The Arab Awakening*, published in 1938. Antonius himself testified to the fact that the 'McMahon Correspondence has remained hidden from public knowledge in England and in the Western world at large. As for Hogarth's message and the Declaration to the Seven, they lie buried in Whitehall in a sea of oblivion'.[27] The Hogarth Message

---

27 Ibid., p. 391. According to Antonius the Hussein-McMahon Correspondence had been circulated in Arab countries, but he failed to provide any evidence to that effect. However, it had been stated in the British Cabinet that 'Unlike the Balfour Declaration, the McMahon Correspondence was not made public at the time and did not become known to the Arabs of Palestine until after the war'. See CAB 24/159, C.P. 106 (23), February 17th 1923, p. 6, para. 10.

deals with the terms to encourage massive Jewish immigration to Palestine but does not assign any territory in Palestine for Arab independence. The Declaration to the Seven, for what it was worth, did not specifically apply to Palestine and was no more than a rhetorical function to appease the Arabs – without any obligation. And finally, the Anglo-French Declaration applied specifically to Syria and Mesopotamia but not to Palestine which was then treated as a separate country.

Notably, the McMahon pledge had no international recognition or validity. None of the Allied Powers was involved in its making, it was not confirmed after the War by the victorious Allied Powers, and was not endorsed by the League of Nations. Its alleged application to Palestine was at best a commitment that the Arabs adhered to which the British Government fully rejected and denied. The Arabs never attached any international foundation to the McMahon pledge. On the contrary, Feisal stated at a Conference held in London on September 19th 1919 that the negotiations prior to the Arab revolt were taken up with Britain and with no other Power. As noted by Feisal at a meeting with members of the British Cabinet:

> When the present rising against the Turks had originally taken place, the Arabs had known of only one great Power, namely Great Britain... There had been no question of France, or the United States, or of any other Power connected with the engagement that his father had entered into. Consequently, he had made a certain agreement with Great Britain, as a result of which the Arabs had taken up arms against Turkey, basing themselves on the pledge of Great Britain.[28]

The Arabs, supported by critics of British policy in Palestine, argued that whatever may have been the pledges given to the Jews, they were rendered null and void by prior promises made to

---

[28] DBFP, op. cit., Vol. IV, Doc. 283, p. 398. Meeting at No. 10 Downing Street, September 19th 1919.

the Arabs. The Arabs argued that the McMahon pledge overrode the Balfour Declaration because chronologically it preceded it. This argument was rightly rejected by the British Government. The McMahon pledge was not universally recognized, was not embodied in a treaty, lacked international significance, and was not, therefore, part of international law. The Balfour Declaration, on the other hand, was of a different category than the McMahon pledge. The significance of the former was well pointed out in a Cabinet session of the British Government as follows:

> The policy of the Balfour Declaration was accepted by the Principal Allied Powers (Great Britain, France, Italy and Japan) at the San Remo Conference in April 1920. A representative of the United States was also present. At the same Conference it was decided that the Mandate for Palestine should be assigned to Great Britain. The text of the Declaration was embodied *verbatim* in the Treaty of Sèvres (August 1920), which was signed by Great Britain and the Dominions (including India), France, Italy, Japan, Armenia, Belgium, Greece, Poland, Portugal, Roumania, Serbia, Czechoslovakia and Turkey. It was also embodied verbatim in the draft Mandate for Palestine which was submitted to the League of Nations in December 1920. The terms of the draft Mandate were eventually approved with some modifications (not affecting the policy of the Declaration) by the Council of the League of Nations in July 1922. The Powers represented on the Council were Great Britain, France, Italy, Japan, China, Belgium, Spain and Brazil... The Mandate has been finally approved by the Council... It may here be added that on the 3rd May 1922, a joint resolution in the following terms was passed by the United States Congress: Resolved by the Senate and House of Representatives ... that the United States favours the establishment in Palestine of the National Home for the Jewish people, it being clearly understood etc.

> We are, in fact, committed to the Zionist policy
> before the whole world in the clearest and most
> unequivocal fashion.
> The terms of the Mandate take us a step further
> than the original Declaration.[29]

In contrast with the McMahon pledge and the three other documents relied upon by the Arabs, the British Government was consistently cognizant of the fact that 'the Balfour Declaration formed an essential part of the conditions on which Great Britain accepted the mandate for Palestine, and thus constitutes an international obligation from which there can be no question of receding'.[30] This was again repeated by Churchill in his address to a delegation representing the Arabs of Palestine at the Middle East Conference on March 28th 1921 in Jerusalem when he flatly refused to repudiate the Balfour Declaration, pointing out that it was a Declaration of the British Government upon which the Mandate had been taken by Britain and upon which the Mandate would ultimately be accepted by the League of Nations.[31]

There could be no doubt that the title conferred upon Britain as Mandatory for Palestine, and the legitimate ground for administering that country, stemmed from the Balfour Declaration, the San Remo Convention and the Mandate for Palestine – not from the McMahon pledge, the Hogarth Message, the declaration to the Seven, or the Anglo-French declaration. None of the international bodies, particularly the League of Nations, mentioned or relied on any of the four documents in any of their decisions with regard to the disposition of Palestine. But they did recognize and endorse the Balfour Declaration as a basis for the establishment of the Jewish National Home in Palestine. International justification for British rule over Palestine was, therefore, based solely on the San Remo Convention and

---

[29] CAB 24/59 , C.P. 106 (23), pp. 3-4, para. 3-5. Memorandum presented to the British Cabinet by the Colonial Secretary, the Duke of Devonshire. February 17th 1923.

[30] CAB 24/162, C.P. 433 (23) October 27th 1923, dispatch from the Colonial Secretary to the High Commissioner for Palestine, Doc. 1, pp. 2, 6.

[31] CAB 24/126, C.P. 3123, March 28th 1921, p. 150.

the Mandate. Whatever the Arab grudge against Britain for assuming the Mandate, a genuine attempt between Hussein and Great Britain should have been made to solve it.[32] But in no way could these differences give the Arab contentions any priority with regard to Palestine over the Balfour Declaration, the San Remo Decision, and the Mandate, which, as pointed out, had been confirmed and endorsed by the international community and the League of Nations.[33]

---

[32] Cmd. 5974, op. cit., March 16th 1939.

[33] See also Benjamin Akzin, *The Palestine Mandate in Practice*, 25 Iowa L. Rev. 32, 1939-1940, p. 47.

Chapter III

The Arabs of Palestine and the Doctrine of Self-Determination

The second pillar upon which the Arabs based their national rights with regard to Palestine was the doctrine of self-determination. This doctrine was impliedly advanced by President Woodrow Wilson during the First World War in his famous Fourteen Points speech delivered on January 8th 1918 to the United States Congress. The Fourteen Points were adopted by the Allied Powers as a basis for the peace settlement with Germany and Turkey, and on November 5th 1918, the Allies made a pledge to President Wilson to the effect that they would negotiate peace with Germany and Turkey on the basis of his Fourteen Points and his *subsequent pronouncements*.[1] The point relevant to the Arab contention regarding their 'right' to self-determination in Palestine was Point XII which stated:

> The Turkish portions of the present Ottoman Empire should be assured a secure sovereignty, but the other nationalities which are now under Turkish rule should be assured an undoubted security of life and an absolutely unmolested opportunity of autonomous development. [2]

Notably, Point XII did not refer specifically to the right of self-determination. However, in his subsequent pronouncement

---

[1] In a joint note dated November 5th 1918, the Principal Allied Powers pledged themselves to President Wilson that they would conclude an armistice with Germany on the basis of his fourteen points. These pronouncements became, in fact, the terms of reference of the Peace Conference. The Allies further promised that the settlement of Turkey would also be made on the basis of these points, and of the President's subsequent pronouncements. BDFA, op. cit., Part II, Series I, Vol. 11, Doc. 34, pp. 136-37, Memorandum by the British Delegation, Paris, on British Policy in the Middle East, February 18th 1919; see also Geddes, op. cit., pp. 49-50.

[2] BDFA, ibid.

on Mount Vernon on July 4th 1918, President Wilson did refer more specifically to this right subject to obvious reservations. His address led to the conclusion that 'Non Turkish populations formerly subject to Turkey... ought to be liberated completely from Turkish rule, and from all political connections, even nominal with the Ottoman Government ... This applies, for example, to the Arab countries formerly under Ottoman rule.'[3] But then he made the following reservations:

> 'Self-determination' as provided for above, is subject to certain inevitable limitations. There may be cases where the area inhabited by a population that wishes to form an independent unit does not constitute a geographical unity that can be administered separately... There are elements, like the Armenians and the Zionist Jews, which for historical reasons or on account of future possibilities, have a claim to special consideration out of proportion to their present numerical strength in the Middle Eastern countries they inhabit. And, finally, there are world interests such as... access to Holy Places in Palestine for all religions... which are so important that they must, if necessary, take precedence over the wishes of the inhabitants of the localities in which they are situated.[4]

From Wilson's Mount Vernon speech and his reservations on the doctrine of self-determination, read in conjunction with Point XII of his Fourteen Points, it is abundantly clear that the doctrine of self-determination could be applied to the Arabs of the Middle East as a whole, but not specifically to the Arabs of Palestine. In the first place, this was because the Arabs of Palestine did not form, at the time the speech was delivered, a separate 'people' eligible to self-determination. Secondly, the Jewish people had a say in Palestine far greater than their numerical power. And,

---

[3]   Ibid., p. 138, para. 10(a).

[4]   Ibid., p. 139, para. 10(f).

finally, the Holy Places were of interest to all three monotheistic religions.

Now, self-determination has been defined as 'the right of cohesive national groups ('peoples') to choose for themselves a form of political organization and their relation to other groups'.[5] The fundamental requirement for self-determination is that a well-defined 'people', as a separate entity, must exist to qualify for it. Defining *'self'* goes to the root of the problem. The test to establish that requirement is two-fold: the objective test and the subjective one. The objective test 'examines common racial backgrounds, ethnicity, language, religion, history and cultural heritage'.[6] The subjective test examines the extent to which the group self-consciously regards itself collectively as a distinct people with common values and goals.[7]

At the time Wilson delivered his Fourteen Points, the Arabs of Palestine did not form, nor were they considered, a distinct 'people' – whether under the objective or the subjective tests. The Arabs were considered one nation and represented as such. None of the States that emerged later on in the Middle East existed then. Palestine was not recognized as a separate territory in the eyes of the Arabs themselves, who regarded it as part of Syria. In the Ottoman period, Palestine formed part of the *Sanjak* of Jerusalem and part of the *vilayet* of Beirut. At the time Wilson made his speeches on self-determination, there were two eligible claimants to this right: The Arab Nation on the one hand, which was represented by Hussein and the Hashemite family, and the Jewish people, on the other hand, represented by the Zionist Organization. The Arab Nation consisted of all Arabs including the Arabs of Palestine, in the name of whom Hussein negotiated

---

5   Ian Brownlie – *Principles of Public International Law*, Oxford University Press, 7th Edition, 2008, p. 580; see also Gideon Boas – *Public International Law, Contemporary Principles and Perspectives*, Edward Elgar Publishing Ltd., Cheltenham U.K., 2012, p. 194.

6   Daniel Luker "On the Borders of Justice: An Examination and Possible Solution to the Doctrine of Uti Possidetis", in Russell A. Miller and Rebecca M. Bratspies, ed. *Progress in International Law*, Leiden Boston, 2008, p. 153.

7   Ibid.

independence with the Allied Powers.

Significantly, at the Paris Peace Conference, Feisal made his appearance as representative of all the Arab peoples including the Arabs of Palestine. He began his speech by asking 'for the independence of *all the Arabic-speaking peoples* in Asia, from the line Alexandretta-Diarbekir southward.'[8] [Italics added]. As a basis for his request, Feisal described the Arab Nation as being one nation, one unit socially and economically, no less homogeneous than any other nation, with the necessary ingredients of language and race. By the same token, in his correspondence with Frankfurter, Feisal spoke on behalf of the Arab Nation as a whole, that 'the Arabs and Jews are cousins', that both movements, Arab and Jewish, are national – not imperialist – movements that complete one another.[9]

Likewise, in the Hussein-McMahon Correspondence, Hussein spoke, as he put it, for 'the whole Arab nation without any exception'.[10] The letters referred constantly to 'the Arab Nation' as a single entity claiming independence on the Arab side. In the Feisal-Weizmann Agreement of January 3rd 1919, the Agreement was concerned with enhancing good relations between the 'Arab State' and Palestine. The Arab State was to extend to all the Middle Eastern territories except for Palestine, which was destined to form a separate entity for the establishment of a National Home for the Jewish people. In speaking for the Arab State, which was repeatedly referred to in the document, Feisal, in the name of his father King Hussein, was, in fact, assuming the position of representative of all Arabs of the Middle East, including the Arabs of Palestine.[11] In this capacity, he was also perceived in his negotiations with the Allied Powers. The Arabs of Palestine were not then in any way perceived as a distinct people eligible for separate independence.[12]

---

[8]   BDFA, op. cit., Part II, Series I, Vol. 2, op. cit., p. 109; Lloyd George testified to this fact, in Lloyd George, op. cit., Vol. II, p. 1039.

[9]   BDFA, ibid.; Lloyd George, ibid.

[10] Cmd. 5957, op. cit., Doc. 1, p. 3, July 14th 1915.

[11] Agreement between Emir Feisal and Dr. Weizmann, Article 1-3.

[12] Julius Stone, op. cit., pp. 13-14.

By the end of the War, the Principal Allied Powers decided to give effect to pledges made to the Arab people, on the one hand, and to the Jewish people, on the other. This was to be carried out under the Mandate System, which had been adopted by the victors of the War to replace a policy of annexation, which had hitherto prevailed. The Principal Allied Powers had the authority to exercise that function since the Ottoman Empire renounced its sovereignty over all the territories of the Middle East, whether explicitly in the Treaty of Sèvres or impliedly in the Treaty of Lausanne in favor of the Allied Powers. The Allies, therefore, had the legal power to dispose of these territories in any way they regarded as appropriate and definitely through the application of the Mandate System. For this purpose, the Principal Allied and Associated Powers gathered at San Remo, where they came to a decision on April 25th 1920, after a long debate, to divide the Middle East between the two nations who were eligible then for independence: the Jewish and Arab nations. The bulk of the Middle East, consisting of Syria, Lebanon, and Mesopotamia, was allocated to the Arab Nation and provisionally recognized as forming independent States, subject to temporary administrative advice and assistance from a Mandatory. This was in addition to the recognition of the independence of the Hedjaz and other Arab entities in the Arabian Peninsula.

Palestine, on the other hand, on both sides of the Jordan River, was entrusted to a Mandatory (Great Britain), that would take upon itself the responsibility for putting into effect the Balfour Declaration for the establishment in Palestine of a National Home for the Jewish people. The Arabs of Palestine, who considered themselves part of Syria and an integral part of the Arab nation, were *ipso facto* represented by Hussein and Feisal in the negotiations that preceded the San Remo Resolutions and the Mandates that followed. Moreover, it would not be irrational to maintain that the British Government had no moral obligation towards the Arabs of Palestine because of siding with the Turks against the British in the Great War, and could have been justified in ignoring them altogether.

The earliest the Arabs of Palestine might have been

considered a separate political body would have been around the proclamation of the Palestinian National Charter in 1964. The Charter solemnly declared that 'Palestine is the homeland of the Palestinian Arab people and an integral part of the great Arab homeland, and the people of Palestine are part of the Arab nation'.[13] The Charter further declared that 'when the liberation of its homeland is completed they [the Arabs of Palestine] will exercise self-determination'.[14] The Arabs of Palestine were not recognized as a nation until 1974, five decades after Wilson's Fourteen Points speech and the San Remo Resolution, when the General Assembly of the United Nations recognized the right of the Palestinian people to self-determination in Resolution 3236 on November 22nd 1974, stating: 'the Palestinian people is entitled to self-determination in accordance with the Charter of the United Nations'.[15]

Resolution 3236, being a resolution of the General Assembly, was declaratory and had no binding effect.[16] Any attempt to implement this Resolution would have required the retroactive annulment of previous international decisions taken half a century earlier, which brought about the creation of Syria, Lebanon, Mesopotamia (Iraq) and Palestine. It would have meant, in actual fact, the total abolition of the decisions taken at the Paris Peace Conference and at San Remo, which shaped the Middle East five decades earlier when the doctrine was first applied. Turning the clock back in these circumstances would have been impractical and, in any case, impossible.

The Arabs were not eligible to the right of self-determination not only because they did not qualify as a 'people' when Wilson announced his Fourteen Points, but also because, at the relevant time, the doctrine of self-determination was not yet recognized as

---

[13] Palestinian National Charter, 1964, Article 1.

[14] Ibid., Article 3.

[15] Julius Stone, op. cit., pp. 9-10.

[16] See Charter of the United Nations, Chapter IV, Article 10. The General Assembly's power was limited in this respect to the making of recommendations to members of the United Nations or to the Security Council on any questions or matters within the scope of the Charter.

a binding principle of international law. Unlike the position which developed after 1945, self-determination was not recognized as a legal right in its first stages and there was no obligation to confer it on any group unit even though that group formed a 'people' within the meaning of the term. In fact, no legal right to self-determination could be established during those years unless it arose under a treaty or a commitment on the part of the sovereign state.[17]

It is generally accepted among jurists to differentiate between the period preceding 1945 during the existence of the League of Nations and the period following 1945 after the establishment of the United Nations. During the period of the League of Nations, the principle of self-determination did not form part of the League's Covenant and was not considered a legal principle with a binding effect. This was explicitly confirmed by the Council of the League of Nations in the *Aaland Islands* dispute in which the legal status of the principle of self-determination was at issue.[18] The League of Nations appointed two Commissions to investigate the dispute: the International Commission of Jurists and the Committee of Rapporteurs. The Report of the Commission of Jurists of October 1920, in its relevant part, read as follows:

> Although the principle of self-determination of peoples plays an important part in modern political thought, especially since the Great War, it must be pointed out that there is no mention of it in the Covenant of the League of Nations. The recognition of this principle in a certain number of international treaties cannot be considered as sufficient to put it upon the same footing as a positive rule of the Law of Nations. On the contrary, in the absence of express provisions in international treaties the right of disposing of national territory is essentially an

---

[17] John O'Brien – *International Law*, Cavendish Publishing Ltd., London, 2001, p. 163.

[18] Max Planck Encyclopedia of Public International Law: Daniel Thurer and Thomas Burri on *Self-Determination*, Oxford University Press, Para. 4; Gideon Boas, op. cit. pp. 195-96.

attribute of the sovereignty of every state.[19]

The Report of the Committee of Rapporteurs had this to say on self-determination (April 16th 1921):

> The principle is not, properly speaking, a rule of international law, and the League of Nations has not entered it in its Covenant. This is also the opinion of the International Commission of Jurists.[20]

The attitude of the international community towards the principle of self-determination changed gradually only after the establishment of the United Nations in 1945 and the issuance of the United Nations Charter, which made the application of this principle part of it in Articles 1 (2) and 55. Crawford asserted that there was little general development of the principle of self-determination before 1945.[21] But after 1945, the doctrine was converted from a general political concept into a binding rule of international law,[22] followed by a General Assembly Recommendation to all State Members, dating December 20th 1952, to 'uphold the principle of self-determination of all peoples and nations'.[23]

---

[19] James Crawford – *The Creation of States in International Law*, 2nd edition, Clarendon Press, Oxford, 2006, text quoted from p. 109.

[20] Ibid., p. 111.

[21] Ibid., p. 112.

[22] Ian Brownlie, op. cit., p. 580: 'Until recently, the majority of Western jurists assumed or asserted that the principle had no legal content, being an ill-defined concept of policy and morality'. See also Robbie Sabel, ed. International Law, Sacher Institute for Legislative Research and Comparative Law, Faculty of Law, The Hebrew University of Jerusalem, Jerusalem 2003, p. 51: Up to the Sixties of the 20th Century, there was much doubt as to whether international law recognized the right to self-determination. But today the right of a nation to self-determination is well recognized in International Law, quoting the East Timor Case, ICJ Reports 1995, p. 102: 'The right of peoples to self-determination... is one of the essential principles of contemporary international law'. See Sabel, ibid., n. 70.

[23] General Assembly Resolution, A/RES/637(VII), December 16th 1952, *the Right of Peoples and Nations to Self-determination*; John O'Brien, op. cit., p. 163.

In conclusion, the Arabs of Palestine were not entitled to the right of self-determination when the principle of self-determination was applied during 1918-1922, for the reasons enumerated above. It is, furthermore, self-evident that any endeavor to apply the doctrine retroactively in favor of the Arabs for the whole area of Palestine five decades after the fact was doomed to failure, since such application would have been impossible or impractical as it would have entailed turning the clock back in total disregard of international resolutions, ignoring the creation of new states, and other structural and political developments that had meanwhile occurred in the Middle East.

Select Bibliography

Books

Aharoni,Yohanan – *Carta's Atlas of the Bible*, Carta, Jerusalem, 2nd ed., 1974

Amery, Leopold Stennett – *My Political Life*, Vol. II, *War and Peace 1914-1929,* Hutchinson & Co. (Publishers) Ltd., London, 1953

Antonius, George – *The Arab Awakening*, Allegro Editions, U.S. 1939

Benvenisti, Eyal – *The International Law of Occupation*, Oxford University Press, 2nd Edition, 2012

Bentwich, Norman – *The Mandates System*, Longmans, Green & Co., London 1930

Biger, Gideon – *The Boundaries of Modern Palestine 1840-1947*, RoutledgeCurzon (Taylor & Francis Group), London and New York, 2004

Boas, Gideon – *Public International Law, Contemporary Principles and Perspectives*, Edward Elgar Publishing Ltd., Cheltenham U.K., 2012

Brierly, J.L. – *The Law of Nations*, 4th ed. The Clarendon Press, Oxford 1950

Brownlie, Ian – *Principles of Public International Law*, Oxford University Press, 7th Edition, 2008

Cheshire and Fifoot – Law of Contract, 8th edition, Butterworths, London, 1972

Clayton, Gilbert – *An Arabian Diary*, University of California Press, CA, 1969

Cohen, Israel – *The Zionist Movement*, edited and revised by Bernard G. Richards, published by Zionist Organization of America, New York, 1946

Cohen, Israel ed. – *Speeches on Zionism*, speech delivered by the Earl of Balfour, Arrowsmith, London, 1928

Cohen, Michael J. – *The Origins and Evolution of the Arab-Zionist Conflict*, University of California Press, Berkeley 1987

Conte, Alex and Burchill, Richard – *Defining Civil and Political Rights: The Jurisprudence of the United Nations Human Rights Committee,* Ashgate Publishing Company, 2nd edition, 2009

Crawford, James – *The Creation of States in International Law*, Clarendon Press, Oxford, 2nd ed. 2006

Dugdale, Blanche E.C. – *Arthur James Balfour 1848-1906*, Vol. I, G.P.Putnam's Sons, New York, 1937

Dugdale, Blanche E.C. – *Arthur James Balfour 1906-1930*, Vol. II, G.P.Putnam's Sons, New York, 1937

Fontaine, Marcel and De Ly, Filip – *Drafting International Contracts*, Martinus Nijhoff Publishers, Leiden – Boston, 2009

Frankenstein, Ernst – *Palestine in the Light of International Law*, Narod Press, London, 1946

Friedman, Isaiah – *The Question of Palestine 1914-1918*, Transaction Publishers, New Brunswick & London, 2nd edition, 1992

Friedman, Isaiah – *Palestine: A Twice Promised Land?* Vol. 1 (1915-1920), Transaction Publishers, New Brunswick & London, 2000

Geddes, Charles, ed. – *A Documentary History of the Arab-Israeli Conflict*, Praeger, New York, 1991

Graves, Philip – *Palestine, the Land of three faiths*, Jonathan Cape, London, 1923

Graves, Philip, ed. – *Memoirs of King Abdullah of Transjordan*, Jonathan Cape, London, 1950

Gribetz, Louis J. – *The Case for the Jews: An Interpretation of their Rights under the Balfour Declaration and the Mandate for Palestine*, Bloch Publishing Company, New York, 1930

Grief, Howard – *The Legal Foundation and Borders of Israel Under International Law*, Mazo Publishers, Jerusalem, 2008

Halpern, Ben – *The Idea of the Jewish State*, Harvard University Press, Cambridge, Massachusetts, 1961

Hanna, Paul L. – *British Policy in Palestine*, Public Affairs Press, Washington D.C. 1942

Herzl, Theodor – *The Jewish State (Der Judenstaat),* Vienna 1896, Jewish Virtual Library. Edition published by the American Zionist Emergency Council in 1946 and translated from German by Sylvie D'Avigdor

Hurewitz, J.C. ed. – *The Middle East and North Africa in World Politics, A Documentary Record*, Vol. 2, British – French Supremacy 1914 – 1915, Yale University Press, New Haven & London, 1979

Jarvis, C.S. – Three *Deserts*, John Murray, London, 1936

Kedourie, Elie – *The Anglo-Arab Labyrinth, the McMahon-Hussein Correspondence and its Interpretation 1914-1939*, Cambridge University Press, 1976

Laqueur, Walter – *History of Zionism*, Weidenfeld and Nicolson, London 1972

Lawrence, Thomas E. – *Seven Pillars of Wisdom*, Wordsworth Editions Ltd. London 1997 [first published 1935]

Lennox, Lady Algernon Gordon ed. – *The Diary of Lord Bertie of Thame, 1914-1918*, Vol. I, George H. Doran Company, New York, 1924

Lloyd George, David – *The Truth About the Peace Treaties*, Victor Gollancz Ltd., London, 1938 (Volumes I & II)

Meinertzhagen, Richard – *Middle East Diary 1917-1956*, The Cresset Press, London, 1959

Miller, David Hunter – *My Diary at the Conference of Paris*, Vol. IV, Appeal Printer Co., New York, 1924

Nahon, S.U. ed. – *The Jubilee of the First Zionist Congress 1897-1947*, the Publishing Department of the Jewish Agency for Palestine, the Jerusalem Press Ltd., Jerusalem, 1947

O'Brien, John – *International Law*, Cavendish Publishing Ltd., London, 2001

Oppenheim, L. – *International Law, A Treatise*, H. Lauterpacht, ed., 7th edition, Longmans, Green & Co., London, 1948, (2 volumes)

Perry, Ralph Barton – *General Theory of Value*, Harvard University Press 1967 (First published 1926)

Sabel, Robbie ed. – International Law, Sacher Institute for Legislative Research and Comparative Law, Faculty of Law, The Hebrew University of Jerusalem, Jerusalem 2003

Samuel, Herbert – *Memoirs*, the Cresset Press, London, 1945

Smith, George Adam – *Atlas of the Historical Geography of the Holy Land*, Hodder and Stoughton, London, 1915

Sokolow, Nahum – *History of Zionism 1600-1918*, Vol. I & II, Ktav Publishing House, New York, 1969 (first published by Longmans, Green & Co., London, 1919)

Starke, J.G. – *An Introduction to International Law*, 5th ed. Butterworths, 1963

Stein, Leonard – *Zionism*, Kegan Paul, Trench, Trubner &Co. Ltd., London 1932

Stein, Leonard – *The Balfour Declaration*, The Magnus Press, Jerusalem & The Jewish Chronicle Publications, London 1983 (first published, 1961)

Stone, Julius – *Israel and Palestine: Assault on the Law of Nations*, Johns Hopkins University Press, Baltimore, 1981

Temperley, Harold W.V, ed. – *A History of the Peace Conference of Paris*, Vol. VI, The British Institute of International Affairs, London, 1924

Webster, Charles Kingsley – "British Policy in the Near East", in Ph. W. Ireland, ed., *The Near East*, Lectures on the Harris Foundation, Chicago, 1942

Webster, Charles Kingsley – *The Founder of the National Home*, Weizmann Science Press, Rehovoth, Israel, 1955

Weiss, Paul – *Nationality and Statelessness in International Law*, 2nd edition, Sijthoff and Noordhoff, 1979

Weizmann, Chaim – *Trial and Error*, Schocken Books, New York, 1949

Wise, Stephen – *The Challenging Years*, London, 1961 [first edition by G.P. Putnam's Sons, New York, 1949]

Articles and Pamphlets

Akzin, Benjamin – *The Palestine Mandate in Practice*, 25 Iowa L. R. 32, 1939-1940

Alexander, Charles Henry – *Israel in Fieri*, 4 Int'l L. Q. 423, 424, 1951

Barak-Erez, Daphne – *Israel: The security barrier – between international law, constitutional law, and domestic judicial law,* 4 Int'l J. Const. L. 540

Biger, Gideon – "Britain's Role as a Boundary Maker in the middle East", in Zach Levy and Elie Podeh eds. – *Britain and the middle East, From Imperial Power to Junior Partner*, Sussex Academic Press, Brighton, U.K., 25, 2008

Brierly, J.L. – *British Year Book of International Law*, Oxford University Press, 217, 1929

Blum, Yehuda – *The Missing Reversioner: Reflections on the Status of Judea and Samaria,* Is.L.R. 3(2)279, 1968

Dinstein, Yoram – *The Arab Israeli Conflict from the Perspective of International Law*, 43 U.N.B.L.J. 301, 1994

Dugdale, Blanche – "The Balfour Declaration: Its Origins", in *The Jewish National Home*, ed., Paul Goodman, J.M. Dent & Sons, London, 1943

Feinberg, Nathan – *The Recognition of the Jewish People in International Law*, 1 Jewish Y.B. Int'l L. 1, 1948

Frankenstein, Ernst – *The Meaning of the Term "National Home for the Jewish People",* 1 Jewish Y.B. Int'l L, 27, 1948

Frankfurter, Felix – *The Palestine Situation Restated*, 9 Foreign Aff. 409, (1930-1931)

Goluboff, Riso L. – *The thirteenth Amendment and the Lost Origins of Civil Rights*, Duke Law Journal, Vol. 50, No. 6, 1609, April 2001

Henriques, Henry S.Q, – *The Civil Rights of English Jews*, The Jewish Quarterly Review, Vol. 18, No. 1, 40, October 1905

Jewish Agency for Palestine – *Documents Relating to the McMahon Letters*, 1939

Jewish Agency for Palestine – *Documents Relating to the Palestine Problem*, 1945

Kliot, Nurit – "The Evolution of the Egypt-Israel Boundary: From Colonial Foundations to Peaceful Borders", in Clive Schofield ed., *International Boundaries Research Unit: Boundary and Territory Briefing*, University of Durham, U.K. 1995. Vol. I, No. 8, p. 5

Lewis, Bernard – "Palestine: On the History and Geography of a Name", *The International History Review,* Vol. 2, No. 1 (Jan. 1980), pp. 1-12

Luker, Daniel – "On the Borders of Justice: An Examination and Possible Solution to the Doctrine of Uti Possidetis", in Russell A. Miller and Rebecca M. Bratspies, ed. *Progress in International Law*, Leiden and Boston, 2008

Maurer, Peter – *Challenges to International Humanitarian Law: Israel's Occupation Policy*, International Review of the Red Cross, Vol. 94, No. 888, Winter 2012

O'Brien, Patricia – *Issues related to General Assembly Resolution 67/19 on the status of Palestine in the United Nations*, United Nations Inter-Office Memorandum, December 21st 2012

Quigley, Carroll – *Lord Balfour's Personal Position on the Balfour Declaration,* Middle East Journal, Vol. 22, No. 3, 340, Summer 1968

Quigley, John – "Britain's Secret Assessment of the Balfour Declaration, The Perfidy of Albion", *Journal of the History of International Law* 13 (2011), 249-283, Nijhoff Publishers, Leiden, 2011

Roberts, Adam – *Prolonged Military Occupation: The Israeli Occupied Territories Since 1967*, AJIL, Vol. 84, No. 1, 79, Jan. 1990

Rostow, Eugene V. – *Are the Settlements Legal? Article 1: Bricks and Stones – Settling for Leverage; Palestinian Autonomy,* The New Republic, April 1990

Wise, Stephen – "The Balfour Declaration – Its significance in the U.S.A". in Paul Goodman ed. – *The Jewish National Home*, J.M. Dent & Sons, London, 1943

Zionist Organization – pamphlet entitled *Zionism: Its Ideals and Practical Hopes*, London, 1919 [Speech by Herbert Samuel]

United Nations Resolutions

Security Council Resolutions

SCR 242, November 22nd 1967
SCR 252, May 21st 1968
SCR 267, July 3rd 1969
SCR 298, September 25th 1971
SCR 338, October 22nd 1973
SCR 446, March 22nd 1979
SCR 452, July 20th 1979
SCR 465, March 1st 1980
SCR 476, June 30th 1980
SCR 478, August 20th 1980
SCR 2334, December 23rd 2016

General Assembly Resolutions
A/RES/181 (II), November 29th 1947
A/RES/637 (VII), December 16th 1952
A/RES/2253 (ES-V), July 4th 1967
A/RES/2254 (ES-V), July 14th 1967
A/RES/3092, December 7th 1973
A/RES/3236(XXIX), November 22nd 1974
A/RES/32/20, November 25th 1977
A/RES/33/29, December 7th 1978
A/RES/3092, December 7th 1978
A/RES/34/65B, December 12th 1979
A/RES/41/63, December 3rd 1986
A/RES/43/58A-G, December 6th 1988
A/RES/ES-10/13, October 27th 2003
A/RES/ES-10/14, December 12th 2003
A/RES/67/19, December 4th 2012

International Bi-lateral and Multi-lateral Agreements

Egyptian-Israeli General Armistice Agreement, February 4th 1949

Jordanian-Israeli General Armistice Agreement, April 3rd 1949

Israel-PLO: Letter of commitment by Yasser Arafat, PLO Chairman to Yitzhak Rabin, Prime Minister of Israel, September 9th 1993

Israel-PLO: Declaration of Principles on Interim Self-Government Arrangements, September 13th 1993

International Institutions and Organizations

League of Nations – *French Mandate for Syria and the Lebanon,* League of Nations Official Journal, August 1922, p. 1013

League of Nations – Treaty Series, No. 565: *Exchange of Notes Constituting an Agreement Between the British and French Governments Respecting the Boundary Line Between Syria and Palestine from the Mediterranean to El Hamme*, March 7th 1923

League of Nations, Permanent Mandates Commission, 15th Session, Minutes, June 15th 1928

League of Nations, Permanent Mandates Commission, 13th Session, Minutes, 1928-1929

League of Nations, Permanent Mandates Commission, 32nd session, Minutes, August 18th 1937

League of Nations – *Statement of Policy on Palestine Issued by His Majesty's Government in the United Kingdom on May 17th 1939*, 20 League of Nations Official Journal (O.J.) 363, 1939

United Nations, British Address before the General Assembly on *the Future of Trans-Jordan*, January 17th 1946, United Nations, Official Records of the General Assembly, First Session, First Part, Plenary Meetings, p. 167

United Nations, Official records of the General Assembly, First Session, First Part, Plenary Meetings, p. 167. Cited in *Trans-Jordan: Attitude of the United States Regarding the Granting of Independence to Trans-Jordan by the United Kingdom*, February 13th 1946, n.1, published in Foreign Relations of the United States: Diplomatic Papers, 1946 (the Near East and Africa), United States Government Printing Office, Washington 1969, Vol. VII, p. 794, n.1

United Nations, General Assembly, Official Records, 2nd Session, Supplement 11, (UNSCOP), Vol. III, Annex A, 21st Public Meeting, July 8th 1947

United Nations Special Committee on Palestine (UNSCOP) Report, General Assembly, September 3rd 1947

Guidelines on *The Eligibility of Israeli Entities and their Activities in the Territories Occupied by Israel since June 1967 for Grants, Prizes and Financial Instruments Funded by the EU from 2014 Onwards*, Official Journal of the European Union, July 19th 2013, C 205/9-11

Declaration of the Conference of High Contracting Parties to the Fourth Geneva Convention, December 17th 2014

Report of the European Union on *Israeli settlements in the occupied West Bank, including East Jerusalem* (reporting period January-June 2019), September 30th 2019

International Treaties

Covenant of the League of Nations, June 28th 1919

Treaty of Versailles, June 28th 1919

Treaty of St. Germain-en-Laye, September 10th 1919

Treaty of Neuilly-sur-Seine, November 27th 1919

Treaty of Trianon, June 4th 1920

Treaty of Sèvres, August 10th 1920

Convention on Certain Points Connected with the Mandates for Syria and the Lebanon, Palestine and Mesopotamia. American Journal of International Law, Vol. 16, No. 3, Supplement: Official Documents, pp. 122-26, July 1922

Treaty of Lausanne, July 24th 1923

Charter of the United Nations, June 26th 1945

Treaty of Alliance between His Majesty in Respect of the United Kingdom and His Highness the Amir of Trans-Jordan, London, March 22nd 1946, United Nations, Treaty Series, 1947, No. 74

International Court Judgments

Permanent Court of International Justice, *the Mavromatis Palestine Concessions*, Collection of Judgments, Series A, No. 2, August 30th 1924

International Court of Justice – the *International Status of South West Africa*, ICJ Rep. 1950, [Judge McNair's separate opinion]

International Court of Justice – *East Timor Case*, ICJ Reports, June 30th 1995

International Court of Justice – *Legal Consequences of the Construction of a Wall in the Occupied Palestinian Territory,* (Request for advisory opinion) July 9th 2004

English Court Judgments

Behn v. Burness (1863) 3 B. & S. 751

Graves v. Legg (1854), 9 Exch. 709

Hyde v. Wrench (1840) 3 Beav. 334

IBM United Kingdom Ltd. v. Rockware Glass Ltd. (1980) FSR 335

Pips (Leisure Productions) Ltd. v. Walton (1980)43 P & CR 415

Sheffield District Railway Co. v. Great Central Railway Co.(1911) 27 TLR, 451

Terrell v. Mabie Todd & Co. Ltd. [1952] 2 TLR 574 (Q.B.D.)

Tweddle v. Atkinson (1861) 1 B. & S. 393

United States Court Judgments

Bloor v. Falstaff Brewing Corp., 454 F. Supp. 258, affirmed 601 F.2d, 609

National Data Payment Systems, Inc. v. Meridian Bank, 212 F. 3d, 849

People v. Barrett, 203 Ill. 99, 67 N.E.742, 96 Am. St. Rep. 296

People v. Morgan, 90 Ill. 563

Stabile v. stabile, 774 N.E.2d, 673, 55 Mass. App. Ct. 724

Winnett v. Adams, 71 Neb. 817, 99 N.W. 681

Commonwealth Court Judgments

Rex v. Christian, South African Law Reports [1924] 121, (Appellate Division, South Africa)

Frost v. Stevenson (1937), 58 Commonwealth Law Reports 528, Annual Digest and Reports of Public International Law Cases 1935-1937, case No. 29, (High Court of Australia)

British Cabinet Papers

War Cabinet Papers, G.T. 1803, July 18th 1917

War Cabinet Papers, G.T. 1803A, August 1917

War Cabinet Papers, No. 227, September 3rd 1917

War Cabinet Papers, G.T. 2015, September 12th, 1917

War Cabinet Papers, G.T. 2191, September 14th, 1917

War Cabinet Papers, G.T.2158, September 26th 1917

War Cabinet Papers, No. 245, October 4th 1917

War Cabinet Papers, G.T. 2263, October 9th 1917

War Cabinet Papers, G.-164, CAB. 24/4/14, October 17th 1917

War Cabinet Papers No. 257, October 25th 1917

War Cabinet Papers, G.T. 2406, October 26th 1917

War Cabinet Papers, No. 261, October 31st 1917

CAB 24/4/33, G. 182, December 12th 1917

CAB 24/68 G.T. 6185, (undated, presumably October or November 1918)

CAB 23/46, November 13th 1919

CAB 24/95, C.P. 391, December 12th 1919

CAB 24/107, C.P. 1470, June 10th 1920

CAB 24/156 British Empire Report, No. 25, September 1st 1920

CAB 24/111, C.P. 1896, September 25th 1920
CAB 24/156 British Empire Report, No. 31, November 24th 1920
CAB 24/115, C.P. 2197, November 30th 1920
CAB 21/186, C.P. 2545, February 7th 1921
CAB 24/156, British Empire Report, No. 37, February 16th 1921
CAB 24/156, British Empire Report, No. 38, March 2nd 1921
CAB 24/121, C.P. 2751. March 18th 1921
CAB 24/121, C.P. 2770, March 22nd-23rd 1921
CAB 24/126, C.P. 3123, March 28th 1921
CAB 24/136, C.P. 3998, May 17th 1922
CAB 24/138, C.P. 4125, July 25th 1922
CAB 24/158, C.P. 60 (23), January 1923
CAB 24/159, C.P. 106(23), February 17th 1923
CAB 24/161, C.P. 351 (23), July 27th 1923
CAB 24/162, C.P. 433 (23), October 27th 1923
CAB 24/165, C.P. 136(24), January 25th 1924.
CAB 24/165, C.P. 121(24), February 12th 1924

Foreign Office Documents

British Documents on Foreign Affairs, Part II: *From the First to the Second World War*, Series I: *The Paris Peace Conference of 1919*, Vol. 2: *Supreme Council Minutes January-March 1919*, gen. ed. Kenneth Bourne & D. Cameron Watt, ed. M. Dockrill, University Publications of America

British Documents on Foreign Affairs, Part II: *From the First to the Second World War*, Series I: *The Paris Peace Conference of 1919*, Vol. 11, ed. Kenneth Bourne & D. Cameron Watt, University Publications of America

British Documents on Foreign Affairs, Part II: *From the First to the Second World War*, Series B: *Turkey, Iran, and the Middle East 1918-1939,* Vol. 15: *Supplement to Eastern Affairs Volumes, 1918-1939*, gen. ed. Kenneth Bourne & D. Cameron Watt, ed. Robin Bidwell, University Publications of America

Documents on British Foreign Policy 1919-1939, First Series, ed. E.L. Woodward & Rohan Butler, HMSO, London, 1952, Vol. IV (1919)

Documents on British Foreign Policy 1919-1939, First Series, ed. E.L. Woodward & Rohan Butler, HMSO, London, 1954, Vol. V (1919)

Documents on British Foreign Policy 1919-1939, First Series, ed. Rohan Butler & J.P.T. Bury, HMSO, London, 1958, Vol. VII (1920)

Documents on British Foreign Policy 1919-1939, First Series, ed. Rohan Butler & J.P.T. Bury, HMSO, London, 1958, Vol. VIII (1920)

Documents on British Foreign Policy 1919-1939, First Series, ed. Rohan Butler & J.P.T. Bury, HMSO, London, 1963, Vol. XIII (1920)

Rise of Israel, Vol. 10 – *Tension in Palestine – Peacemaking in Paris 1919*, ed. Isaiah Friedman, Garland Publishing Inc., New York & London, 1987

Rise of Israel, Vol. 12 – *Riots in Jerusalem – San Remo Conference April 1920*, ed. Isaiah Friedman, Garland Publishing Inc., New York & London, 1987

Rise of Israel, Vol. 13 – Great Britain and Palestine 1920-1925, ed. Aaron S. Klieman, Garland Publishing Inc., New York & London, 1987

F.O. 371/356 No. 40321 (n. 62), November 16th 1907

F.O. 371/3083/143082, undated, presumably end of August 1917

F.O. 371/3388/1396, p. No. 30340, February 17th 1918

F.O. 371/3388/1495, July 30th 1918

F.O. 371/3383/747, August 16th 1918

F.O. 371/3386/856, November 15th 1918

F.O. 371/4179/2117, February 19th 1919

F.O. 608/99, March 24th 1919

F.O. 608/98, April 9th 1919

F.O. 371/4231/100141, July 9th 1919

F.O. 371/5121, April 12th 1920

F.O. 371/6342, March 22nd-23rd 1921

Parliamentary Debates

H.L., Vol. 50, cc. 994-1033, June 21st 1922

H.L., Vol. 54, cc. 654-682, June 27th 1923

H.C., Vol. 248, cc. 751-757, February 13th 1931

H.C., Vol. 347, cc. 1937-2056. May 22nd 1939

H.C., Vol. 347, cc. 2129-2197, May 23rd 1939

Command Papers, Royal Commissions

Cmd. 1176, *Draft Mandates for Mesopotamia and Palestine*, Miscellaneous No. 3, HMSO, London, 1921

Cmd. 1195, *The Franco-British Convention on Certain Points Connected with the Mandates for Syria, Lebanon, Palestine and Mesopotamia*, December 23rd 1920, HMSO, London, 1921

Cmd. 1540, *Palestine, Disturbances in May 1921: Reports of the Commission of Inquiry with Correspondence Relating Thereto*, HMSO, London, October 1921

Cmd. 1700 – *Palestine: Correspondence with the Palestine Arab Delegation and the Zionist Organization,* HMSO, London, June 1922

Cmd. 1700, Doc. No. 5, *British Policy in Palestine*, June 3rd 1922, [the Churchill White Paper]

Cmd. 1785, League of Nations: *The Mandate for Palestine, (together with a Note by the Secretary-General relating to its application to the territory known as Trans-Jordan under the provisions of Article 25)*, HMSO, London, December 1922

Cmd. 1989, *Palestine: Proposed Formation of an Arab Agency – Correspondence with the High Commissioner for Palestine*, HMSO, London, November 1923

Cmd. 2559, *Convention between the United Kingdom and the United States of America Respecting the Rights of the Governments of the Two Countries and their Respective Nationals in Palestine,* HMSO, London, December 3rd 1925

Cmd. 3069, *Trans-Jordan: Agreement between the United Kingdom and Trans-Jordan*, HMSO, London, 1928

Cmd. 3229, *The Western or Wailing Wall in Jerusalem*, Memorandum by the Secretary of State for the Colonies, HMSO, November 1928

Cmd. 3530, *Report of the Commission on the Palestine Disturbances of August 1929,* HMSO, London, March 1930

Cmd. 3686, *Palestine: Report on Immigration, Land Settlement and Development,* HMSO, London, October 1st 1930, [the Hope-Simpson Report]

Cmd. 3692, *Statement of Policy by His Majesty's Government in the United Kingdom,* HMSO, October 1930, [the Passfield White Paper]

Cmd. 4661, *Agreement Between His Britannic Majesty and His Highness the Amir of Trans-Jordan Supplementary to the Agreement Signed on 20th February 1928.* HMSO, London, June 2nd 1934

Cmd. 5479, *Palestine Royal Commission Report*, chaired by William Robert Wellesley, Earl Peel, HMSO, London, July 1937, [the Peel Report]

Cmd. 5513, Palestine Statement of Policy, HMSO, London, July 1937, p. 3

Cmd. 5634, *Policy in Palestine: Despatch dated 23rd December 1937, from the Secretary of State for the Colonies to the High Commissioner for Palestine*, HMSO, London, January 4th 1938

Cmd. 5854, *Palestine Partition Commission Report*, HMSO, London, October 1938, [the Woodhead Commission]

Cmd. 5957, *Correspondence between Sir Henry McMahon, His Majesty's High Commissioner at Cairo, and the Sherif Hussein of Mecca,* July 1915-March 1916, Miscellaneous No. 3, HMSO, London, 1939

Cmd. 5974, *Report of a Committee set up to Consider Certain Correspondence between Sir Henry McMahon and the Sharif of Mecca in 1915 and 1916*, HMSO, London, March 16th 1939

Cmd. 6019, *Palestine Statement of Policy*, May 17th 1939, HMSO, London, 1939 [the MacDonald White Paper]

Cmd. 6916, *Treaty of Alliance Between His Majesty in Respect of the United Kingdom and His Highness the Amir of Trans-Jordan*, Treaty Series No. 32 (1946), March 22nd 1946

Press Reports

The Times, May 28th 1917
The Manchester Guardian, December 10th 1917
The Jewish Chronicle, April 12th 1918
The *Jewish Chronicle*, July 26th 1918
The *Jewish Chronicle*, August 16th 1918
The Jewish Chronicle, September 13th 1918
The *Jewish Chronicle*, November 1st 1918
The Jewish Chronicle, November 18th 1918
The Times, January 16th 1919

The Jewish Chronicle, January 17th 1919
The Times, January 18th 1919
The Illustrated Sunday Herald, February 8th 1920
The Times, November 19th 1930
The Manchester Guardian, May 20th 1935
The Times, February 7th 1937
The Times, February 21st 1939

British Archives

Destani, Beitullah, ed. – *The Zionist Movement and the Foundation of Israel 1839-1972*, Vol. II, 1917-1918, Archive Editions, 2004

Foreign (Non-British) Documentation

Duwel, C.L.Torley ed., – *Bulletin de L'Institut Intermediaire International*, Publication trimestrielle, the Hague, 1919
Statutes of the United States of America, Vol. XLII, Sixty Seventh Congress, Session II, Chap. 372, p. 1012, Joint Resolution by the Senate and House of Representatives, September 21st 1922
Organic Law of Transjordan, Official Gazette, No. 188, April 19th 1928
Palestinian National Charter, 1964

Dictionaries and Encyclopedias

Stanford Encyclopedia of Philosophy, *Civil Rights*, ed. Andrew Altman, Stanford University, U.S.A. 2003 (substantive revision 2012).
Black, Henry Campbell – Black's Law Dictionary, Revised 4th Edition, West Publishing Co. Minn. U.S.A., 1968
Planck, Max – Encyclopedia of Public International Law: Daniel Thurer and Thomas Burri on Self-Determination Oxford University Press, (last updated December 2008)

Index

Made in the USA
Middletown, DE
23 December 2021

56774611R00245